Wanderers United
and the
Year They Nearly Pulled Out
of the
F.A. Cup

A footballing farce
by
Tom Trust

British Library Cataloguing In Publication Data
A Record of this Publication is available
from the British Library

ISBN 1846850797
978-1-84685-079-0

First Published February 2006 by

Exposure Publishing, an imprint of Diggory Press,
Three Rivers, Minions, Liskeard, Cornwall, PL14 5LE, UK
WWW.DIGGORYPRESS.COM

Set in 11pt Garamond; cover titles in Joinks! © Font-a-licious Fonts and FullyCompletely from ÆNIGMA FONTS.
Back cover notes and spine in Comic Sans.

Foreword

Okay, so at first you thought this was about Manchester United. Sorry. Had to catch your eye somehow. No; this is about an entirely fictitious team, Wanderers United, existing in a parallel universe if you like, who have dominated the Premiership for years. Having taken the title once again in 1999 they find themselves entering FIFA's World Club Championship the following season. Like Manchester United did.

Only in my confusion of fact and fiction, Wanderers United managed to avoid having to pull out of that season's FA Cup. You'll have to read the book to find out how.

Most of the other football teams mentioned do exist, of course, especially Porthleven of the Carlsberg South Western League. I know the chances of any South Western League team reaching the fourth round of the FA Cup are extremely slim but this *is* a work of fiction.

The tale begins slowly but picks up some pace towards the middle, so stick with it. The proof-reader laughed out loud at some bits and said she was keen to read the sequel. There isn't one planned! It wasn't written as part of a saga; just a one-idea yarn to give football fans all over the world a laugh.

Acknowledgements

Firstly, I'd like to express my gratitude to Lord Stratford (Tony Banks), for background information about events in the 1999-2000 season, and for allowing me to include him in this book. He read a draft of Chapters 12 and 16, 'phoned with advice and sent me a useful document; what a tragedy he couldn't read the whole book;

Then, thanks to:
The Tenth Floor, for giving me the encouragement to publish;
The members of the Porthleven AFC team of 1999-2000 that I was able to trace and the club's officers for their permission to be included in this book;
BBC Radio Cornwall for the Saturday job;
Ed Harry of BBC's World Service for finding Tim Vickery (a freelance football broadcaster) who suggested a suitable venue for the walk-over scene;
Kevin Stevens, Resources Manager of Redruth School, and Scott Jenkin of Cornwall Multimedia Services for invaluable IT help;
Elsa Rutter for proof-reading and editing advice;
Rosalind of Diggory Press for masses of technical advice;
Charlotte Rashleigh of Redruth School Sixth Form for the cover design;
Ellie Chrisanti, one time student in Venice, for the inspiration behind one character;

Venice in general but especially Venezia Football Club, just for existing – you've got to see their ground!

All former players of Illogan Women's Football Club (later Truro City Ladies) which I coached for nine memorable years, for valuable insight into the women's game.

Nige of Perth, Western Australia (and the Tenth Floor), for advice about Australian idiom and for discovering Useless Loop;

Hootch of Wimbledon (and the Tenth Floor), for information about the inside of Concorde and a Boeing 747;

My Godson Caspar and his mum Elsebeth for the loan of their names; and his brother Seb for background information about the airport at Capetown;

Rob Hornung of Caldy in the Wirral for advice about progression through the medical profession;

Mick Mahon, Newlyn fisherman, for advice about fishing quotas;

Manchester United for the idea;

The agents of Lenny Henry, Ron "Chopper" Harris and Gary Lineker for permission to use their clients' names;

To the Chelsea sides of the sixties and seventies, for the many peaks and troughs of delight and despair;

To the beautiful game;

And to Jackie, my wife, for putting up with everything and giving some sound, practical advice, not all of it to do with this book, even though she doesn't like football (except for the time I took her to watch England at Wembley just so she could get a glimpse of Gary Lineker's legs).

Chapter 1 - Sharon, Jenny and Club-coloured Knickers

"So will we get good seats, then?"

Sir Fabian Blankopf winced, as he often did at the sound of Sharon's voice: it put him in mind of fingernails scratching a blackboard.

"What?"

"Good seats. At all the games. Will we get good ones?"

He turned to look at her. Sometimes he wondered what he......

Her breasts wobbled to the combined vibrations of the movement of the stretch limousine and her nail-filing. The honey-tanned cleavage put him in mind of the Grand Canyon. Those breasts had cost him a fortune. Both in entertainment and in cosmetic surgery.

* * * * * * * * * *

"I don't like the shape," she had said after their first re-sculpting. "They look like ruddy steamed puddings." Blankopf tried unsuccessfully to suppress images of golden syrup slowly trickling down these huge new monuments to the more trivial branches of private medicine (Sharon had insisted on being done in Harley Street), just waiting for him to remove with his tongue.

"Well what damned shape *should* they be, then?" His attempts to mask his heavy Afrikaans accent always failed. It constantly bedevilled his attempts to gain British citizenship. That and his total lack of manners, both at the table and in company. The flecks of saliva that escaped his lips every time he spoke didn't help much, either. His knighthood was an honorary one, a bit like Bob Geldof's, due to the many good works many of his companies had performed throughout the Commonwealth; and although he wasn't entitled to, he insisted on being addressed as "Sir" Fabian at every opportunity, not realising that this didn't exactly help his attempts to gain the citizenship he craved.

"Where's that Tarzan and Jane porn film you like so much?" pouted Sharon. Blankopf, in his fifties now, though late thirties to anyone who asked, needed a little help to get it up for Sharon - or any other pretty young female who was prepared to succumb to his multi-billion pound wallet.

"I haven't got time for a screw," he growled. "You should have warned me. I'd have popped a Viagra." He could never get enough sex, a habit he acquired during his late teens in his first job as a gofer in an adult bar in Johannesburg. The trouble was, the inconvenient spectre of stress-induced impotence had reared its ugly head years ago. Well, drooped its ugly head, more precisely. His personal doctor had expensively warned him that he couldn't just take one Viagra three times a day like they were antibiotics. It would kill him.

"At least I could shag any time," Blankopf had pleaded, nevertheless.

"Maybe," replied the doctor, mentally adding another hundred pounds - no, *guineas* - to his bill for the trouble of answering the point. "But you'd never hit the pan when you had a wee unless you stood several feet back. And with your blood pressure you'd be dead in weeks." And I can't allow that, can I. I've got to keep you alive as long as possible, with what I charge you. How else could a man keep four children in private school, with the prospect of having to sub them through University, too, as well as a mistress?

"*Nnnnoooo!*" screeched Sharon's nerve-jarring voice. "In that film, there's that actress, the one 'oo plays Jane's long-lost odd sister wiv the willy *and* a fanny. *Her* tits. I want 'em shaped like hers."

So they had later run the tape, Blankopf taking a preparatory Viagra half-an-hour before, copied a number of photos of the actress (or was it act*or*? Blankopf could never be sure) via his P.C. onto paper and Sharon had gone back to Harley Street.

"How can you put up with having it done *twice?*" an incredulous friend of hers had asked, visiting her after the operation. Actually, she mumbled the question through a mouthful of grapes she was eating. It was what you did when you visited someone in hospital.

"Well, Blanky can afford it. It was 'is idea, too. 'E reckons the size of a girl's tits have got something to do wiv 'ow brainy she is. I can't remember 'xactly wot 'e said but 'e *defnitly* said in my case nature 'ad got it wrong an' I ought to 'ave big ones." She smiled a smug smile. "I fort that was nice, so I 'ad it done. But I fort if I do, I'll 'ave 'em the shape I want."

"Well, I hope he's worth it," mumbled the friend through more grapes.

A very smug smile. "Blanky's worth *billions*! 'Ere! Where's me grapes?"

* * * * * * * * *

"Of *course* we'll get good seats," sprayed Blankopf. "I've just *bought* the whole damned club!" He still felt a huge buzz of excitement at the thought. Owning the biggest satellite T.V. company in the world - Digital International - as well as an airline, two major newspapers in each of the U.K., U.S.A. and Germany, plus three in his native South Africa as well as his five major international publishing companies, major brewing and distilling companies on every continent and four international tobacco companies, gave him plenty of satisfaction. None, though, had given him the thrill that buying Wanderers United had. And anyway, all the media giants were buying into English Premiership Soccer. Granada owned ten percent of Liverpool, NTL owned a bit of Newcastle United, and Murdoch had bits of several clubs, like Leeds United and Chelsea. There was money to be made!

As *the* major team in the English Premiership over the last decade, there was a waiting list for season tickets greater than the number available as well as a massive turnover in merchandising.

Those replica shirts which cost £3.24 to buy from the supplier in Korea and retailed at £39.99 were a real goer, changed every season, both home and away - and there was that young Commercial Manager at Wanderers. She was someone Blankopf certainly intended to keep on. Her idea of a different home and away shirt for F.A. Cup matches as well as for Premiership games, plus others for the League Cup, UEFA Cup, Champion's League *and* the new FIFA World Club Championship was a master stroke; better still, the wheeze to even have different shirts for *floodlit* games in each competition! She had great thighs, too.

Plus, there was a reserve side that could probably come second in the Premiership. Yes, Wanderers United were a world-wide legend, greater than Juventus, Real Madrid, Manchester United and Santos all rolled into one. Half of all people surveyed world-wide who expressed an interest in soccer at all claimed to be Wanderers fans (most of the other half opting for Man. U., of course).

Blankopf saw them as the huge captive market that they were. And there was a little sweatshop on the outskirts of Jo'burg owned by one of his tobacco companies (well, they had to diversify in the face of increasing anti-smoking attitudes in the western world) that could knock out those replica shirts for £2.89 a unit. Selling five million new shirts a year throughout the world would net another six million profit to add to the £183.75 millions already made.

"Well," Blankopf had mused, "Look after the millions and the billions will look after themselves!"

Sharon had finished filing the nails on her left hand and now struggled to file the ones on her right. She always struggled to do this which is why she almost always had them done at an expensively chic little beautician's in Beauchamp Place. So handy for a coffee at Harrod's afterwards.

"Well, yer own the Rumpy Pumpy Club," (this, the Jo'burg club that Blankopf had started his working life in. When wealthy enough, at age 22, he had bought it just so he could sack the manager who had been a complete bastard towards him when he joined the staff at the tender age of seventeen. He also allowed his rugby club free use of it as their regular post-match watering hole which assured him of many good contacts in the years ahead as he built his business empire up.) "an' yer once said ter me, yer can't find room fer a standin' fuck on a Sat'day night. I'd have fort they would 'ave made room fer the *owner*. So I jus' wondered if we'd get good seats in this football gra'nd. Anyway, 'ow do yer 'ave a standin' fuck?" In the three years that Sharon had graced Blankopf with her company, sex had always been a horizontal affair whether Sharon was underneath or on top - which to be fair was more often than not the latter due to Blankopf's marked lack of both stamina and leg strength.

At the age of twenty, Sharon had not had time to explore the more exotic types of sex before meeting Blankopf three years earlier, even though standing knee-tremblers were a fairly standard type of congress in her native Barking. No, Sharon had been quite determined that she would *never* have sex outside. That was for animals. Of course, when "outside" could now mean the deck of Blanky's 145ft yacht cruising off the Florida Keys (especially with that deliciously bronzed and muscular Navigator that Blanky employed on board), she was prepared to concede that perhaps her earlier view of outdoor sex had been a little rash. But standing up with her back pressed against a scruffy brick wall in a side alley outside a disco, amidst the take-away cartons and used condoms and in between the pungent wheelie-bins was not for her.

Her fourteen-year-old cherry had been popped in a patchwork Capri with threadbare seat covers and threadbare tyres to match. The acned youth who had deflowered her had "borrowed" the car specially for the occasion. Thereafter, her reputation freely broadcast around the borough by said spotty youth, Sharon got to know the roof linings of most of the Capris in Southern Essex. She also sampled a couple of Cortina Mark Vs (preferring their larger back seat) and knew she was "in lerve" when, at almost sixteen, she was serviced several dozen times over four or five weeks by the same lad - unusual enough in her free-shagging, one-night-stand circle of friends - in no less than an A-reg Sierra Ghia. *Real* class, this, as *this* lad's fluffy dice didn't dangle predictably from the driving mirror but were suspended from the centre of the rear window, hung from a suction cup held on by superglue.

"Why 'ave yer got one 'ung lower than the uvver?" she had fatally asked one evening, looking at them over her paramour's shoulder as he sweated away on top of her. She never understood why that shag had ended right there and then with the lad's sudden flaccidity, nor the reason for the silent, sulky drive home, least of all why she never saw him again.

Blankopf knew none of this history, though. He had found Sharon as an innocent young lap dancer in the infamous Pimlico Sporting Club. She was amazed he was so incredibly rich at only thirty-five. He was amazed that a girl in such a club could still be a virgin. Such was the firm foundation of honesty upon which their relationship was built.

"Standing fu.... for crying out loud! I didn't mean it literally!" He wanted to add "You brainless tart" but there was no need to upset her. She was such a good shag, and even if her voice did make him wince, there were many times when she gave him the utmost pleasure just by opening her mouth.

Sharon looked up from her clumsy attempts at left-handed nail filing. She leant towards Blankopf, giving him a perfect view of the second-time-lucky cleavage, and kissed him on his bulbous, vein-strewn nose.

"Ooh, Blanky!" she squealed. "Yer do tease me! I luv it when yer tease me! Yer on'y do it 'cos yer luv me, don'tcha!"

"Yeah, that's it!" Love to shag you, that is. Time to change the subject, he thought. He looked out of the window.

"We have to be getting close now."

"Oooh, Blanky, luv!"

Sharon snuggled up to Sir Fabian on the soft leather seat.

"What're you doing, Shaz?"

"Yer said we 'ad ter be gettin' close - so 'ere I am!"

"Bloody hell, girl, I meant we must be getting close to the stadium!"

Sharon pouted and slid away again. "Oooh, *Blanky*, I fort yer wanted a cuddle!" Then she smiled. "Yer mus' fink I'm a *right* divvy!"

"Course not, sweetheart!" Sir Fabian lied. Oh, give me strength, he thought. He pressed a button on the centre console. The glass partition behind the chauffeur slid open.

"Are we nearly there, James?"

The chauffeur turned to reveal a face topped by a traditional chauffeur's cap. Chauffeuse, really, for the face was beautiful, a perfect oval framed by a mane of startling red hair, hanging long, shiny and straight. It swung freely, like a shampoo advert, as she turned her head back to keep an eye on the road ahead.

"Just a couple of minutes, Sir Fabian."

"Right."

The glass partition slid shut again.

"Right!" repeated James, sighing a little sigh and hoping that this thing with the football club didn't mean spending less time driving for Sir Fabian in more exotic places abroad.

As an economics graduate from the L.S.E., Jennifer James was aware that she ought not to be doing this! But she was just one of an increasing number of University students who had graduated onto the dole queue. With so many new Universities and so many graduates, it was no surprise.

"They give degrees out like they did O-levels in my day," said her father when Jennifer told him how hard she was finding it to get a job. "The bloody questions are probably about as hard, too!" He had gone to a "proper" University - Essex - read politics, helped organise a few sit-ins and protest marches, graduated with a third, then sold out and became an estate agent; which at least had provided him with a good living. He had insisted that Jennifer went to a "proper" University too, but it hadn't helped her to get a job once she'd graduated.

Her mother gave more practical advice once she was alone with her daughter. "Use your body," she said, taking Jennifer by surprise. "Strip, be a hostess, even go on the game! With your looks and figure, you'd make a fortune."

"Mum!"

"Oh, don't pretend to be so shocked. You've been at it since you were fifteen. So was I!"

"Mum! How did....?"

"I'm your mother. Mothers know these things instinctively. And what do you think *I* was doing when I met your father?"

"You always told me you were working in the hotel where dad went for some conference."

"That's right. I *was* working in the hotel. But not *for* the hotel. I was on the game. Your dad turned my head! He got it for nothing that night." She laughed. "He's bloody paid for it since, though!"

"Mum!"

But Jennifer had more or less taken her mother's advice. Some work as a policewoman-o-gram led to proper stripping, which in turn led to her meeting Blankopf at a special party celebrating the fortieth birthday of a business acquaintance (who was really fifty-three). Jennifer knew who he was. She read the Sunday Times. Somehow he had mentioned that he needed a chauffeur, she had suggested herself, he had looked unimpressed, she had mentioned her economics degree, he had seemed slightly impressed, she had pointed out that very few chauffeurs could offer striptease as an extra, his face had brightened considerably, she (remembering her mother's advice) had said (so that there was absolutely no chance of his misunderstanding) "and I would sleep with you if you wanted" and he had said "You're hired!"

"What's the salary?" Economics graduate, after all.

"Sa...well, how much do you make now? I'll double it!"

"Well, that would be about £52,000 a year," she lied.

"Is that *all?*" Blankopf spent that much a week on bits and pieces. "O.K., you're hired!"

Jennifer almost fainted. "I'd have to live in, of course."

"Well, yes, all my chauffeurs have to. There are chauffeurs' quarters at all my places. And if you were needed to meet my 'plane or yacht, well, I've got a lady who sorts out all that sort of thing."

"What sort of thing?"

"Eh? Oh, 'plane tickets to get you to where I need you, hotel rooms - that sort of thing."

"Like, where do you go that you might need your chauffeurs?"

"Jo'burg, the States, Hong Kong - places I've got offices or deals. Australia, Japan. Usual sorts of places. Why?"

"Just interested, thank you, Sir Fabian."

So Jennifer was banking at least £35,000 a year, having to buy just the odd bit of make-up, a few tops, sometimes some new jeans. She had simple tastes in clothes and had to wear a uniform when on duty. It didn't really do justice to her 36C 24 35 figure, but hell! She was earning far more than her former classmates and getting to travel at Sir Fabian's expense all over the world, and the sex was great, too. Not the sex with Blankopf, the impotent old fart. She had to wear a uniform then, too, and put up with his calling her "James" all the time. He got a kick out of having a chauffeur called James. No, it was the sex with Roger she enjoyed, one of the other chauffeurs - a Cornish zoology graduate from Plymouth University. (How he became one of Sir Fabian's chauffeurs is not *nearly* as interesting.) Roger was a sun-bleached blond who loved Jennifer as much as he loved Cornwall. "One day I'll take you there, and the rest of the world will seem pale by comparison. Only the sex will be as good....."

She loved a good Rogering.

Waking from her reverie, Jennifer realised the stadium gates were just a couple of hundred yards away. She had reconnoitred the route the day before in her 1971 MGB roadster, a superb ground-up rebuild that she had treated herself to in her stripping days. Her parents had owned one, and all the old photos she had seen it in had made her fall in love with the car.

She punched out a stored number code on a mobile 'phone held in a dashboard clip. The number rang three or four times and was then answered.

"Arnie Robinson."

* * * * * * * *

"Mr Robinson," said Jennifer, "This is Sir Fabian Blankopf's driver speaking. We are about a hundred yards from the stadium gates. You told Sir Fabian's secretary that we should let you know we had arrived."

"Yes, right, I'll get down to the gates and have them opened for you. Er - what sort of car are you in?"

"A white stretch limousine."

"How will I recognise it?"

Good grief, thought Jennifer. "It is white, it is very long, it has black windows and a red-headed female chauffeur driving it."

"Well, O.K." Mr Robinson sounded doubtful.

"We're nearly there," said Jennifer. "I don't want to have to park outside."

"No, no, of course not. I'm on my way down to the main gate. Don't worry."

Jennifer could tell by the way his voice wobbled that he was running.

"Right. See you." Jennifer rang off. She steered the monster car the last few yards to the large iron gates that led into the stadium's private car park. A tall, white moustached man in an ornate uniform stood behind them, staring balefully at the limousine. Jennifer smiled at him. He stared balefully back at her. She broadened her smile and tilted her head slightly, lifting her eyebrows in a mute plea for him to open the gates. He stared balefully back. A little, worried-looking man in a crumpled suit, clutching a mobile 'phone, approached the baleful gatekeeper from behind. He spoke a few words to the much taller uniformed man, who inclined his head downwards towards the little worried man to show that he was listening, without removing his baleful glare from Jennifer. His faced acquired a frown now - still baleful - and he grudgingly unfastened the gates, swinging them open to let the limousine in. He indicated with a sweep of his arm that the car could proceed, managing to convey in that simple gesture that he regarded the car and its occupants with suspicion and contempt. Jennifer also felt, uncannily, that there was a hint of balefulness in the gesture, too. Baleful. She would have to look it up in a dictionary to see what it meant. It hadn't cropped up in any of her economics text books.

The car glided through the gates. The little worried man trotted ahead of it, pointing to where he wanted the car to park. Beyond the space he had indicated, broad ornate marble steps swept up towards a huge glass and chrome entrance. Above the huge doors, in huge yellow and blue lettering, was the legend "NEW STAMFORD STADIUM - HOME OF WANDERERS UNITED". Jennifer drew the car up to the foot of the steps, ignoring the little worried man's frantic gestures. In the door mirror, she saw him gallop after the car. She stopped the car, got out, walked round to the side facing the steps and opened the rear door. Blankopf climbed out, followed by Sharon. He stood by the open door of the car, still held open by Jennifer, and looked up at the huge main entrance.

It was situated in the middle of the back of the main stand, still not quite finished judging by the contractor's huts nearby and the workmen scurrying about. Blankopf knew it held two restaurants, a bar, swimming pool and gymnasium for the use of supporters. Well, those who could afford the £950 membership fee (reviewed annually). It also housed the players' and officials' facilities, of course, including a new Board Room that had windows above the main entrance. Blankopf looked along the full length of this stupendous erection - recognised as the most magnificent part of the most magnificent football stadium in the world, bar none now its lengthy rebuilding programme was all but complete. He gave a great sigh of satisfaction.

"Well, here we are, Shaz. All mine."

"Mmm, luvly," she declared. "I'm dyin' fer a pee!"

"Well, put a cork in it. You'll have to wait!" He looked around again. "Where is everybody. There's no-one to meet the new owner. Some poor bastard is going to be sorry."

At that moment, the poor bastard in question arrived by the car in the form of the little worried man, breathless and still worried-looking. As well he might, in the circumstances.

"Er... Sir Fabian Blankopf?"

Blankopf turned and examined the breathless, worried-looking little man.

"Who the fuck are you?"

"My name's Arnie Robinson, the Club Secretary. Are you Sir Fabian Blankopf?"

Behind him, still holding the car door open, Jennifer winced.

"No, *she* is!" roared Blankopf, spittle flying, nodding towards Sharon.

Taken aback, Sharon looked confused. "No I'm not, silly. *You* are!"

"Of course I bloody am!" Blankopf roared even more loudly, directing an even heavier shower of saliva at the worried-looking poor bastard, "and you're bloody fired!"

"Huh?"

"You heard me, you're fired. I've just paid umpty billion Rand for this outfit and when I get here there's no-one to bloody show me in. What kind of a half-assed outfit is this, anyway?"

"*I'm* here to meet you, Sir Fabian," stammered the even more worried-looking poor bastard, or Arnold Robinson as he was Christened. Well, not actually Christened as such. His parents had bought all the special Christening gowns, sorted out the catering, provisionally booked the Vicar and Church, invited all the guests, then at the last minute, with all the said guests waiting round the font and all the buffet food drying out as it fed flies on the tables in the hired community hall, the vicar reminded the proud parents that he hadn't yet had sight of their marriage certificate (which he had asked for when they provisionally booked him). They hadn't quite registered that particular point, each thinking he had said something like "if you can". Whatever. As they weren't married, there was no certificate, the vicar said he didn't Christen bastards, Arnie's father had hit the vicar, his mum had burst into tears and the guests all had to be told that the Christening was off.

Although as a baby of just a few weeks Arnie obviously had no memory of the event, he got to know of it later when various malicious spinster aunts had related the tale to him, and it was no surprise to any of them when, twenty-two years after this first fiasco in a Church, Arnie suffered a similar sort of mishap when he was jilted at the altar by one Debra (sic) Whittingstall (her parents obviously couldn't spell) whose period started unexpectedly an hour before the time booked for the service, making her realise that she wasn't pregnant after all, so therefore needn't marry Arnie. Which was only fair, as she had only shagged him after she thought she was pregnant, because he was at least a reasonable example of a human being, which is more than could have been said about any of the deviant characters that could have been the father, if she *had* been pregnant.

Such traumas in his life had perhaps contributed to his almost terminal hypochondria. As, for example, now, because with the exertion of running after the car and the shock of Sir Fabian's summary sacking of him, he thought he felt a pain developing in his chest. That plus his sweating were surely symptoms of a heart attack! He was one of the few people in the world to have 999 programmed as a speed-dial number on his mobile 'phone. He didn't have time to think about whether he needed to use it, though. Sir Fabian was yelling at him again.

"What's the point in you being here to meet me when you don't bloody work for me?"

"Blanky, I *need* a *pee!*"

"Oh, for Christ's sake, Shaz, bloody wait!"

"If you'd like to follow me," offered the confused, very worried-looking poor bastard known as Arnie Robinson, now convinced he was suffering from the onset of a coronary, "I'll show madam where the facilities are."

"Ooooh, Blanky, they've got *facilities*! Ain't that posh!"

Even Blankopf was impressed by words like "facilities", boor that he was. He had been called a boor once, by a gentleman he had drunkenly bumped into in a bar a few years earlier.

"Mind out, you old boor!" the gentleman had exclaimed. Sir Fabian had been about to punch the man as, in his drunken state, he had imagined that the gentleman had bumped into him, and deliberately at that. All aggression immediately evaporated, however, and a misty nostalgia clouded his eyes as he had clasped the gentleman around the shoulders.

"Boer! I'll say I am! How the hell did you know?"

Buying the puzzled gentleman a drink he had stumbled off, suddenly mellowed by memories of his father's tales of beating uppity kaffirs.

Arnie led the way up the huge marble stairway towards the equally huge glass and chrome doors, hoping he could lead the new owner to the Boardroom before the heart attack claimed him. Sharon followed. Blankopf turned to Jennifer, still holding the car door open.

"Park the car, James," he said. He loved that name. "I'll see you later."

"Certainly, sir. How will you let me know when you are ready to go?"

He nodded towards Arnie. "I'll tell that little wanker to come and get you."

"Thank you, sir."

Blankopf made his way up the steps behind Sharon. This wasn't how he had pictured arriving at the United's stadium for the first time after he'd bought it. He had expected the full works, red carpets, staff lined up, masses of photographers, T.V. cameras, Kate Adie..... Okay, he knew she only really did wars and other dangerous stuff, but he'd have *paid* for her to be there. Perhaps it was in his Boer genes to fancy women who scorned bullets, bombs, spears..... Still, looking up the steps at Sharon's backside was compensation enough.

13

"Fuck me!" he chuckled as he realised, thanks to the shortness of her mini - or rather micro - skirt and her being several steps above him on the stairway, that she was wearing yellow and blue pants - Wanderers' colours.

Running to catch her up, he put his arm round her.

"What a girl, Shaz! Yer knickers are in the team's colours!"

Sharon giggled. "Ssh, Blanky! Don't tell everyone!"

Ahead of them, the ex Club Secretary thought of a way he just *might* get to keep his job. That's if he survived his heart attack first.

Chapter 2 - A Deal is Struck

In the main Board Room, above the huge glass and chrome entrance, with its proportionately huge yellow and blue lettering that informed the uninitiated visitor that this was "NEW STAMFORD STADIUM - HOME OF WANDERERS UNITED" (just in case anyone arriving at the massive stadium hadn't been aware that that was where they were heading for when they set out), a fattish, balding late middle-aged man looked down on the arrival of the stretch limmo. He couldn't resist a chuckle at the obvious discomfort of that poor bastard Robinson, running about the director's car park like a headless chicken, then running after the limmo which had refused to park where he wanted it to.

He watched the small procession of Robinson, a blonde tart and Sir Fabian Blankopf, whom the observer immediately recognised even from that far above. Not many wheelers and dealers in U.K. business circles would have failed to recognise the most widely detested non-politician in the world.

"Our new boss is here," he said over his shoulder to the room in general. "Do we line up in order of the size of the bung we took?"

"You speak for yourself," said a sly-looking oily little man, dressed in a tasteless check suit. "He never had to buy *me*."

The sly-looking oily little man was one Malcolm Black, Managing Director of Consolidated Solids, brought up from early childhood to watch Wanderers United in their second division days. He used to watch his idols training by bunking off school; dreamt of playing for them one day, but wasn't good enough. Well, actually, he was crap. In P.E. lessons, when they weren't on United training days, the bull-necked P.E. teacher (once a free-transfer reject of Accrington Stanley's), used to make Malcolm stand on the pitch as one of the goal posts.

"An' yer no dam' good at *that*, Black," he would yell in that encouraging way so typical of P.E. teachers everywhere in the nineteen sixties. Malcolm's partnering goal post was a stupendously obese lad called Clarence Draper who always seemed to have a cold. He would stand at the other side of the goal and if the action was down the other end they would chat. If, on the other hand, their goal was being bombarded they would duck, weave and wince, afraid of being struck by the ball, especially if the sadistic Accrington Stanley free-transfer reject was helping the team kicking their way.

"With what I put into this place, Sefton, I was more than happy to accept the going price for my little contribution." Malcolm continued. He often reminded the Board how cheaply Consolidated Solids had tendered for the job of constructing the New Millennium Stand, as the huge structure that housed the main Board Room, completed only weeks before, was called. The smell of fresh paint and varnish was evident in the Board Room, a testimony to the newness of everything as the stand was still being finished off. According to Malcolm, Consolidated Solids had made a *loss* for the privilege of building the stand, the difference being made up out of Malcolm's own pocket. Since Malcolm had made many millions in the construction industry, his pocket was capacious.

"You're a real brick, Mal, a real brick." Sefton Perkins, the fattish balding, late middle-aged man didn't sound particularly sincere. He was thinking "prick" rather than "brick". Sefton was the Chairman of Wanderers United - or, at least, had been until late the previous week when Blankopf's long campaign to take the club over had reached its triumphant conclusion with the final signing of the deal. Sefton had been a steelworker, working his way up through the rank and file until he became a Managing Director. He sold his share options just before the collapse of the British steel industry but really made his fortune from the value of the land on which the old steelworks lay, cannily bought up by Sefton for a knock-down price to be sold on later at a huge profit to Supermarkets, industrial estate developers and the like.

As United had not been launched on the Stock Market like two or three other Premiership clubs, its purchase by Blankopf was fairly straightforward. At first, though, back in the January, none of the Board had wanted to sell, except for Malcolm Black, who had seemed almost suspiciously keen. The deal on offer at the special Board meeting, convened (in the middle of what turned out to be the Wanderers' treble-winning season) to discuss Blankopf's approach, was for Blankopf to buy fifty-one percent of each Board member's stake in the club. The seven Board members would all become even more wealthy than they already were and still be Board members, or so Blankopf had promised.

"What's the bloody point of that if Blankopf owns fifty-one percent," asked Ernie Arscott, a sallow-complexioned, cadaverous figure of indeterminate age (most would have simply called him "old", or, less simply, "one foot in the grave"). "Anything he wants, he'll get. How could we outvote the bugger?"

Muttered agreement around the table.

"Well, I think it will be great for the club," stated Malcolm, trying to ignore an insistent spasm in his colon. He seemed eager to accept Sir Fabian's offer. "Blankopf's got a hundred times more cash than all of us put together. Think of who we could buy. We'd clean up. We'd walk the Champions League every season. Think of that!"

"Yes, but if he decided to kick the soccer into touch and replace it with a rugby team, he could do it. After all, he's a South African, and what do they know about football, eh? Rugby's their game." The speaker was a youngish-looking man compared to the rest of the men around the table. At thirty four, Cecil Norris had made his money in recycling. Plastics were his main money-spinner, but he would handle most materials. His breakthrough had come when he won contracts to collect broken chairs from schools up and down the country. It brought in thousands every week, so destructive are today's school pupils. In addition to this, every time a soccer club moved its ground, it was Cecil's men who moved in to clear the seats from the old site. Once or twice, with a bit of helpful cash in the right hands, he'd even managed to clinch a deal to clear the seats before the site was sold (usually to a shopping developer) and then negotiate another contract for the same job with the purchaser.

"If you buy the old stadium, we'll clear all the old plastic seating out for a *very* good price...."

What they couldn't sell on for reprocessing, or reprocess themselves, Cecil's company dumped down a disused coal mine (as closed by Margaret Thatcher), purchased for that very purpose. His company - Elastic Plastic plc - had, of course, disposed of all the old seats and ironwork from the Old Stamford Stadium, demolished bit by bit as the ground was redeveloped gradually into United's hugely-publicised and specially re-named New Stamford Stadium. Mind, those stubborn old bastards that had wanted to buy their old regular seat as a keepsake had been a headache - until Cecil realised he could sell them for fifty times their scrap value. Some seventeen thousand or so punters had coughed up £25 each for their old plastic folding seat. That was some bonus!

Another sallow-faced, not-quite-so-cadaverous man, next to Ernie Arscott, spoke up next. "That's very true," he said. "Are there any guarantees that he'll keep the football going?" He was Reginald Arscott, younger brother of Ernie, hence his not-quite-so-cadaverous appearance. Together, the brothers ran Arscott and Arscott, a chain of butchers all round England's major towns and cities. They made their own black puddings and sausages, as well as producing a range of cold meats. "If the meat in yer bangers tastes right fair, there must be some Arscott in it somewhere" ran their longest-running billboard advert. No Saatchi and Saatchi fees paid for that little gem: it was all their own work! For some reason, though, commercial television stations wouldn't carry it. Both men being scraggy and stooped, Ernie more so than Reginald, they did not exactly make out a strong case against vegetarianism.

"Oh, he wouldn't dare do that," replied Sefton. "Let's face it. The bugger's unpopular enough now. Think what people would think of him if he closed the team down! And the stadium due to be finished in time for the start of next season!"

"Come off it," laughed Cecil. "He wouldn't give a shit! He couldn't *be* more unpopular world wide. He wouldn't notice the difference!"

"Right! He wouldn't give a toss. I reckon, if he could get a good mark up on this place, then he would, and bugger the consequences!" The speaker, one Jack Grimethorpe, was the only man not dressed in a suit and tie. Mind, he was the only man present who looked comfortable in what he *was* wearing: a check shirt under a boiler suit. All the others, solid working class men bar none, were squeezed into collars and jackets they'd no business to trifle with. Jack had come to the meeting in the tractor unit of one of his huge fleet of trucks, the business built up by his father who, now in semi-retirement, had handed over to Jack. Despite this inherited position, Jack was a hands-on man and drove as much as he could, delegating all the office work to others. He loved nothing more than swinging a truck onto the ferry at Dover en route for foreign destinations. "You'll never get me down that damn tunnel again. It's just as well you haven't got time to eat the food, its crap anyway." The ferry gave his drivers a suitable break to keep their tacho cards legal, time to sink a bloody good fry-up or, if you'd picked up one of the road groupies, you had over an hour for a shag in your bunk. Perfect!

The only other man present, who hadn't yet spoken, was a tough, rugged-looking man with a ragged mane of white hair framing his weather-beaten face. He was Dick Fosset, one-time United centre-forward who still held the club's goal-scoring record of fifty-one goals in a season. That had been in the 1947-48 season, in forty-seven league and F.A. Cup games. After he hung up his boots, he went to sea and then went coal mining until he was sixty-five. His big stroke of luck came when a Wanderers fan, who also happened to be the writer of scores of best-sellers, wrote Dick's biography and willed all its proceeds to him when he died. With the fortune it amassed due to its world-wide sales (translated into thirty-three languages) Dick had bought himself a place on his beloved club's board.

"What does a bloke with these satellite thingy T.V. stations, airlines and all sorts want with United?" he asked. "Sounds bloody fishy to me. Mind, he wants us to switch our Sky TV channel to Digital International so I suppose that ties in. But no - I'm against."

And so the Board voted against Blankopf's approach by five to one (Sefton, as Chairman, not voting. He only voted if a casting vote was needed).

"How's the women's team coming on?" asked Dick. Now that the serious business was over, it was time for a bit of light relief.

"I'll give Christine a buzz," replied Sefton. He called a number on the internal 'phone beside him. "Christine, could you come up to the Boardroom to give us the latest on the women's team? ....Thanks."

"I hope she's got that short-skirted executive suit of hers on again," chuckled Jack Grimethorpe.

"I think that's unanimous!" laughed Sefton.

Commercial Manager Christine Goodley entered the room and was offered a chair round the table.

"Gentlemen," she hailed them, icily. They were hardly that, the lecherous bunch of old farts. She was sure she had only got the job because of her looks and figure, rather than for her previous experience as a sales team leader for a major kitchen appliance manufacturer.

"What's the latest, Christine?" prompted Sefton.

"I have negotiated with Midford Town Ladies, a fairly local side who play in the Second Division of the National Women's League," replied Christine. "They finished sixth last season and got to the quarter finals of the Women's F.A. Cup. They haven't fully agreed yet - but I'm sure I can talk them round for the start of next season. They'd prefer to play here, of course, not at the reserves' ground. We'll have to cultivate them a bit for the rest of this season, help them with coaching, etc., a bit of financial support - that sort of thing."

"I'm not sure them playing here will be that straightforward, but there'll be no trouble with the other bits, eh, lads?" said Dick, beaming round at the other members of the Board.

I'll *bet* there won't be, you lecherous old bastards, thought Christine.

"Why can't they play here?" she asked.

"Well," began Sefton, "It costs a bit to open the ground up. We'd have to open up a stand for just a handful of people, and somehow cut off the rest of the stadium. But we'd have to have ball-boys in the closed stands - it would be very difficult...."

"Perhaps they could play the odd special game here," persisted Christine.

"Well..... maybe, eh, lads?" suggested Sefton.

Nods of agreement all round. Even the two Arscott brothers were quite perked up at the prospect of what they imagined would be twenty two nubile young things running up and down their pitch

So that was all right, then.

Refusing Sir Fabian's first approach meant that as the rest of the season passed by, with the achievement of the treble seeming more and more likely, he gradually upped his offer to the five dissenters - and to Sefton, just to be on the safe side - in the certain knowledge that sooner or later, one by one, they would give in.

"Every man has his price, Shaz," he explained one night from beneath her groin.

"Oh? An' what's yours, Blanky?" she squirmed.

"I'll have a Foster's!" he chortled. The old ones were the best! The chortle turned into a fit of coughing. A hair had gone down his throat.

Bouncing around above him due to the tidal waves set up in the water bed (an optional extra in their Bangkok hotel suite) by Blankopf's coughing fit, Sharon looked puzzled. Surely *she* was supposed to do the bouncing when she was on top. "Are yer sneezin'? Did I tickle yer nose? Or is it a cold? I don' wannit!"

Blankopf, purple by now, extricated himself from between Sharon's legs and started to breathe more normally as his coughing subsided.

"Cold my arse! How can you catch a cold in your fanny?" Another cough and he could distinctly feel something break free from the back of his throat. He started to try to work the hair forwards to his tongue. "Gah! I keep telling you to shave it, for Christ's sake!"

"If I shave it, it *will* get cold, Blanky."

"Then I'll buy you a fur G-string, sweetheart!"

"Oooh, Blanky!"

She tried to kiss him to show her appreciation, but Blankopf was too busy making little spitting sounds and poking his fingers into his mouth.

* * * * * * * *

Only Malcolm Black failed to get an increased offer for 51% of his stake in United. He had gone straight to his car 'phone after that special Board meeting and contacted Blankopf's P.A. with the news (pinching the number off Blankopf's letter which still lay on the table where Sefton, the Chairman, had been sitting), emphasising that he alone was willing to sell fifty-one percent of his stake. It hadn't been easy. He was nervous going behind the Board's back, though he had his reasons. They had worked together for many years, master-minding the emergence of Wanderers United from being just another first division side of the sixties to the most successful and therefore widely supported club side in the world. It was privately owned between the seven Directors but was reckoned by financial pundits to be worth something like one and a half billion pounds if it was ever made into a plc. The seven men had become friends over the years and Malcolm suffered a great deal of stress as he made contact with Sir Fabian's office but he needed a lifeline if the worst happened. He had to 'phone from his toilet, so violently did his large intestine behave as he contemplated the treachery he planned. Unknown to Malcolm, Sir Fabian had always planned to raise his offer until he found each man's price.

"Silly boy," he thought after being told about Malcolm's call. "No need to try to buy *him*, then, is there!"

Each new offer of more cash that was made to each of the Board members was made very discreetly as if no-one else was being made the offer. Pretty soon, Arscott and Arscott, who shared everything including the services of the same blowsy pro who entertained each of them every Thursday afternoon (half-closing day for their traditional family business), came to the conclusion that the bribes *they* were being offered must be being made to the rest of the Board. This was confirmed when Reg the younger Arscott encountered Cecil in their Golf Club gents. Watering the porcelain together, they got chatting, as men do.

"We've been getting little personal calls from Blankopf," said Reg, worried when he saw that his stream was far less powerful than Cecil's. Did that mean prostate trouble?

"Oh?" replied Cecil, noting with pleasure, out of the corner of his eye (as men do) that Reggie's willy was somewhat smaller than his own.

"Yes, he's offered us a sight more than the face value of our shares. What about you?" Bloody hell, my stream *is* feeble. I can't even shift that fag end that he's washed in my direction.

"Well, now you mention it, he's been on at me, too." Poor sod. That fag end I floated down to him has gone aground. Small willy, can't pee! Is that what old age does to you, makes your willy shrink? " Er - what's he offering?"

"He went from twenty percent more, to forty, then to fifty. We haven't accepted." I'm *sure* a weak stream is a sign of prostate trouble.

"Me neither. He's gone to fifty with me, too." Having finished peeing, Cecil shook his willy flamboyantly, just to emphasise how much bigger his was than poor old Reggie's - which was still trickling feebly. The poor bugger must have prostate trouble! That was it!

"We'd better have a word with the others," concluded a now desperate Reg, as his stream dribbled to an inconclusive end. "Except Malcolm. He was in favour of selling. But if Blankopf is trying to buy us off, we could all hold out for, say, a hundred percent mark up. I mean, a few million isn't to be sneezed at. And us all still on the board. If he sells the club in a fortnight, well, bollocks. We'd get even more cash, more than we'd know what to do with. Bloody tens of millions! Canaries, me!" Only after I use some of the cash for a top surgeon to look at my prostate.

"Right. I'll ring you." As Cecil left, Reg struggled with his flies, praying that he'd have no late dribbles that would leave him having to try to use the hand dryer to dry his fly fronts, never an easy task and bound to coincide with someone else coming in to use the toilet. And surely only queers waved their willies like Cecil had in a public bog? Was Cecil queer? He had a big bastard, though.

Cecil contacted the others - except Malcolm - and quickly gleaned that they were all being quietly harassed by Blankopf, offering the same increases to all of them.

"What's his game?" asked Dick Fosset of the rest of the conspirators a few days later as they all sweated in the United Sports Centre's newly-built sauna. It wasn't really big enough for six adults, four of whom were of above-average girth, but it was thought to be the only safe place they could all "happen to" meet, just in case anyone saw them all together and let a stray comment go in Malcolm's earshot. It was also impossible for them to be overheard. Tightly-packed in the pine-panelled cubicle, there was no room for anyone else to sit, so their secrecy was assured.

"Well, he certainly wants to buy the club." Jack Grimethorpe was a simple pragmatist.

"Yes, obviously," gasped Reginald Arscott, wilting somewhat in the heat. "But why doesn't he just try to buy off half of us?"

"Perhaps he's just waiting for us to give in one by one until he's got a majority," suggested Jack.

"Yes, but hang on." said Sefton, squinting as sweat filled his eyes. "He's only asking for fifty-one percent from each of us. If he had *all* mine as well as all shares from any two of you, he'd have his fifty-one percent. He must want us all to stay on the board."

"Clever bastard!" Ernie Arscott, sitting next to his brother so that the two of them together could be seen to be taking up barely more room than Sefton did on his own, looked particularly unhappy in the hot, maximum humidity atmosphere. At least the others could reckon to lose some of their fat in this sweat box, consolation for the discomfort they were being forced to endure in the name of confidentiality. He and his brother were merely hot and uncomfortable. And the smell was ten times worse than the average post-match changing room. "He wants the club, but he also wants all of us on the board. It'll look like he's just *joined* the board. Let's face it, we never get any grief from the fans like some Directors do at other clubs, so we're the perfect Board to join. If he bought us out and replaced us, well, he'd have to start from scratch. The fans - and the media, for that matter - *trust* us."

A murmured agreement laboured its way through the steam.

"You're right there," squinted Sefton. "Look at all the flak Ken Bates had to take at Chelsea that time. You're right, Ernie. He wants to use us as a popular front because he knows what a shit everyone thinks *he* is."

"It's perfect," wheezed Cecil, trying to make it look as if his towel was slipping off accidentally, just to give the others a view of his Hampton, which after his encounter with Reg in the Golf Club loo confirmed his belief that his must be larger than most. "I'll make 'em all jealous!" he thought. He said, "He saw how much opposition Murdoch had when he tried to take over *Manchester United*." (He had to emphasise the "Manchester". In the world of football, if anyone referred to "United" most assumed they meant Wanderers United - a constant niggle to fans of Leeds, Newcastle, Hereford and all the other "Uniteds".) "Of course, their being listed on the Stock Market meant there were rules, controls, that sort of thing. It couldn't be kept secret. The Department of Trade and Industry got involved, remember? The Monopolies Mergers Commission. The F.A. blocked it in the end. But with us he can do it. He can get one over on Murdoch. Digital International will have their team. Not just any team, but *us*! By 'eck, it's perfect!"

"If we *never* sell, he can still buy in via half of Malc's share," said Reginald.

"Yes, but he wouldn't have *control*," replied his brother, visibly more sickly than usual after twenty minutes in the sauna. "Blokes like him have to have control."

"The way I see it, then," said Dick Fosset, the rugged record goal scorer, "We can either keep saying no until he goes away, or agree here and now how much we want. I say we hold out for, say, twice what fifty-one percent of our stake is worth."

"Three times!" Ernie Arscott thought like a butcher. Might as well be hung for a sheep as a lamb. That didn't sound right, but who cared?

"Is that a proposition?" Sefton assumed the chair.

"Seconded," said Reginald, who would always support his brother, of course. Although he had suggested a one hundred percent mark-up to Cecil in the Golf Club loo, he was happy to hold out for more. Rather a sheep than a lamb, he thought. Well, he was a butcher, too.

Sefton called for a vote. "Those in favour?"

All six men raised their hands. Cecil Norris's towel slipped off his lap as he shifted on his sweaty backside whilst casting his vote. "Not before time," he smugly thought. "Blimey," thought Dick Fosset. "If mine was that small I'd keep it covered." Upon seeing the size of his son's equipment when he was born, Dick's father had named him accordingly. Over the years, few team-mates were willing to shower alongside him. Comparisons can be cruel, especially if the water is a bit cold.

"Carried!"

* * * * * * * *

Blankopf was onto their little game as soon as one, and then all the others, accepted an offer of three times the value of fifty-one percent of their individual stakes in United. Actually, it didn't seem unreasonable as, with the season at an end, Wanderers had done the treble of Premiership, FA Cup and European Champions Cup. What had Murdoch offered for Man United? £623 million? *His* outlay for fifty-one percent of Wanderers United came to just £36 million. A snip! Blankopf positively *glowed* with pleasure. When Murdoch's attempt to buy Man. Utd. had been blocked, he had laid out about £14 million for just under ten percent of Leeds United. For a bit more than twice that, he, Blankopf, had not only acquired a whole club, but no lesser one than Wanderers, the finest club in Europe, the most famous club in the world.

"That new stadium of theirs will be worth ten times that alone when it's finished!" chortled Blankopf. "And they've just won lots of cups - they're bloody huge, Shaz! This deal will pay back big time!" He and Sharon were relaxing on a huge sofa in their Hong Kong hotel penthouse suite, celebrating the deal.

"*Reeelly?*" said Sharon. She knew that Blankopf got, well, excited when he had pulled off a big deal. She knew she was in for a session on the waterbed (also an optional extra). She had shaved her pubic hair off as per Blankopf's earlier demand.

"Are we goin' next door, then, Blanky darlin'?"

"How'd you guess, Shaz!" He patted her tightly-clad backside as he got up from the sofa they had been lounging on.

"I'll jus' go an' pahder me nose, then."

"And the other end, sweetheart!"

Sharon also put on her new fake fur G-string. She had insisted on fake fur. She couldn't bear the thought of mink farms. Sharon might be brainless, but she wasn't heartless. Mind, Blankopf had said he hadn't been thinking of mink. He'd suggested beaver fur, but Sharon didn't know why.

"Can yer *get* beaver fur, then?"

"You sure can, babe! But not from you!"

"I know, Blanky. You told me this is fake fur."

God! But she was gormless!

Chapter 3 - Meeting the New Chairman

So now Arnie Robinson led the small procession through the impressive corridors of the New Millennium Stadium. The chrome and glass entrance doors were complemented by the chrome and glass lift that took anyone privileged enough to have got past the doorman guarding the entrance up to the various levels within the stand. At one level there was the long row of terribly expensive executive boxes that backed onto an extremely long bar and fast *posh* food servery. Then there were the extortionately expensive so-called Private Boxes - a bit like boxes in a theatre, with huge double-glazed patio doors that could be kept shut against the worst winter weather, but opened if desired to let in the atmosphere of a live game, though with soft upholstered seats and a call button to summons waitress service during the match. In addition there was a set of "special guest boxes" for the private use of each of the club's Directors.

There was also, of course, the Main Board Room, into which Arnie led Blankopf and Sharon. As he entered, Arnie stepped to one side and announced to the room: "Gentlemen! May I introduce Sir Fabian Blankopf and........ er ...." Christ, what was the bimbo's name? The pain in his chest intensified. He scrabbled through his pockets to find the envelope he had written the details on when he had liaised with Jennifer about today's arrangements. Finding it with a surge of relief, he scoured his scribbled notes. "......and Miss......" Shit! *How* could he have forgotten *that* name! "......Smith, Sir Fabian's Personal Assistant."

Sefton Perkins stepped forward. "Well, here you are, Sir Fabian." He offered his hand. Blankopf shook it. Both men had expected to crush the other's hand. It was Boer versus Steelworker. The two held on, increasing their grip until sweat began to break out on both mens' faces. They stared fixedly into one anothers' eyes, each with a sickly, insincere smile.

Malcolm Black stepped forward.

"Welcome, Sir Fabian, welcome Miss.... er..... Smith!"

"Oooh, fanks," squealed Sharon. "Where's the bogs?"

"The bo....? Oh, of course. The ladies. Arnie, would you show Miss *Smith* to the Lady V.I.P.'s Cloakroom?" Personal Assistant? Just *how* personal, wondered Malcolm, pleased that a recent dose of Imodium seemed to be keeping his bowels under control.

"No, I don't want ter 'ang me coat up, mate. I wan' a pee!" Sharon hopped from leg to leg.

Malcolm was unused to Sharon's Essex charm. He thought all birds from down South were posh. He thought only Northern bints said things like "I want a pee".

"Arnie," he asked. "Would you.....?"

"Would you like to come this way, miss?" invited Arnie, all politeness despite his pain. Was it spreading along his arm? Which arm was it for a heart attack? He began to sweat again. *That* was another symptom, he knew. Despite his conviction that he was about to have a heart attack, he still needed to pull out all the stops to make sure he'd still got a job (if only he could survive this heart attack) even if the idea he'd had on the front steps worked. He led her out of the Board Room.

Blankopf and Sefton were by now both purple in the face and white in the knuckles, sweat dripping from them as neither would let go of their terrible handshake.

"You know everyone, of course," gushed Malcolm unnecessarily.

"Of course," snarled Blankopf from between gritted teeth. Why wouldn't this stubborn British bastard admit he was beaten? He knew he couldn't keep this up for much longer. Sharon had taken too much out of him this morning.

"These are Ernie and Reggie Arscott," Malcolm went on regardless, waving a hand in their direction. Both offered guarded nods of greeting, both glad they didn't have the opportunity to shake hands with the uncouth, unloved South African; though Reg was thinking that perhaps Sir Fabian might be a good contact for a decent prostate surgeon. Didn't they have brilliant surgeons in South Africa? Surely the first heart transplant was performed there if his memory served him well?

Malcolm grovelled on. "That's Cecil Norris." More nods. "That's Jack Grimethorpe." Nod, nod. "And that's Dick Fosset, a legend in his own lifetime, our Dick. His goal scoring record for the club still stands." Final nods.

Both Sefton and Blankopf had completely numb right hands by now, so drained of blood were they due to the immense pressure of their combined grip. In that state, both hands, lubricated by sweat, slid easily apart as neither was under the control of its owner. As neither man could feel his right hand, neither was aware of having let go so both felt they had won the encounter. They kept their sickly, insincere smiles in place for one another.

"Drink?" offered Sefton.

"Don't mind if I do. Fosters."

"Fosters. I'm not sure...We don't have that Australian stuff, do we?"

"Yes, yes, of course we do," Malcolm butted in quickly. "I saw to it as soon as I heard it was Sir Fabian's favourite tipple!" With Arnie Robinson out of the room he could take the credit for what had in fact been Arnie's earnest suggestion that the Board Room should lay in a plentiful supply of Fosters. He in turn would never have revealed that he had been given the advice by Jennifer, Blankopf's driver.

"Oh, right, well Fosters it is, then, Fabian," tried Sefton.

A pin dropped. You could hear it. Sefton had dropped the "Sir". What would the South African's reaction be?

The sickly, insincere smile on Blankopf's face became even more insincere.

"Members of *my* boards call me F.B. Anyone else in the outfit calls me *Sir* Fabian." Someone was in danger of losing their trousers or something, because, in the silence which followed, another pin was heard crashing to the floor.

Sefton knew when he had hit a nerve. He poured some iced water onto it, just out of malice. "So who calls you Fabian, then?"

An avalanche of pins cascaded to the floor.

"What the fucking hell are you doing with all those bloody pins?" Blankopf pounced on the opportunity to change the subject.

A red faced Malcolm grinned ingratiatingly at Blankopf as he dropped to his rickety knees and began scrabbling to retrieve the scattered pins from the floor.

"I thought we'd need pins - to pin our rosettes on."

"Rosettes?" Blankopf looked confused. "What are we? Bloody racehorses?"

Sefton, too, welcomed this diversion. "No, it's just that supporters often wear rosettes in their team's colours." The directors never wore them though. What was Malcolm playing at? "We don't normally wear rosettes, Malc. What's the idea?"

"I thought this was a rather special occasion," said Malcolm, still trying to pick up the errant pins. "First meeting between the new Chairman and the rest of the Directors. I thought we could all pose up in the Director's Box in our rosettes. Sort of show the supporters that we have something in common with them. Have our photo taken by our Club Photographer to be passed on to the papers - for a fee, of course - when we decide the time is right."

"Bloody stupid idea," Sir Fabian growled.

Malcolm looked deflated. Perhaps he had pricked himself on one of his own pins. He certainly felt that perhaps he had been a bit premature with his pleasure at the effects of the Imodium he had taken. He felt a distinct twinge in his bowels.

"Well, if you say so, er, FB," he said. He began to struggle to his feet, abandoning the few remaining pins. Yes, he could definitely feel his irritable bowel syndrome kicking in.

"I do. We'll need a board meeting as soon as possible. Who will liaise with my secretary?"

Sefton, considering himself to be the next most senior man present since the arrival of Sir Fabian had uprooted him from the Chairmanship, felt the need to take over.

"That's Arnie Robinson...."

"Which one of you is him? I know that name!" Sir Fabian glowered round at everyone.

"He's the chap who showed your - er - personal assistant - to the cloakroom."

"*Him?* I fired him downstairs."

"Ah!" Sefton was a little nonplussed, but only a little. "Well, we'll replace him as soon as possible. Meanwhile, as he works his notice out he can organise the date of our meeting. After all, he's already made the acquaintance of your - er - personal assistant, so that shouldn't take long, if she's got your diary on her...." Sefton knew he was trying it on.

"*Her?* She doesn't know anything about my business or appointments. Get him to 'phone my office today to sort something out."

"Oh, sorry," Sefton laboured the point. "When she was introduced as your personal assistant, I thought..."

"She's 'is bit o' stuff, Sefton, you know full well!" Jack Grimethorpe didn't go for subtlety.

Sir Fabian rounded on him. "Right first time! You're a bloke after my own heart, mate. Who are you again?"

"Jack. Jack Grimethorpe."

"You and me understand one another!" And for the first time since he'd arrived, he broke into a genuine smile. He clapped Jack on the back. "Tell me. Where's that Commercial Manager of yours? Bloody fine-looking bit of skirt, that. Very shrewd of someone, appointing her. Great thighs, eh?"

"Well, yes," agreed Jack. "I think we all agree with you there! Christine Goodley is her name. Mind, she's not just a pretty face - or a great pair of thighs. She's good at her job, too."

"I know," sprayed Sir Fabian, getting a bit excited. "Which one of you bastards is shagging her, eh?" Looking at this lot, though, he doubted any of them were.

"Well, er, none of us, Sir Fabian," replied Jack. "Fact is, she's a bit of a feminist - a bit unapproachable. Bit like a female spider! But like I say, she's good at her job, and she *is* good to look at, so it's nice having her on board."

"Be nice to have her on *any*thing," laughed Sir Fabian lewdly. "Where is she?"

"Actually, she's paying a visit to a local women's team that will hopefully be coming under our wing for next season."

"Women's team of *what?*" asked Sir Fabian.

"A women's soccer team. It's a growing sport in the UK."

"*Women?* Playing *football?* What are they - bloody Amazons?" Sir Fabian held the view that women should cook, clean and shag, and be on hand to lay on the food and drink for the rugby players after cheering dutifully from the touchline. He'd imagined that the same would apply in this football game that his new acquisition played.

"None of us has seen them, Sir Fabian, but I think they're just ordinary women and girls who play sport - like tennis players, or hockey." Mind, Jack wasn't the only member of the Wanderers board looking forward to seeing the women play.

"Hmmph!" was all Sir Fabian managed in reply. It was time to get back to serious business.

"Now! Who runs the team? I must meet him today."

"That's Ronnie Bone. He'll be at the training ground." Jack looked at Sefton as he spoke, aware that, as Sir Fabian's chosen one, he was going to have to take up the running. Sefton returned Jack's look. The old Board had found a weakness already: Sir Fabian imagined he'd found an ally.

"How soon can you get him here?"

"We can get him on his mobile."

Chapter 4 - Ronnie and Joker

The posed photo, with or without rosettes, forgotten, Sir Fabian was taken down to the palatial home dressing room. There was Ronnie Bone,

The Wanderers Manager for the last six seasons, Ronnie Bone enjoyed an enviable reputation in the world of football. Not just in the world of football: in the world full stop. Ronnie Bone was a household name and face, recognised wherever he went. Holidays were a problem. In all the usual jet-setters' sun spots he was as well known as in England. Spain, Italy, Mexico, South Africa, wherever. You name it, he couldn't go there and simply lie on a sun-lounger by a pool or on a beach without being besieged by autograph hunters, weirdos, people offering team or tactical advice, crawlers, hangers-on, creeps, nerds and babes.

Well, the babes were O.K. as long as his wife Fanny wasn't with him. Except he had only to look at a gorgeous, pouting, young, nubile, virtually naked, sun-bronzed, preferably blonde bit of talent and fifty telephoto lenses immediately sprung out of nowhere to record the moment, so his wife and the world got to know anyway.

Not that Ronnie was likely to stray, female-wise. Fanny was his life-long choice. Or the other way around, really. He had been picked up by her in a Glasgow night-club in his Celtic days when still a raw nineteen-year-old. Fanny was a year younger but already knew where she was going: upmarket! Fortune had favoured her, of course. In her dancing gear of micro skirt and cut-off vest, she burst into Ronnie's life, a vision of his very dreams: a gorgeous, pouting, young, nubile, virtually naked, sun-bronzed blonde bit of talent gyrating seductively on the dance floor. She knew who *he* was: Celtic's new wonder-boy goal-scoring teenaged striker who was (a) being paid £110 a week (this *was* in 1968), (b) famous, (c) single and (d) allegedly very shy, so as helpless and vulnerable as a baby seal. Oh, and (e), he was also quite good looking - a bonus but hardly compulsory for a girl just interested in getting a big house with a swimming pool plus an E-type and an Aston Martin in the double garage.

She gyrated with a couple of tame ex-school friends that she always encouraged to accompany her to dance halls and clubs. Take *one* friend and it could get awkward if the right chap came along. Scheming she may be, but Fanny was at least a little considerate. It wasn't nice to be abandoned in a dance hall and have to worry about getting home alone. So her scheming included bringing *two* friends who would still be company for one another if she decided to go off with a likely lad.

Many Saturday nights went by without Fanny being in the least bit interested in the many lads who tried to get off with her. Then she read in the Daily Record that this Ronnie Bone had been seen in "Nae Troosers", a trendy club in the centre of town. There was his photo, and suddenly Fanny's scheming mind was in overdrive. Footballers were heroes, famous, rich! Just the job!

Hence the outing to "Nae Troosers" and her dance routine which she was certain would catch the eye of young Bone. Which it did, of course, only he was too shy to do anything about it, despite raucous encouragement from his friends.

She had to go to him, of course. She got him out on the dance floor. She suggested he ought to buy a girl a drink. She asked him to take her home because the friends she had come with had disappeared. Ronnie didn't have an E-type, but he did have an MGB roadster. Fanny was well satisfied with that and, to cut a long story short, after a relatively short time she suggested that Ronnie ought to propose to her; which he did and was delighted when Fanny accepted.

Only after all *that* did he discover that all was not *quite* what it had seemed with his gorgeous, pouting, young, nubile, sun-bronzed, blonde fiancée. He only got to see her naked once he had made things official with a suitably chunky engagement ring and discovered that the sun-bronze *and* blonde were out of a bottle. Fanny had carefully kept herself to herself whilst hunting down her quarry. Just a bit of light petting was all she allowed the sexually inexperienced Ronnie, and the MGB helped with its large transmission tunnel between the bucket seats.

"Ah thought *all* o' ye hair wid be blonde," he had stammered, Fanny now naked at his side on the bed of a borrowed flat (for Ronnie, the young Highlander signed from Forres Mechanics and cared for in the big city by a motherly landlady employed by the vast Celtic club, had only his room in the landlady's house and was allowed no visitors upstairs). With such an expensive engagement ring on her finger and an extensively publicised engagement, Fanny felt able to allow Ronnie a few pre-marital delights safe in the belief that not turning out to be a real blonde wouldn't cause any problems. By then, though, Ronnie didn't care. Ronnie was in love.

"Ah didn'ae realise that *every*one's - well - private hair - wasn'ae black," continued Ronnie, not at that moment remembering that his team mate Jock Campbell, a fiery redhead, was in fact covered in a mass of ginger body hair, pubes and all.

"Really?" replied Fanny. Good grief, she thought.

But on a football field, Ronnie was a different person. Fast, skilful, two-footed, hard, uncompromising, quick thinking and with almost mystical vision, he was fast making a name for himself in the Scottish League, Celtic having beaten several clubs to his signature from his Highland League side, the whole Board of which were drunk for a week as a perk out of what was a record fee for the club.

Once engaged to Fanny he was rarely out of the tabloid papers. She went everywhere with him.

Forres Mechanics, Celtic, Leeds United, Chelsea, Celtic again and forty-two appearances for Scotland led him to the end of his playing career and his first crack at management with Hamilton Academicals. Then he was tempted south again to manage Newcastle United and after a successful spell there Wanderers made him an offer he couldn't refuse.

Summoned on his mobile 'phone, he had left the training ground and now found himself face-to-face with Wanderers' new Chairman. Polite introductions over, Sir Fabian got down to business.

"I want you to build a new team, Ron," ordered Sir Fabian. "World beaters."

"They already are," replied Ronnie.

"As I understand it, Wanderers are only European Champions. Am I right?" He looked around the assembled company as if daring to be contradicted, his coarse voice booming off the bare changing room walls and floor. Hearing no contradiction, he went on. "I said *world* beaters, Ron, not just Europe."

"There's only tha' silly Toyota Cup thing in Japan, then." explained Ronnie. "We're due tae play some South American side fo' that, but its a tuppenny ha'penny thing, nae worth the cost o' gettin' there."

"Ah, but it *will* be. Digital International have bought the rights to televise it and believe you me, because Wanderers are in it, the whole world wants to see the game. It'll be worth millions to the winner."

"Fine." Ronnie seemed unimpressed, mainly because he *was* unimpressed.

"Then there's that world club thing in Brazil next year," continued Sir Fabian. "You'll be expected to win that, so I say again, I want you to build a world beating team. Money no object."

"The FIFA World Club Championship? We cann'ae play in that, man," said Ronnie. "It clashes wi' the F.A. Cup and we're defendin' that."

"Which one's the F.A. Cup?" Sir Fabian's staff had briefed him on the big money-making opportunities that buying Wanderers United would bring, which is why he knew of the Brazil tournament, but he hadn't yet got his head round the names of the various competitions that Wanderers played in.

Ronnie's eyebrows disappeared up into his hair. "*Which one's* the F.A. Cup? Wha's the use o' a Chairman who has tae ask *that!*" It was a rhetorical question.

Sir Fabian's face took on a thunderous expression. Jack Grimethorpe leapt in, clapping Ronnie affably on the back and laughing fit to burst. Falsely, but still fit to burst. "Your sense of humour, Ronnie, you kill me!" More false laughter accompanied by desperate facial signals to the rest of the board, who, fearing that somehow their anticipated fortunes from their sell-out to Sir Fabian might be snatched out of their grasp before they even had it, slowly took the hint and began to laugh too. Synchronised false laughing.

"That Ronnie!" said Dick Fosset, "Always had the dressing room in fits in his playing days. Worth a goal start in any game!" Sir Fabian was unlikely to know that Dick and Ronnie had never shared a dressing room. He'd probably even forgotten Dick's goal scoring record for the club.

Malcolm chipped in. His irritable bowel syndrome was beginning to flare up again. He was desperate that Sir Fabian should not be upset, so he thought he'd better do something quickly, and removing Ronnie from the scene immediately seemed the wisest thing he could do.

"Well, now you've met Sir Fabian and broken us up with that uncanny wit of yours, Ronnie, you'd better get on and start building the team that Sir Fabian wants." Malcolm began to lead Ronnie out of the dressing room. "No time like the present!"

He led Ronnie down the corridor to the match-day office. When the new Millennium stand was being built with its palatial Managerial Suite on the same level as the Board room, Ronnie had been a bit nonplussed.

"Ah need an office by the dressin' rooms," he had complained as the building was taking shape. "On match days ah need tae get tae stuff sometimes. Ah dinn'ae need carpets an' all that."

Some rapid redesigning had allowed for there to be a "match-day office" for the manager and his assistant in the same corridor as the dressing rooms and Ronnie was placated. As long as he had a base near to the action on match days, he could put up with a centrally-heated, carpeted, double-glazed four hundred square foot office overlooking the pitch from which to carry out many of his every day activities. There was even a separate office (only two hundred square feet) for his Assistant Manager Joker Wallace.

"Somewhat different from facilities at the Accie's, eh, Joker?" Ronnie had said when they had moved into their new offices. Ronnie had played with Joker at Celtic and taken him with him as his Assistant Manager since that first job at Hamilton.

"Tell you what, mate," observed Joker. "In the Accie's little cubby-hole it was a doddle to throw empty cups into the bin in the corner. It'll be a bastard in your new office."

Joker was in the match day office when Malcolm and Ronnie arrived. Six foot tall and with a face like a bag of nails framed by a mane of long greying hair, he was pinning a large and colourful "Football Manager's Calendar 1999 - 2000 Season" on the wall. The photo for August was an equally large and colourful silicone enhanced redhead, naked except for a strategically placed green and white rosette.

"Joker!" greeted Malcolm. "You came as well. Why didn't you come to meet Sir Fabian?"

"Left that to the Boss," replied Joker. "I had things to do."

"So I see," said Malcolm, smirking towards the calendar. "Who's she?" He leaned forward and squinted at the caption. "Nineteen year old Tiffani Clitheroe, known as 'Clith' to her friends," he read. "Clith!" he laughed, turning to the other two with a laddish wink. "I'll bet, eh, lads?" He read on. "Clith is a Celtic fan and loves nothing better than a good long ball up the middle and admires players like Mark Viduka with that perfect first touch." Malcolm straightened up. "We ought to have one of these for the board room!" He could enjoy looking at such images but his unpredictable intestines made any kind of liaison with the opposite sex rather difficult. His wife had long since ceased to allow him any access to her bed. His nocturnal snoring, gut-rumbling and farting had disqualified him from sex years ago.

His one attempt to gain satisfaction from a prostitute was during a trade conference in London and had been a monumental flop. He had chosen a number at random from a card in a Tottenham Court Road 'phone box and arranged for the girl to come to his hotel. So nervous was he at the infidelity he contemplated that he was stricken by a cripplingly painful bout of wind and diarrhoea just at the moment when the girl arrived at his door. Doubled up with agony on the toilet, he was helpless to do anything and had to just listen to her insistent knocking and eventual unladylike curse as she gave up and went away.

"Well you're not having this one," Joker snorted. "A kit firm sends one out to each club, specifically for the manager, so hands off! What's the new Chairman like, boss?"

"Wha' a *wanker!*" Ronnie gave vent to his feelings. "How come we get a noo Chairman who disn'ae know wha' the fochin' F.A. Cup is?"

"Well," tried Malcolm, "Give him a chance, lad. He's South African. He's got a few things to learn yet."

Joker looked puzzled. "Doesn't know what the F.A. Cup is? Who?"

"This Blankopf chappie, our new Chairman. Bluidy hell, Malcolm, why did ye sell out tae *him?*"

Malcolm felt uncomfortable, not just in his intestines but mentally as well. "He's got loads of cash, Ronnie. With his money you can get any player you want."

"We don't need any players at the moment, do we boss," stated Joker. "We won the League, the Cup and the European Champions Cup with the squad we've got. If it ain't broke, don't fix it." This last point was directed towards Malcolm.

"Well, Sir Fabian seems very insistent that you rebuild the side and win the FIFA World Club Championship in the coming season. Look, I'd better get back to the rest. I'll leave you two to start your plans, eh? Draw up a list of the greatest players in the world - and then we'll get 'em all here for the start of the season. See you later!"

Malcolm scuttled out of the match day office, undecided about whether or not to fit in a quick visit to the loo in response to the insistent churning of his bowels. He left behind him two very disgruntled men.

"Wha' total *bollocks!*" growled Ronnie. "Yon new Chairman wants us tae get rid o' the lads we've got noo and put taegether a bluidy World XI as Wanderers United."

"I reckon," said Joker, "that we should just ignore him. Since when have you put up with any interference from the board?"

"Ye're right, laddie. The Board sets limits on wages and provides the cash for buying new players, but that's it. Aye, bollocks. Hey! I wonder wha's goin' on in the dressin' room." He quickly shut the door, then went behind one of the two small desks in the room and pressed a button on the intercom.

* * * * * * * * *

In the home dressing room, Malcolm arrived back to find Sir Fabian inspecting the treatment area, Jack Grimethorpe by his elbow explaining everything and answering his questions.

"Massage couches?" he was saying, his bombastic voice amplified by the echo of the large tiled room. "We can improve *that* facility. I'll get some massage girls in from one of my little establishments in Bangkok! Cheer the team up, eh?"

"Well, it's not exactly *that* sort of massage, Sir Fabian," explained Jack. "It'd take the lads' minds off the game a bit, eh? Mind," he looked thoughtful. "It'd be a great way of relaxing the lads *after* a game." And a few Thai massage girls at the club could become a Director's perk, too. He'd point that out to the rest of the Board later, when Blankopf had gone.

Sir Fabian turned and saw that Malcolm was back with them. "Where's that manager of yours, then? On the 'phone recruiting a world beating team?"

"I think so, Sir Fabian."

"*Think? THINK!*" Sir Fabian's roar echoing round the dressing room was doubly deafening, hiding the sound of his spittle hitting the tiled walls and floor. "He'd better be! I want this club to dominate the *world*!"

Malcolm looked unusually cowed. "What I meant was, yes, he is. He's with our Assistant Manager, they're talking about it now."

"*Talking* about it? They should have started 'phoning clubs. I've no time for wasters. I didn't get where I am today by sitting on my arse talking about doing something. I got on and *did* it!"

"Well, yes, they were talking names as I left. You know, making a list of players they want," Malcolm lied.

"Yes, well if you ask me, that Ron bloke is trouble. He bloody *criticised* me back there. We'll get rid of him."

There was a moment's stunned silence in the dressing room, broken eventually by Sefton.

"As your *vice*-Chairman, I think I ought to point out that Ronnie has been the most successful Premiership manager there has ever been. We did the treble last season. If anyone can put together a world-beating side, he can."

Blankopf glared at him. "Are you saying that he's the man to build the team I want?"

"Exactly."

"Right, then we'll let him do that. *Then* we'll sack him!"

There were looks of disquiet amongst the Board members present, though none of them actually made a sound. Except for Sefton.

"Sack him after he's built up a new team? You can't do that!"

"No? Then I'll pull out of the deal, gentlemen. If you look at the microscopic print in the contracts......"

"You can pull out at any time in the first twelve months with all your money back from us plus interest." Ernie Arscott, ever vigilant, had found a magnifying glass and read the microscopic print. He wasn't too bothered by it because as far as he was concerned, once Blankopf's cash was in his bank he didn't care *what* the conditions of the contract were. His brother Reginald had agreed with him. Let Blankopf have his way for twelve months and the money was in the bag. Who cared what happened to Wanderers after that. If the club continued to prosper, then so would they. If it went to the wall, they would each still have a few million to their name.

"Right! So we let him build the team, then get rid and bring in someone who'll do as he's told! Agreed?" Blankopf glared at the assembled board, daring them to defy him.

No-one voiced dissent.

* * * * * * * *

In the match-day office, Ronnie and Joker looked at one another with mounting fury. They'd heard it all over the intercom, installed so that Ronnie or Joker could talk to one another between the dressing room and the office. It saved shouting along the corridor. Ronnie released the button.

"The bastards! The whole fucking board has just caved in to that wanker Blankopf! Get rid of us!" It was Joker speaking. Talk of getting rid of Ronnie meant him as well. They were a double act. Joker wouldn't stay without Ronnie, not for a million pounds a week.

"Money!" gritted Ronnie. "Did ye hear that? They caved in because Blankopf threatened tae pull out an' take his money *from them*! He's bought the bloody lot o' them!"

"We may as well get out now," sighed Joker.

"No; no, I've another idea. What d'ye think o' this?"

Ronnie began to explain his idea to Joker. Joker's eyes slowly widened and a grin creased his ugly features as Ronnie revealed his plan.

Chapter 5 - Flashback

Some two years earlier, in a dusty office upstairs in a Portakabin sprawl, Malcolm Black sat in a scruffy office chair at a scruffy office desk facing a scruffily dressed man: Bert Barnard, the Senior Foreman at Consolidated Solids. Bert had been Malcolm's right hand man for more than twenty years as Malcolm had nursed his building firm up into a huge enterprise that had recently begun to tender for contracts abroad. Malcolm and Bert had dug footings, mixed cement and concrete, laid bricks, lifted lintels into place, secured roof trusses, secured roof tiles and shagged crumpet together in the early years, and as the business expanded it was Bert who took charge on the various sites whilst Malcolm got on with the wheeling, dealing and tendering.

The crumpet-shagging stopped as each of them married and then there was more time to devote to the business. With not a single paper qualification between them, they had nevertheless become wealthy due to a lot of hard work as well as some pretty risky deals that bordered on the fraudulent. Neither man was beyond using a bit of knocked off stuff. Paying labourers cash in hand to avoid tax and national insurance complications was routine practice, as was letting some men have a few hours off so that they could go and sign on.

The cost to Malcolm was his martyrdom to irritable bowel syndrome, probably brought on by the increasing stresses that grew with the business. At first, he just thought he was getting more than his fair share of diarrhoea, but his wife eventually persuaded him to visit his GP in case it was something more serious. Thus began a series of investigations that led to the conclusion that Malcolm was suffering from nothing more serious than IBS. Much relieved, his wife simply began to buy Andrex in nine-packs.

"I want to build that stand for Wanderers, Bert." The final stage in the rebuilding of Wanderers' stadium was the replacement of the old West Stand by a state-of-the-art showpiece stand that would be the envy of football clubs the world over.

"I know, Mal, but it's a bloody big job. Millions. We've never done anything like it. Do you know the right sort of architects and engineers for that sort of job?"

"Yes, I reckon so. I just want the job, though. It's my bloody club, after all. You know what it means to me." Malcolm looked forward to the increased prestige he would have on the Board if his company built the proposed new West Stand. It would make the New Stamford Stadium the best in Europe. It would certainly be used if England got the World Cup in 2006. It would make Old Trafford and Stamford Bridge look second rate.

A frown suddenly creased Malcolm's brow. "Excuse me. I must go to the bog."

Bert was the only person apart from Malcolm's wife who knew about his martyrdom to IBS, though at first he had been confused when Malcolm had told him about it because he wasn't aware that his long-term friend knew any Conservative politicians.

So: architects and engineers were commissioned and over the next few months a design was produced, costed and submitted to the Wanderers United Board by the deadline stated in the Invitation to Tender. Malcolm had wanted to buy and include the twin towers from Wembley but Wembley Stadium Limited wouldn't sell them at the time. Twelve months after the conversation in the Portakabin office, the Wanderers United Board (with Malcolm waiting outside, as an interested party) accepted the design and tender from Consolidated Solids.

The Arscott brothers had expressed reservations. "Won't people think it stinks if we give the contract to Malcolm's firm?" asked Ernie, with Reg nodding agreement beside him.

"It'll be all open and above board," reassured Sefton exercising his authority as Chairman. "Everything made public. If any of the other companies want to challenge our decision, we've nothing to hide. Mal's was easily the cheapest tender, and meets all our requirements with respect to seating capacity, refreshment facilities, bogs, all the other stuff. He's even included a special guest box for each of us to use as we wish - nice touch, that. You know, perks for people who work for us, favours to mates, gestures to promote good P.A."

So the vote went three in favour of awarding the contract to Consolidated Solids, two against, with Sefton, as Chairman, not voting. Malcolm was summoned into the board room.

"We're giving you the contract, Malcolm lad. At least we know you'll do us proud."

Malcolm was delighted, not least because of the little idea of his about the private guest boxes for the Board members. He had already planned which one would be his: one by a support column that would contain various service connections, not least important of which was a pipe from a VIP lounge toilet on the level above. At the appropriate time, he would secretly have his own WC installed into his box, plumbed into the downpipe in the column. He'd position it so he could watch the game whilst seated on it. No more missing large chunks of a game if his condition flared up. Only sufferers of IBS would understand.

He felt a disturbance in his bowels right then. Of course, it had been a stressful few weeks leading up to this day and the tension as he'd waited outside the meeting had been almost unbearable. He scrabbled in his pocket for his Imodium and threw one down his throat. Swallowing awkwardly, he beamed round at his fellow Board members.

"Er - gentlemen," stammered Reginald, the younger, less cadaverous Arscott. He and his brother had been the only voices and votes against awarding the contract and they felt the need to regain some credibility amongst their colleagues.

Their colleagues all turned to face them, a little peevishly if truth be told.

"Can I - er - *we* - suggest a name for Malcolm's stand? Could we call it the 'Millennium Stand'?" The brothers were nothing if not unoriginal. Sefton allowed a patronising smile to creep across his features.

"Great idea! The 'Millennium Stand'. I like that! We hadn't thought about a name - other than just 'West Stand'. What do people think?"

People apparently thought it was a good idea.

"That's carried, then. Proposed by Reg, seconded by Ernie, carried unanimously!"

Club Secretary Arnie Robinson duly minuted the decision.

"Thanks, lads. You've made my day!" beamed Malcolm. Hands were heartily shaken around the room and the meeting moved to the next item on the agenda: an approach from the F.A.'s Developments Officer for Women's Football, hoping to encourage Wanderers United to begin or adopt a women's team to help boost the image of the women's game.

Sefton read out the letter. "Who'd do it?" he asked.

"We could pass it onto Christine," suggested Dick Fossett.

"Commercial Manager?" queried Cecil Norris. "Is that really her job?"

"She's a raving women's libber," explained Dick.

"Oh, of course."

"Those in favour, then?" asked Sefton.

All hands went up, even Sefton's, so carried away was he at the thought of young, athletic women in Wanderers United kit, running around, working up a sweat, their football shirts sticking to their bodies..........

"Sefton? My arm's getting tired!" Ernie's plea jolted Sefton back to reality.

"Carried!"

* * * * * * * * *

Malcolm had to sub-contract all the work, of course. Demolishing the old stand was no problem. Cecil Norris's Elastic Plastic plc did its usual job with the old seats, although there was no chance of a fraudulent double contract on *this* job! Faithful Wanderers season ticket holders were allowed to buy their old seat for £25. If they did (Commercial Manager Christine Goodley's idea, this) they were allowed to choose which seat they wanted in the new Millennium Stand.

"We can't yet tell them how much the season tickets in the new stand will be," she explained to the Board one day. God, what a leering, lecherous bunch of old farts they were, she found herself thinking. Male chauvinist pigs, the lot of them. All that "pet" and "love" and "lolly dolly" and arms round her shoulder - typical sexist behaviour. Ugh! Presumably "lolly dolly" was their patronising way of describing her job as Commercial Manager. "That shouldn't matter, though. We'll definitely be charging them more - quite a lot more - but by the time we've got a price for them they'll feel really tight if they don't cough up. We've got them by the balls, really, gentlemen." She knew they hated her using "laddish" expressions.

Wouldn't mind you having me by *my* balls, Sefton, Cecil, Jack and Dick all happened to be thinking. Has *any*one ever cracked her? Tasty but frosty! Like an ice lolly! They often wondered if she knew why they called her "lolly dolly".

"Well done, love," said Sefton. "You have some great ideas for a wo....." Shit! Can't say that!

"For a what, Mr Perkins?" Christine looked belligerent.

"Now, we've told you before, Chris....." Sefton was buying time.

"Chris*tine*!"

".....Sorry, Christine." Oh, thank God! Inspiration! "For a *way*....... some great ideas for a *way* to squeeze an extra quid or two out of the punters."

Christine looked suspicious but said no more. Sefton was just grateful that he'd managed to get himself out of a tight corner.

Soon afterwards, problems arose with the construction work. First of all, the reinforced concrete support columns had to be erected. The company that got the contract, Stressed Erections, had recently relocated from northern Turkey where it had built countless blocks of flats and offices. It's Chief Engineer wasn't that experienced in building enterprises, having cut his teeth installing a number of flood defence schemes along the coast of Venezuela. The company had submitted the cheapest tender and as its workers swarmed over the site, the foundations quickly went in and the support columns began to rise.

The site foreman for Stressed Erections was a bitter man. He'd been with them for years but they had never promoted him beyond Site Foreman. He had seen spotty-faced young newcomers join the company and get promoted over him time after time. This was to be his last job for Stressed Erections before he retired, so he felt no particular enthusiasm for what he was doing. Plus, he was a Man. United fan, so bitterly anti-Wanderers. So he saw to it that the concrete poured into the foundations was what might generously be described as a rather anaemic mix.

The Chief Engineer had to do all the calculations concerning stresses and loads to determine the gauge of steel to be used in the support columns. Somewhere in the middle of his deliberations his Paraguayan girlfriend had an exceptionally loud orgasm. She was a particularly demanding nymphomaniac and one strategy the Chief Engineer had found useful was to work whilst on the job, so to speak – strumping her doggy-fashion so he could make notes or use his calculator without her tits getting in the way. He could even use her back to rest his paperwork on. Because of her untimely distraction, however, he misplaced a decimal point.

"Cara mia!" he exclaimed. "You alla right, bambino?" He kept right on thrusting, though.

His girlfriend, kneeling on the carpet with her head and shoulders resting on the sofa, breathlessly assured him that she was fine. Kneeling behind her, his paperwork and calculator conveniently to hand, the Chief Engineer resumed his calculations. He'd nearly finished - the calculations, that is - and his knees were getting carpet burns. When he *had* finished, he'd change positions. The sooner the better, so he didn't bother to check his calculations. Her knees must be hurting, too, so he decided on a side-to-side on the sofa. Considerate lover; crap engineer.

Consequently, the girders, when they arrived, looked very slender for the job they were meant to do.

"Never mind," said the disaffected, Man. United-supporting site foreman. "All this modern bloody architecture is made to look like a bloody spider's web." He was only glad that Bert Barnard, the Chief Foreman for the main contractors, had chosen to take his three-week holiday at this time. He was away in Canada, studying the engineering on the Rockie Mountain railways.

The concrete to be poured into shuttering around the slender girders wasn't mixed on site. It had to be poured in one continuous stream around each girder, from bottom to top. It couldn't be allowed to set halfway up: that would create a weak spot.

Bert Crapper's Concrete got the contract. Cheapest tender again. Bert's family was not connected to the famous sanitary-ware merchants, but the name helped him to get work. So much, at that time, that he had to *sub* sub contract. He took the first offer he got as there were tight deadlines to meet. The new stand had to be ready for the start of the new season. A call from a man offering to do the job for a fraction of the price he had tendered was received and, with the prospect of making a profit for doing nothing, Bert accepted. He wasn't to know that the gangers mixing the loads for the convoy of cement trucks that took the concrete to the Wanderers stadium were cowboys. They had written instructions but few of them could read. They just added miscellaneous proportions of sand, cement and aggregate so that the strength of concrete that ended up being poured into the support columns was extremely variable.

But of course, the Board knew nothing of this. They just saw a magnificent new stand rising in the place of the old West Stand, as did the fans who regularly packed the other three stands. That season, 1998-99, went superbly well, of course, despite the lack of atmosphere created by the open side where the Millennium Stand was being built. The stand rose, keeping pace with the Wanderers' chances of winning the treble as well as with Sir Fabian's offers to the Directors as he sought to buy the club. By the time Wanderers were playing out the final games of the season the bulk of the *New* Millennium Stand (as the Board had later decided it should be named) was in place, a huge stressed steel and concrete construction that acted as a sounding board for the roar of the home fans, echoing their noise and creating a unique new atmosphere.

By the time the treble was in the bag and Sir Fabian had bought the fifty-one percent of each Director's stake in the club, most of the internal work was complete: new Board room, Manager's suite, training room, treatment room, fitness centre, sauna, changing rooms, manager's match day office (hastily included), restaurants, bar areas and fast food serveries, press room - all these and more. The executive boxes, private boxes and the Board members' special guest boxes were being kitted out with appropriately comfortable furniture. Malcolm made sure his was next to the required support column with its down pipe from the toilets on the level above. He then got Bert Barnard himself to see to the installation of his customised toilet.

Up in the box itself, the newly varnished door shutting off the bustle of workmen passing to and fro along the corridor, Malcolm explained to Bert what he wanted.

"I want the lav *here*," he said, marking a spot with the toe of his boot on the dusty cement floor. "That way, I can see the whole game from the karsi if I want to. You've no idea, Bert. It's torture, this IBS. I've tried everything. I've seen specialists. They pumped stuff up my arse so they could see my intestines on an X-ray. They pump it in, then they pump bloody gas in after it, *then* they put you on a bloody table like a fairground ride that twists you in every bloody direction. D'you know why they do that?"

Bert was sympathetic towards his friend of many years, but he had no real desire to be told the intricacies of a colonoscopy. He was trying to shut out the images that Malcolm's account was conjuring up in his mind.

"Do what?"

"Twist you about in all directions after they've pumped the X-ray stuff and gas up your arse."

"No, no idea, mate."

"Get this." Clearly, Malcolm was building up to a revelation he found embarrassing. He glanced in the direction of the door to make sure it was shut. "It is to make sure all the insides of your bowels are coated with the stuff. They might as well shake you like a bloody cocktail shaker!"

"Sounds a bit like slip casting to me," said Bert, eyeing up the floor and wall where he was to fit this secret thunder box for Malcolm.

"Slip casting? What's that?"

"What? Oh, my daughter does pottery at Art School. She's told me about it. You have a mould, and you put runny clay in and sort of turn the mould over and over to coat the inside. Then you pour out the surplus, let the lining dry and you've got a hollow shape you can fire in a kiln."

Malcolm's brow furrowed as he tried to follow Bert's description. "You'd have a bloody funny looking ornament to put on your sideboard if you did that with your bowels!"

Bert's mind switched from images of Malcolm with a funnel up his backside, to the estimates of how Malcolm's special toilet would look when it was done, to one of a shiny, luridly coloured model of Malcolm's large intestine occupying the centre of his sideboard. For Christ's sake! Malcolm *was* an old mate, so Bert just forced a laugh.

"Do 'em in club colours, Mal! You could get 'em done from all yer star players! One up from replica shirts!"

"Its not funny, Bert. It was bloody degrading, if you want to know. Two bloody technicians and a doctor and *all* bloody women. Even when they've finished, they send you to a cubicle with a karsi in to get rid of the X-ray stuff and the gas. All you do for five bloody minutes is *fart!* You can hear the women talking outside, so *they* can hear *you!*"

"So what did they find out?" There was some concern in Bert's voice.

"Nothing! Bloody nothing!"

"That's good, isn't it? No cancer, like?"

"Well - yes, I suppose so. You do wonder about that. They want to eliminate things like that. They just end up ruling loads of nasty things out and you're left with this bloody irritable bowel syndrome. Not life threatening, true, but a *bloody* nuisance. You know what the bloody doctor said while she was photographing my guts? She said I had a very photogenic bowel! I told her I hadn't been paid a compliment by a bird for some time, so I'd settle for that!"

"Photogenic bowel? That's not exactly a bird-puller, Mal!"

At least Malcolm managed a smile. "Yea, right!. So, what about this job then? Karsi there, a partition wall across here - just to hide the loo: a concealed door so if anyone visits, they don't see it. Hardly anyone knows about my problem, and I don't want them to."

"Yeh, no problem. You say there's a soil pipe down this column?"

"That's right. All you have to do is cut through that panel and there's a duct inside for pipes and wires and stuff. The soil pipe should be in there too."

"Seems straightforward enough. You've got a water supply plumbed into the box already, haven't you?"

"Yes, all the boxes have so people can have a brew if they want without having to leave the box." Malcolm had thought of everything where the Directors' guest boxes were concerned. He'd planned to have his loo with a view from the very start. Supplying each Director's guest box with running water was hardly necessary. The pretext of it allowing them to make a cup of tea for their guests was pretty feeble but it allowed for a water supply to be available in each box with no questions asked. Vital to his plan, and oh! the relief of not having to suffer agonies during games. Malcolm couldn't wait! He very rarely went to away games. You couldn't always be sure of the toilets. At home games he could always find an excuse to dash out of the Directors' Box if his bowels played him up - which was frequently. He always carried a roll of Andrex and some wet wipes in his briefcase in addition to the Imodium capsules he kept in his pocket. One of the side effects of prolonged use of some anti-diarrhoea drugs was, according to some sources, irritable bowel syndrome itself, but as Malcolm already suffered from it, he didn't worry about that. He would shun most away games, saying that "some of us ought to show an interest in the reserves," which was true, of course. It did mean, too, that whenever a player was drafted into the first team from the reserves, Malcolm was able to talk authoritatively about him to the others. It always impressed visiting Directors, few of whom bothered to watch their reserves.

"So," said Bert. "I'll get started straight away. Well, first thing tomorrow."

"No, not tomorrow." Malcolm looked a little anxious. "Start Sunday. I've got the karsi at my place. I bought it at B & Q. You've got to get it up here with nobody seeing." He was desperate that no-one should see it and start asking questions. "And make sure you keep this door *locked* when you aren't working - *and* when you are." They were leaving the box, opening the door on the corridor with its busy workmen carrying tools and fittings past every few minutes.

And so it was that by the beginning of April in the Wanderers treble-winning season, Malcolm's loo was up and running. Although the New Millennium Stand was nowhere near finished, Malcolm did have a sneak preview from his guest box, hidden from view behind one-way glass. Bliss! Made even more blissful by the 2 - 0 win over title contenders Leeds.

As he was leaving, Bert, whom Malcolm had informed of his intention to try out his box, hailed him from along the corridor. There was a worried frown on his face. "Mal, I'm glad I caught you. I think you ought to see something.

Down here." He led Malcolm along the corridor, past a number of doors that led into other guest boxes. "In here." He led Malcolm into a box much like Malcolm's, except that it seemed larger. No partitioned-off secret karsi! "What's up?" Malcolm sensed the worry in Bert and had become worried himself.

"I'm fitting this box out - it's Dick Fossett's. He's asked for Sky TV to be installed. I was drilling here to fit a couple of rawl bolts for the TV shelf and - well, look for yourself." Bert picked up a large screwdriver and pushed it into a hole in the wall. When he made a few stabbing movements, coarse dust and small chunks fell out of the hole. "See?"

"Not really, no."

"This hole is drilled into the concrete of one of the support columns," explained Bert. "It's soft as shit, Mal. I used a tungsten bit on me hammer drill, leant me full weight on it and nearly did meself a mischief. It was like drilling through putty. This stuff was done by that crew that just 'phoned up, wasn't it? Paid in cash? Who were they?"

"Search me, Bert. They 'phoned, gave a quote, Crapper said yes. He just gave a name, apparently. John. Crapper told him when to start delivering and on the due date the trucks started to roll up. Our lads did the shuttering and supervised the pouring, but yes, you're right, the concrete was mixed by that bloke John. He came here for his money when the job was done, asked for cash - a bit more than we usually give cash in hand, but there were deadlines. What do we do?" Now Malcolm *was* worried.

"I'll just make some random checks on the concrete used in each of the columns. I'll let you know. In the meantime, don't panic. The girders inside are what really support the weight. The concrete just covers them and gives you something to fix things to."

So Bert set about his checks with Malcolm at least half reassured by his explanation about the importance of the girders rather than the concrete.

Chapter 6 - Team Building

"....So ye're all free tae leave."

It hadn't been an easy speech for Ronnie to make. He was glad to have Joker, as ever, by his elbow. Which was better than being by Joker's elbow. Joker's name came from his playing days as an uncompromising central defender. He had a reputation for being particularly efficient with his elbow, especially when defending set pieces. Not the nasty, cheek-bone breaking elbow that seems to have crept into the modern game. No, Joker's elbow was far more subtle, used to find the solar plexus, kidneys or testicles to lay opponents out with no visible damage. Joker's skill was no doubt helped by the lack of multiple close-up slow motion cameras that tend to expose skulduggery these days. Players would tumble, gasping for breath (solar plexus), back arched (kidneys) or with eyes watering in foetal position (nuts). The referee and linesmen saw nothing, the cold spray was applied and the victim was likely to have a quieter game.

"That bastard Wallace," a wheezing forward might croak from the ground as the cold spray was judiciously used by the trainer.

"Caught you wiv' 'is funny bone, did 'e?" one well-known Premiership physio asked on one occasion, wielding the magic aerosol (this was not that long ago: magic sponges were a thing of the past) and making the kind of medical diagnosis somewhat removed from the level of attention heaped upon the pampered, overpaid stars of today.

"I'll give 'im funny bone, if that's 'is idea of a joke!"

Hence the name.

Next to Ronnie, Joker looked every bit as uncomfortable as his manager. Ronnie had just explained to his treble-winning squad that the new club Chairman, Sir Fabian Blankopf, had told him to completely rebuild the team.

"It'll cost the club a bloody fortune." The speaker was a squat, shaven headed individual sporting a five o'clock shadow. It was midfielder and captain Troy Hard. He had recently negotiated a new contract for two years, rumoured (accurately) to be worth £52,000 a week, making him the Wanderers' highest paid player.

"Blankopf knows. Ah told 'im. Money's nae object. Ye'll all get what's due tae ye."

Which in all cases was the full balance of their contract plus variable sums to recompense them for projected loss of extra earnings from appearances in Champions League matches, should Wanderers qualify - which of course, they had done.

"Ye know we wouldn't normally do this," Ronnie went on, referring to himself as well as Joker. "We'd normally tell a chairman like that tae get stuffed. But we've got our reasons. It'll make interesting reading in the papers, and it'll be tragic tae break up what I reckon is the greatest team in England. Still, ye're all internationals, ye've all won loads o' cups an' that. Ye've all got more money than's guid fer ye...." some gentle laughter round the room at that ".... an' now ye're bloody agents are set to make more money themselves!" Louder laughter. "So make *their* day and give 'em a bell. Good luck to ye all!"

"D'you reckon to have this new team together for the start of the season?" Fred Menzies, "Bruce" to his team mates, was the newest member of the squad, having been drafted in as reserve 'keeper midway through the treble winning season. At only £12,000 a week he was the pauper of the squad, but as an Australian international he had done remarkably well for himself at only twenty three years of age.

Most of his money was sent home to his mum in Useless Loop, a little cluster of weatherboard shacks near Shark Bay, over 120 miles of dirt road from the main Great Northern Highway in remote Western Australia. When his mum had tried to cash Bruce's first cheque in the little post office agency they didn't have enough cash for her. Since then they had made sure they did.

"If you don't mind my saying, Mrs Menzies, that's a lot of cash. Are you sure it wouldn't be better off in the bank?" suggested the concerned cashier one day, counting out sixty thousand Australian dollars, a monthly routine.

"Stone the crows, no. I don't trust banks. Never needed one, neither has Mr Menzies. Always deal in cash. Fred may want some dosh when he pays a visit. You never know." Bruce's mum, of course called him Fred, his given name, and couldn't understand why all references to him in the British press cuttings that she regularly received with her cheque, as well as on the satellite TV sports programmes, were as "Bruce". She was characteristically suspicious of city habits and ways. Banks could cheat you. They could even go bust. She preferred to keep the cash under the floor of her shack - in a metal box, so the termites wouldn't get it.

"You'll have to go flat out like a lizard drinking; and paying compo to clubs to sign more world-class players will cost another fortune," continued Bruce. "The guy must be dumb as a drover's dog-shit!"

"Blankopf knows all that," said Ronnie. "I think he feels that wi' a team made up of players fra' all over the world, it'll get T.V. viewers fra' all over the world. As long as the Wanderers keep winnin' things, the cash'll roll in, an' wi' him owning Digital International he'll clean up. We're gonnae have tae switch oor TV channel tae Digital International TV, o' course."

"Well, lads," said Troy Hard, "let's get on with it. Poor Boss, stuck with a wanker as Chairman telling him what to do, and a load of temperamental foreign nancy boys!" Wanderers United was fairly unique in the Premiership. A couple of Scotsmen, a Welshman, Bruce, right wing back Charlie Wong, whose Birmingham accent you could cut with a knife due to his being a third generation descendant of a back street take-away owner, and brothers Winston and Selwyn Chamberlain whose great grandparents had emigrated from Jamaica in the fifties, were as exotic as they got. The rest were all English, which probably accounted for their huge popularity and support both in the U.K. and all over the world amongst Commonwealth nations and in the United States. A multinational Wanderers team would be something quite new.

"Well, we'll see." Ronnie and Joker didn't want anyone to know that they, too were surplus to Sir Fabian's requirements. "Guid luck t'ye all!"

The team meeting broke up, the players shaking hands warmly with Ronnie and Joker as they filed out, some already on their mobile 'phones to their soon-to-be-even-richer agents.

Ronnie and Joker also faced a busy time on the 'phone as they sought to put together a new team of the calibre they considered that Blankopf deserved. They had not been idle since hearing of Sir Fabian's perfidy. Like all managers, they knew who the best players were. Although opinions count for a lot in matters like this, and can vary from person to person, virtually all managers of clubs in the top divisions of the major footballing nations would have come up with much the same list of the world's best players. They would have all come up with the same list of all the fakes, duds, has-beens, trouble-makers, drinkers, drug addicts, womanisers and general wastes of money, as well as those players hiding career-threatening injuries. Some of the names would be of players popularly regarded as amongst the world's greatest by fans and - more importantly from Ronnie's and Jokers' point of view - the average club Director.

It was a list of the latter category of player that Ronnie and Joker had put together.

"Ye know?" Ronnie had mused, sitting in his lounge facing Joker across a coffee table strewn with cups and sheaves of paper. It was the evening of the day they had overheard Sir Fabian telling the Board that he was going to get rid of them. "I dinnae expect we'll have trouble wi' any of their clubs. They're all players ye'd want rid of if the price was right. We'll approach, they'll suggest a silly figure, we'll accept it - its fochin' Blankopf's money after all - and bingo."

Joker looked down the list. "One or two might not play ball. Some are at clubs that are struggling. This Antonio Genitile at Venezia. A clogger, suspect knee, vision of a rocking horse in blinkers, but he did a job at the back for them last season. Kept them in Serie A. They'll not let go of him easily. There are others in that category."

"Aye, so they say no, we offer a silly price and raise it until they say yes. We could even ask any of our lads if they fancy a year in Venice - do a swap."

"Not Bruce, though," concluded Joker. "Just think of him sending all his wages back to his mum! Think how many bloody lira that'd be! And by the way - what's a drover's dog?"

* * * * * * * * *

Jesus Bastardi idly paddled his inflatable woman around his pool, cool shades shielding his eyes from the sun. Head pillowed on her bulbous breasts, he languidly splashed at the limpid water. The inflatable right hand held a large iced Bacardi and coke. Jesus prised it from her pneumatic grip and took a mouthful. Life was great. All he had to do was play football, staying in all the best hotels as he travelled round Spain. At every away match there were lissom young nymphomaniacs that made themselves available, eager to make it with a big star. He always took his training seriously - no shirker, he. He was, admittedly, near the end of his career which spanned some twenty years in

Spain's top division including spells with Barcelona and Real Madrid with whom he won many trophies to go with his collection of international appearances. Still he trained, and one day during the previous season he had taken a rising young star to one side, on the eve of the lad's transfer to Barcelona.

"Bit of advice before you go. You don't seem to train as hard as you could. The football, that's easy. You need to train to cope with the women after the game!"

Whether the lad took his advice or not he wasn't sure. The young, they know everything. After making an early splash, though, the youngster disappeared from Barcelona's first team. No stamina, was the word.

Jesus was just reflecting on the lad's fate and drawing his own conclusions when there was a shout from his villa.

"Telephone!"

"Bring it here, then."

An unbelievably sun tanned, topless girl in the tiniest scrap of material imaginable masquerading as bikini briefs ran across the patio, large breasts bouncing in what looked a rather uncomfortable fashion as she did so. Bloody hell, thought Jesus, I wish she wouldn't do that.

"Juanita!" he scolded as he paddled to the edge of the pool. "Cover yourself! The neighbours!"

"Oh, papa, don't be so old fashioned!"

Jesus took the 'phone. It was his agent with exciting news. Jesus sat upright on his inflatable women, his more concentrated weight causing her to sit up as well, as if she was looking over his shoulder. Jesus' face bore an expression of excited disbelief. Hers just looked emptily happy.

"Wanderers? Me? I don't believe you. Someone's winding you up."

No, his agent had suspected a wind-up and had cut off the call and immediately 'phoned back to the Wanderers. It was genuine. The Wanderers' manager wanted Jesus Bastardi to join the English treble-winners and current European Champions on a two-year contract. They'd pay him twice what F.C. Calvados were paying him. Would he be interested?

"Of course I'm bloody interested, but when they find out about my knee they won't want to know." Twenty years of top flight football had taken its toll and Jesus' left knee was a mess, liable to go at any time and end his career. It could take just one tackle - by him or on him. He'd lasted last season, bolstering the feeble F.C. Calvados defence behind its ineffective midfield and toothless attack, saving them from relegation by just one point from Spain's first division (some say earned by the 0 - 0 draw in the last game of the season against the already relegated bottom side, when in the last minute Jesus had cleared a shot off the line. "Jesus saves!" screamed the local paper's headline....). He had one more season on his contract on a very good wage, but double that over two years? Mama mia!

"They aren't worried about your knee, Jesus!" laughed his agent. "Señor Ronnie Bone himself said to not worry about your little problem. He said he was sure they could find a doctor to give you the all clear!"

"Well I still think it's suspicious," replied Jesus, "but I'll go. Do the necessary. What do Calvados want for me?"

"More than you're worth, Jesus, when they hear who's after you, but Señor Ronnie said money was no object - they have a new Chairman with millions of English pounds to spend! I'll get back to you."

Jesus let himself drift on his inflatable woman for several minutes as he tried to get his head round the conversation he'd just had. His almost naked, sun-tanned seventeen year old daughter called to him from the pool's edge.

"What's wrong, papa?"

"Uh? Oh, that was my agent. How do you fancy two years in England?"

"Where?"

"Wanderers United!"

"Wanderers want *you*?" Her huge, huge brown eyes became - well, even *more* huge. "Nicky Bickham! Oh, *wow*!" She could not believe that in a couple of months time her own father would be a team mate of *the* sexiest footballer in the *world* (except to the girls who loved Ronaldo's teeth). "Oh, papa, brilliant! Will mama let me come?"

"Hmm. Well, she might kick up. You'll have to work on her. Here, take the 'phone. See what she says."

Juanita's mother's first reaction was that she had better move to England as well. Divorced from Jesus sixteen years earlier, not long after Juanita was born, she had found his incessant womanising impossible to put up with; plus, her marriage greatly interfered with her being able to entertain the many male admirers who continued to flock round her even after she was married to Jesus in Spain's sporting marriage of the century: international footballer to international show jumper. At thirty six, a year younger than Jesus, she looked ten years younger and was often taken for Juanita's sister by people who didn't immediately recognise her.

When she put the 'phone down from talking to her daughter, she thought, yes, I *will* go to England if the transfer takes place. She *really* fancied trying her luck with that gorgeous Nicky Bickham. She lay back and imagined that the attractive young groom whose head was currently buried between her thighs was the fabulous Nicky.

"Mmmmmm!" she sighed at the mere thought.

"Women just can't resist me!" thought the groom.

Jesus Bastardi's transfer was arranged, a fee agreed (exorbitant), his terms agreed (even more exorbitant) and Ronnie was able to put a tick by his name on the list.

Other star buys included Manuel Sardinhas from Oporto in Portugal. He was a midfield player in his late twenties who had made several appearances for his country before a drop in form threatened his place even in Oporto's reserves. The P.R. reason given was that he had clashed with his manager and was just out of favour. Only the managerial grapevine knew that he was in danger of becoming a chronic alcoholic. Oporto were delighted to get rid of him.

Then there was Lim Po, an enormously popular Chinese International who had been snapped up by F.C. Bruges on the crest of a huge wave of popularity enjoyed by the player in question. F.C. Bruges did a summer tour of the People's Republic and played a series of games against the National side, winning them all. Lim Po scored a goal against them and in a fit of euphoria and good will, he was signed, despite having an all-too-easily dislocated shoulder as a result of a tussle he had when, a conscript in the Peoples' Army, he'd tried to arrest a pro-democracy demonstrator in Tiananmen Square. He had not lived up to expectations, though, and had become a bit of an embarrassment. For Wanderers, he was a snip, really.

As a striking partner for Lim Po, Ronnie and Joker thought they were being particularly brilliant in signing Sum Wun from Panathiniakos. He wasn't exactly a capped player unless you count the fact that he had represented Taiwan. He had made a name for himself in a European Championship match against Lazio when he was the absolute star on the night with a hat trick in the home leg, sustaining a bad knee injury in the last minute after which he hadn't done very much for the rest of the season. He was still under treatment when Ronnie's call came through, so the sale was straightforward. There was little chance of Lim Po wanting to have anything to do with someone from Taiwan, and vice versa. Plus they both stood five foot three in their football boots and hardly rated as target men.

Italy was a good source of players. Napoli's surge back towards Serie A had not been helped *too* much by their lunatic Colombian goalkeeper Antonio La Pazbaq. He had been an internationally known character in the nineteen nineties with his totally unorthodox style. He'd take free kicks on the half way line, come up for corners at virtually any time during a game and frequently saved goal-bound shots by deliberately turning to knock the ball away with his mooning backside. Napoli had enjoyed his presence until he began to leak goals. The whisper soon got round that his eyesight had suddenly gone, and the simple truth was that without pebble-thick glasses he was as blind as a bat. He made a point of never emerging from his home in fashionable Ravello, high above the azure Mediterranean Sea on the Amalfi coast south of Naples, wearing his glasses. He didn't want the media to find out. He always made sure his wife Conchita was at his side, always with her arm linked to his in a display of togetherness, whenever he left his house. She would accompany him to his Ferrari with its blacked out windows (so no-one could see him put his glasses on) and off they would roar; to training, to the stadium for home matches, to the meeting venue for away travel: everywhere.

"The clown is tamed by romance," the gossip magazines gushed, interpreting the constant presence of Conchita in the only way possible.

Napoli were happy to get rid of him. "I suppose he could get contact lenses, you know, those flexible ones," suggested Joker when he and Ronnie were discussing him.

"Well, I suppose he could, but he's a crap 'keeper anyway," replied Ronnie. "We'll welcome him wi' open wallet, eh? He's probably o' of the few players that Blankopf has heard of, and if he has, it'll be because he's a character, lots o' publicity, lots o' media attention - good box office, eh?"

And so it proved. Ronnie mentioned to the now Vice-Chairman, Sefton Perkins, that he had signed La Pazbaq.

"Really? He's quite a character, isn't he? Remember that save he made in the last World Cup? Cheeky would be one way to describe it, eh?" Sefton chuckled. Ronnie was right about how those not in the know viewed the legendary Colombian goalkeeper. Sefton was delighted. What a catch! He'd let Sir Fabian know. He'd be bound to have heard of him. Sir Fabian was in the United States on business, but Sefton knew how to contact him and dialled the number of the hotel.

Sharon took the call as she was on top, as usual.

"Hello?" she squealed. "Who? Mr Sefton? Sir who? Sir Fabian who? Oh, you mean Blanky?" She looked down. "He's a bit tied up at the moment." Not that she or Sir Fabian were into bondage or anything kinky like that. Spray cream, ring doughnuts, chocolate body paint, golden syrup (Sir Fabian had sprung that one on her one evening when they got home from a meal at the renowned "School Dinners" restaurant in London), all the normal edible accessories that every couple uses. Don't they? Not liquorice boot laces any more, though, which was the closest they'd ever got to bondage. Sir Fabian had tied Sharon up with yards of the stuff and then enjoyed freeing her using his teeth until he had eaten the lot. What with the laxative effect of liquorice, he had the trots for the next three days, so that little snack got kicked into touch.

"This is Sharon, 'is Personal Assistant. Can I give 'im a message?" Sharon was nothing if not willing to please. Which is why she was gyrating her hips, gently but with increasing tempo, over Sir Fabian's face. She knew that as long as he thought he was giving her a good time, he would feel that he wasn't losing his touch, and a man who thinks he is God's gift to women is a happy man. And anyway, he deserved some reward for having got his yacht to meet them at Boston. She could look forward to a nice romp with that lovely young Navigator.

At the other end of the line in the Wanderers Director's Office, Sefton passed on his message. "Wanderers have signed the Colombian goal keeper called Antonio La Pazbaq from Napoli - and my surname is *Perkins*! Got that?" God, she was simple. Must be a good screw. Why else would Blankopf keep her in tow?

"Okay, Mr Sefton, I've got that. Fank you for calling. Byeee!"

Something told Sefton that the call had been a waste of time.

On the other side of the Atlantic Sharon put the receiver back on its cradle and looked down at Sir Fabian who was completely unaware that there had been a 'phone call as no sound could reach his ears, gripped as they were between Sharon's to-die-for thighs. She looked at her watch. "Dinner time!" she thought. It was all right for Sir Fabian, making a right meal of it down there, but she realised that she was hungry. She allowed Sir Fabian to bring her to a fake orgasm and lifted herself free.

"Bingo, eh, Shaz?" spluttered Sir Fabian, a little purple faced. Brought her off again! As long as I've still got it, she'll stick around. And with a shaved fanny, no chance of choking on a hair down me throat.

Sharon headed for the shower, as she usually did after sex. Even in her Ford Capri days she'd always had a shower when she got home.

"There was a 'phone call," she called from the bathroom.

"When?"

Oh shit! 'E'll go spare if 'e finks I was on the 'phone while 'e was tryin' to reach me G-spot! "Oh, er - earlier today. I forgot."

"Who from?"

"Mr Sefton."

"*Who?*"

Tracey couldn't hear Sir Fabian too well over the sound of the shower. " 'E said Wanderers 'ave signed a Canadian gamekeeper called Ant'nee 'oo passes the buck - um - 'appily, and 'is surname is Perkins." Ooh, the hot water was lovely! She lathered the soap over her siliconised breasts and imagined her hands belonged to the Navigator. She was quickly in a world of her own.

"A Canadian gamekeeper? What the fuck do they need a *game*keeper for?" called Sir Fabian.

"Uh huh," murmured Sharon, dreamily allowing the Navigator's hands to soap other parts of her body.

"Anthony Perkins is bloody film star, isn't he?"

"Mmmm." The Navigator was getting quite naughty, now, especially as he had reached for the loofah.

"And what's the point of hiring someone who just passes the buck? If there's a job to do you need someone who'll take responsibility, for Christ's sake!"

"Mmmmmmmm!" The Navigator and the loofah had helped Sharon to a *real* orgasm. If only the Navigator knew! But at least Sharon now began to return to the land of the living. She rinsed off the remains of the suds and turned the shower off.

"Are you sure you got that message right?" she heard Sir Fabian call.

"Yea, 'f course," she replied, unconcernedly towelling herself dry. "Why?"

Sir Fabian was about to reply when Sharon emerged from the bathroom. Just the sight of her magnificent body stifled the words in his throat. She was a thick cow, but bloody hell! Those tits! Gaining his composure and breath, he was able to answer. "It just seems odd that my football club should employ a gamekeeper. None of the rugby clubs I played for ever had one. I mean, sometimes you had to clear a few wildebeest off more remote grounds, but it wasn't worth having someone do it full time. And what sort of wildlife is there around Wanderers' ground? How would they get in? I'll 'phone and ask."

"Okay, luv."

So he did, and got the correct version, leaving him, the club Chairman on one side of the Atlantic and Sefton, the Vice-Chairman, on the other side of the Atlantic both thinking the same thing: God, what a *thick* cow! But as Sharon was still padding round the hotel suite in her birthday suit, Sir Fabian bore no grudge. Instead, he was delighted by the news that Ronnie Bone had actually signed a player he had heard of. He was that brilliant Colombian goalkeeper. Bone was still getting the chop, mind, as soon as the new team was assembled. After all, the bastard had questioned his suitability as a club Chairman! No. He's out. Antonio La Pazbaq. Brilliant!

"Canadian gamekeeper!" he chuckled as he stood behind Sharon whilst she looked for something to put on. Happily for Sir Fabian, she found it necessary to work her way down the dresser to the bottom drawer before she found something she fancied.

"Where are me Viagra, Shaz?"

* * * * * * * * *

The new Wanderers team took shape. A larger collection of over the hill drinkers, drug addicts, hot heads, has-beens and medical time bombs had never before been registered with one club. There was midfielder Enrique Mouette of Marseilles, a former French international who specialised in red cards and practising martial arts on people on the opposition's bench, who had in fact needed surgery on torn ankle ligaments the last time he did it; and Papa Médecin, a wing-back from Haiti, whose pre-match preparations for French League side Nancy were strange to say the least, involving as they did a skull, two bones, an urn of grey ashes and bundles of smouldering leaves that had a distinctive herbal smell familiar to students all over the Western world. Just as Ronnie and Joker thought that signing a player from Taiwan as well as one from the People's Republic of China might give whoever took over the manager's mantle a bit of bother, so, too, were they quite pleased with their two signings from the former Yugoslavia: Serbian Stefan Milosovitch, conveniently sacked by Red Star Belgrade for his involvement in drug pushing, and Croatian Milo Opec of Port Vale, both midfielders.

Heinrich Schickelgrüber was a good signing. An Austrian International centre-back with Sturm Graz, he had a reputation for not taking any prisoners, which was something of a family trait as it happened, as his grandfather had been in the SS, something the family didn't actually advertise. Heinrich had a weakness, in that he was absolutely shitless about flying. This wasn't too much of a problem while he played for Sturm Graz. Even when they did qualify for European competitions, travel by car or train was possible. It was going to pose a lot of problems for him and the club once he was based at Wanderers. Every European game would involve a sea crossing which would slow things down. He wouldn't use the Eurotunnel. As an enthusiastic member of Austria's Freedom Party - something he kept quiet for some reason - he eschewed anything that could be construed as to do with the European Union. European football competitions were all right: they pre-dated the EU and so did not conflict with his principles. Ronnie and Joker weren't bothered by his travelling arrangements. They would provide headaches for whoever was appointed in their place.

Edmund Edmunsen, the Icelander who kept goal for Venice was part of a complicated deal, Wanderers paying Venice millions and millions of lire plus Fred Menzies, not just in exchange for Edmunsen but also for the clogging, blinkered rocking horse of their central defence Genitile, and there was also the additional condition that Wanderers would play a pre-season friendly in Venice, bringing their full squad.

St. Johnstone provided Peter McGrath, a Geordie. A genius at free kicks, his international career had come to a premature end due to the fact that he was quite simply a complete piss artist. Some men are born yobs, and if fate makes them rich and famous they carry their yobbishness onto the front pages of tabloids the world over. They crash fast cars, have several high-profile girlfriends (all of which leave them because of their violence, drinking and womanising), fall out of night clubs drunk in the early hours of the morning of a big match, swear and carry on in posh restaurants, sniff coke and so on. Peter McGrath - "Macca" to the front-page headline writers - had done all these and been sent off several times each season.

Various managers had chanced their reputations by signing him meaning that his list of clubs was prodigious. He'd let all of them down. He had his fans, though. A diminishing number, true, but they were still around. Ronnie and Joker could justify signing him by claiming that maturity had at last caught up with him. After all, when was the last time he'd thrown a hissy fit at being sent off? Extra weight due to his excesses of alcohol led to his inability to last ninety minutes but that, Ronnie and Joker could claim, was irrelevant in these days of tactical substitutions.

The new Wanderers attack was completed by strikers Georgi Strupinski from Katowice, a Pole with an eye for other peoples' wives - especially team-mates' wives, a rapid withdrawal from one as her husband arrived home unexpectedly leaving him with a suspect lumbar disc; and Republic of Ireland international Seamus O'Hooligan. He occasionally scored goals for Brentford and Ireland and many in the lower divisions of the Nationwide League had expected him to be "discovered" before long by a Premiership outfit. Wanderers United, though! Brentford hadn't had so much money to spend in all their long history.

The midfield was completed by Jerome McZane, a Trinidad & Tobago international from a team called Khelwalaas in the Trinidad & Tobago Professional League, who had had trials with Nottingham Forest and had made the news because he played for a famous Reggae band called "Aftah de Tone" as a tribute to Lenny Henry; and Dutchman Johann van Dyke of Ajax. Ajax had just heard of his connections with a thriving pornography exporting business and the possibility of his arrest. A solid performer on the field, Ronnie and Joker thought he would be ideal. Imagine the scandal Blankopf would have to put up with if it hit the fan!

Caspar Hansen, the "Great Dane" in international footballing circles, was another fine player at centre back. It was just that he had sustained so many head injuries that he was actually becoming punch drunk. Again, only a very few people in the game knew. Arsenal were happy to let him go, though George

Graham was puzzled as to why his old mate Ronnie had offered to buy him when he told him of the player's problem. He was the last but one piece in the jigsaw: another wing-back, Zaire International Kwasi Ankomo who had played all his senior football for Celtic Brazzaville, completed the shopping list.

The huge transformation within the legendary treble-winning club presented headline writers with plenty of overtime.

"New United can Rule the World!" - The Daily Mail.

"United - Kings of the World!" - The Daily Express.

"Wanderers can Rule the World!" - The Mirror.

"United can Dominate the World!" - The Star.

"United can Rule the World!" - The Sun.

"Macca's Double Hat trick in One Night, claims Model!" - The Daily Sport.

"United to Rule the World!" - The Universe.

"Wanderers Try to Buy Success!" - The Globe.

"Wi' a bit o' luck," Ronnie said, as he and Joker surveyed the portfolios of their new acquisitions, "That lot'll look brilliant to the punter and the Board, but do bugger all in the league. The poor bastard who they appoint in our place might even face relegation!"

"I wonder how many of them will last the season?" replied Joker.

"Not our problem, laddie; not our problem!"

Chapter 7 - Midford Town Ladies

"Look, Elaine, if you're going to put it in, keep yer eye on the bloody ball!" Elaine was getting sore.

"If I stare at it much more I'll go cross eyed!" she snapped. "If I'm not doing it right, *you* bloody do it yourself!"

"Well that would hardly help, would it!"

Manager Marty Fozzard once again felt he was losing control. The team just didn't seem to want to do what they were supposed to be doing and were getting argumentative. "Just try once more then we'll move on." He shouted to a track-suited man some distance away. "One more, Rex!"

The man Rex swung his leg and sent over yet another cross from the right wing. It dropped towards Elaine who, petulantly, watched it carefully and, dropping her hip at the right moment, lashed the ball goalwards. The muddied 'keeper getting cold in the goalmouth leapt acrobatically up and to her right and tipped the ball over the bar.

"Brilliant! Brilliant, brilliant, brilliant! Both of you!" Marty felt a little better. "*What* a shot, Elaine, and *brilliant* save, Jan!"

Begrudgingly, Elaine Richards looked at Janine Morris, now lifting herself once more from the mud. "You cow, Jan! That was in!"

"Sorry," shrugged the 'keeper. "Instinct."

"Don't underestimate yerself, Jan, that save was out of the top drawer," enthused Marty. "Now, let's do some heading and then you can finish up with a game. Then we need to talk about Bromsgrove on Sunday."

Midford Town Ladies Football Club were in their first season in the National Women's Premier League, and were struggling to get out of the relegation places. Bromsgrove were their next opponents and were unbeaten so far, a tough prospect for newcomers Midford even though they were at home. They'd lost away to Bromsgrove seven - nil in their first match in the Premier League.

"Home" to Midford was a windswept council pitch in the middle of an industrial estate with the almost completely rebuilt New Stamford Stadium one of the shapes on their horizon. When Midford was just a girl's team in a junior league the towering floodlights of the Wanderers' unmodernised stadium had been the most prominent feature in sight, but as the lights were now incorporated into the roofs of the new stands, Midford's skyline had changed.

Midford Town was still a small outfit compared to many of the top women's teams in the country, many of whom were attached to league clubs. Martin Fozzard was their long-suffering manager, helped by his mate Rex Holden mainly because Rex was married to midfielder and captain Barbara. The club's paper work was dealt with by the unfortunately Christened Ricky Head, whose relatively straightforward rôle of club secretary was a genuine labour of love. He was in love with Josie Smith, the ball-winner of Midford's midfield. If she was aware of Ricky's infatuation she didn't show it; nor was she likely to be flattered by it, never mind return it. If Ricky had been able to see Josie's bedroom - which he certainly never would - he might have been puzzled by her choice of pinups. No boy bands, no David Beckham, no Nicky Bickham, no David Ginola. Various women's singles champions, the female Gladiators, Madonna and other similar female icons adorned Josie's bedroom walls. Without hormone treatment and drastic cosmetic surgery, Ricky had no chance.

And so to the heading session. "Two areas where the women's game really lags behind, Rex," Marty had once opined. "Goal keeping and heading." Marty made sure that no team outdid his when it came to dealing with high balls.

The team arranged themselves in two semi-circles, one around Rex, the other around Marty, and for the next fifteen minutes the two men each threw a ball high into the air for each girl in turn. Sometimes they were told to "clear" the ball, heading it as far away as they could, sometimes they had to "shoot", getting as much power into putting it as close to the thrower's feet as they could. They'd beaten better sides just because their defenders got to crosses and route one balls first or their strikers would blast crosses past the other 'keeper with their head whilst defenders around them waited for the ball to drop to the ground.

By the time they divided up for their final small-sided game, all the girls had well-muddied foreheads, even the diminutive Daisy Trickett, not yet fifteen and the baby of the team.

"They're coming on brilliantly," said Rex as he and Marty watched them enjoy their warm-down game. "All seventeen at training again, and I know for a fact that Linda's kid is still poorly. I told her a couple of days ago not to worry about things until she was better."

"I know," said Marty. "Brilliant team spirit. I thought there'd be a problem when Sharon arrived but Kylie's not said a word even though she isn't first choice any more."

Sharon Onslow was a nineteen year old student who had moved to the area when she enrolled at Midford University (formerly Midford Tech., formerly Midford Sixth Form Community Technology College, formerly Midford Sixth Form College, formerly Midford Girls Grammar School, est. 1932) to study a Sports Science degree. Five feet eleven inches tall and of Steffi Graf proportions, she had turned up to a training session two or three games into the season and asked to join.

It was soon obvious that Midford had uncovered a diamond as she naturally fell back to play in the centre of the defence. After a couple of appearances off the substitutes' bench she had started to dominate the games she played in. Opposing strikers soon learned that her Naomi Campbell-length legs would deny them the ball when they thought they were clear and her solid frame would jar the teeth out of their heads if they collided with her. Every ball in the air was *"SHARON'S!"*

Defences became uncomfortable when she approached their goal for corners and free kicks. When Lou Purdey, Midford's playmaker with a number of England trials under her belt, placed corners at just the right height at the edge of the penalty area, Sharon would time her run from well outside the box to reach full speed by the time she met the ball with her head. If she got it on target, it was a goal.

Once, a hapless defender on a post found such a shot directed her way and tried to head it off the line. She came round in an ambulance on her way to hospital, having been knocked out as the ball propelled her over the line. She was kept in overnight for observation, though it turned out to be nothing more than mild concussion.

Sharon's footballing ability as well as her fabulously long legs, gorgeous figure, child-like face framed by long, straight, dark, shiny hair – worn in a pony-tail for matches and training – oh, and sexy suntan, made quite a difference to the sizes of the crowds who watched the girls play. She was considered a major factor in helping Midford to lift themselves off the bottom of the table, giving them hopes of avoiding relegation after just one season. She was having a bit of fun this evening, though, playing in goal for one of the teams whilst the normal second choice 'keeper Linda Lawson honed up her outfield skills. Besides, Sharon had been known to injure her own team in her enthusiasm for the game during training matches.

As the session wound to an end, a figure made its way towards Martin and Rex.

"Excuse me," she said. "I presume you two are in charge?"

"He's the manager," answered Rex. "I just help."

"I'm Martin Fozzard," Marty introduced himself. "This is Rex Holden, he shares the coaching with me." It wasn't technically true, but Rex was his long-time mate and although he avoided any official responsibility in the club, he never missed a game or training session. "His wife, Barbara, is our captain. Do you want to join? We're always happy to welcome new players."

The woman sighed wistfully. "I'd like to think I could, but I've never played, so I'd be hopeless. I'm a bit old, too."

"Nonsense. Rex's wife is thirty four, Kylie Livermore is thirty three with two kids in secondary school and we think Janine Morris, our 'keeper, is forty only she doesn't let on!"

"Thank you, but I didn't come here to join. Sort of the other way round, really. I've been watching you. Your girls can really play, can't they. I mean, proper football. I'm not sure you'll actually welcome my suggestion, but I'm going to ask anyway."

"Er, we don't know who you are," interrupted Marty.

"Oh, sorry. I'm Christine Goodley. I'm th..."

"You're the Commercial Manager for Wanderers!" exclaimed Rex. "I *thought* I knew your face. I've seen your photo in the papers!"

"Yes, usually with some silly comment about me being a woman in a man's world," said Christine, who resented any such references as male chauvinist drivel.

"Well what can we do for you?" asked Marty.

"Would you like some help from Wanderers?"

"Help? What sort of help?" Martin was aware of just how much of a shoestring affair Midford Town was. "We're always scratching around for money."

"Yes, well, some financial help would be possible. What about coaching?"

"Marty does the coaching," said Rex.

"Yes, but be fair, Rex. What's my expertise compared to what Wanderers could do? I'd *love* to have some help coaching the girls, except it wouldn't be help, exactly. It would be me learning as well. Yes, er, Christine - can I call you that, we've only just met..."

"That's fine," said Christine. "So you'd like some coaching, and a bit of financial help, yes?"

"Well, yes," said Marty. "Can I get the girls round to introduce you and tell them what you've said?"

"By all means."

Marty walked into the middle of the practice game and clapped his hands.

"Okay girls, that'll do. There's someone over here I want you to meet."

The team, muddied and panting, surrounded Martin, Rex and Christine.

"I know you," gasped Jackie Lowson, petite but dynamic midfielder that she was. "You're that woman in charge of all the merchandising and so on at Wanderers!"

"That's right," said Marty. "Girls, this is Christine Goodley. Her official title is - er..."

"Commercial Manager," supplied Christine.

"Right," Marty continued. "She's offering some financial help for Midford, as well as some coaching! What d'you think about that?"

"Great, if we get to train with the team and share the team bath with them afterwards," said left wing back Zöe Pryde.

"We can't really discuss it here, can we," said Marty. "Can you give us time to get changed and then go to a pub or somewhere?"

"Better than that," smiled Christine. "Come and see me at the club. I'll tell the man on the door to expect you. How many of you? About half a dozen?"

"Well, more like a dozen, at least...." Marty wasn't quite sure how many of the Midford Town Ladies should be at the meeting. Obviously Josie Smith as Treasurer – but they'd probably all want to go.

"That's okay! As many as you like. Let's say an hour's time?"

"Right. Thanks. Yes, that should be O.K." Marty felt a bit stunned. "In fact, it'll be brilliant!"

* * * * * * * * *

Much later that evening a deal was struck. Midford Town Ladies would become Wanderers United Ladies for the following season (whether or not they managed to stay in the National Women's Premier League - Marty had insisted on that being understood, just in case). Their small bank balance, shrewdly managed by Josie who doubled as Treasurer as well as midfielder, would receive an immediate, generous cash injection and one of the Wanderers coaching staff would attend each training session henceforth to show Marty and Rex the ropes.

The girls were thrilled at this unexpected turn of events.

"Imagine! We'll be playing for the same club as Nicky Bickham and Stevie Grigg!" squawked Zöe Pryde after training the following week. "If we are Wanderers United players, then we'll get to use all the facilities and *that* means mixing with the players! Can you *imagine getting off* with one of them?"

"*I* can't," said utility player Penny Rickard, one of the four lesbians in the team. There was a ripple of laughter round the dressing room.

"All the more for me!" said Valentina Materazzi, grinning. She was the right wing back and, perhaps after Sharon, was the most attractive girl in the squad with her Italian background having bequeathed her a permanently tanned skin, long, long shiny black hair and long, long legs. She was known to the team as "Maserati" due to her speed on the right wing.

"Hey, steady on, you," warned Barbara, " You're only sixteen!"

Valentina pouted. "Well, some of those players aren't much older. How old's that Mark Bowen? Nineteen?"

"Yeh, an' he's *mine*," claimed the petite midfielder Jackie Lowson.

And so the banter continued, the spirit in the team sky high. That weekend, they had held Bromsgrove one-all, the goal an equaliser from Sharon off Penny Rickard's second half corner after Midford had gone behind to a dubious penalty. The point had lifted them to third from bottom, the first time they'd been out of the relegation places all season.

Sharon's goal hadn't quite been one of her specialities. True, she had sprinted up to the edge of the Bromsgrove box to meet Penny's corner with her head. The ball had crashed against the bar, rebounded and hit the 'keeper and flown almost vertically high into the air. The speed of Sharon's run-in brought her to the centre of the scramble that awaited the ball's return to earth, and she leapt majestically again to head past the 'keeper who even with outstretched arms could not reach the ball before Sharon.

Thereafter Bromsgrove made sure she never got a clear run for corners or free-kicks, and Sharon finished the game elated but bruised.

Chapter 8 – Preparations

Having put together the new Wanderers squad of assorted misfits, deadbeats, has-beens, alcoholics, etc., and with the new season just a few weeks away, Ronnie stopped Sefton one morning in the palatial entrance hall of the New Millennium Stand.

"Sefton! The noo team is more or less complete. Jest a few loose en's tae tie up, contract-waise, ye understand."

Jesus Bastardi wanted *two* houses, one for him and his daughter (palatial) and one for his estranged wife (not so palatial); Antonio La Pazbaq was insisting that if he *had* to wear contact lenses, Wanderers should pick up the tab for new soft ones every day plus the services of an optician to fit them; Enrique Mouette demanded fresh sardines to be delivered to him on the eve of every match, wherever it was; Papa Médecin insisted on a completely isolated house that faced the rising sun, six live hens every new moon and the freedom to return to his native Haiti whenever the moon rose in Orion; Edmun Edmunsen had to have whale meat flown in regularly, which wasn't that easy what with the world-wide embargo on whaling (Arnie Robinson tracked down a shady-sounding supplier who dealt with the disposal of the whales Japan insists on harpooning for "research"); Johann van Dyke insisted on a return flight to Amsterdam every Monday; Jerome McZane demanded a house with a recording studio in situ.

Because Heinrich Schickelgrüber was scared of flying he had to have a limmo and two drivers at his disposal for all away matches, including those in Europe; Lim Po and Sum Wun insisted on separate interpreters, and Lim Po insisted on a house within smelling distance of a MacDonald's. All in all, a complicated package of deals to be negotiated all at the same time. Many top players make what to normal people are outrageous demands of their clubs, but at least these normally have to be dealt with one at a time as a player is bought during a season, or even in the closed season when a squad is strengthened. Poor old Ronnie and Joker and their office staff, with an entire new squad to cater for, had been burning the midnight oil for a couple of months.

"Looks brilliant on paper, Ron," Sefton responded. "Cost a lot, mind!"

"Aye, but it's Blankopf's money, and we got quite a lot back from selling the old team. What are we? Sixty million down?"

"Sixty one." Sefton didn't think it sounded very much if he remembered it was all Blankopf's money. "We've got far and away the biggest wage bill in the Premiership, mind."

In the world, actually, thought Ronnie, but I don't think you need worry about that. I certainly won't. All Ronnie was waiting for now was the chop, and surely the fact that the new team was assembled was the cue.

Sefton said nothing about that, of course, because it was up to Blankopf. Sefton, like the rest of the Board, felt a bit guilty about it all because Ronnie - and Joker - had been a bloody good management team, bringing them loads of silverware culminating with the treble last season. They'd be all right, though. They'd get a job anywhere in the world.

He duly reported to Blankopf by 'phone, as the new Chairman was in New York on business. "The team is all set up, Sir Fabian. All ready for the pre-season friendlies."

"Right! Now that cocky Scotchman has attracted the world's best players, he can go! Calling me useless! No-one talks back to me like that!" Sir Fabian never stood for that. Sefton was glad that the ether protected him from the shower of saliva that was no doubt accompanying Sir Fabian's outburst.

Actually, though, at that moment Sir Fabian wasn't standing for anything at all, not even for Sharon. He had mislaid his Viagra and a few moments earlier, in their Hilton Penthouse in New York, none of Sharon's efforts, ranging from her school uniform with the peep-hole blouse to the generous application of her lipstick on his limp member without using her hands, had stirred a response. So he had sent her shopping. That always made up for her disappointment. She had skipped into the lift planning a raid on Macey's with no apparent cares in the world.

"We'd best keep him on until we've sounded out a replacement," advised Sefton. "We can't afford to be without a manager for the start of the season."

"If you say so. I'll get my boys onto it."

Which later led to a rather uncomfortable telephone conversation for one of Sir Fabian's minions from the board of Digital International.

"I've - er - tried all of the biggest names in football, F.B. No-one is interested!"

"*Whaddya mean?*" Sir Fabian had no time for failure. The one difference between him and a Mafia boss was that he couldn't have people liquidated when they failed to deliver. This Widdelow, Weddelow, whatever his bloody name was, had been given the task of engaging a replacement manager for Ronnie. The Wanderers board had furnished him with a short list of names, managers of the top clubs in the world, in the order they felt reflected their status in the world of football.

Waddilove, for that was his name, had tried the first, Sir Alex Ferguson of Manchester United, and he simply wasn't interested. No, not even *five* million a year, thanks, he was happy at Old Trafford. Yes, he *did* know which players had recently joined Wanderers, but it was still no (*especially* as he knew which players had been signed - what were Ronnie and Joker up to? He had been delighted to sign Nicky Bickham and wasn't about to leave Manchester United when it seemed likely that in the coming season they'd not have to play second fiddle to Wanderers).

The story was the same with David O'Leary at Leeds and Bobby Robson at Newcastle. Parma coach Alberto Malesani gave the thumbs down, Louis van Gaal at Barcelona had apparently laughed at the idea. Waddilove got to the end of the list he had been given. He went back to Sefton Perkins.

"What, none of them?" Sefton was taken aback. The unanimous opinion of the board was that with what Sir Fabian was offering, they could have got the Pope. A hurried meeting produced a further list, longer this time.

"What's the matter with 'em all?" snorted Sefton when Waddilove got back to him with a second blank. "Look, lad, no offence, but you're not a footballer, are you. No-one knows you. Let *me* try. I won't let on to Sir Fabian."

Sefton suffered the same set of rejections as Waddilove. Not so much as a nibble. Kevin Keegan let slip one comment. "Sorry, Sefton old mate. Not with that bunch that Ronnie has signed."

So that was it! It was the squad that Ronnie had put together that was putting everyone off! Absolutely no-one had the balls to take on such a world-beating side!

"That's the problem, Sir Fabian. Ronnie and Joker have put together such an amazing squad that there is no-one confident enough to assume the responsibility to coach them. It's such a helluva prospect, no-one's up to it. You'll have to stick with Ronnie until we can talk someone round."

"I'll get back to you!" Sir Fabian was not happy. He was used to getting what he wanted. The English season was about to begin. Sir Fabian had expected to get back to England in time for the opening league match of the season under the best manager in the world. He had given that little arse Widdelow or whatever his bloody name was the simple task of getting whoever it was the Wanderers board recommended. He punched out a number on his mobile and clapped the unfortunate instrument to his ear. "Get me Widdelow!" he bellowed after a few seconds. "Well, whatever his bloody name is! Just get him!"

Which led to Waddilove's second uncomfortable telephone conversation with Sir Fabian.

"Whaddya mean?"

"None of the managers or coaches of any of the top clubs in every major league in the best footballing nations in the world want the job, nor any national coaches. At *any* salary. Sefton Perkins says..."

"I *know* what bloody Sefton Perkins says, I've just been talking to him. Did you tell 'em it was *me, personally*, who wanted them?" How *could* anyone turn down an offer from Sir Fabian Blankopf?

"Y-yes, of course," stammered Waddilove. "I c-can't understand how anyone can turn down an offer from you, F.B."

Good grief, the idiot thinks the same as me. He can't be that much of an idiot after all. They weren't saying no to him, they were saying no to *me. Me! Sir Fabian Blankopf!* Right!

"Okay, Widdelow. Not your fault. I'll be back the day after tomorrow." With which, Sir Fabian rang off.

"Th-thank you, F.B.," mumbled Waddilove into the dead 'phone his end. He still waited until he'd put his receiver down before correcting Sir Fabian. "And it's Waddilove, sir."

Sir Fabian brooded in his hotel suite. He didn't like to be pushed into changing his mind. He had said to the Wanderers board that Ronnie would be sacked. Now he couldn't do that because none of those feeble minded football managers would take a job with him. Sod them all, then. That Sefton Perkins had suggested keeping Ronnie until a replacement was found. O.K. That was what they'd do. He, Sir Fabian, wouldn't be seen to have changed his mind. A replacement could not be found straight away, so Ronnie would be kept on. He didn't know he was for the chop anyway. He'd got all those world-beating players together, perhaps only he had the balls to handle them. Why, he'd questioned his suitability as a football club chairman, hadn't he? If that didn't prove he had balls, then what did?

"Right!" Sir Fabian had made a decision. Now he needed a treat. Sharon was shopping. Not due back until he sent James to collect her from somewhere or other, whenever she 'phoned. She usually needed a car to pick her up after a shopping trip to carry all her bags and boxes. Jenny James! He called her up.

"James? Step up to my suite, babe, and bring your special uniform!"

Jenny sighed. Oh, well, it was her suggestion when persuading Sir Fabian to employ her that not many men had chauffeuses they could screw. He didn't trouble her much. She fetched her "special" uniform from her room en route to Sir Fabian's suite. There was nothing that special about it: it was just one of the Anne Summers range of uniforms - nurse, traffic warden, policewoman, chambermaid, schoolgirl, French waitress, Wren, teacher, chauffeuse - just the normal sort of skimpy, transparent, fun-filled fancy dress. She looked at her watch. It wouldn't be a long session. It never was.

In fact, Jenny was no more successful than Sharon at stirring Sir Fabian's naughty bits. Poor Sir Fabian (not fiscally speaking, of course). He loved being important: hated being impotent.

After a not very satisfactory romp he sent Jenny on her way and got back to Sefton. "You're right. We can't sack Ronnie before we find a replacement. We'll keep him on."

"Right, Sir Fabian. I'll keep Mr Waddilove informed of any new names we come up with, let him know if any of our men get the sack, you know, come onto the market, so to speak."

"Let who know?"

"Mr Waddilove."

"Mr Wa...... oh, Widdelow, or whatever his bloody name is! See you in a couple of days."

"Are you coming to Venice for the opening friendly?"

"No, beastly place. Can't use the fucking car, got to walk everywhere or piss around in boats. It smells, too. No, first league game. And I wanna see *blood!*"

Sefton, sitting in his sun lounger by his fragrantly-smelling rose garden, turned off his 'phone and pondered. So Sir Fabian wasn't going to sack Ronnie - yet. He felt a sense of relief first of all, but doubt slowly clouded his mind. Getting rid of him after the season had started might be worse than letting him go now. He'd served the club exceptionally well: no-one could have done better, in fact. He and the rest of the Board had done very nicely, thank you, out of the sale of Wanderers to Digital International. Ronnie - and Joker - would have got very little by comparison under the condition of their contracts. That was it! Their contracts! An idea of how the blow of their sacking could be softened suddenly crystallised in his mind. He 'phoned back to Sir Fabian.

"Just a quick one, Sir Fabian. With Ronnie and Joker having put this shit-hot side together, we ought to offer them new contracts."

"What's the use of that if we're going to let 'em go in a few weeks' time?"

"Well, if we weren't going to sack them it would be normal to offer them better money. We'll not be paying it for long, anyway." Sefton hoped that Sir Fabian was unfamiliar with football contracts, with their compensatory clauses. He needn't have worried. In Sir Fabian's world, he hired and fired on the spot. "I'm a bit surprised they haven't asked for a pay rise already," concluded Sefton.

"I pay by results. They haven't had any yet," snorted Sir Fabian.

"Football's a bit different, Sir Fabian. That team he's got us - every one a household name." Well, almost. Jerome McZane?

"Well, okay. Whatever. Give him and his mate new contracts so they won't expect the chop." Sir Fabian wanted an afternoon nap. Two unsuccessful attempts at a leg-over had made him disgruntled. Perhaps a snooze would help him to perform when Sharon got back.

Sefton quickly 'phoned round to arrange the necessary Board meeting. Only Reggie couldn't make it. He was in a private hospital "Having his waterworks MoT'd," explained brother Ernie.

Next day in the new Boardroom in the New Millennium Stadium, the Board meeting quickly drew up generous new terms for Ronnie and Joker, doubling their salaries and writing in a clause for huge compensation if Wanderers sacked them. Each one of them felt the same guilt as Sefton about Sir Fabian's decision to sack Ronnie, which was the same as sacking Joker as well, so apart from the hike in salary there were things like win bonuses of a week's wages, a draw worth half that, half a million for Ronnie, £300,000 for Joker for winning the league, the same for the FA Cup, the same for the European Championship, the same for the World Club Championship - it was a mind-boggling package for each man.

"I'll fetch 'em up," said Sefton, when all was settled. He picked up the 'phone. "Who knows the number of the Managerial Suite?" he asked, enjoying the use of the name of the palatial-sounding new facility. Dick Fossett consulted his diary. "442."

General chuckles all round. "Who thought that one up?" asked Malcolm.

"Some herbert from the 'phone company," answered Arnie Robinson, still somehow the Club Secretary despite his unfortunate meeting with Sir Fabian a few weeks earlier. "The match day office is 532."

Sefton punched in the number. There was a pregnant silence round the table, broken only by Malcolm's colon loudly relocating a quantity of gas. His hasty rustling of the meeting papers in front of him only drew attention to it. He was saved from any embarrassment he might have suffered by Sefton's booming voice. "Ronnie, lad, can you and Joker step up to the Board room a moment?" Pause. "We'd rather you both came up here, face to face, like. Right, see you in a minute." He looked round at the others. "They're on their way."

On the floor below, Ronnie hung up and rubbed his hands together. "Here we go, Joker! We're fo' the sack! Dinnae fergit tae look devastated!"

Joker laughed. "Never thought getting the sack would be so satisfying!"

They were still chuckling as they approached the imposing-looking Board Room door. "Steady the buffs!" whispered Joker. "Straight faces, now."

"No, lad," whispered Ronnie in reply. "We can smile. We dinnae knaw we're gettin' the boot!" He knocked, and they both went in.

There they were, all sitting along one side of the mirror-polished mahogany table, all smiling fixedly at Ronnie and Joker.

Sefton indicated two chairs on Ronnie and Joker's side of the table. "Sit down, lads. We've got something to say to you." Ronnie and Joker sat down.

"Now I'll not beat about the bush, lads," Sefton went on, speaking for the rest as the now Vice-Chairman. Here we go, thought Ronnie. I'm going to laugh if I'm not careful, thought Joker.

"You've put together this - er - amazing squad, and yer've sold well, too, so the net outlay is only about sixty million quid."

Sixty-one, thought Ronnie.

"I don't want the two of you thinking we're ungrateful or anything," Sefton went on. Here it comes, thought Joker. "Only yesterday I had direct instructions from Sir Fabian himself, who unfortunately can't be here today." I'll bet he isn't, thought Joker. Get someone else to do your dirty work, thought Ronnie. "So it falls to me - er, well - us," That's right, spread the blame, thought Ronnie. "to offer you both new contracts on greatly improved terms."

The silence was long. Ronnie and Joker sat as if carved from stone, the smiles frozen on their faces. Again, the peristalsis of Malcolm's colon provided the interruption that broke the spell.

"I'll explain what we're offering, then you can think about it."

Sefton summarised the terms the Board had hammered out earlier. The feeling of numbness deepened in both Ronnie and Joker. They sat frozen by shock.

"Well, I'm sure you'll both want to chew it over, but I hope you think we've been generous." Sefton slid the new contracts over the table to the two statues opposite. "I think we've taken the wind out of their sails, lads," he said to the rest of the Board. "We'd better leave 'em to talk it over. Let Arnie have the signed contracts, boys - unless you don't think you can accept the terms!" He laughed good-naturedly in a manner that encouraged sympathetic laughter from the others, and rose in a manner that brought the meeting to a conclusion.

Ronnie and Joker remained rooted to the spot for a minute or two after the Directors left. It was Ronnie who broke the silence.

"Aw, fochin' hell! Ah mean - fochin' *hell!*"

"What the fuck are we going to *do?*" gasped Joker. Then he started to giggle, slowly at first, then with increasing helplessness as the giggle evolved into a laugh. Then the laugh became hysterical as Ronnie joined in until both men were leaning against one another, gasping for breathe between guffaws, tears streaming down their cheeks.

Chapter 9 – Training

The first training session was a complete nightmare. Only Enrique Mouette, Milo Opec, Seamus O'Hooligan, Caspar Hansen, Johann van Dyke, Jerome McZane and of course Macca spoke any form of English. Jerome's was a West Indian patois, Enrique sounded like the presenter of Eurotrash, Caspar's pronunciation was like the policeman from " 'Allo 'Allo" and Seamus' accent could have been cut with a knife.

After half an hour of total chaos, Lim Po and Sum Wun stood and had a blazing row in Mandarin in the centre of the pitch. No-one had a clue what they were arguing about but when they came to blows the others had to pull them apart. Unfortunately, Stefan Milosovitch and Milo Opec both happened to grab Lim Po and there began a second slanging match in Serbo-Croat which also resulted in punches being thrown and the others having to pull them apart.

"This is no fucking good," said Joker. "It's just like we reckoned it would be for the schmuck who took over from us."

"We'll have tae get bloody interpreters," said Ronnie. "Ah cannae think o' anythin' else. What a fochin' game, eh? Let's call it a day fer a wee while." He whistled loudly to get everyone's attention. With Lim Po and Sum Wun still glowering at one another and Stefan and Milo also looking murderous, the players, as confused as Ronnie and Joker, became still and waited for something to happen. Ronnie made signs with his hand indicating a drink. "I hope that doesn't mean 'you're a bunch of wankers' in any of their languages," whispered Joker. He went over to the touchline to fetch drinking bottles whilst Ronnie made for the Manager's Suite.

"We need interpreters for yon bloody crew outside," he said to the three secretaries filing their nails in front of flickering word processors. "Where d'you get them from, then?" asked the brassiest of the three, Alliss.

"Ah don't know! Look in bluidy Yellow Pages!"

Which Alliss did, after she had satisfied herself that all her nails were neat. There were lots of interpreters in the Yellow Pages, though Alliss was annoyed to find that having found "Interpreters" - no mean feat as she had inherited her parents' spelling skills - she had to scour through the directory again until she'd found "Translators and Interpreters". She closed her eyes and plonked her finger randomly on the page. Opening her eyes, she looked at the number. Pressing a button on her desk, she waited for Ronnie to answer from his office.

"What?" his voice crackled.

"I've found one. Shall I get 'em for you?"

"That was quick. Yes please."

So Alliss dialled the randomly selected number and as it rang she transferred the line to Ronnie's 'phone. She was supposed to wait until the call was answered, then tell them that it was a call from Ronny Bone of Wanderers United, flick Ronnie's connecting switch and tell him his call was ready, and then transfer the call. Except she couldn't be arsed.

Ronnie picked up the receiver just in time to hear the ringing end. A voice greeted him. "Cunning Linguists. This is Letitia. How may I help you?"

"What?"

"Cunning Linguists. This is Letitia. H......"

"Are you takin' the piss?"

Letitia wasn't, of course. She hadn't invented the bloody name of the business. She'd just graduated in Spanish and French a year ago and had hoped to get a job earning a disgracefully huge salary translating somewhere for the European Union only to find that her student membership of the United Kingdom Independence Party unfortunately seemed to count against her. Still, she'd found this job easily enough, run by a couple of lads from her year whose addiction to a stupid bloody football team meant that they didn't want to be based abroad. They went absolutely ballistic when she told them they'd had an enquiry from their stupid bloody football team.

They both kissed and hugged Letitia. "I don't care what bloody language they want, we'll do it!"

After which the training sessions, though resembling at times a religious re-enactment of the chaos of Babel, became a little more organised. The one mistake was in having an utterly delicious bilingual twenty three year old raven haired babe called Ellie as the Italian interpreter. Antonio Genitile and Jesus Bastardi both came on strong to her and now they wouldn't talk to one another, pass to one another or do anything together without there being a risk of them beating the crap out of one another, all over the macho question of which of them was likely to win Ellie's favours (i.e. shag her) first. Neither was likely to succeed. Ellie, from Treviso in Northern Italy, lived with her artist boyfriend Andrea, a lad from nearby Udine, whom she adored.

Lim Po and Sum Wun had already insisted on separate translators.

"Good job there's a thousand million Chinese," observed Joker.

* * * * * * * * *

The former Midford Town Ladies, however, were enjoying some excellent pre-season training. Now officially Wanderers United Ladies, even down to the Digital International logo on their shirts, they were looking forward to the 1999-2000 season with great optimism. After their adoption midway through the previous season they had gone from strength to strength and were unbeaten in their last ten Premier League games, finishing not just clear of the relegation zone but healthily in mid-table.

The Wanderers United coaching staff had taught them and Marty Fozzard a great deal. They got to meet with the United players to such an extent that by the season's end they took it all for granted. Except perhaps for petite midfielder Jackie Lowson, who had succeeded in catching the eye and, later, all of the more important bits of nineteen year old England International Mark Bowen. They became an item; Jackie went everywhere with him and watched all his games, he did likewise for her and attended most of the Ladies' training sessions as well - just to "help out" with the coaching.

Valentina Materazzi wasn't that put out - she became the centre of attention of Welsh International Stevie Grigg for several months.

When Mark was sold to Liverpool during Ronnie and Joker's enforced team rebuilding, the Ladies lost out as Jackie went with him, joining Liverpool Ladies. Stevie Grigg was bought by Aston Villa.

"You may as well stay with your team," he had muttered to Valentina one hot July night as they lay on top of his duvet. Gazing adoringly at the reflection of the moonlight on the sheen of sweat on his body, Valentina considered this for a moment.

"You don't want me to come with you?" She pushed herself up onto one elbow to look down at his face, monochrome in the dim light. She had small breasts, as uniformly olive-tanned as the rest of her skin (she made good use of Wanderers United's fitness room sunbeds). "Small breasts must be a great asset to a wing back," Stevie had suggested the first time they slept together. Luckily for Valentina he was not a breasts man.

"Why?"

"All that sprinting up and down the wing. Not very much to bounce around and get uncomfortable. Your body...." He paused to run his tongue from her left shoulder to her left big toe. "....was meant to be a wing back!"

"D'you mean that?"

"Course. It was meant to be something else, too."

"What?"

"Shagged! C'm 'ere!"

Was all that over? "Why don't you want me to come with you?" Feelings ranging from desolation to fury juggled for position in her mind.

Stevie smiled. "Because I'm not going anywhere, silly!"

"You're going to Villa. They've paid eleven million quid for you!"

"Yes, but I'm not selling *this* place! Villa's only in Birmingham, three quarters of an hour away. When you move in, this'll be our home. And you can stay with the team. Wouldn't you like that?"

Love surfaced and pushed all those earlier unnecessary emotions aside. "Yes, oh *yes!* Move in with you? My mum will go mad! But I don't care! Oh, Stevie!" Valentina threw herself on top of Stevie and began to kiss him.

Their second session of lovemaking for the night completed - quite quickly due to Valentina's excitement - they lay tightly cuddled together.

"Actually, your mum *won't* go mad. I've already asked her. She made me promise to look after you because you are still so young, and *she* promised to break both my legs if I hurt you."

"Oh, Stevie!"

Marty Fozzard had to replace Jackie Lowson and wanted to recruit enough new players to start a second team. A few youngsters were spotted at various summer soccer schools run in the area - no-one to match the first-choice Jackie, true, but then young Daisy Trickett was getting better all the time and would soon be sixteen. His only worry was the keen interest shown by some of Wanderers new signings. The trouble was, not many of these new players were that young. Of the most obvious womanisers, the two Italians, Genitile and Bastardi, were both in their thirties, as was the Pole Strupinski. He thought the Dutchman was a bit younger, late twenties, perhaps, but he had about five girls of twenty or younger whose heads might easily be turned by these experienced foreign womanisers.

Antonio Genitile had indeed already tried it on with striker Laura Kitson.

"You-a striker, me-a defend, I teach-a you many things, eh?"

His English was extremely poor, so conversation was very limited, but he managed to make it clear that not all the "things" he wanted to teach her were to do with football.

"I teach-a you make-a love, eh? You no-a have Italiano make-a love, eh?"

"Piss off!"

Antonio was not used to being turned down.

"Hey, what-a piss-off-a, eh? You lesbica, hey?"

Laura spoke no Italian, but the first syllable of the word was enough for her to cotton on to the fact that Antonio, perhaps unwittingly, had stumbled across the reason for her refusing his advances.

"Got it in one, Romeo. I don't go for men, and if I did I wouldn't go for a smarmy tosser like you!"

"Non capisco."

"What?"

"You lesbica?"

"*Yes!*"

Thus Antonio's first foray into the women's team. For a while he was convinced that all of the players were "lesbicas" until he realised that Caspar Hansen was seeing a lot of his central defending counterpart Sharon Onslow.

The Wanderers players past and present who had hit it off with some of the women players all played their part in helping to improve the ball skills and tactical knowledge of the women's team. Where Stevie Grigg had helped out with the Midford Town Ladies training the previous season, Caspar Hansen took over with the now Wanderers United Ladies once his relationship with Sharon blossomed so Marty and Rex continued to benefit from Wanderers having taken the women on board.

"D'ye no think the lassies may interfere wi' the lads concentration, Joker?" Ronnie had asked one day.

"No, I don't think so. The other way round, really. The lads all want to look good and impress the women's team, and Caspar has certainly settled in well. He's thinking about his game more than at any time in his career because he's started coaching, and the reason for that is that Sharon girl. She's a bit of a sort, and you should see her head a ball! She and Caspar were mucking about with a ball in the car park the other day. She was heading almost as hard as he was."

* * * * * * * *

The 1999-2000 season was about to get underway for the new Wanderers United team. Ronnie and Joker were wondering what was in store for them.

They weren't looking forward to it as much as Marty and Rex were!

Chapter 10 - Mile High Club

"So, I s'pose all you people are in the mile 'igh club, then?"

Sharon was bored on the flight back to England after the New York trip. Next to her, in the fully-reclined window seat, Sir Fabian was snoring.

The *gorgeous* young Virgin steward looked somewhat taken aback. All their training centred around dealing politely and correctly with the passengers in all sorts of situations, from serving coffee to getting them down the emergency chutes after a crash landing. But none of their rôle play exercises had prepared him for this.

"Er - I beg your pardon, Madam?"

"You know - 'aving a bit of 'ow's yer farver durin' a flight. It's orl right. I'm jus' bein' nosy." Sharon was happy to note that the gorgeous young Virgin steward was staring her straight in the cleavage. "Lots of people I know are in the club and I jus' fort that all you air stewards and stewardesses are in the right job to join the club yerselves."

The gorgeous young Virgin steward let his professional veneer slip a little. "Are *you*, then, Madam?"

"I'm Sharon. *Shorley* you c'n call me Sharon? An' I arst you first."

"Well, er - Sharon - I'm not supposed to use your first name, you know. No-one must hear me saying anything other than 'Madam'. And, well, yes, most of us have taken advantage of the facilities, so to speak."

Sharon gave her little squealing giggle. "Ooh, I *fort* so!"

"And what about you, then," asked the gorgeous young Virgin steward.

"Oh, no, not me. Them toilets is too cramped fer my liking. 'Ow d'yer manage it in there?"

"Er, well, standing up, of course."

"Standin' up?" Sharon wrinkled her cute little nose with distaste.

"Well, you don't *have* to do it standing up." The gorgeous young Virgin steward looked round the Upper Class cabin. Half the seats were empty and most of the occupied ones were fully reclined, like Sir Fabian's, as most of the fat, balding businessmen in them slumbered. A couple of men at the back were conversing quietly. No-one was taking any notice of Sharon and the gorgeous young Virgin steward.

"Follow me - *madam*." Sharon followed him back through the cabin and through a curtain. He led her along the length of the economy cabin, past rows of sleeping, eating, reading adults and sleeping, eating, pissed-off, screaming and rebellious children, until at the rear of the 'plane he opened a narrow door to a compartment behind the rear central row of four seats. The door was marked "Crew Only". He told Sharon to wait a minute whilst he disappeared inside. Sharon barely had time to notice the sleeping couple in the seat across the narrow aisle from the door before he was back.

"All clear," he whispered. "Come in." Sharon squeezed past him and found herself in a tiny little cabin with tiers of bunks set against the walls.

"Woss this?" she asked.

"Crew's quarters for sleeping in on long haul flights. We can carry a replacement pilot and co-pilot. They kip in here and take over in mid flight. Or the cabin staff can sometimes grab forty winks - or do our shagging in here. The bunks are small, but much more comfortable than the toilets!"

Sharon looked at the gorgeous young Virgin steward.

"Woss yer name?"

"Stewart."

"Gorgeous young V.... gorgeous young Stewart, then," muttered Sharon, thinking aloud.

"Pardon?"

"Nuffink! It looks luvly - er - Stewart."

"I'll make sure we aren't disturbed," said Stewart. He picked up a telephone receiver from its wall mounting and pressed a button.

"Hullo, Rita? Stew here. I'm in the doss house. Can you make sure I'm not disturbed for ten minutes? What? A passenger. Joining the club. Thanks, I owe you."

Something of the old feelings she associated with Ford Capris came over Sharon. This would be one way to relieve her in-flight boredom. But ten minutes! Why had gorgeous young Stewart asked for *that* long? "He must like me," she thought. "He must want to chat to me afterwards."

* * * * * * * * *

When Sharon got back to her seat in the front of the 'plane in Virgin's Upper Class section, Sir Fabian was still asleep. The dull background sound of the engines was enough to send anyone off to sleep, that is if the effects of too much champagne on top of a paté starter, steamed cod in a cream and mushroom sauce, prime Scottish roast beef with French beans, petits pois and baby new boiled Jersey potatoes, with a pleasantly sharp summer pudding topped with a generous helping of thick, yellow clotted cream to round off with, weren't enough on their own to send an Upper Class passenger off to the land of nod.

Sharon settled back in her seat and reflected on her encounter with the gorgeous young steward Stewart. He had taken more like *twenty* minutes and no time for a chat afterwards! She sighed with contentment. Not only had she joined the Mile High club but she had broken a personal best. None of her experiences in Capris, the Cortina or with the multitude of other one-offs she had managed from amongst Sir Fabian's entourage had prepared her for such lengthy sex. Not even the yacht Navigator, who always seemed to be so busy. Twenty minutes! In some ways, her life was so full; in others, so empty. She dozed off.

The 747 approached the U.K. through cloudless skies, pulling long fluffy vapour trails behind it making its path easy to follow from 37,000 feet below. The crew of a trawler making towards Newlyn round the Scillies looked up from their labours with the fish they had caught, watching sunlight glint off the shiny fuselage far above. The boat was tattered and battered by the Atlantic, the flaked paint showing its name as the "Stuff EU" - a newly registered name-change that defied the sea-faring superstition about renaming vessels, but which adequately summed up the popularity of the EU amongst Cornish fishermen.

"747," said a particularly grizzled man laconically. He absently picked up another dead cod and threw it into a black plastic tray.

"Where do 'ee reckon 'ee's come from?" asked a young fresh-faced but tanned youngster.

"States? Mexico? Depends on winds," replied Grizzled, throwing another cod into the black tray. " 'Ere, Treve, this 'un's full. Put 'im in the 'eavy box." He turned to the youngster, whose first trip this was. "We're over quota, see. Got to leave some cod for those fuckin' Spaniards to 'ave." He hawked and gobbed over the side. "So we sink these under a short buoy an' pick 'em up in a launch after the fuckin' Maff man 'as checked our catch. Bastards!"

"Maff man?"

"Ministry of Agriculture, Fisheries and Farming, boy. Spies for Brussels, they Maff men. *Bastards!*" Grizzled hawked flamboyantly into the ocean again.

"Oh. Right. What's a short buoy?"

Grizzled laughed bronchially. "You will be if I cut yer fuckin' legs orf!" He laughed even louder and more bronchially at his own oft-repeated joke until he fell into a spate of wheezing coughs. Another hawk, another flamboyant gob over the side, and he was better. "It's a buoy with a chain not long enough to reach the surface, not even at low tide," he went on. "No-one can see it, see, but we knows where it is an' we can go an' get it. We go out in a sailin' boat an' 'ook it up with a long boat 'ook. The tide 'as ter be right, mind. Then we tie up somewhere like Porthleven or even Falmouth. The fish goes into suitcases an' rucksacks an' we steps off like emmets. Beats the fuckin' Maff man somethin' pretty. Bastard!"

No-one could have possibly known that some of Grizzled's last lot of illicit cod - known as black fish in the trade - had somehow ended up at Billingsgate, been bought by a buyer for the caterer contracted by Virgin Atlantic, turned into mouth-watering steamed fillets in a cream and mushroom sauce, frozen, loaded onto a plane, thawed out, re-heated and served to Sharon and Sir Fabian on board the U.K. bound flight that had just passed over the battered trawler that caught it.

* * * * * * * *

Sir Fabian Blankopf stirred in his reclined seat and slipped from his food and alcohol induced stupor into befuddled consciousness. Christ! His mouth felt like the inside of a Jo'burg hooker's thong. No idle comparison, that. He'd often heard contemporaries (there *were* a few, he acknowledged) and subordinates (almost the entire population of the world in his opinion) boast or complain about mouths feeling like the inside of various nationalities of prostitute's underwear. What did *they* know? He *knew* the taste of the inside of a Jo'burg hooker's thong from personal experience. Well, lots of thongs, actually, as well as leather shorts and latex French knickers. And not just from his youth, of course. Once he became grotesquely wealthy he simply attracted skirt like a magnet. Still, he needed a drink. He struggled to raise his seat so that he could call the steward. A young man answered his insistent pushing of the service button.

"Yes, sir. May I help you?"

"Got any Alka Seltzer? Your shit champagne has left my mouth feeling like a public toilet."

"Certainly, sir," said Stewart benignly, glancing down at the sleeping Sharon. Sir Fabian noticed the look in Stewart's eye.

"Don't look at her like that, you smutty little bastard!"

"I'm sorry, sir? I don't know what you mean. I was wondering if your grand-daughter was feeling under the weather as well." Sir Fabian went purple.

"Grand....." he spluttered. "I'll give you fucking grand-daughter. She is my personal assistant, you cheeky young bastard!"

"Oh, I *see*, sir," smirked Stewart, feigning apology. "An unforgivable mistake. I thought you must be related as you seemed so.....shall I fetch you your Alka Seltzer, sir? We're over Cornwall now. We land in about thirty-five minutes."

Stewart went back towards the galley.

Bloody cheek! thought Sir Fabian. Bloody grand-daughter! Still, he had to admit he was actually old enough to be Sharon's grandfather at a pinch. Not many men of his age - his real age - got to regularly shag girls as young and as beautiful as Sharon. He looked at her. What a beautiful face! Her big baby-blue eyes were closed as she slept. Her cute little nose complemented the generous and expertly made-up mouth which had a tiny smile on it in repose. The skin of her neck was soft and smooth, partly hidden by the sweep of her fine golden-blonde hair that tumbled around her head in a way that got Sir Fabian's pulse racing. As it began to race he forced himself not to contemplate the rest of her body, thankful that her casual Armani outfit actually camouflaged her expensively sculpted 36D breasts, natural 23 inch waist and 34 inch hips. Her long, lean thighs...

"Your Alka Seltzer, sir."

Sir Fabian was sweating. "About bloody time," he growled.

"I hope it does the trick, sir," said Stewart.

Sir Fabian knocked back the fizzing tumbler and screwed up his face in disgust. "Bloody hell! What the fucking hell was that?"

"Just our particular type of Seltzer, sir. I don't think they taste the same in different parts of the world. Something to do with the different pharmaceutical regulations in different countries, I suppose."

"Well, bugger that one, boy!" said Sir Fabian, still trying to get the taste out of his mouth. "When do we land?"

"About thirty five minutes' time, sir."

Sir Fabian peered out of his window. "Where's that down there?"

"Cornwall, sir."

"Never heard of it! Is it in England?"

"Well, yes, sir, but a lot of Cornish might dispute that. They think of Cornwall as a country in its own right."

"Fighting for independence from the Brits, eh?" In Sir Fabian's brain, tales of his Grandfather's began to surface, the Boers rising against the British.

"The cream on your sweet was made in Cornwall, sir."

"*Was* it, now?" Always the businessman, Sir Fabian pushed the Boer War out of his mind and made a mental note to buy that cream factory, wherever it was. There must be a fortune to be made there, especially as he also owned a drugs company that made, amongst other things, slimming and cholesterol-dispersing drugs. The two would complement one another extremely well!

The steward went off to answer another call; jauntily, because only he knew that the obnoxious Sir Fabian's "Alka Seltzer" had really been a cocktail of tonic water and an obscure but potent spirit called Aquadent, distilled in the Azores from figs, so well known for its laxative effect.....

* * * * * * * * * *

Six miles below the Jumbo and about twenty five miles as the seagull flies from the homeward-bound "Stuff EU", Denzil Chegwidden patiently plodded behind the line-marking machine, leaving an unerringly straight line behind him as he marked out the touchline in front of Porthleven Football Club's little covered terrace.

"Where d'you think that one's come from, Mr Chegwidden?"

The speaker was a boy of about twelve, looking up at the jet far above, still leaving its vapour trail behind it.

Denzil stopped, wiped his brow and squinted upwards. "We-ell," he drawled. "Oi'd say America or the West Indies, Treve."

"America?" There was a tinge of wistfulness in the boy's voice.

"Prob'ly. We've flied in over Cornwall a couple of toimes comin' back from our 'olidays. It depends on the winds."

His mobile 'phone rang.

"Denzil Chegwidden," he said into it. A pause. " 'Ess, Oi've put the extra yard and a 'alf on each soide. It fits lovely." Another pause. " 'Ess, it'll be ready. You could play bowls on un now!" Then "Ar!" and he hung up.

"That were the manager," he explained to Treve. " 'Ee wants the pitch woider fer this comin' season. Signed a couple of noo boys 'oo'll play woide an' worry a foo defences. Tactics! An' that's a secret, see! Not a word."

Treve valued being allowed to help Denzil look after the pitch. A village boy who played a fair game at the back for his school team and Porthleven's under thirteens, his ambition was to play for the first team in the South Western League.

"Don't worry!" He touched a finger to the side of his nose. "Not a word!"

Denzil got on with his line marking. Treve made his farewells, jumped on his bike and cycled furiously home to his cottage just off the harbour. He went straight onto his dad's computer, trawling through the Internet comparing the pitch dimensions of all the Premiership clubs.

Chapter 11 – Venice

After the chaos of the early training sessions Sefton Perkins was relieved to see things appearing to sort themselves out. Some crash English lessons in football jargon as well as the introduction of the interpreters seemed to have paid off so that instructions during training were understood and the players could communicate reasonably well on the pitch. Those that would communicate with one another, that is. Lim Po and Sum Wun would only trade insults in Chinese which tended to diminish their effectiveness as a striking partnership, as if it were not diminished enough already by their diminutive build. Similarly, things tended to break down in midfield if Stefan Milosovitch and Milo Opec found themselves too close to one another. In training, the various players carrying injuries were lucky. Genitile's knee held out, so did Mouette's ankle (though to be fair, in training sessions there is no opposition bench to attack), Strupinski didn't overstrain his back, Lim Po's shoulder stayed in place and Macca's excess weight wasn't as much of a hindrance to him in training as it had been in the few games he had played in the previous season.

"They're shaping up nicely, Mal," Sefton said one July afternoon as they stood in the New Millennium Stand's Executive Viewing Lounge looking down on the training match taking place below them. The view was stunning, the players looking like table soccer figures from that height.

"I suppose so," responded Malcolm.

He was mentally measuring the distance between where he was and the nearest toilet. His irritable bowel syndrome had been flaring up a lot recently.

Bert Barnard, his Senior Foreman at Consolidated Solids, had been carefully poking around the new structure and what he had found out on the day he had been working at the back of the new press box, chasing out some channelling for some ISDN wiring, was worrying to say the least. He was on his own, luckily, when a huge chunk of concrete fell out from around the support column he was chipping into. He had already discovered that the concrete in the columns varied from granite hard to plaster soft and had consoled himself with the thought that at least the steel girders would be carrying the weight of the new structure. This huge chunk of displaced concrete shook that view, however. It revealed the complete width of the girder within. Bert looked in annoyance at the gaping hole and exposed metal and was about to get up to fetch some ready-mix to slap in the gap when his long years of instinct made him hesitate and look again.

Something about the girder worried him. He stared at it, trying to narrow down the problem. It hit him like a cold shower. That feeling of fear hit the pit of his stomach and he broke into a cold sweat.

"Shit, no! Shit, shit, *shit!*" His trembling hands scrabbled in his overalls for a tape measure. He made a few measurements of the exposed girder and jotted them down in a tattered notebook from his breast pocket. Then, leaning a convenient piece of plywood against the hole in the wall, he hurried out of the press box.

A couple of hours later, after much deliberation with calculator and a book entitled "Stressed Steel and Concrete for HND" - a valuable treatise from his night school days - he sat back and sank his face into his hands.

"If I'm right it's going to be a fucking close call!"

He'd 'phoned Malcolm who had a violent attack of diarrhoea as soon as the short call was finished. What's more, he suffered an increase in the severity of his IBS thereafter.

"What d'you mean, you suppose so?" Sefton brought Malcolm back from his miserable reverie.

"Eh? Oh, I mean, until they actually play a match it's hard to judge how much better they are than last season's team."

"You think they are, then? Better?" Sefton looked encouraged.

"Well, yes, stands to reason, doesn't it, all those foreign internationals. They'll clean up. They'll do well in that FIFA World Club thing in Brazil next January."

"We aren't definitely in that yet. It clashes with the fourth round of the cup."

"I thought Tony Blair wanted us to go in it to boost our chances of getting the World Cup in 2006?"

"That's the word. Tony Banks is supposed to be meeting Blankopf next month to say something about it. Blankopf will be all for it. Money." Sefton watched the training game for a few silent seconds. "Well, you'll get your chance to see how they do in a game. We've got that pre-season game in Venice to play, you know, part of the transfer deal for Bruce. Going?"

Malcolm wasn't sure about Venice. What were the toilets like? Where did all the toilet flushes actually *go*? "I don't know that I can. Pity, but work may get in the way."

"Ooh, I'm going. Never been to Venice. Looks marvellous."

"Where's their ground?" All Malcolm could think of was all that water. "On the mainland somewhere?"

"No, its actually in Venice. Can't wait to see it. I don't see how you can get a football stadium on the place."

* * * * * * * * *

The trip to Venice was not without incident. The Alitalia flight from Gatwick to Marco Polo airport ought to have been routine enough for such travelled players. As a pre-season friendly the idea was to create a relaxed atmosphere, so players' wives and girlfriends were allowed to come, paid for by Wanderers. Many were thrilled at the prospect of visiting such a romantic place. Jesus Bastardi had a problem on his hands when the tabloids got wind of the trip.

"Anyone for Venice?" - The Mail (Wanderers were paying to take wives and girlfriends on this romantic pre-season friendly.)

"Sinking feeling for Gondoliers!" - The Express (Venice wouldn't be confident about facing Wanderers, even in a friendly.)

"Canal do you now, sir?" - The Mirror (Wanderers' hard-man defence was going to knock the Venetians for six.)

"From Doges' Palace to Crystal Palace" - The Star (referring to Wanderers' next pre-season friendly.)

"Death in Venice!" - The Sun (Wanderers band of international stars was going to annihilate what was a very struggling Serie A team.)

"Sex and soccer in sinking city stadium sensation!" - The Daily Sport (whose correspondent looked up Venice on the internet and booked a flight to the U.S. as a consequence of having paid absolutely no notice of any Geography or English Literature lessons at school.)

"Wanderers On Show to the World!" - The Universe (After all the changes, the new Wanderers line-up would at last be showing what it was capable of.)

"Venice This Team Going to Face Real Opposition?" - The Globe (After all the hype, it is time for the new Wanderers United team to prove itself.)

Three young football groupies who had all been given the impression that they were the only girl in Jesus' life each wanted to go. There was Tracey from Essex, Stacey from Middlesex and Lacey who just loved sex. Lacey was eighteen, Stacey was seventeen and Tracey was younger than Jesus' daughter Juanita. Certainly the importance of training was no less now than in previous seasons where Jesus was concerned, but no amount of training could prepare a man for dealing with three nubile girls all wanting a freebie to the most romantic city in the world. He got around it very nicely by deciding to take Juanita.

"I did promise she could go," he separately told each of the sulking trio. Juanita was sulking as well, mind. Thrilled at the prospect of being able to have a crack at the sexiest footballer in the world, Nicky Bickham, she had been well put out when she found out that he had been transferred to Manchester United.

"Well, Okay, papa," she had agreed when offered the trip. "But don't forget you promised to introduce me to Nicky when you play against him!"

"Of course not, my little peach." Problem solved.

Sharon Onslow was with Caspar Hansen, of course, having first of all excused herself from her team's first pre-season friendly.

"Well, I can't begrudge a girl a romantic trip to Venice," Marty had said to her. "It's the most beautiful city in the world. Just come back raring to go, eh? Not too much pasta!"

On the 'plane, the rather tarty-looking girl brought along by Macca was looking very nervous as she sat by a window, watching everyone else settling in, chatting and laughing excitedly. She was Rosie from Lambeth and had never flown before. She was terrified. Trembling, blinking back tears and stifling a sob, she looked for a sympathetic face. Beside her, Macca was already quietly pissed.

A female flight attendant made her way along the crowded aisle and spotted Rosie. "Is some-a thing-a wrong, madam?"

Macca focussed in. "Oh, she'll be all right, luv. She's never flown before, that's all. Don't fuss, girl."

A male flight attendant had also arrived and asked his colleague what the problem was. Upon hearing that the damsel was in distress his Italian male genes kicked in. He leant across Macca, smiling into his face as if to say "You British! Let me show you how to treat a lady!" Taking one of Rosie's hands in both of his, he turned it on.

"You donta worry! You-a be safe-a wit' me! We no-a crash! Iss quite-a safe, you see. Less-a than-a two-a hours, you be in Venezia. Iss so-a romantica, you no-a be afraid again!" with which he drew Rosie's hand to his lips and kissed it.

Macca didn't have enough room to swing a good punch, which was just as well, but he still caught the flight attendant a fourpenny-one on his nose.

"Ya greasy spic bastard! That's my bird your kissing!" The bloodied nose withdrew and Macca struggled to go after him. Quite a disturbance followed during which Macca was pinned down by Antonio Genitile who not unreasonably remonstrated with him over the disparaging language directed towards his fellow coutryman by Macca. At least, that's what most people nearby thought Antonio was probably saying as his hands tightened round Macca's throat. His former team mate Edmun Edmunsen pulled him off and a three-way struggle ensued for a few seconds until Ronnie and Joker got to the scene and, in the confined space of the first class cabin, pulled them all apart. Rosie, momentarily placated by the gallant flight attendant, was now having hysterics.

"Let me off, let me off!" she shrieked, climbing over Macca, Antonio, Edmun, Ronnie and Joker with surprising agility for a girl encumbered with a combination of overgenerous breasts and over tight skirt. Forcing her way through the mêlée of players, wives, girl friends, club officials and flight crew she reached the door and, finding the steps were still in place, got off, which hardly improved Macca's mood as he now faced the prospect of a trip away with everyone having a shag except him.

Until he remembered that Jesus Bastardi had brought his daughter, who looked extremely shaggable and was bound to be at a loose end with no lad in tow. He was sure Jesus would be away chatting up the local talent. No, could be all right there.

"The bastard shouldn't have kissed my bird," he complained again as he stopped struggling and went back to his seat. "Just keep him away from me, that's all! You know how it is, Antonio. I'm a fat Geordie bastard and you're likely to call me that if you get mad at me." If he'd known what Antonio really *had* called him....!

Then there was the small matter of a two-hour delay whilst all the luggage was unloaded from the 'plane so that they could remove Rosie's suitcase.

"Well, *that* was a bloody good team building exercise," said Joker as things quietened down. "What a shame our Heinrich wasn't with us!"

Heinrich Schickelgrüber, afraid of flying, had set off the evening before last to make the journey by road in the powerful limmo hired by Wanderers as part of Heinrich's contract. The two drivers were on duty so that there was no chance of fatigue leading to an accident. There were hotels to book for overnight stops, too. Altogether a complicated business which had fallen into

Arnie Robinson's lap, still working as the Club Secretary. As Arnie was still not very certain about the security of his job, he was keen to take on any new task that made him more difficult to replace. Mind, it didn't help to improve his hypochondria. More stress and longer hours tended to make him feel more tired, so he was convinced he had M.E. Then there were the more frequent headaches, which were presumably brain tumours.

"The trouble is, Mr Robinson," said his exasperated G.P. after yet another visit to his surgery by Arnie, "You are just a bloody hypochondriac!"

"Oh, God! Is that serious?" gasped Arnie; then "Hang on! Hypochondria? Yes I know I suffer from that! You don't know what it's like, doctor. I tell you, the doctor who discovers a cure for hypochondria will be doing mankind a huge favour!"

Needless to say, Arnie had not travelled to this first pre-season friendly. He was tracking Heinrich every step of the way, electing to stay in his office so that if the unexpected happened, he would be better placed to deal with it than if he were in Venice.

Macca's fight put rather a cloud over the two-hour flight to Marco Polo airport – once it took off. Passengers on the right hand side of the 'plane had a stunning view of the lagoon and Venice as they came into land, with the setting sun glinting on countless windows in the tightly packed buildings.

Transfer to a specially chartered water bus was achieved without too much trouble, though Macca was in need of support as he had continued drinking on the 'plane.

The water bus took them round the eastern side of Venice, giving the players a preliminary glimpse of where they would be playing, the floodlights visible above the surprising number of trees. The sombre mood of the party evaporated as the beauty of the city's southern aspect came into view. The water bus headed for the landing stage of their five-star hotel, the world famous Cipriani in quiet gardens on the eastern end of Giudecca, an island on the south side of the city and off the tourist track. Wanderers wanted their new clutch of stars to have some peace and quiet to prepare for this first match of the season, even though it was just a friendly.

The evening meal was pleasant, almost all players well used to the luxurious surroundings provided by top international hotels. Those that weren't just quietly followed whatever the others did. The hotel is named after the founder of the world famous Harry's Bar in Venice. This fact wasn't lost on the players - Antonio and Edmun had been regulars there during the previous season.

An expedition to Harry's was planned without Ronnie or Joker knowing. At a suitably late hour when the expeditioners felt safe, a fleet of specially hired water taxis arrived and the players, plus some of their ladies, departed. Macca still needed support as he had continued to drink during and after the meal. He managed to survive the short crossing to Harry's without throwing up.

A great time was enjoyed by all. The staff were delighted to see Antonio and Edmun again, and honoured that they had been visited by most of the widely publicised new Wanderers team, universally tipped to win everything they played for. As a consequence, drinks flowed and measures were generous.

Well after midnight — well, a long way past 3 a.m., really - a considerably-pissed gaggle of giggling players, players' wives and girlfriends staggered onto the waterfront to take the water taxis back to the hotel.

Macca was being carried, and not very well at that, as his body fluids were by now about 40° proof and those of his team mates carrying him not a great deal less. Their struggles meant that they got into the last of the convoy of water taxis.

"WhereamI?" spluttered Macca.

"Taxi," replied several in chorus.

Macca surveyed the stars above him from his place on the floor of the boat. "Fantashtic! Bloody cabriolet fer a tackshi! Magic, theesh Eyetyesh!"

Their taxi gurgled away from the landing stage and the engine promptly cut. There was a moment's silence broken only by the pleasant sounds of water lapping against the sides of the taxi and the unsynchronised farting of the drunk passengers. Then a stream of Italian invective poured forth from the mouth of the taxi's helmsman.

"Engine, she-a fucked," translated Antonio Genitile, paraphrasing the technical details provided by the distraught helmsman.

In the bottom of the boat, Macca stirred. "Wassermarrer? Whyerwestopped?"

Seamus O'Hooligan enlightened him. "Taxi's broken down, bhoyo."

Lurching manfully to his feet, Macca took charge. "S'awright! We'll gerroutanpush!"

As the others were trying to register what he had said, not helped by the amount of alcohol in their bloodstreams and, in some cases, an absence of translation, Macca half-staggered, half fell, towards where he thought the taxi door should be. Finding none, he simply muttered "Great idea, shoft top tackshis," and hopped out over the side.

Splash!

"What the fuck...?" Never had five completely intoxicated people sobered up so fast as pandemonium broke out in the drifting taxi.

"Where's the life belt?"

"Call the police!"

"Where the fuck *is* he?"

"Hold me coat!"

"Can he swim?"

"Can you see him?"

"Get this bloody boat started!"

"Throw him a rope!"

"Can you *see* him?"

"Get off me foot!"

"Careful, you nearly had *me* in!"

The disorganisation was complete as everyone, in their panic, was shouting in his own language. The taxi lurched dangerously, threatening to throw all the occupants into the water.

"Blaaargh! Flurphlgluurgh! Bastards! Grooluurgh!"

"He's-a over there!" yelled Antonio in English. At that second, flashing lights over a dark, speeding shape, the sound of a powerful diesel and a swirl of bow wash ghosted past the rocking taxi.

"*POLIZEI*" was visible in the lights from the city. A pair of uniformed arms stretched over the side of the police launch and grabbed at the threshing form in the centre of a patch of foaming water. Macca was hauled unceremoniously into the launch, cursing and swearing at the top of his voice, still struggling.

It wouldn't have been so bad if the police launch hadn't had to make a quick U-turn to pick up Seamus O'Hooligan and Manuel Sardhinas who had been thrown out of the taxi which, already rocking alarmingly due to the chaos on board, was tipped even further by the wash of the police launch.

With three soaking wet revellers on board the police prepared to deal severely with them They drew their launch alongside the unfortunate taxi. A quick dialogue between one of the policemen and the taxi man soon established two things: the taxi needed a tow, and the men on board (and in the water) were the world famous footballers of Wanderers United. Much shoulder-shrugging, face contorting and arm waving later, the taxi was taken in tow and the party was delivered to the Cipriani. The three soaking wet players sploshed their way through the elegant foyer and up the expensively carpeted stairs.

The night receptionist looked on in dismay (or was it disgust?) and shook his head. The players had been escorted to the door by the fawning police, who gave the Receptionist a brief account of the little incident. Antonio filled in the details. Back at his desk, the Receptionist picked up the 'phone, punched out a number, waited, then spoke. "Desk here. You'll need to bring carpet-cleaning equipment here. Puddles of water across the floor and up the stairs. Our football team, the mighty Wanderers. That fat slob McGrath and two others. Sorry."

Putting the receiver down, he settled back into his chair and carried on reading the soft-porn magazine hidden inside "La Gazzetta dello Sport".

Somehow the incident was kept from Ronnie and Joker. Those at breakfast just a few hours later numbered just a few, the ones who hadn't been out until the small hours. By the time Macca surfaced, thankfully free of his customary hangover, it was almost lunchtime.

"All right, bhoyo?" Seamus also had a clear head and had quite an appetite as they began to sit down in the dining room even though it was still a bit early.

"Right as rain," replied Macca. "Cold bath does the trick, eh? Why didn't anyone stop me?"

"Shure, we were all too far gone, Macca. Ah'll tell yer what, though, the poh-lice were so cool about it. It would have given the papers a field day."

Macca was well used to damning publicity, whether true or not, so couldn't care less about it. Seamus hadn't experienced the heady heights of the Premiership and its attraction to the paparazzi so was a bit more sensitive.

"What happened to your face, Macca?" asked Johann van Dyke, the Dutch porn star.

Macca had the early signs of a black eye and his left cheek was bright red.

"I guess the cops must have been a bit rough when they hauled me out of the water last night," replied Macca. Close observers might have noticed the tell-tale body language of lying.

Sitting with her father at another table, Juanita Bastardi had noted both the absence of Macca at breakfast and his jovial arrival just before lunch. The fat bastard! He'd come creeping to her room last night as somehow she'd forgotten to lock her door. To be honest, in such a magnificent hotel in such a wonderful city, widely acknowledged as being safe even for unaccompanied women, it hadn't crossed her mind.

"Ah've seen yers watchin' me, lass," Macca had said as he came, uninvited, into her room. She was in bed but not asleep, and had sat up, alarmed at the intrusion. She always slept in the nude so Macca got a brief, wonderful eyeful before she pulled the bedclothes up. Enough to notice that she obviously sunbathed topless. "Well, Ah'm here, pet. It's your lucky day!"

Well, she *had* been watching him, it was true. His behaviour on the 'plane had been so bad that a lot of people had been looking at him. His increasingly drunken demeanour had made him an obvious object of interest.

"Of-a course I watch-a you!" she shouted in her broken English. "You are-a bad-a boy, all-a people-a watch you. You drink-a much, is not-a good!"

Though considerably sobered up by his drenching, Macca nevertheless didn't detect any signs of a potential brush-off. Mind, he was one of those obnoxious types where girls are concerned, a firm believer in the notion that when a girl says 'no', she really means 'yes' unless she's a lesbian.

"Now, pet, shift over. Lerrus in an' Ah'll show yers a good time!" Macca made as if to get into Juanita's bed.

She screamed and smacked his face hard, which stopped him in his tracks; but as she did so, the bedclothes slipped down to give Macca another tempting eyeful.

"Frisky, eh, lass?" chortled Macca, still not perceiving the girl's mood.

She punched him in the right eye, one knuckle slightly protruding to dig into the orbit as she had been shown by her dad. "To protect yourself, my angel," he had explained at the time.

This time Macca stepped back. "Nah, coom on lass. It's late. Let's get doon to it, eh?"

He thought he was making progress as she flew out of her bed, magnificent breasts jiggling and heaving with her anger.

"Ooh, tha' din't sunbathe in the nuddy, then. Ah thowt ye might....Oooooof!"

Juanita had brought her scrumptiously sculptured knee sharply up into Macca's goolies, bending him double. He clasped his injured manhood with both hands.

"No rub-a them! *Count*-a them! And-a *fuck off!*" She shoved him backwards and, off balance, he fell. Juanita kicked him where he was still holding himself. Despite the protection of his hands, his discomfort was greatly increased by the kick. Tears streaming from his eyes, Macca began to crawl towards the door.

"All reet, all reet, Ah'm goin'! You're crazy, pet, p'raps you's are too young anyway!" He reached for the door handle and hoisted himself onto his feet and made a hurried exit. Juanita quickly locked the door behind him and stood, panting with rage, for a minute or two while she calmed down. She decided not to tell her father if only not to upset the team. Even at her age she recognised how important it was for the players not to fall out. It was her father's livelihood, after all.

So that explained Macca's visible injuries, and only Juanita and he knew the real cause. Of course, only Macca knew how tender his goolies were that morning. Juanita could only wonder if she hadn't imagined Macca's gait as being slightly nautical that day.

A small commotion occurred just then which some thought heralded the arrival of their lunch, but it was Heinrich arriving, reasonably relaxed after his long drive, but with the car parked at the other end of Venice, he'd had the stiffness and boredom blown out of him by the water taxi journey to the hotel and he was in a good mood - and hungry. He sat down with Macca, Seamus and Johann, completing the Wanderers party.

The pasta arrived, the meal already ordered for them by the Wanderers new nutritionist, Nita.

"One thing about the Eyeties," mumbled Macca through a mouthful of fusilli. "Pasta! I love it! I eat loads of it at home. It's good for you."

Not in the quantities you stuff it down, thought Nita, sitting at the next table and therefore overhearing him. That's why you're such a fat bastard. Wonder you didn't sink last night and a bloody good job if you had. Nita had entertained the night receptionist after he was relieved at seven that morning. He had crept up to her room and told her all about the night's fun and games as he fed her the kind of diet she couldn't have recommended to a vegetarian.

It was with that much preparation that the team set out for a light training session at the Campo Sportivo where Venezia play. Situated on the easternmost of the Venetian islands, it proved something of a surprise when the Wanderers party walked out onto the immaculate pitch for the first time.

The Directors who had travelled ahead of the team stood a little apart from the players: Sefton Perkins stood with Malcolm Black, Cecil Norris, Jack Grimethorpe and Dick Fossett, surveying the Venice pitch. Malcolm had decided to make the trip after all. He had researched the toilet availability in the team hotel and at the ground and had dosed himself up for the trip with an inadvisable combination of Imodium and Kaolin suspension. Antonio Genitile and Edmun Edmunsen were happy enough to be back at the ground they had left less that two months earlier. The few fans already in the ground had greeted them reasonably well. Not many seemed to begrudge them their move to the most famous club in the world. They had got the Wanderers' Australian 'keeper in exchange who many thought was better than Edmunsen - which in fact he was - and enough cash to buy a very competent striker.

"Bloody hell!"

Dick Fossett, gritty ex-player that he was, had never seen the like and spoke for them all. The pitch was fine. Excellent, in fact. The little stand behind them was O.K. A bit third division, perhaps, but quite modern looking and comfortable enough. It was the seating opposite and at both ends. It was entirely constructed of scaffolding, like the temporary stands erected for things like Royal Weddings and intended for perhaps just one day only. At each end the spidery stands stood about four storeys high. Behind the left hand goal there was a huge gap in the scaffolding, dividing it into two sections.

"I suppose that bloody gap keeps opposing fans apart," suggested Jack. "By 'eck, Cecil, all that bloody scaffolding. You couldn't charge much for knocking that lot down, eh, lad?" He and Cecil chuckled.

"Wouldn't take much," suggested Dick. "Get the fans a bit bloody wound up and all singing and stamping and it'd come down of its own accord! No joke, that, a bloody stand full of fans collapsing!"

Rueful smiles from him, Sefton, Cecil and Dick. Malcolm had suddenly gone white, muttered "Bloody hell!" and dashed into the players' tunnel, seeking out the nearest toilet.

The match itself was nothing remarkable. The little ground was packed to its capacity of just under 16,000 with screaming, chanting fans, the visiting fans' section filled with wandering Wanderers fans who belligerently followed their team anywhere. The only unpleasant episode was the sinking of a Vaporetto, one of Venice's water buses. Wanderers fans simply smothered it, climbing onto the roof when no more could be packed inside. It capsized without leaving the bus stop landing stage. Fortunately, at each stop the water buses are tied to the landing stage, so the stricken vessel just wallowed sideways and hung from the two ropes which manfully resisted the complete immersion of the vessel. No lives were lost but it was a close thing, the fans in the two cabins smashing windows to escape. They were the wet ones in the ground that day.

As for the game itself, Venezia went ahead in the thirty first minute when La Pazbaq failed to connect with a shot by the home striker. He'd tried his "mooning backside" save but mistimed it, the ball skimming up off his left cheek into the roof of the net.

And the crowd went wild.

Sefton, sitting next to Malcolm in the Directors' Box of the neat little covered grandstand, said to those around him: "I wouldn't fancy being in that stand behind the goal there," referring to the end to his right where the goal had been scored. "Listen, they're going mad. How that scaffolding stands up to it I don't know. Wonder the whole bloody thing doesn't collapse!"

He didn't understand why Malcolm leapt to his feet and charged past him, disappearing into the stand. Malcolm was, of course, heading for the nearest toilet again (quietly reconnoitred in advance), crippled with the pain of a sudden attack of his irritable bowel syndrome. Slamming the door and dropping his trousers at the same time he sat, partly relieved, partly sweating. He wished he hadn't come! He wished Sefton hadn't made that remark about a collapsing stand, not after Dick had made the same comment earlier! He wished he could think of a way to somehow put things right. But as Bert had told him, the only way to do that was to knock the whole New Millennium Stand down and start again. As the waves of diarrhoea subsided he couldn't help thinking about the shit he was in.

Venezia held their lead until half time and a contented buzz went around the ground, spoiled only by the singing from the Wanderers crowd: "Just one goal-ee-o, that's all you've got; just one goal-ee-o, it's not a lot! We are United, we are not Crewe, and if you beat us, we'll slaughter you!" - to the tune of that ice cream cornet advert popularly sung by obnoxious British tourists in Venice. Some joker had put the words out on the Wanderers Unofficial Web Site as well as in "Wanderers Are Naturally Kings", the unofficial fanzine. Of course, none of the Italians knew what words the Wanderers fans were singing, so just joined in with the proper words. The Wanderers fans naturally thought the home fans were singing the same threatening song back to them, only in Italian, so everyone was happy.

"Translated it quick, didn't they?" commented one soaking-wet, shaven-headed, tattooed, scarred, gap-toothed thug in a Wanderers shirt. He was a City dealer by trade, accounting for his ability to afford to follow Wanderers everywhere and the fact that his club shirt was a *genuine* one and not a bootlegged cheapo.

"Yes, well these Eyeties are much better than us at languages, aren't they," explained his companion, similar in appearance in terms of haircut and tattoos but with added eyebrow, nasal and ear jewellery, an unemployed Philosophy and Sociology graduate from the University of Neasden (formerly Neasden Polytechnic, formerly Neasden Tech., formerly Neasden Community School and Technology College, formerly Neasden Secondary Modern School, est. 1961). He could afford to follow Wanderers everywhere because he was a skilled Social Security fraudster, though to be fair his replica shirt was a bootlegged cheapo.

As the teams came out for the second half, Ronnie muttered to Joker, "Like we said in the dressing room, when Lim Po gets the ball, he never passes to Sum Wun and vice versa. What a striking partnership, eh, laddie?"

"Yes," agreed Joker. "When either of them has the ball, the other one is left completely unmarked. Look."

From kick off, the ball had reached Sum Wun in the left channel. Lim Po was in acres of space to his right. He wouldn't call for the ball. He wasn't going to speak to that revisionist capitalist running dog. Venezia's defence swarmed round Sum Wun and he lost possession. Even if he had seen Lim Po, he wouldn't pass to him, the Communist pig!

"I've had an idea, boss. Leave it for another quarter of an hour."

The score remained the same until Joker said, "Bring Sum Wun off, put Georgi Strupinski on, boss."

"Who d'ye think we should take off?"

"The bloody Chinaman Sum Wun!"

"Oh, right. Ah thought ye meant 'some one'. Whatever ye say, Joker. Ah've lost the will tae live, ye ken! This is fochin' agony!"

The swap was made. Through the interpreter, Georgi had brief instructions from Joker. He ran on to take the place of the withdrawn striker.

In Wanderers' next attack, Lim Po got the ball and headed for goal. By now the Venezia defence had got used to converging on the Chinaman. Lim Po looked up, saw Georgi in acres of space to his left and poked a wicked little ball between the approaching crowd of Venezia shirts straight into Georgi's path. A touch to control it, and wallop!

One-all.

"How about that, boss!"

"Ye're a fochin' genius, laddie! It's almost funny!"

Habits established during a match are hard to change just like that, and despite the hysterical antics of the Venezia coach on the touchline, three minutes later exactly the same thing happened. Two - one to Wanderers.

Venezia, tipped to struggle in Serie A again that season, were happy with just a two - one defeat. The game had been played at something like exhibition pace with the result that none of Wanderers' medical risks suffered any injuries by the time the referee blew for time. Wanderers had started their season with the expected win from their newly-built squad of international superstars and so everyone was happy. Except for Ronnie and Joker, perhaps, who were more bemused than happy.

Chapter 12 - Brazil?

It was just coincidence that while Wanderers were in Venice, Arnie Robinson, the Club Secretary, received a call from the office of the Minister for Sport.

"Could the Minister have a word with you, Mr. Robinson?"

"Well, yes, of course." Arnie was puzzled. The Minister didn't support Wanderers. He was used to getting memos from Westminster suggesting that, for example, as Chelsea were due to visit Wanderers on such and such a date, the MP for somewhere or other would like to obtain a couple of tickets. This always meant that an MP, or sometimes a Minister, wanted a freebie. It was always good politics (with a small "p") to invite them along and give them the full VIP treatment including the meal in the Committee Room with all the players afterwards. You never knew which MP, Minister or Shadow Minister might be of some value to the club at some time in the future: Labour and Conservative ones, at any rate. The Lib Dems were sold the best tickets at the ticket's face value. They were unlikely to form the Government so didn't need to be cultivated.

"When does he want to speak to me?" asked Arnie.

"Well, now," replied the starched voice at the other end of the 'phone. "I'll put him through."

Click. Pause. Click. "Arnie?" the unmistakable voice of Tony Banks.

"Er - yes." Who was he, making with the first names? Arnie hadn't even *voted* New Labour. He was a socialist. "Arnie Robinson speaking. What can I do for you, Mr Banks?"

"I won't beat about the bush, Arnie. It's about our bid to host the 2006 World Cup. We'd like you to enter the new FIFA World Club Championship in Brazil in January."

"I see." Arnie didn't see. What had the World Cup bid of 2006 got to do with the FIFA tournament in Brazil?

"We felt that FIFA would look more positively at our bid if we co-operated by taking part in their little tournament. It could become huge in the future and the chances of that happening would be greatly increased by the presence of Wanderers in the first one. There's two million quid in it for each participating club..... though I don't suppose that will be much of an incentive for a club like Wanderers, eh?"

"Look, Mr Banks, I think you'd better put it in writing, then the Board can discuss it at their next Board Meeting. Of course, I'll mention it..."

"Er, well, Arnie, I don't want anything in writing yet. This is just - errrrm - a personal view we have. Something we'd very mush like Wanderers to do."

"Who's this 'we' you keep mentioning, Mr Banks?"

"Tony, please. I know the Prime Minister thinks it will help. Tell you what, why don't you drop in to the Ministry for a chat?"

"It'd be better if you spoke to the Chairman, Mr Banks. Something like that is way outside my terms of reference."

"Tony, *please*, Arnie. That'd be - er - Sefton Perkins. Speak to my secretary and arrange a meeting."

"Well, Mr Banks, actually Mr Perkins is the *Vice*-Chairman now." Shit. Sir Fabian's ownership of the club was supposed to be a secret. Arnie broke into a sweat. Normally he would immediately suspect that it was the symptom of something serious, but his brain was so busy grappling with the dilemma he was in it didn't have time to put his hypochondria into gear. Could he at least tell the Minister for Sport? Surely *he* wouldn't blab to the press? He became aware of the voice on the 'phone again.

"Are you there? Hello? Arnie?"

"Sorry, Mr Banks, what did you say?"

"*Tony!* I said who is the Chairman now?"

Gulp! "Sir Fabian Blankopf, only we aren't letting the public know until the season starts," blurted Arnie. There! It was done. Oh God! What have I done? "You mustn't let on, Mr Banks. Only he's the guy in the Chair now. And he'll be the one to talk to. What he says goes, so to speak."

"*Fabian Blankopf?*" The Minister did not sound pleased. He wasn't. Blankopf was further right than Margaret Thatcher. He owned Digital International. He owned that bloody rag the Daily Universe with its tits on every other page, anti-Labour slant, anti-EU editorials. How the hell had he managed to get control of the biggest football club in the world? "How did he manage to get control of Wanderers, for God's sake?"

"Well, that's not for me to say, Mr Banks. Do you want me to set up a meeting?"

The Minister was uncertain. Sir Fabian bloody Blankopf had been trying to get British Citizenship for several years now. He always referred to himself as *Sir* Fabian even though he wasn't entitled to as his was only an honorary knighthood. No doubt he'd love to have pictures of himself smiling and shaking hands with a Government Minister plastered all over the papers and TV screens. Better have a word with Tony. "Yes, do that. Cheers, Arnie." He rang off. If Tony wasn't happy, he could cancel the meeting.

Tony *wasn't* happy. "We mustn't let him be seen with any of us in public, Tony. That chap Sefton Perkins was a different undertaking altogether. An ex-steelworker. Good 'old labour' background, you know. We could have got some good mileage out of him. We *must* have Wanderers in that FIFA tournament, though. If it begins to look like we've a good chance of landing the World Cup in 2006 - what do our people say it's worth?"

"Nought point eight five percent," supplied the Minister for Sport.

"Right, nought point eight five percent on the vote in the next general election. It'll help the marginals." The Prime Minister made a decision. "You'd better see Blankopf, but for God's sake don't step outside, don't even go near a bloody window while you're with him. Just get him to agree to put Wanderers in that tournament."

* * * * * * * * *

"How did the British Government get involved in us playing in Brazil?" Sir Fabian bellowed down his 'phone to Sefton Perkins.

"It was Arnie Robinson who made the first - er - approach, Sir Fabian," replied Sefton. Here was a chance to save Arnie's job after his summary sacking by Sir Fabian outside the stadium. "He wondered if our taking part wouldn't help England's bid to stage the 2006 World Cup. We're bound to win it. The FIFA tournament, that is: not the World Cup. Not that we *can't* win the World Cup, of course." Sefton was getting off the point. He got back on track. "Great idea of Arnie's. He's even set up a meeting between you and Tony Banks - the Minister for Sport." He knew Sir Fabian wouldn't know who Tony Banks was even though he was desperately keen to gain British Citizenship. The Minister for Sport wasn't likely to have much influence in the Foreign Office so he wasn't worth knowing.

"I think Arnie deserves a pat on the back."

"Sure, great guy!" Sir Fabian had presumably put his sacking of Arnie out of his mind. "When do I see this Minister fellow?"

"You'll have to get your people to contact Arnie, I think, Sir Fabian. There is one small problem to resolve, however."

"So resolve it!"

"Yes, well it won't be as easy as that. If we play in Brazil, we'll be out of the country for the fourth round of the FA Cup." Sefton couldn't see a way round that one.

"What cup?" Sir Fabian still had not grasped the importance of the FA Cup despite his meeting with Ronnie.

"The FA Cup, Sir Fabian. Ronnie - er - mentioned it. One of the things in the treble we won last season. It's the biggest thing in English football. We'd have to clear it with the F.A."

"The who? F.A?" Sir Fabian still had much to learn about the new industry he had bought into. "Where I come from that means f..."

"Football Association," supplied Sefton. "They run football in this country, Sir Fabian. F.A. for short."

Of course, Sir Fabian had been overwhelmingly in favour of Wanderers playing in Brazil once the projection of the likely TV income was made clear to him by his team of accountants. If only Digital International could get the TV rights. With Wanderers in it and likely to win it, the demand would be huge. He barked down the 'phone, his mind made up.

"Sort it out. As far as I'm concerned, we play in Brazil!"

Chapter 13 - Brazil!

The FA weren't that happy with the Wanderer's preliminary enquiry about the possibility of their entering the FIFA World Club Tournament in Brazil.

"It clashes with the fourth round of the FA Cup," said their President. "They can't."

"You can't," said their Secretary to Arnie over the 'phone. "You've the FA Cup to defend. How could you go to Brazil and still play in round four? You'd be flying to and fro like Lancaster bombers in the war."

"We could get knocked out in round three," suggested Arnie. Oh God, his palpitations were setting in. He was *sure* he had heart trouble. He'd noticed that every time he got stressed out about something, his heart started to pound.

He broke out into a sweat again.

Oh no! That *was* that a symptom of an imminent heart attack. He'd looked it up. He couldn't feel any pain in his chest, but there was a bit of an ache in his left arm. Was it or wasn't it? He'd better soldier on. He got out his mobile 'phone and turned it on, keying in the speed-dial code for 999. If he felt himself going he'd just have to press "call" as he blacked out and they would trace his 'phone...

The FA Secretary on the other end of the line was disagreeing with him. "Yea, very likely. Drawn to play Tamworth or some such. Look, we don't see how it can be done."

"Why can't you just let us play round four when we get back?"

"We talked about that. It would mess up the fixtures of whoever you played, and we won't know who that is until the middle of December at the earliest. It could be another Premiership club, it could be a Nationwide club. It could even be a bloody non-league club. Their league would have to fiddle about with its fixtures just to accommodate Wanderers. It might prove very unpopular. We decided against it."

Arnie's fluttering heart sank. "Okay, I'll get back to you," he moaned, replacing the receiver. If I don't drop dead first, he thought. He called in the Directors.

The Wanderers Board, minus Sir Fabian who had gone to Brussels for something or other, debated the situation.

Dick Fossett, record goal scorer, wasn't mincing his words. He looked determined, his mind made up. "Get onto Banks. Tell him to lean on the FA. We can tell him we're only talking about this because he wants us to play in that bloody tournament. It'll be summer in Brazil in January. Hotter than hell. I'd rather not go. Next FA Cup Final is the last under Wembley's twin towers. We've got to win that one. Tell Sir bloody Fabian it wasn't possible to fix it."

"Er, careful, lad," warned Sefton. "Remember he can pull the rug from under us at any time in the first twelve months. He made it very clear that as far as he's concerned, we play in Brazil. If we upset him and he goes, we're up shit creek with a wage bill of over three-quarters of a million a week. Even we don't make enough to sustain that kind of outlay. It's only Blankopf's money that's keeping us afloat and he reckons to get his money back in the short term from the TV rights from jamborees such as this Brazilian thing."

"Well, get bloody Banks to talk to the FA, then," repeated Dick.

The machinations of Government are far too complicated for the ordinary mortal to understand. They can sway big business, they can influence individuals, they can certainly lean successfully on all manner of institutions - but not the FA. Having operated more or less as a law unto themselves since the nineteenth century, they were not about to allow a club to alter the date of an FA Cup match by two weeks just because Tony Blair asked them personally. Well, almost personally.

So It was back to the Wanderers Board, still with Sir Fabian giving apologies for absence but with his presence felt very strongly nevertheless.

"We'll have to enter the FIFA thing," sighed Malcolm, not enjoying this pre-season upheaval which was playing hell with his large intestines. "We'll have to pull out of the FA Cup."

"That's bloody unheard of," snarled Dick. "No-one's ever done that, not that I know of, anyway."

There was a murmur of unhappy agreement around the table.

"Who's going to propose it, then?" asked Sefton, in the chair in Sir Fabian's absence.

"I reckon," suggested Jack Grimethorpe, "that Blankopf has already proposed it. He told us to 'sort it', didn't he? Put his bloody name down."

"Bloody right," agreed Dick.

"Yes, do that," said Malcolm to Arnie who was taking the minutes. It was difficult to write whilst taking your pulse, but he was sure his heart was playing up again. This FA Cup thing was very stressful. Put Sir Fabian's name down even though he wasn't there? There was that sweat breaking out again. "Sefton?" he squeaked, pleadingly.

"Yes, make it his proposal *in absentia*," said Sefton, "so who's going to second it?"

No-one wanted to. They drew straws (hurriedly fetched from the bar in the Hospitality suite by Arnie, who was convinced that rushing about like that was only going to precipitate his heart attack) and Malcolm lost, so his name went in the minutes. They all voted in favour. No point Sir Fabian reading that anyone had voted against. God knows what he might do.

The media uproar was phenomenal. Wanderers, so big and successful for the last two decades, were unpopular in certain quarters. People hated their success and loved an opportunity to knock them.

The Daily Mirror mounted a campaign to make Wanderers reconsider and enter the FA Cup. Premiership sides didn't enter until the third round, of course, so the Mirror's Sports Editor and others planned to keep up the pressure until at least November when the draw would be made.

Of course, the FA came in for a lot of stick for not being willing to move the dates of Wanderer's fourth round game. They demonstrated their empathy with the millions of fans and players up and down the country that actually made their existence possible by completely ignoring them. The Government came in for criticism for putting pressure on Wanderers. Ronnie Bone made it known that he didn't want to go to Brazil but that he was powerless in the face of the Board's decision. The Directors were vilified for betraying fans of all clubs up and down the country.

"MAN. UTD. WILL WIN CUP!" yelled a Mirror back-page headline, "BUT VICTORY WILL BE EMPTY", it concluded over an article that pointed out that, without the holders Wanderers defending it, the FA Cup would be a meaningless competition that season. Although Manchester United were now bound to win it, it would mean nothing to them if Wanderers hadn't been involved."

Of course, the more publicity there was, the better Sir Fabian liked it. Now back in London, in his recently-bought mansion overlooking Wimbledon Common, he was a happy man.

"The bloody cash'll roll in, Shaz," he chortled, looking at the array of sports pages spread out on the floor by his bed in his huge first-floor bedroom. Sharon didn't respond. Working class she may be, but she never spoke with her mouth full. She just wished Blanky would put those bloody papers away and *concentrate*. Her cheek muscles were getting tired and his Viagra seemed to be wearing off. She felt like giving up. She gave up.

"Blanky, yer Viagra ain't workin', luv."

"What? Oh, Christ, Shaz, sorry. I wasn't concentrating. This Wanderers thing is going so well. All you Brits are really worked up about this bloody FA Cup thing. You gotta realise, there's so much more money to be made in Brazil."

"Why can't yer do boaf of 'em?"

"None of those stupid bastards in that FA would take a bung to change their rules. Imagine that, Shaz. I couldn't buy 'em. I think FA stands for fuckin' arse'oles! Mind, like I say, it isn't worth that much to me so we didn't tempt them too much!"

Which at least meant that our men of the FA are above reproach in terms of ethics, which is nice.

"'Ave I got this right, Blanky?" Probably not, thought Sir Fabian. "We'll be in Brazil when Wanderers should be playin' someone in the cup."

Bloody hell, she's got it! "Right, Shaz. Don't worry your pretty little head, gal."

"No, *lissen*!" shrilled Sharon. "Why don't yer jus' fly the uvver team aht ter play yer in Brazil?"

"Yea, sure, Shaz. Like I said, don't worry your head. I don't have you round me for your brains. Let's turn in."

An hour or so later, Sir Fabian, suddenly wide awake, sat bolt upright in bed, about the only way any part of him could easily become bolt upright in bed. Fuck me, he thought, she's a fucking *genius!*. Fly the opposing team out to Brazil! He'd get his tacky tabloid, the Daily Universe, to do it. Great publicity for the paper: sales would soar! His mind raced over the idea. Fly the team out on Concorde, include some "lucky prize winners" - more increase in sales. And supporters. Wanderers would already have some supporters out there. Fly a

Jumbo jet - no, *two* Jumbo jets, one for each team, out to Brazil full of supporters. Leave each club to work out how to fill the seats free of charge - with a few more seats set aside for more "lucky prize winners" chosen through the pages of the Daily Universe. Oh, this is brilliant!

Sir Fabian leapt out of bed and went to his 'phone. A few minutes' ringing conjured up a befuddled voice at the other end. "Yes? Do you know what the time is?"

"Fuck the time," yelled Sir Fabian. The voice at the other end spluttered into fawning mode. "Shuttup and listen," commanded Sir Fabian. "Get me prices on chartering Concorde to Rio for, say, four days, and two 747s, maximum seating capacity, also Rio, for, say, three days. Then get me that Arnie wanker at Wanderers."

The voice at the other end squeaked deferentially.

"No I *don't* care what the fucking time is. Get on with it!"

Sir Fabian's next door neighbour, a Managing Director of an international merchant bank in the City, was giving his pet collie a late walk on the Common in front of his own mansion. He saw the light in Sir Fabian's bedroom window. Back home, his wife already in bed, he commented as he undressed: "That bastard Blankopf is at home for once. His light is on."

"Couldn't be burglars, could it?" asked his wife.

"No such luck. That bloody awful stretch limmo of his is there. Bloody thing is so long, it nearly took the nose off my Bristol once when I met it turning in front of me." His classic 1970s Bristol 411 Saloon was his pride and joy.

"Do you think we should invite him round for a drink, as a new neighbour?"

"Don't even think about it! The man's a wanker. I didn't tell you, did I. My last trip back from New York, the bloody 'plane had to circle over the North Downs for nearly an hour because that sod was having an attack of the shits in one of the toilets. They wouldn't land until all the loos were empty and he was in there for half a bloody hour, refusing to come out. Couldn't have been the food, no-one else was ill. Must have drunk too much. I don't want him near me!"

Chapter 14 - The New Season Starts

In the next pre-season friendly at Crystal Palace there was another 2 - 1 win for Wanderers, Seamus O'Hooligan scoring with a goal set up for him by Sum Wun in circumstances similar to those that created Georgi Strupinski's chances against Venezia, with Macca scoring the second direct from a free kick thirty five yards out. Ronnie and Joker decided to put him on when the free kick was awarded ten minutes from time. They took off Milo Opec who had taken a knock from the foul, and stuck Macca on because, overweight as he was, if he couldn't do anything else he was world-class at free kicks, and he didn't let them down.

After that second goal, Antonio La Pazbaq saved a shot with his bare backside again and was immediately arrested by a policewoman behind his goal for indecent exposure and behaviour likely to cause a breach of the peace. This had resulted in his having to be substituted with Edmun Edmunsen whose bobble hat looked rather out of place in the South London August sunshine. Too many of the Wanderers team were laughing at this to concentrate fully and Palace had hit back two minutes from time.

A little friendly diplomacy involving the local Chief Inspector and the promise of appearing as Guest Speakers at the local Police Ball by Ronnie and Joker smoothed out the mooning incident and the charges were dropped.

"Ye'll have tae get some flesh-coloured Y-fronts!" bellowed Ronnie at the confused Columbian through his interpreter, though how that translated into Colombian or whatever bloody language they spoke there Ronnie could only wonder at, or might have if he cared a jot, which he didn't.

Another win over Hamilton Academicals (Ronnie and Joker's first club as managers) set them up for their Charity Shield match against Arsenal at Wembley. There was some discussion in the tabloid press about the unfair advantage Arsenal would enjoy because they had used the venerable old stadium as their "home" ground for European Champions League games, so their players would be more used to playing there. In fact it worked against the Arsenal's interests because set against their complete lack of nerves at playing there was the excitement virtually all of Wanderers' new squad felt at the prospect. Only Milo Opec, Johann van Dyke and Caspar Hansen had played there before: Opec in a Division Two play-off with Port Vale, van Dyke a couple of times for Holland against England and Hansen, of course, as a former Arsenal player.

In the event, Wanderers won 1 - 0, Hansen heading a corner home in the forty-ninth minute to defeat his former club. He did behave a little strangely after the game, suffering the effects of heading clear the succession of high balls put his way by the Arsenal team who knew of his problem. He'd scored the goal, though, so no-one minded him standing and peeing in the bath afterwards. They just good-naturedly threw him in it and had a shower instead.

On the coach back to their hotel afterwards Ronnie and Joker sat together at the front and had a quiet chat.

"This is bizarre," said Ronnie. "Ah mean, winnin' the friendlies wasn'ae a surprise: we didn'ae play anyone. But that was amazin' today."

"I know," agreed Joker. "They played their fucking hearts out. The passing was amazing. And I'm not sure what Papa Médecin was doing down that right side. He seemed to have Petit hypnotised."

Which in fact he had, invoking some weird spirit to mesmerise Emanuel Petit into having a particularly ordinary game, wiping his memory afterwards so that in the gloomy Arsenal dressing room afterwards he had to ask what the score had been.

"Look." Ronnie appeared thoughtful. "We're stuck wi' this bloody shambles. How we've got this far wi'out any of the crocks breaking down is a miracle. We need tae strengthen the squad, and quick. Only this time we need some decent players."

"Right. I don't suppose the Board will mind because our squad is smaller than most."

"Aye. Mind. Who in his right mind will join *this* bunch o' wankers? Let's face it, all this lot thought they were joinin' oor treble-winnin' team. Even though they didn'ae, they've all got such huge wages, they dinnae care. They're just enjoyin' their football, and who can blame them?"

"You're probably right," said Joker. "I can't see any decent player wanting to join us now."

Which, over the next few weeks, proved correct.

The first Premiership fixture was at home to newly promoted Sunderland, and it was to this game that Sir Fabian went as his introduction to association football. He and Sharon were comfortably ensconced in the back of his stretched limousine with the darkened windows, approaching the ground through increasingly congested streets.

"I hope you're right about us getting good seats, Blanky luv," Sharon remarked, remembering her uncertainty about it from a few months earlier. "I want a good view. Some of those footballers are quite sexy. Will I be able to meet them?"

" 'Course you will, Shaz, 'course you will. Since I've bought the club, I'm the boss, so you wanna meet them, you can."

"Some of my mates from home support Wanderers," said Sharon. "They'll puke when they see me in the papers with the players. There will be photographers, won't there, Blanky?" Sharon quite fancied being splashed all over the papers. Let the folks back home see she'd made it!. She didn't know offside from her backside, but she knew Wanderers were bigger than big in the football world.

"There'll be photographers, my TV cameras, the whole shooting works. You can have yer photo taken with the players if you want. The papers will love that!" Sir Fabian recognised the value of Sharon's figure to the cause of promoting the club. There was no other soccer team in the world that got more publicity than Wanderers, but photos of players with the new Chairman's "Personal Assistant," would simply be a refreshing new angle to re-sharpen jaded public interest in items about Wanderers. The new squad had already generated enormous publicity world-wide. The papers had been full of squad photos, individual photos, predictions about just exactly *how* many trophies the new Wanderers team would win, past scandals about some of the new players (sour grapes and hot air, Sefton had assured Sir Fabian) and more. Having the new owner's young bit of stuff draped round various players would just further whet the public's more salacious appetites.

"*Your* TV cameras, Blanky?" Sharon looked around the inside of the car. Spacious as it was, she could see no cameras. She struck a pose and smiled widely, though, just in case. "Where are they?"

Oh, God, she's at it again, thought Sir Fabian. "No, Shaz, I mean Digital International cameras. That's all there'll be to televise the game. No BBC, no Sky, *no* bugger except *mine*!"

Sir Fabian had got his biggest guns out when it came to dealing with the TV rights for games involving Wanderers. The Premiership's deal with Sky, worth millions to each club, had been a tough nut to crack, but Sir Fabian had done it. He and Wanderers didn't need Sky's millions, and Digital International negotiated a deal to compensate Sky for all games involving Wanderers. Negotiations had been tough: Sky and Digital International were about as friendly and communicative as Hitler and Churchill might have been, had they ever met. Sir Fabian had grudgingly given in to the rest of the Wanderers Board over the question of letting the BBC show highlights of Wanderers games on "Match of the Day".

"Our name'll be shit, Sir Fabian." Dick Fossett pulled no punches. "Look, we'll be doing our fans a favour. Those that can *get* tickets still like to go home and watch the highlights on TV. They like to spot themselves in the crowd, see the goals again from all the angles and in slow motion, that sort of thing."

Cecil Norris was equally persuasive. "There's blokes I know that watch Wanderers highlights while they're shagging. The better we do, the better they shag. Honest. You don't want to spoil anyone's sex life, do you?"

Partial to a bit of unorthodox stimulation himself, Viagra permitting, Sir Fabian wavered. He *could* have overruled the entire Board due to his having bought fifty one percent of each Directors' shares, but even he recognised that there was still a lot to learn about this British soccer. Christine Goodley, invited to join most Board Meetings by Sir Fabian because she *did* have good ideas as well as those superb thighs, finally persuaded him.

"I know Gary Lineker *very* well," she drawled. "I'm sure I could get him to agree to interview our new Chairman on the first 'Match of the Day'."

"Who...?" Sir Fabian began.

"Gary Lineker is the programme's presenter. He used to play for England. Second highest scorer. I know him personally. I'm *sure* he would do it for me," explained Christine.

I bet he bloody would, thought just about every Director present.

"Get me on his show as well, would he, sweetheart?" joked Sir Fabian.

Christine, feminist, politically correct, stifled her instinct to give Sir Fabian a piece of her mind and made do with an icy stare. "I'm sure he would, Sir Fabian."

Which Gary agreed to do as a favour to Christine. She was a woman with a good footballing head on her shoulders and Gary had a lot of time for her, more than he did for some Football Club staff. Plus, she did have great thighs.

At least the name and logo of Digital International would be emblazoned over the world's TV screens and sports pages. They adorned the shirts of Wanderers United and featured on every alternate advertising hoarding around the Wanderers pitch.

Outside the car, there were plenty of the Wanderers shirts in evidence as the crowds increased in density.

"Look at all the fans, Shaz." Blankopf waved a hand to draw Sharon's attention to the thickening throng that overflowed the pavements on either side of the stretch limmo. There they were, those thousands of loyal (probably "mindless" would be a better word, thought Blankopf) fans, making their regular pilgrimage to Old Stamford Stadium, home of the invincible Wanderers United. Well, almost invincible. Being beaten in the season before last's F.A. Cup 3-0 by Wimbledon wasn't in the script, but the ensuing riots and accompanying vandalism in the Wanderers Shopping Mall had only lasted two nights, and anyway, it was re-opened in time for Christmas.

Blankopf observed how close the knuckles of some of the fans were to the ground. You could almost measure their I.Q. by that yardstick - except very few of them would make the full yard. One point of I.Q. per centimetre above the paving stones would be about right, he thought. And the longer their arms were, the deeper they would reach into their pockets (or, more likely, someone else's - he didn't really care) to pay for all those new home and away strips and other money-making scams that the gullible bastards hadn't heard of because he, Blankopf, or the lovely Christine hadn't thought of them yet.

"Coo!" cooed Sharon. "There's *fahsands* of 'em! Shall we wave?" she started to fumble for the window-opening switch. She still sometimes found herself absent-mindedly looking for the rubber wedge that had held the windows up in so many cars she had once graced, forgetting that she was in a state-of-the-art limmo rather than an A-reg Sierra Ghia with fluffy dice in the back window.

"Christ, no, Shazza!" *Christ* no! He didn't want the Neanderthals out there seeing him arrive! Although there had been those damned photos taken on his first visit to the ground a couple of months earlier, the take-over had not been made public and it had been decided that the Board would announce Sir Fabian's arrival on the Board as the new Chairman at the first Premiership game - which meant today.

Rumour abounded, of course, but the new club sponsorship shown on the shirts was easily explained away - sponsors change from time to time - and the money to pay for the complete rebuilding of the team was said to have been "almost" paid for by the income from selling the old squad, with the balance being provided by the Directors, which was not exactly untrue. Sir Fabian's advisers had suggested, nervously, that the faithful may not take too kindly to their idols being owned by him and Digital International.

"Why the fuck not?" Blankopf had demanded at the last D.I. board meeting, staring straight at Weddelow, Widdelow, whatever his bloody name was, picking on him because he was sure he was a poofter.

Waddilove swallowed heavily, feeling the sweat breaking out on his head. Well, everywhere, actually. The back of his shirt suddenly felt soaked. How do you tell Blankopf that he is the single most unpopular businessman in the *world*, never mind the U.K., except amongst the readers of his never-underestimate-the-intelligence-of-the-readers Daily Universe. Perhaps they didn't actually know who owned the rag and didn't care as long as the girls on each odd-numbered page from 3 to 11 had either suitably large or, more perversely, suitably small breasts.

"*WELL?*"

"Squeak! Er, I mean, well, like, you know......."

"Do you write for the fucking Universe or something? Say something I can fucking understand!"

Waddilove looked around the table for help. All other members of the Board present were completely absorbed in their briefing papers, the wallpaper, the Secretary's hemline, the number of heat-resistant tiles on the ceiling - anything but meet the stricken Waddilove's eyes as he struggled to tell Blankopf the truth. Bad luck on Waddilove, of course, but the woofter deserved no better, and anyway, it could have been any of them.

Inspiration! "Er, well, see....."

"Yes, yes, *yes*! You've said that already!"

"It's just that in England the public don't view their football clubs as businesses. They're just used to the clubs being owned by...." Oh, thank you, God! *More* inspiration! ".....owned by bumbling, inefficient chaps who....er....just own the club because they support the team. That's why so many clubs in the U.K. lose money. They aren't run as viable businesses, even though some owners are actually quite successful businessmen in their own right - outside of football, that is." Yes! That was it! "Having their club run by a slick, no-nonsense, efficient team of top businessmen like we of Digital International...." He gestured around the table. "..........." Shit! Nearly a serious faux pas. ".....led by no lesser person than yourself, F.B., known as the most shrewd businessman in the world," (Phew!) "will be quite a major departure from the norm. And you know how conservative we Brits are!"

"How you lot won the fucking war, God knows!" spat Blankopf. "So what you're saying is, keep it under our hats until the ink's dry, right?"

"Er, exactly, F.B."

The use of initials by Company Chairmen is widespread in the world of business and commerce, lending as it does a sense of informality tempered with just the right suggestion of superiority to ensure the right degree of grovelling. Or so such initialled fat cats believe. For Blankopf, having been Christened Fabian was something of millstone when his initials were used in the English speaking world. F.B. by name, F.B. by nature, thought many of those forced into contact with him.

The rest of the board ground their teeth in silent rage. How had that wanker Waddilove thought *that* one up, the jammy faggot! Now he would be F.B.'s pet, for God's Sake!

So no-one yet knew about the sale of Wanderers United to Digital International. It had taken a lot to buy off the club's Board of Directors. Still, a few millions invested here and there.......

"Speculate to accumulate," Blankopf sometimes muttered. He often muttered it at moments of extreme excitement, like when he bought up yet another little company to strip the assets from, or when he was getting there or thereabouts in a session of horizontal P.E. with Sharon - or any other girl, really. Sharon thought it was *really* sexy and had something to do with the male orgasm, and would scream it in the Yacht Navigator's ear at the appropriate moment. He thought she was slightly barmy, but certainly good looking enough for a quick shag.

The progress of the car was impeded somewhat by the thickening crowds as they got nearer to the stadium. The fans, decked out in the famous blue and yellow stripes of Wanderers, overflowed onto the road from both pavements. Any vehicle trying to make its way through the crowd attracted attention, but a stretch-limmo with blacked-out windows: was it a player? Was it one of the well-known T.V. sports presenters? Was it the Prime Minister or Minister for Sport, both known as avid football fans? Faces began to peer into the limousine windows. The blackened glass meant that they couldn't see in, of course. To Blankopf and Sharon, though, it was a bit disconcerting to find all those curious faces peering in. The expressions on most of them were hostile, too. To some, anyone inside a stretch limmo with blackened windows must be a rich bastard who didn't deserve his money. Faces of all shapes, colours and ages snarled, tongues poked out, hands waved their one and two-fingered salutes.

And she wanted to wave at this lot? What a bunch! Blankopf couldn't wait to start taking their money. Never mind getting the replica shirts made more cheaply. He'd put the selling price up, too, the sad bastards!

The crowd was really dense now. The glass partition behind the driver slid open.

"Do you want me to stop, sir?" Jenny's face appeared,

"Christ, no, James. Plough the bastards down, for all I care!"

"I can't do that, sir," said James through the back of her head. "We aren't in Jo'burg now!"

"Hmph!" If the crowds there got too ugly you could just push the kaffirs out of the way. A few Rand compensation - *if* there was any comeback, which there usually wasn't - was all it took. Things hadn't changed *that* much since Mandela took over. The car quietly crept forward.

Jenny James touched the button on the dashboard to close the partition behind her. The polished bodywork of the car was going to take a hell of a lot of cleaning after this little lot, and it was her responsibility. She sighed.

The baleful gatekeeper was waiting and opened the ornate gates so that Jenny could slide the car through. She stopped at the foot of the ornate marble steps once again. Sefton Perkins was there to escort Sir Fabian and Sharon to their place in the Director's Box.

"Well, if you want some evidence of how well *we* think we are doing, I think it's time to tell the world that Digital International own Wanderers," said

Sefton as they settled into their luxurious seats. "We've kept quiet about it all this time. Didn't you tell us that it was because the fans might suspect your motives, Sir Fabian?"

"Something like that," replied Sir Fabian, who couldn't quite remember what it was Waddelow, Widdelow or whatever his bloody name was, had come up with at that meeting.

But that first Premiership game for the defending champions had been a dream. Admittedly, Wanderers had played at home to newly-promoted Sunderland who'd been a bit overcome by the occasion. Sir Fabian had been introduced as the new Chairman who had provided the money that allowed the fantastic array of new stars to be signed. Any reservations that supporters had about shedding all of the previous season's squad and about the business reputation of Sir Fabian were allayed by full time. Keen to impress now that they had started the season, the players totally bamboozled the Premiership new boys, thumping them four-nil. Georgi Strupinski got a hat-trick and Macca hit a peach of a free kick from almost thirty yards which scraped both the cross bar and upright as it flew into the very top corner of the Sunderland goal.

It had been a full-blooded encounter, Sunderland contesting every ball, and Lim Po was an early casualty, his shoulder dislocating when he fell heavily in a tackle, but that was all and he was likely to be fit for the following Saturday.

"Well, the fans are *more* than happy with that. Time to talk to the press boys now." Sefton moved towards the door.

"Hang on!" barked Sir Fabian. "Talk to the guy from 'The Universe' first."

"Why that ra... spected journal, Sir Fabian?" Sefton remembered just in time that Sir Fabian owned 'The Universe'.

"Because I *own* the bloody thing! They might as well have the exclusive. We'll have to do the other interviews later."

Afterwards, Match of the Day man Garth Crooks interviewed Ronnie about his completely new team. Sir Fabian, by arrangement through Christine Goodley and Gary Lineker, hovered by Ronnie's elbow.

"We'd met all challenges las' season," lied Ronnie. "an' decided tae poot a completely noo team taegether."

"World beaters!" interrupted Sir Fabian, spraying the camera lens with saliva. "This man is the finest manager in the world. No other man could have got this team together *or* coach them - Wanderers will take on the world and beat them, you'll see." He had clapped a comradely arm around Ronnie's shoulders during this outburst.

"Garth, I just need to clean the lens," the cameraman said. He knew the editor would cut out the shot.

Sir Fabian turned to Ronnie. "Christine didn't tell me this Gary Lineker....." nodding towards Garth Crooks ".....was a fucking kaffir!"

The programme editor, an Arsenal fan about to move to a new job on Sky Sport, left the comment in.

Sir Fabian, of course, was oblivious to the howler he'd let slip.

The Sunday sports supplements and pages all had the exclusive news about the take-over at Wanderers United:

"World's Biggest Business Empire Takes Wanderers Into Its Fold - Exclusive!" – The Universe.

"D. I. Own Wanderers Outright - Exclusive!" - The Mail.

"Media Giant Swallows Football Giant - Exclusive" - The Express.

"New Owner of Wanderers is F.B. - Exclusive!" - The Mirror.

"Blankopf gets his Digitals on Wanderers - Exclusive" - The Star.

"F.B. Snatches F.C. - Exclusive!" - The Sun.

"Student Sleeps with Entire Wanderers Squad - Exclusive!" - The Daily Sport.

"Should TV Companies Own Football Clubs? Exclusive" - The Globe.

* * * * * * * * *

The women's team had enjoyed a good run of pre-season friendlies as well, winning them all, and looked forward to their first Premiership game with great optimism. No longer did the likes of Arsenal, Doncaster Belles or Charlton hold any fears for them. Their opening match was at home to Southampton Saints. The Saints tore into them and were two - nil up after half an hour but ran out of steam and were lucky not to concede a goal before half time. In the fourth minute of the second half, Penny Rickard swung a corner over and, yes, the statuesque Sharon Onslow powered in to hammer home a header from the edge of the box. On the bare touchline of the pitch in the shadow of the New Stamford Stadium Caspar Hansen jumped highest and cheered loudest, then staggered back as Sharon hit him with a running hug, having sprinted over to him to celebrate her goal, Wanderers United Ladies' first competitive goal of the season.

Ten minutes later the equally statuesque Lou Purdey struck the equaliser from outside the box off a cross from Zöe Pryde who then provided the cross from which Laura Kitson headed Wanderers into the lead with twenty-five minutes to go. Elaine Richards played a one-two into the box with Josie Smith, known more for her ball-winning tackles than for her one-touch play, and slid the ball past the 'keeper for 4-2 and Lou Purdey rounded off the scoring in the eighty-fifth minute with a powerful run from midfield, riding two tackles before rounding the 'keeper and walking the ball into the net.

The celebrations in the dressing room afterwards were long and loud. Marty, Rex and Caspar couldn't get in to join them for ages because the girls wouldn't stop singing in the showers. They knew verses to rugby songs that men didn't know.......

Chapter 15 - The Season Progresses

The next match brought Ronnie and Joker's squad down to earth with a bump. Unfancied Leicester City forced a draw. Heskey put them ahead. Enrique Mouette weaved some magic to equalise early in the second half and Sum Wun wriggled through nine minutes from time to put Wanderers ahead. That seemed to be enough until in injury time Antonio Genitile stretched to tackle Heskey in the box. His knee went and he toppled against Heskey, bringing him down. Penalty! Izzet coolly beat La Pazbaq from the spot and the Wanderers' three points became one.

The next two Saturdays brought wins, though: one-nil at home to Aston Villa (another dazzling Macca free kick) and away to no-nonsense Wimbledon by the same score (Seamus O'Hooligan getting off the mark thanks to a brilliantly placed forty five yard pass from Macca, whose fitness was slowly improving). Ten points from four games put them in third place behind Arsenal and Manchester United, which had the fans happy enough, the old Board members content but Sir Fabian dissatisfied that they weren't sweeping all before them.

"Nothing to worry about, Sir Fabian," soothed Sefton over drinks in the Selhurst Park hospitality suite after the win over Wimbledon. "That's a completely new team and all they've done is drop two points thanks to a dodgy penalty decision at Leicester. Ronnie and Joker have done wonders." He looked around the room, crowded with Directors, players, wives, girlfriends and hangers-on. "I wonder where they are? Remember that not a single one of the top men in the world had the balls to take Ronnie's squad on. Proves that he's the best!"

"Hmph!" Sir Fabian liked to *win*.

As for Ronnie and Joker, they couldn't believe their luck - so far.

"We still need tae get cover for when the knees, booze, drugs and womanising begin tae take their toll," said Ronnie to Joker as they sat in the empty Selhurst Park "away" dressing room. "Did ye speak to Ginola?"

"Yes. He said no." Joker sounded gloomy. "I spoke to George Weah's agent, too. He laughed. He said George wanted to win something this year. Mind, I've one idea. I might have suggested adding him to our old squad anyway. What about Alex Smith?"

"Pickaxe? He's just a bloody thug."

"He's no injury problems, his last suspension is finished and his contract is out. He hasn't agreed terms with Bradford. He could be some cover for the middle."

Alex "Pickaxe" Smith was a late developer, having been spotted by a Millwall scout whilst playing on Hackney Marshes for Bermondsey Villa in the East London Midweek League. A bricklayer by trade, he was catapulted from Hackney Marshes into the old Second Division. He helped Millwall into the old First Division, then moved to Arsenal where he spent several high profile seasons besmirching the Arsenal's ancient image of respectability built up in the Herbert Chapman years.

Whilst at Highbury he managed a few games for the Republic of Ireland, allegedly on the grounds that one of his grandparents had a stepmother who was Irish. As his career suffered from his rapid assault not only on any creative midfield player who lost concentration long enough to allow Pickaxe to get near him but also on the Football League's record for red cards by one player, he was consigned to the reserves for a couple of seasons until Bradford rescued him in their attempt to win promotion to the Premiership. Since then, Pickaxe had been bickering about a new contract, hence his availability. His nickname of Pickaxe was a deliberate reference to Chopper Harris of Chelsea. Whatever a chopper could do, well, a pickaxe could do it with knobs on, or so Alex's mates told him. Chopper Harris used to tame opposing ball-winners for Chelsea. Pickaxe Smith, it was claimed, would have had Chopper Harris for breakfast.

There was no Premiership programme the following Saturday because of the Euro 2000 Qualifying games. Ronnie and Joker thus had a bit of spare time and found Pickaxe in a drinking club in Bethnal Green. Six foot two, grade one haircut, gold tooth, part of one ear bitten off (not by Mike Tyson. He wouldn't have dared), he was easy to spot. He recognised Ronnie and Joker straight away, and over a vodka and Red Bull listened to their proposition. "Twelve grand a week? Make it fifteen plus the usual benefits and I'll sign." He'd been hoping for six thousand from Bradford. Ronnie and Joker knew this. "Twelve," he said. He looked at Ronnie and pointed to the door with his eyebrows. The two men began to rise. "O.K., twelve it is," agreed Pickaxe, with which, barring the paperwork, he joined Wanderers.

Mind, he missed Wanderers next game. After Ronnie and Joker left, Pickaxe had a couple more drinks with his mates and then decided to leave early so he could tell his dear grey-haired old mother the good news. He loved his mum and his mum loved him. Pickaxe would have been mortified if he'd known that it was mainly his antics that had turned his mum's hair grey. As he mounted the few steps that led up from the bar and dance floor area to the foyer and exit, he turned to wave to his mates. He didn't see the shortish, middle-aged man coming in the opposite direction. This other man, for his part, didn't see Pickaxe as he was talking to his friend Geoff behind him.

Pickaxe and the middle aged man collided. Pickaxe went down, having cracked his knee against the other man's shin, overbalanced and twisted his ankle. It happened so quickly that the other man had gone down a couple more steps before he stopped and turned round. Pickaxe looked up and saw Geoff, whom he also knew.

"Oi, Geoff, did you see that?"

"You all right, Pickaxe?"

"Aren't you going to do 'im, Geoff?"

"I never saw anything, Pickaxe. You just lost your footing or something."

"Oh, come on, Geoff. He tripped me!"

The culprit looked down at Pickaxe. "Never touched 'im, Geoff!" he said.

"Best walk away, then," said Geoff. He and a few onlookers helped Pickaxe up and out to the street, where a taxi was hailed to take him home.

Back inside the club, Geoff found the other man at the bar. "That was Pickaxe Smith, Chopper."

Chopper Harris just raised his eyebrows, shook his head dismissively and sipped his lager.

* * * * * * * * *

Some three hundred miles away on the same afternoon, young Treve Hocking waited excitedly for the game to start. He leant over the railing on the half-way line, waiting to see which way Porthleven would be kicking in the first half. Leaning casually against the wall of the clubhouse behind the goal to Treve's right was Denzil Chegwidden, quietly surveying the pitch he had so lovingly prepared for today's game. It was a special day for the South Western League side: the first qualifying round of the F.A. Cup. Drawn at home to Tiverton of the Doctor Marten's Western Premier Division, they faced a stern test. Treve didn't see a lot of the game. As usual, he went behind the goal Porthleven were attacking, but ninety percent of the play was at the other end, the clubhouse end, as Tiverton pounded the Porthleven goal. The 'keeper, Gary Penhaligon, made several fine saves, his bar and both posts were hit, he was fouled as Tiverton netted the ball so that the goal didn't count and it was nil - nil at half time.

Treve changed ends for the second half and saw about the same amount of action; until injury time when, with the game still goalless despite the battering the goal at the harbour end had suffered (more great saves, more shots against the woodwork, two open goals missed), an umpteenth clearance by veteran sweeper George Torrance found striker Charlie Legge who quite frankly had almost forgotten what the ball looked like. He raced onto it, outstripping the Tiverton defence which had been gradually drawn forward as the second half went on, and slid the ball past the visiting 'keeper. It was possibly his first touch of the ball when he picked it out of his net. The crowd of some five hundred, swollen by the visit of so prestigious a team, went mad. Tiverton kicked off, the referee blew time and Porthleven were through! There were long interviews on BBC Radio Cornwall's live sports programme with Porthleven's manager, Alan Carey, their goal-scorer Charlie Legge and one or two supporters, including young Treve who was thrilled at the thought that he was live on radio.

It was a huge day for the Cornish fishing village's team, but in footballing terms it was a mere flyspeck on the grand scheme of things.

* * * * * * * * *

The Wanderers' next game was at home to a stumbling Newcastle United side, nestling uncomfortably close to the bottom of the Premiership. With only one point from six games and having conceded twelve goals in three away games the Northern giants were struggling. Wanderers managed an unconvincing one - nil win but it took a very late and somewhat desperate strike by Jesus Bastardi, charging up from the back to meet a Macca free kick. Sir

Fabian's "Daily Universe" couldn't resist the back page headline: "Jesus saves Wanderers!" and there were critical match reports in the tabloids owned by other moguls, perhaps jealous of Sir Fabian's coup in buying the world's most famous club from under the noses of others inclined to try their hand at taking over control of a major football club.

Some sports journalists, under orders from their paper's owner, predicted annihilation for Wanderers in their opening UEFA Champions League match at home to AC Milan. Secretly, Ronnie and Joker thought the game would be up at last against such formidable opposition.

Bastardi had suffered a cracked rib heading that winner against Newcastle, something to do with a collision between said rib and an unidentified bony piece of Alan Shearer's anatomy, or so he alleged. However it happened, Bastardi was now on the casualty list and perhaps it was still tremendously lucky that none of the other players with suspect medical problems had, as yet, broken down.

"This has to be Pickaxe's chance," suggested Joker as he and Ronnie discussed the team. "He's over that sprained ankle of his. He'll put the fear of God into the centre of the park, they can't create, we route one it."

"Aye, why not?" Ronnie agreed. "Ah wouldn'ae do it wi' a proper team, but at least this noo manager o' theirs....."

"Zaccheroni," supplied Joker.

"Aye, Macaroni, whatever, well he's had us watched an' seen all the videos an' all, an' these pillocks ha' been playing some sweet stuff when all's said an' done. Except Sat'day against Newcastle. Tha' was dire."

The tactics proved adequate. AC Milan played tight, controlled football, patiently building from the back and raising the pressure from midfield. Until, that is, Pickaxe got busy. By the time Schevchenko, Bierhof and Maldini were limping around unwilling to go anywhere near a ball that Pickaxe might also reach, Heinrich Schickelgrüber's delivery of long balls over the top to a front three of Lim Po, Seamus O'Hooligan and Sum Wun proved devastating. At this level, the notion that a club would field two strikers who wouldn't pass to one another just didn't sound credible so Milan's defence was stretched and chances appeared. O'Hooligan hit the first after a one-two on the edge of the box with Sum Wun, Lim Po the second on the stroke of half time, a far post header off O'Hooligan's cross and Sum Wun headed the third directly off one of Schickelgrüber's huge clearances. At not much over five feet tall, he was able to get under the ball after its first bounce and deflect it over the 'keeper who had come to safely gather it at the edge of his box.

A packed New Stamford Stadium went wild. The thunder of stamping feet echoed around the ground. On his loo-with-a-view in his Guest Box, Malcolm went white and grimaced at the effect of another painful spasm in his colon.

"Oh God!" he moaned to himself. "The bloody stand'll collapse if they don't stop their stamping!"

* * * * * * * * *

The women's team had a good start to the season after the win over Southampton Saints. Their next match was at Liverpool where they were greeted by Jackie Lowson. They caught up with all her gossip (which mainly centred around her impending engagement to Mark Bowen) and then had to part company to get changed.

Jackie was a bit subdued at the end of the game, Liverpool Ladies having done well to hold Wanderers to just 3-0. Twenty-year-old Gina Perry, Laura Kitson's striking partner, got all three and after the game was seen in deep discussion with Sharon, Caspar and Johann van Dyke, who had kept Caspar company on the touchline and begun to show an interest in the women's team.

Goalkeeper Janine Morris called for Gina on the way to training that week, to give her a lift.

"I've got to take this microwave to my Auntie on the way. Is that OK?" asked Gina, struggling with a big cardboard box as well as her kitbag.

Janine took the kitbag and they got into her car. Gina directed her to her Aunt's bungalow.

"Won't be long!" said Gina as she got out. A few minutes later she was back, a sweet-looking grey-haired old lady with her.

"Hullo," she called through the driver's door window. "I'm Gina's Auntie. I just thought I'd come out and meet one of her friends. Do you play football too?"

"Yes," replied Janine, immediately taking to Gina's Auntie. "I'm the goalie."

"Oooh, lovely! I wish I was young enough to play! It sounds such *fun*! And wasn't Gina clever? She tells me she scored *four times* last Sunday!"

"Er - we must go, Auntie!" Gina gave her a hurried kiss and leapt into the car.

As they drove off, Janine looked puzzled. "We won three - nil last Sunday and you got a hat trick. I remember you talking about it to Sharon, Caspar and Johann after the match, just before you got into... oh!"

"Yes, he gave me a lift," said Gina, smiling to herself. "I scored again!"

Chapter 16 - Pressure from the Ministry

Sir Fabian looked forward to his meeting with Tony Banks. He tried to think how he could turn the meeting to his advantage in his quest to gain British citizenship. He had suffered several knock backs over the years in his attempts to become British. Owning a couple of British newspapers ought to have helped him because he could use them to publicise his various acts of charity. He had paid for children to have life-saving surgery, had his photo taken with baby seals saved from being bludgeoned by seal hunters, funded a couple of air ambulances and generally let himself be reported as an all round good egg and it had all gone some way, in the early days, towards gaining him his honorary knighthood.

His ownership of some tobacco companies busy developing their market in third world countries – since the award of his honorary knighthood, it has to be pointed out - tended to work against his attempts to get his British passport and there was too much gossip about the tendency of his companies to be over-generous towards any individual, be he Government Minister or Company President, that they were trying to influence.

So a legitimate meeting with a Government Minister was an opportunity he didn't want to waste. How to work it to his advantage, that was the question.

The appointment was for a Monday morning at eleven, so Sir Fabian made sure he was outside the Ministry early and was somewhat annoyed to find that although there were photographers outside to snap him arriving (obviously the press knew because his own newspapers had been instructed to send cameramen and to "leak" the story of Sir Fabian's date with the Minister of Sport), he wasn't greeted by the Minister himself. Instead, a uniformed doorman demanded proof of identity before admitting him to an inner hall where a desk clerk bade him wait whilst someone was fetched to take him to the Minister. So no photo opportunity there. Never mind, Sir Fabian had one or two other tricks up his sleeve.

Tony Banks had arranged to use a Junior Minister's office at the rear of the building for the meeting. Its only window looked out over the quadrangle at the back and, being on the top floor, it wasn't over-looked so there was no chance of even the longest telephoto lens recording the meeting.

"There is the chance that he may have a concealed camera himself, Minister," suggested an over-cautious aide.

"Better have the lights dimmed, then," decided Tony, more to placate the aide than because he thought it likely that this Blankopf character would have his own camera. I mean, how would he be able to use it to get a photo of the two of them together? Unless, of course, it was in a brief case that he could put down and...... "See to it, will you? Get a twenty five watt bulb put into the main light. Shift the desk and chair so that my back is to the window. Raise the Venetian blind and pull the curtains almost to, so that there's just small gap."

"Bad Feng Shui, Minister, to have your back to the window," advised the aide.

"Even worse Feng Shui if this Blankopf bloke gets any photos of himself with me. The PM will have my guts for garters! Let's just make it impossible for him to use his Brownie, eh, if he's got one?"

And so Sir Fabian found himself being ushered into a drab little office with such a dim light that most of the room was in deep shadow except for the bright daylight coming through the gap in the curtains behind the desk. It was just as well he hadn't thought of bringing his own camera. He had anticipated that opportunities would arise for the press photographers outside, and anyway his understanding was that the Minister's office was at the front of the building and it was no coincidence that the Goodyear airship was heading towards a position in view of the office window.

Specially chartered by Traffic Surveys Ltd., which didn't exist, it was carrying a couple of photographers who were snapping the traffic jams around popular tourist spots. Big Ben and Whitehall were naturally on the itinerary. The pilot wondered why he had been given such an exact timetable for being over certain points, but it was easily explained by the need to be over certain places at their peak popularity time. Or so the two photographers from 'The Universe' told him, preparing to take the telephoto shots of the Minister for Sport's office windows in the expectation that the Minister and Sir Fabian would both be in view, talking amiably.

Meanwhile, in the rear office, the shadow in front of the curtains rose.

"Sir Fabian!" It wasn't really right to use the title, but the Minister was being diplomatic. He wanted something from this odious man.

Sir Fabian's eyes were having difficulty adjusting themselves to the gloom but he did just manage to make out Tony Banks's proffered hand. He had been briefed by the aide who had brought him up to just lightly shake the proffered Ministerial hand.

"Ministers have to shake hands with hundreds of people a week," he explained. "We can't risk them getting any injuries from over-zealous members of the public."

"I'm not a member of the bloody public!" growled Sir Fabian.

"Of course not, Mr Blankopf," smarmed the aide, "but nevertheless in Britain we do have - er - certain protocols to observe. I'm sure you understand."

Certain protocols? That could be a subtle reference to how British people behave, and Sir Fabian desperately wanted to become British. Probably why the fawning bastard had called him "Mister" and not "Sir". So when Tony Banks offered his hand and greeted him as Sir Fabian, he suppressed his boorish Boer instincts and limply shook it.

"Minister. Can I say how pleasant it is for me to have been invited to meet you?" Sir Fabian began to gush in his enthusiasm to make a good impression. Unfortunately he gushed saliva too. He affected pleasure, though his mood was less than favourable as he realised that the office he was in was at the rear of the building and not at the front. Someone had ballsed up! Was it the Widdelow, Waddelow, whatever his bloody name was? His men on the airship wouldn't see him! And even if they *did* know where he was, the way the curtains were almost shut would make it *very* difficult for them. Damn, damn, *damn*!

No, Sir Fabian wasn't used to having to make a good impression. His life had been spent surrounded by people who had to impress him. The house and garden servants of his boyhood in Johannesburg, the other pupils at school where he had been a tyrannical bully, players in the rugby teams he'd usually captained, employees, directors of companies he was about to gobble up, the list was endless. But here he was having to try to impress someone and he didn't know how to. So he gushed. And when he gushed, his tendency to project little droplets of spittle as he spoke came to the fore.

Tony Banks was very struck by the extremely limp-wristed handshake given by Sir Fabian. Surely this tough businessman ought to have a really firm grip. He was also struck (literally) by Sir Fabian's saliva.

"Well, I'm glad you could find the time to see me," he began. "I know how busy you are, with all your business interests. And now you are the Chairman of Wanderers United, eh? I won't ask you how you managed that, but it must be a terrific thrill."

"Thrill? Well, shit - I mean I don't know about that. The return on my investment should be pretty damn' thrilling, if that's what you mean."

Tony Banks's heart sank. As he had feared, this South African pillock was only interested in profit, not in the Wanderers as a football team.

"Yes, I'm sure, Sir Fabian."

Mind you, if he was only interested in money, it might be easy to talk him into getting Wanderers to play in the FIFA tournament in Brazil in the coming season.

"It's quite simple, Sir Fabian. I'd very much like Wanderers to play in the FIFA World Club Championships in Brazil in January. We're bidding for the 2006 World Cup and we think that having the Wanderers play in the first FIFA World Club Championship might help our cause."

"So where's the problem?" asked Sir Fabian, who was thinking only of how he could come out of this with something to strengthen his case for becoming British.

"You'd have to pull out of the coming season's FA Cup."

"So?"

"Er - well, it might not go down too well with the FA, and it might not go down too well with your fans. The media will crucify Wanderers and we accept that this might be too much for Wanderers to stand. We tried asking the FA to be a bit flexible with your fixture dates, but they wouldn't budge."

"Look, I don't understand why you can't just *tell* this bloody FA or who ever they are to go jump. You're the Government, for Christ's sake!" Sir Fabian felt he might have gone too far. "I mean, surely this FA would listen to *you*, Minister."

"Well no, unfortunately. We've already tried, as I said. But we'd still like you to think hard about playing in Brazil even though it would mean withdrawing from the FA Cup."

"Who d'you mean by 'we'?"

"The Prime Minister is very keen for us to get the 2006 World Cup...."

"Tony Blair? Tony Blair wants Wanderers to play in Brazil? Well, *any*thing for Tony. I mean, I've never actually met the guy, but he's obviously a good bloke." Any bloke who could kid the voters into thinking he was an alternative to a Conservative Prime Minister, whilst actually being almost as much of a Tory as Margaret Thatcher, *had* to be an okay bloke. "We'll do it!" Sir Fabian thought it wise not to tell the Minister that the Wanderers' Board had already decided to pull out of this bloody FA Cup thing. "But there'll obviously be a lot of publicity when we announce it. Perhaps Tony would like to break the news himself, you know, to get the most out of it."

"Get the most out of it? What do you mean?" Tony Banks already knew, of course.

"Well, you politicians are all the same! If you want Wanderers in this Brazil thing, there's obviously something in it for you."

"I told you," explained the Minister. "We think it will help our bid to hold the 2006 World Cup in England."

"Yea, but since when did politicians have an interest in sport to the extent of getting hold of a club and asking them to enter a particular competition? It's like me. I've bought Wanderers. I don't even know anything about football. To me, the word 'football' means what you call 'rugby'. But I do know a good business proposition when I see one, and buying Wanderers is a good crack. So what do *you* guys want, eh? Votes! Am I right? Course I am! *You* want votes, *I* want profit. Both those needs are best met by Wanderers playing in Brazil. So, you scratch my back, I'll scratch yours. Eh? Whaddya say?"

Sir Fabian envisaged an eternally grateful Tony Blair instructing the bloody Foreign Office to stop blocking his application for British citizenship. Of course, Wanderers would have to win in Brazil, but he was assured that the team they had would be able to do that, and a few back-handers here and there to key players in the opposition could oil a few wheels; and FIFA would have to award the 2006 World Cup to England. That might take a bit more in bribes but he had people good at sorting out who was most likely to have a price. It had frequently worked for Sir Fabian in sorting out deals in Third World countries; less frequently in more developed parts of the world, true, but nevertheless bribery was a key feature in a lot of the deals involving Sir Fabian's many and varied companies.

"I'm not sure I understand you, Sir Fabian," said the Minister, who knew exactly what Sir Fabian meant.

"You know, this World Cup thing means a lot to you Brits. A bloke who helps to make it happen will come in for a lot of gratitude, if you follow me. For you, it means votes, for me...."

"Money?" suggested Tony.

"No - well, *yes*, but you know what I want more than anything else. Do I have to spell it out?"

"I don't think so. Well, we'll have to see, won't we? All I can say is, we'll be *very* grateful if you can persuade your Board to enter the FIFA tournament."

The Minister got up. The two men understood one another. Well, no, actually, they didn't. Sir Fabian thought they did and that all he had to do was get Wanderers in the FIFA tournament and no less a person than the British Prime Minister would be supporting his application for citizenship. Tony Banks understood that Sir Fabian was going to get his Board to enter the FIFA World Club Championship and would be getting absolutely nothing in return apart from any millions he might make out of TV rights. That couldn't be helped, but getting the World Cup in England again would be a great coup for the New Labour Government.

It was time to get rid of this obnoxious Boer.

"Let me show you out, Sir Fabian," he smiled.

Great, thought Sir Fabian. A photo opportunity after all! Those bastards from his papers had better be there even if there were none from any other rags.   "Thank you, Mr Banks. I think we understand one another."

The two men left the dingy office and headed for the lift. After the gloom of the little rear office, the light in the corridor and lift was blinding. They left the lift at the ground floor and Tony Banks ushered Sir Fabian in the direction of the foyer. Sir Fabian prepared to grasp the Minister's hand as soon as he saw the light from the front door. He had been assured that even from outside the photographers could get something useable as long as Sir Fabian and the Minister were in view of the door. Sir Fabian slipped his hand into his jacket pocket and found his keys. On the fob was a small transmitter that looked like an ordinary car remote locking key. A press on its button would alert his men outside that he was in view of the door and they would start snapping. Apparently, computer enhancement would do the rest.

A flustered middle-aged woman suddenly confronted them. "I'm sorry, Minister, but an emergency has occurred!"

"Emergency, Emily? What emergency?" Tony Banks looked concerned.

"The - er - footballs for Gambia, sir. They haven't arrived!" Emily looked distraught. Sir Fabian could see they were just a few steps from the foyer. Just a few steps. Damn the bloody woman.

"Haven't arrived? That's terrible! Tell me what you know," demanded Tony Banks, a hand to his face, his look of concern deepening.

"The balls were supposed to have been sent by the - er- British Council but they thought - um - Sport England were doing it and vice versa. They were promised for today for distribution to schools and youth teams by - the Red Nose day people. You'll have to intervene!"

The Minister looked thunderous. "Right! Thank you, Emily, I'll do that now! We can't have all those poor children in Ghana...."

"Gambia, Minister!"

"....What? Oh, yes, of course: Gambia. Those poor kids have got to have those footballs, Emily. I'll kick a few backsides. In fact, I'll do it right now!" He turned to Sir Fabian, still fretting about those last few feet between him and a superb photo opportunity. "I'm sorry, Sir Fabian. I'd better get on to this straight away. Keep in touch."

With that, Sir Fabian felt his hand being grabbed and shaken and then looked in dismay at the figure of Tony Banks disappearing back into the lift with Emily. Bloody Gambia!

He was in a foul, foul mood all the way back to Wimbledon Common, but then Jenny, driving him in the stretched limmo, was used to Sir Fabian's moods.

* * * * * * * * *

"Where did you get all that stuff about Gambia from?" Tony Banks had asked Emily as he escaped back up to his proper office in the lift.

"You said to waylay you before you got to the foyer, Minister. It was the first thing that came into my head!" Emily was worried that she had upset Mr Banks.

"Well, you were brilliant!" smiled the Minister. "It worked a treat. He didn't get any photos. Well done!"

Emily beamed.

Tony Banks didn't beam, though, when 'The Universe' carried a front page story about how a Government cock-up had deprived thousands of needy, underprivileged Gambian school children of much needed footballs. How were the Third World countries supposed to compete on the world sporting stage when they couldn't rely on a simple act of aid from countries like the U.K.? Never mind, 'The Universe' would come up with the goods where the British Council, Sport England and Red Nose Day had all failed. They sent five thousand size four match balls to The Gambia.

The General Secretary of the British Council wanted someone's head. Who had cocked up? He wanted answers! And meanwhile, better buy and send some footballs to Gambia to make up for the mistake. Five thousand size four match balls were quickly ordered and sent.

The Director of the relatively new Sport England was furious. Who had fouled up? A new organisation like theirs had to be seen to be working efficiently. Send some footballs quick. Five thousand size four match balls were hastily purchased and sent to the Gambia.

Lenny Henry kicked some arse in the Red Nose organisation. He didn't like it getting bad publicity. "Just get some footballs to them bloody quick!" he yelled down his 'phone. "I've had the press and TV boys nagging me about it. Five thousand footballs, not full sized ones. Smaller, for kids. Okay? Spondicious!"

Tony Banks buzzed for Emily. "That was a brilliant idea of yours, Emily, but it has kind of backfired on us! Blankopf obviously let 'The Universe' know what he heard us talking about and now we're being bollocked for not managing to get some footballs to the Gambia. See to it, will you?"

Emily looked up the population of the Gambia and did some sums. Then she ordered fifteen thousand footballs. The wholesaler asked what the Ministry for Sport wanted them for.

"They're for school children, young man. In the Gambia. Do you know where that is?"

Oh, yes. The wholesaler's 'phone had been red hot these last couple of days. He knew where Gambia was.

"You'll need size fours, then. And yes, I do know where the Gambia is." Not many! That meant thirty five thousand size four match balls, all for the Gambia. It was going to be a hectic week.

A couple of days later, a bemused Minister for Sport in Gambia was called by the Chairman of the Gambian Football Federation.

"I'm at Independence Stadium. Can you come down here?"

The affairs of state of a country of less than a million people are not so time-consuming as they are in a major world economy such as the United Kingdom, so the Minister was able to drop what he was doing and get along to the stadium in another part of Banjul, the capital. He might even get to kick a ball around for a few minutes with the Football Federation's Chairman, an old friend of his. When he got there, an amazing sight met his eyes. At least half the pitch was covered in dazzling white, brand new footballs. Closer inspection revealed them to be size fours. A TV camera team was there and - good Lord, wasn't that the British comedian Lenny Henry, with his back to the sea of footballs, talking animatedly to the camera?

"What's happening?" asked the Minister of the Chairman.

"Thirty five thousand size four footballs - for developing soccer in The Gambia," he explained. "We had *no* notice of their arrival other than a 'phone call this morning that a couple of Jumbo Jets full of footballs were arriving. It took us hours with a fleet of lorries to get them here. We couldn't think of anywhere else to put them for now!"

"What's Lenny Henry doing here?"

"Something to do with the charity that provided them."

"How many, did you say?" The Minister looked gob-smacked.

"Thirty five thousand. That's one for every fourteen year old in the country, boys and girls!"

The Minister shook his head and turned away. He'd leave it to the Football Federation to sort out.

Over by the camera, Lenny Henry had finished his piece for a Red Nose Day update video. He turned to look at the sea of footballs on the pitch.

"Are you *sure* that's five thousand footballs? It looks like a lot more to me."

"Yea, well it certainly looks like a lot of balls," agreed the sound man.

Chapter 17 - Five Nil!

Whilst August, the opening month of the season, had been a good one for Wanderers, September brought mixed fortunes. It was an anticlimax to travel to Vicarage Road after the three-nil trouncing of A.C. Milan. Not surprising, then, that the players didn't lift themselves for the game and provided newly-promoted and already struggling Watford with one of their few wins all season. It was only one-nil, but the performance had Ronnie and Joker grinding their teeth.

"Ah knaw we're only doin' this 'cos nae one else wants tae tak' on yon bunch o' cripples and dead beats bu' tha' was tragic!" moaned Ronnie on the coach back to New Stamford Stadium. "Tha' Watford team are dead an' buried already. We were pathetic!"

Next to him, Joker could only agree. "They've all got their minds on next Wednesday."

That was the Wanderers' next Champion's League game, in Berlin. Heinrich Schickelgrüber, who wouldn't fly, had already got his route planned and ferries booked. The game was Wednesday evening; he would set off on Tuesday morning. Berlin isn't that far.

Hertha Berlin proved to be less troublesome for Wanderers than Watford: a comfortable two-one win kept them on top of their group. Seamus O'Hooligan was on target again, making him joint top scorer and confounding speculation that he was well past his prime, playing out his twilight international career at Brentford when Wanderers rescued him. The other goal was scored by Heinrich Schickelgrüber who, although Austrian by birth, felt strangely at home in Berlin. It made it worth the long drive there and back.

But the players were a bit chastened by that defeat at Watford. The criticism they had suffered, from Ronnie, from Joker, from the media and from a bellowing Sir Fabian, seemed to strike home as they trotted out onto Middlesborough's new ground and turned in a competent one-nil win thanks to a goal by Sum Wun.

"Wanderers struggle to overcome 'Boro" - The Globe.

"Just because that rag is owned by Ootgers, he uses it to rubbish everything Wanderers do!" growled Sir Fabian at a Board meeting. "It'd be something if that so-called bloody world-beating team began to actually *win* something!"

Malcolm's bowels gave a gripe. Every time Sir Fabian threw a wobbly at the less-than-poetic football played by Wanderers, he had visions of the bombastic Boer withdrawing his money and leaving them all up shit creek.

"They're doing very well in the Champion's League," he said, hoping to console the Chairman.

"Two games! That's all! And if they're *that* bloody good, how come they didn't beat that village team? Whitford? Waddiford?" A feeling of déjà vu flashed across Sir Fabian's memory. "Or whatever its bloody name is....."

"Watford," supplied Sefton Perkins.

"Well: them! From what I've heard, if they can beat that Eyetie outfit, they should beat anyone."

113

"They say it's about motivation," explained Dick Fossett. "In my day each game was as big as another. We never got worked up about beating foreign sides, quite the opposite. We were better than them anyway."

"I think the buggers ought to have all the bloody motivation they need with the wages we're paying," suggested Cecil Norris. "We'll see what they're made of when that Turkish lot comes here on Wednesday."

"The women's team is doing well." Malcolm decided to change the subject. Sir Fabian liked winning and he like women, so Malcolm thought it prudent to try to divert Sir Fabian onto safe ground.

"Ay, that's true," agreed Sefton. "Have you watched 'em play, Sir Fabian?"

"No. They play Sundays, don't they? I'm always busy Sundays." Which was true. By some unspoken agreement, Sharon and Sir Fabian often had their Saturday nights apart especially when they were in England. Sharon was free to go and visit her mother or sister in Essex and Sir Fabian was free to go to his club in the West End; or that was what they told one another. Sharon usually ended up liaising with one or another of the various young men she encountered here and there. At this particular time, since Sir Fabian's take-over of Wanderers, she was currently investigating the potential of Jerome McZane, the Trinidadian midfielder. She had always found black athletes a turn on but had never had the chance to try one for size, so to speak, until now. She couldn't understand why Sir Fabian always got so short tempered whenever she made a complimentary remark about a coloured bloke. It had all started with Lynford Christie's lunch box.

"They *are* s'posed ter be big, ain't they, Blanky?" she had asked one day as they watched a "Sporting Heroes" programme on Digital One Sport. Sir Fabian had yelled something about "fucking kaffirs" and stormed out, leaving her completely confused, which, to be fair, wasn't very hard, another condition in which, to be even more fair, Sir Fabian often wasn't, hence his anger at references to a the famous man's lunch box.

Sharon's first target had been the enigmatic and vaguely frightening Papa Médecin, but she found his eyes so - well, strange once she got close, and although she had no memory of drinking very much, she found the next morning that she couldn't remember anything of what they might have got up to the night before, but had the overwhelming feeling that it had had something to do with chickens. Jerome McZane was a far better prospect, jovial and laid back. The previous Saturday night and Sunday morning, she had been laid back with him, smoking some lovely-tasting roll-ups and enjoying her discoveries about what was and was not true about black men. Actually, as far as her herbally-affected brain could judge, it was all true!

Whilst all this was going down, so was Sir Fabian, at his club. Not exactly the Garrick, it was a very exclusive gentlemen's club in Knightsbridge that only advertised abroad, and very discreetly at that in countries where it was not illegal to advertise such facilities. The management provided free Viagra for such of its members who required it, so to speak. Sir Fabian had been enjoying an epicurean feast for breakfast on the Sunday, the subject of his mastication and slurping making suitably delighted "cooing" and "oohing" sounds just for encouragement. When his tongue felt like it was about to suffer cramp he had stopped. His "hostess" affected disappointment. "Oh, Sir Fabian! You are a teaser, aren't you! I was just going into my fourth climax!" she lied, stifling a yawn. "There! You've worn me out, and I've got to go out this afternoon."

"Talulah, you've got just about the most stupendous thighs a bloke could ever hope to get his head between! Do you work out?"

"Oh, yes, Sir Fabian," fluttered Talulah, for that was indeed her name. "I work out and train. I like to work up a bit of a sweat sometimes, know what I mean?"

"Don't I just!" leered Sir Fabian. "D'you know, I own a club like this in Jo'berg. How d'you fancy a job there? I'll pay you twice what you get here!"

"Lovely offer, Sir Fabian, but I couldn't. I've got commitments here, see. But if things change, is the offer open?"

"Sure it is! You're a top shag, Talulah. In fact, can I book you this afternoon as well?"

"Oh, what a shame! I'd *love* to, but I can't. Sunday afternoons I have off, see. Like I said, commitments."

God, he was awful. He was fat, spat when he talked, needed Viagra to get anything approaching an erection (probably, two lolly sticks and a reel of sticky tape would be more effective) and, even more than most of the sad middle-aged men who frequented the club, he thought he was God's gift to women. She gratefully accepted the tip he pressed into her hand - it was usually a hundred quid, always useful and tax free, of course - and looked suitably morose at his departure.

Once he had gone, Talulah went into the little ensuite shower room that all the "private conference rooms" had and enjoyed a good hot shower. Then she dressed in Falmer's stretch jeans - an old but much-loved pair that showed off the lower half of her athletic figure nicely but not tartily - and a sleeveless vest top that showed off her tan and revealed what lovely arms and shoulders she had. Grabbing a large Nike bag, she left.

Thus Sir Fabian's Sundays.

"Well, you ought to give 'em a look, Sir Fabian," continued Sefton at the post-Middlesborough discussion. "There are one or two cracking-looking girls. That girl that Caspar Hansen goes around with is one of them. Stunning looking, legs up to her armpits! Some of them are lezzies, of course, but you always get that in women's sport."

"I'm more concerned about beating the Turkish lot this week, and some decent bloody results in the English league," said Sir Fabian.

In the event, he watched with grudging pleasure as Wanderers dealt comfortably with the physical Galatasaray side, a goal from O'Hooligan early in the second half keeping his team comfortably on the top of their group.

"That Irish feller is getting some points, isn't he," stated Sir Fabian, forgetting as he often did what you called the scores in soccer. Mind, it had caused no small surprise in the inner circles of football management that the Eire international had carried on knocking in goals with the apparent ease he had experienced with Brentford the previous season. The fans, of course, simply saw him as another international player producing the expected goods. Although there was some concern that the Wanderers' completely new team of various nationalities and hues wasn't already running away with the Premiership, you couldn't argue with their results in Europe. However, their next match, the first in October, would be a big test of their mettle: at home to Manchester United, the other British team with pretensions of being the world's best.

"You promised to introduce me to Nicky Bickham," pouted Juanita Bastardi to her father when they got home after the Galatasaray match.

"Don't worry, my little chicken. I will." Jesus adored his nubile daughter and would certainly honour his promise to her. It is the custom for any two Premiership teams to gather in the Boardroom after each match (unless the visitors were so pissed off that they got straight on their bus) and that was when he would introduce Juanita to the young man who had featured so prominently in the Wanderers' treble win the season before. There was also that young England player married to that pop singer. He'd like to meet *her*! No-one would guess, if they didn't already know (which the whole world did anyway except for certain mountainous regions of Tibet and parts of the Amazonian and Papua New Guinean rain forests), that she had recently had a baby. What a figure! He'd introduce Juanita to Nicky, get Nicky to introduce him to his young England international team-mate and then spend a happy hour or two chatting to the pop singer.

"Premiership Showdown! - Off-form Wanderers in sternest test yet!" - Daily Mail.

"Battle of the Giants! - Now we'll see who's best!" - Daily Express.

"War is Declared! - Big Two to Clash in Mortal Combat!" - Daily Mirror.

"Match of the Season - Wanderers Play the Title Pretenders" - The Star.

"D-Day! - Big match could settle title already!" - The Sun.

"Who's Got The Biggest One? - W.U. and M.U. in Battle of the Bulge!" - Daily Sport.

"Man. Utd. in for a Shock! - Wanderers have them beaten already!" - The Universe.

"Wanderers in for a Shock! - Man. U. will murder them!" - The Globe.

It turned out to be just about the most amazing Premiership match of the season. The archives would just coldly record it as "Wanderers United 5, Manchester United 0." If the Wanderers' performance against Milan had been good, their defeat of Manchester United was mesmerising. The Mighty Reds didn't get a kick. Well, that's not strictly true. Pickaxe ran amuck amongst their midfield, leaving neutral observers who were watching the game on Digital One Sport TVs all over the world wondering where the Reds' alleged hard men were that night. Once Pickaxe had inflicted a limited amount of actual bodily harm and been booked for his endeavours, he was tactfully substituted and replaced rather strangely by Papa Médecin who had never up to that point played a strictly midfield rôle.

Nevertheless, on he came five minutes into the second half with Wanderers hanging on to a slender one goal lead, a Mouette free kick from an impossible angle by the edge of the penalty area on the left. From that point on the centre of Man. United's team just fell apart as players seemed half a yard slower and even appeared to allow particularly Médecin to just take the ball off them. The second goal came from a Mouette corner on the right. Médecin placed himself in the centre of the goal area and appeared to be giving orders or at least talking to someone, judging by what the cameras showed. The Man. United players nearest to him closed up tight around him, including the 'keeper and Bastardi just strolled unchallenged into the penalty area to head into an unguarded net.

Howls of dismay from the visiting fans were drowned out by the noise from the Wanderers' fans as their team ran back to the halfway line. Médecin was clapping the goal as he ran. The Man. United players who had been marking him to the exclusion of all others looked around in bewilderment and saw the ball in the net.

To say they were dispirited when they kicked off would be an understatement.

Médecin continued to be the dominant figure in the Wanderers side and he scored a deserved hat trick in the last twenty minutes.

"Did you see that?" drooled Sir Fabian at the final whistle, to anyone who could hear him in the Directors' Box. "Those other bastards didn't have a bloody look in!"

All the other Directors were there, except for Malcolm who, customarily, was in his private guest box. They were all almost as delirious with delight as Sir Fabian. Up in his box, on his unseen loo, Malcolm was wishing the win had been less emphatic. Those bloody fans, banging their bloody feet and jumping up and down! He'd have to get Bert Barnard to do some more checks for signs of cracking and impending structural failure. He'd also have to get another nine-pack of Andrex up to his box. What with the worrying possibility of Sir Fabian pulling out of the club if Wanderers didn't win anything and wondering what to do about the dangerous state of the stand, his secret loo had taken quite a hammering that afternoon.

The result sent shock waves all round the world, as Manchester United had almost as much world-wide support as Wanderers. Certainly in the Premiership a few eyebrows were raised in the light of Wanderers' rather indifferent results so far, leaving aside their European games.

* * * * * * * * *

More than two hundred and fifty miles away, big headlines were also being made, admittedly only in the local press, as the Cornish side Porthleven had beaten Conference side Woking one - nil in the second qualifying round of the FA Cup. Having survived a non-stop onslaught in the first half, Porthleven went in at half-time drawing nil-nil. Wing back Alan Roberts overlapped and scored virtually from the kick off in the second half after which it was all Woking again but they still did everything but score, and the crowd of several hundred invaded the pitch to celebrate Porthleven's success at reaching the First Round Proper at their first attempt.

* * * * * * * * *

Meanwhile, in the plush new Wanderers' Boardroom it was a rather subdued Man. United party gathering amidst the jubilant Wanderers people.

"Never mind," commiserated Sefton to Martin Edwards. "We've got to come to you later on."

"Yes, but today your lads seemed have mine completely mesmerised."

He didn't know how close he was to the truth.

Sharon Onslow was on Caspar's arm, still partly mesmerised by her ability, through her relationship with the punch-drunk centre back, to mix with the Premiership's household names; and with the players of both Wanderers United *and* Manchester United in the same room, there were a lot of household names there.

Martin Edwards recognised Caspar from his club's games against Arsenal the previous season, and was taken by the pretty young girl on his arm.

"Hello, Caspar," he called. Caspar and Sharon went over to him. "Who's this, then?"

"This is my girlfriend, Sharon. She plays centre back for our women's team."

"My word, do you really? Of course, women's football is getting more popular, isn't it."

"I'm told you lot are doing well," interrupted Sir Fabian, his interest in the women's team suddenly aroused now that he had a close-up of one of the players.

"Yes, we haven't been beaten yet this season - er..." Sharon didn't know who Sir Fabian was.

"This is our club Chairman, Sharon, Sir Fabian Blankopf!" whispered an embarrassed Caspar.

".... yes, we've beaten Southampton and Liverpool, and drawn with Doncaster and Arsenal. Caspar helps with the coaching."

"I'll bet he does, eh?" sprayed Sir Fabian, turning to give Martin Edwards a conspiratorial wink. "Wouldn't mind trying to teach you a thing or two myself!" Another Sharon! He chuckled lewdly to himself.

Sharon smiled falsely and gave Caspar a push sideways. "Nice meeting you, Mr Chairman. Get me a drink, Cas."

The couple moved towards the bar.

"What an awful creep!" hissed Sharon to Caspar. "Yeuch!"

"You should see his lady friend. She's not much older than you. Her name's Sharon, too."

"Is she here?"

Caspar looked around.

"There she is, by the door talking to Jerome McZane." As Caspar's Sharon spotted Sir Fabian's Sharon, she and Jerome McZane slipped out of the crowded Boardroom together. Caspar and his Sharon just raised eyebrows at one another and went for another drink.

In a corner, a crestfallen-looking Nicky Bickham was talking to Ronnie and Joker. "Got to hand it to you, Boss; Joker." He still felt that Ronnie was his Boss especially after all they had gone through in the treble-winning season before. "You must both know what it's like to come back to play against your former club. You want to do well!"

"Sorry, lad," said Ronnie. "They even surprised us taeday!"

"He's right," agreed Joker. "We *did* put Pickaxe on to quieten your midfield down a bit. We had to bring him off once he got booked - that was pre-arranged - but I don't know why Ronnie put Papa on in his place."

"Ah thought *you* put 'im on!" said Ronnie, looking puzzled.

"No, nothing to do with me."

"Ah cuid have *sworn*....."

"He certainly did the business," said Nicky. "I was marking him for that corner. Mind, where Jesus came from I don't know. I never saw him. I was tight on Papa and the next thing I know, he's clapping and the ball's in the net. And he ran where he liked for the rest of the match, like he was invisible. He seemed to just keep appearing out of nowhere and score. Bloody good signing!"

Ronnie and Joker exchanged glances and just drank their lemon and lime.

That was when Jesus approached, with just about the most sensational-looking girl Nicky had ever seen hanging back behind him.

"Nicky, I theenk we-a gonna play in same-a team, but Ronnie, 'e sell-a you to Manchester. This my daughter Juanita, she like-a to meet-a you. "

"I'd like to meet her, Jesus," replied Nicky. Jesus, I'd like to shag her, he thought.

"You-a help-a me meet your man who is with-a pop singer?" asked Jesus.

"With a pop sing... oh, right! Come with me. Excuse us, Boss, Joker."

Ronnie and Joker lifted their glasses in salute and were left alone.

"Let me guess," mused Ronnie. "Nicky shags Jesus's wee girl, Jesus tries to shag pop star."

"Right," nodded Joker.

Much later, and in the privacy of her bedroom, Juanita looked at the card which bore Nicky Bickam's private mobile number, together with his postal and e-mail addresses. She also examined Nicky's autograph. She had to use a mirror to see it. Before it had a chance to wear off, she'd go and get a discrete tattoo artist to go over it.

Chapter 18 - Highs and Lows

If the September had its ups and downs, October was worse. Malcolm spent a fortune on toilet paper. Bert's unobtrusive examination of the New Millennium Stand's structure revealed no new problems beyond some hairline cracks in some of the concrete.

"And you would put that down to drying out if you didn't know what we know," he reported to Malcolm.

"What's that supposed to mean?" asked Malcolm, who was hardly consoled by Bert's comments. He winced as a spasm contorted his colon.

Bert sensed he had said the wrong thing. "Well, it means you always get drying cracks in concrete structures, and I can't see any signs of things giving way."

"It's bad enough having that to worry about. If only the bloody team would put together a long sequence of wins in the Premiership. Sir Fabian could pull out any time he likes, you know, Bert. Where would that leave us?"

"Up shit creek?"

"Yes, without a paddle and heading for white water!"

But after the heady heights of the five - nil defeat of Manchester United the Wanderers team just could not get it together. They had a week without a game, then had to play host to First Division Huddersfield Town in the Worthington Cup.

"Bloody thing's not worth getting worked up about," said Joker as he and Ronnie contemplated the game in the plush Managerial Suite. "In our day it meant something, the League Cup. What d'you think, Boss?"

"Aye, ye're right. We'll stick in the boys who dinnae get a game much. They shuid see off the likes o' Huddersfield!"

He was wrong, unfortunately. The Wanderers side clearly had more flair and skill, but the Yorkshire side, playing with typical grit and determination, fired up by the indignation they felt at not being taken seriously enough to face the Wanderer's first team, put up the shutters and sneaked a one-nil win.

The Premiership match at home to Liverpool the following Saturday turned out to be just as disappointing, the Anfield outfit deserving more than their one-nil win.

"They need another bollockin'," sighed Ronnie as he and Joker headed for the dressing room after the final whistle, "but it's a fochin' waste o' time!"

"It's the damn' Champions League again," moaned Joker. "Last season's squad were decent grafters. This lot are just glory boys, only interested in the big stuff!

"Aye, an' if they dinnae think the fochin' Premiership is big enough then it's a wonder they can get their fochin' heads through the door!"

"Well, we're getting good money, Boss, for managing a side we bought in to cause Blankopf and the Board trouble. They're certainly doing that!"

"Aye, but some other focher shuid be runnin' the show!"

"Think of the money, Boss!"

"Aye."

So there was the routine bollocking for the team after their poor performance followed by the usual exhortations to pull their fingers out for the mid-week match in Turkey, the return match in the Champions League.

Heinrich Schickelgrüber set off on the Sunday afternoon. It is a long drive to Turkey. The rest of the team had the opportunity to savour the press reports of what the Galatasaray team and fans were going to do to the Wanderers team and supporters. The fans were warned to stay at home. So, in effect, were the team.

"They dinnae like losin'," observed Ronnie.

"No, they're just fucking savages," growled Joker. Political correctness was not his forte.

The team flew out and met up with Heinrich at the chosen hotel. They had a look at the ground the following day, facing hostile fans on the coach journey from their hotel to the stadium and back. On the evening of the match their coach was stoned when they arrived at the ground.

"Oi didn't know they was Prods," said Seamus O'Hooligan.

"No, canny lad," replied Macca. "They're just fucking savages."

Wanderers were unrecognisable from the side that lost to Liverpool a few days earlier. By the time they were three-nil up with half an hour left (O'Hooligan, Mouette, Macca) many of the Galatasaray fans were leaving in shame or disgust. The ones that stayed booed their team mercilessly. It was almost cruel when O'Hooligan completed his hat trick.

"Now for bloody Arsenal!" chortled Seamus in the riotous dressing room afterwards. Arsenal had sold him to Brentford, a move that hadn't pleased him at the time.

New Stamford Stadium was packed for the visit of Arsenal, and Wanderers losing three-two would not have necessarily have been a disaster if Wanderers had won most of their other games in the Premiership up to that point. It was a showpiece for the Premiership, a draw might have been a fair result, it could have gone either way, but it went Arsenal's. Georgi Strupinski and Enrique Mouette had each scored, Arsenal had equalised each time and then nicked the winner. Some blamed the decision to "rest" Heinrich Schickelgrüber so that he could simply join the side in Milan for the next Champions League match.

Milan's San Siro stadium is no place for faint-hearted visiting players. The point is, none of the Wanderers team could be described as that and the one-all draw they earned was all they needed to top their group. Kwasi Ankoma chose the occasion to score his first goal for the Wanderers, somehow appearing unexpectedly at the far post to volley home Enrique Mouette's free kick from out on the left. It equalised A.C. Milan's earlier goal.

Three days later, Wanderers went to Derby and lost three-one. In the Premiership in October, then, a win and a draw were all Ronnie and Joker's team of has-beens and dead beats could manage. The fact that they easily topped their Champions League group gave sports journalists something to spin up, but their dismal Premiership run provided plenty of ammunition for those who like to see the top teams falter.

* * * * * * * * *

As the Wanderers team made its glum way to the team coach after the Derby game, down in Cornwall little Porthleven were beginning to break into the national papers. In the First Round of the FA Cup at their first attempt, they had just beaten Guisley of the Unibond Premier League one-nil. Guisley had bombarded the Porthleven goal for ninety minutes, hitting the posts, the crossbar, defenders on the line, missing a penalty, the lot. Interviewed by BBC Radio Cornwall's Tommy Matthews after the game, lone striker Charlie Legge excitedly described his injury time goal. "I'd almost forgotten what the ball looked like, Tommy, then all of a sudden Darren Holsey whacked a clearance my way and I just headed for goal. It was about the first clearance that came anywhere near me. I didn't know my marker had slipped. I just saw the 'keeper come and then hesitate, so I tried a lob. Brilliant!"

Late that night Malcolm sat on his en suite toilet at home and watched the goalmouth escapes and winning goal of Porthleven. It was the FA Cup First Round highlights on "Match of the Day" and Gary Lineker was naturally focussing on the giant-killing games.

Malcolm thought that it was all right for them, enjoying their moment of glory. The main match on the programme had been Wanderers' dismal performance at Derby and Malcolm's bowels insisted that he sat on his loo with the door open so that he could watch the programme on his bedroom TV from there. At this rate, Blankopf was bound to pull out. Now, not only did his colon go into convulsions, but he broke out in a cold sweat at the thought of what would happen if Blankopf pulled the plug.

* * * * * * * * *

Fortunately, Sir Fabian, blazing mad at the team's league performances, was not reminded of them because he was unable to watch "Match of the Day". They do have television sets at his Club, but they just show non-stop hard-core porn to supplement the effects of the Viagra swallowed by many of its members. Sir Fabian couldn't see much of anything where his head was. He was having second helpings of Talulah whose magnificently toned and tanned thighs blocked not only the sight but also the sound of the TV from his musky little world.

Chapter 19 - Ups and Downs

There was only one more game in the first phase of the Champions League Group matches, at home to Hertha Berlin and it was a fairly straightforward two-nil win, Macca once again producing the magic from one of his free kicks and Seamus O'Hooligan adding the second. The New Stamford Stadium was full as usual despite the fact that Wanderers could not be overtaken at the top of their group, and the fans were chanting "Champions, champions!" before the end. They tended not to chant the same thing at the end of most of the Wanderers' Premiership games, though things picked up a little with two draws in successive weeks, nil-nil at home to West Ham and one each at Everton thanks to a Jesus Bastardi header off a Macca corner. This left them ninth in the Premiership and had Sir Fabian grumbling away to those he felt were in some way responsible.

* * * * * * * * *

Way down in Cornwall, hangovers were being developed in and around Porthleven as their Committee began to contemplate the arrangements for the eleventh of December. It was beyond belief, but as Wanderers were grinding out their draw at Everton, Porthleven faced the impossible task of competing with Hayes of the Conference in the Second Round of the FA Cup. True, they'd beaten Woking from the same league two rounds earlier, but it had been well against the run of play - one of those occasional freak results. It had been the same in the First Round against Guisley and the word was that the village side's luck had been used up for several seasons to come. This turned out to be wrong: the game was a carbon copy of Porthleven's previous FA Cup games. They soaked up pressure for ninety minutes, relied a lot on the woodwork, inspired goalkeeping, off-target shooting and luck, then sneaked an unlikely winner courtesy of a break away by Charlie Legge again and found themselves in the Third Round draw the following evening. They'd wanted a Premiership side away to ensure a huge payday, but they drew Hereford at home.

"Do we opt to play it at Hereford?" asked Chairman Len Williams at the weekly Committee Meeting.

The consensus was that it wouldn't be worth it. They'd play at their own Gala Park so that as many of their supporters as possible could enjoy the spectacle.

* * * * * * * * *

Wanderers were drawn away to Hull of the Nationwide Third Division.

"A tricky one," said Ronnie, interviewed on TV after the draw. "The cup is a great leveller. Ye dinnae know where th' giant killers are waitin'." Public relations had never been his strong point, but that was bollocks. If Wanderers lost to Hull, he and Joker would pack it in, World Club Championship or not!

The next day, the actions of the Wanderers manager were being discussed elsewhere.

"Can't you tell that manager of ours to get some other players in," demanded Sir Fabian at a Board meeting.

"Well," suggested Sefton, "that would require more capital, of course, but if we were to casually mention to Ronnie that more funds were available.....that's if they are, Sir Fabian."

"I said he had to get a world-beating team together whatever it cost," replied Sir Fabian. "I didn't tell him to stop buying. He just did, so if there are players out there he could get, then tell him to get them."

"I imagine there will be no shortage of players who'd like to join us now we've qualified for the next stage in the Champions League," said Dick Fossett. "The chance to play in Brazil might tempt some, too."

"Our League position is bound to improve soon," ventured Malcolm, hoping to lull Sir Fabian into a better mood. He was having a wretched time with his intestines at the moment. "And our women's team has only lost one game in the last couple of months." Not that that had anything to do with the matter in hand, but knowing of Sir Fabian's liking for the ladies he harboured the hope that he could get him to watch the women play. If he did, Malcolm was sure he would be hooked, which might lessen the chances of his abandoning the club before the season ended.

"Oh, that reminds me, Sir Fabian," said Cecil Norris. "I've a matter to raise under Any Other Business."

"Yes? Well, we've decided the team is to have some extra players bought to try and make our League position better. Got that down?" Sir Fabian turned to Arnie Robinson, taking the minutes in his rôle as Club Secretary. "Can I take it everything is in hand for this European thing this week?"

"The next phase of the Champions' League?" asked Arnie.

"Whatever. Is it all arranged?"

Arnie nodded as he quietly jotted down the decision about buying new players, wishing that the pain in his right testicle would go away. That had to be cancer. The only other time he'd felt such discomfort was in his fumbling teenaged days when girls tolerated a clumsy grope above the belt but maintained a strict demilitarized zone at waist level. Hot balls, he and his mates had called it. But this was nothing to do with that. All this inane prattle about players and the Premiership and here he was needing to see a specialist about a possibly life-threatening condition.

"Yes, I've got that," he said. But I haven't managed to even get an appointment with my GP yet. The Receptionist at the Surgery had been less than helpful.

"A pain where, Mr Robinson?"

"What? Can't you just make me an appointment, please?" Damn the woman! Was she going to decide if he could see his doctor or not?

"Well, if it's an emergency you *could* come at ten past six, but if it's not urgent...."

"How do *I* know if it's urgent or not? You don't know that until you get a diagnosis!"

"You aren't bleeding anywhere?"

"No, I told you, I have this nagging pain, three days now."

"Not vomiting or passing blood?"

"No! Look...."

"No dizziness, pains in the chest or left arm?"

"No! Just...."

"No blackouts, loss of vision, difficulty with breathing?"

"No! All I...."

"No broken bones, loss of sensation in......"

"Look, I just want to see my bloody Doctor!"

"Really, Mr Robinson, there's no need to be rude. I'm just trying to establish whether or not you need an emergency appointment."

"It's a pain in the balls!"

"Well if you are going to continue to be offensive I shall hang up on you. The practice takes a dim view of abusive patients. Looking at your medical records....." Arnie suspected she was looking at the immensely dog-eared and swollen folder that bore the record of his martyrdom to hypochondria. ".......I'd say that it is unlikely to be anything serious. There doesn't seem to be a part of your body or physiological function that hasn't been investigated in the past few years. Now where's this pain you are suffering from?"

Arnie didn't want to have to go to the trouble of finding another Doctor. "I've told you, but you obviously misunderstood. If you must know, the pain is in my left testicle. Just the left one, not the right one. Now, can I see my Doctor, please?"

"Can you think of any reason why the pain might have occurred? Have you done any heavy lifting?"

"No, it just...."

"Have you sustained any injury to the groin?"

"No, I just...."

"Did you have a suddenly curtailed sexual experience just before you noticed the pain?"

"Hot balls! You're talking about bloody hot balls, aren't you!"

"Mr Robinson, I shan't warn you again about your tone!"

"I would very much like to see my Doctor, please. I have a pain in my left testicle, not the right one, not both of them, just the left one, and I can think of no reason why it has started, I am grateful to you for allowing me to complete a sentence once in a while, I do not have a sex life, I am single, I am not gay, and for your information, since, as a woman, you have no experience of such things, a 'suddenly curtailed sexual experience' leads to a pain in both testicles, a condition colloquially referred to by men and adolescent boys as 'hot balls'. I'm afraid I may have testicular cancer and would like to be referred to a specialist. Please."

"I see. Hold on, please." Dreary music filled Arnie's ears. Mercifully, it stopped after just a few seconds. "Mr Robinson?"

"Who else?"

"Mr Robinson, if the pain is still there in two days' time, 'phone again. Thank you for calling."

"Two days? Look, all......" The 'phone had gone dead.

"Arnie?" Sefton was speaking quite loudly.

"Oh, sorry, Mr Perkins. I was miles away! I was - er - thinking of memos I've seen concerning available players." A plausible lie: it worked.

"Cecil's got something he wants to raise under 'Any Other Business'," said Sefton.

"Yes," Cecil responded to his prompt. "The Women's team have asked if they can play a game here immediately before one of our Premiership games."

Arnie jotted the request down in his minutes and waited for the decision.

"I thought they played on Sundays," asked Dick Fossett. "Would it have to be one of our Sunday games?"

"I think they just want to see if we'll let them do it at all, first," explained Cecil. "If we do, and I think we should, they'll sort out the details. If it was a Saturday and they persuaded a team to play a day early and then the weather turned bad they could still play on their usual pitch on the Sunday."

"Won't they cut up the pitch? We can't have that. The Premiership won't stand for that." Jack Grimethorpe voiced what some of the others felt.

"We'd have to consult the groundsman and Ronnie - it won't be easy," added Ernie Arscott, who had been to see the women play and was all for them. "But are we against the idea in principle? Couldn't they kick off *after* a Premiership game? Or, it's been very dry of late and the pitch is very hard - the girls wouldn't leave a mark. I've seen them play and you wouldn't think there'd been a game on the pitch after they've finished."

"Anyone against the idea?" asked Sir Fabian. No-one spoke. "So we aren't against the idea in principle. Just a question of sorting out the detail."

"It'd make a nice little extra feature on Digital TV's Wanderers Channel, Sir Fabian," suggested Malcolm, to take his mind off the fact that he couldn't take another couple of Imodium capsules for at least two hours despite the fact that his colon appeared to be in need of another dose. "You could feature a few of the girls, glam 'em up a bit....."

"How do you 'glam up' dykes?" Sir Fabian did not seem convinced.

"They aren't dykes," explained Malcolm. "Well, not all of them. Well, only a few of them, really."

"One or two of them are very nice," Ernie pointed out.

"That Lou is extremely pleasant to the eye," added Reginald, who had accompanied his brother to a few of the womens' games. "And that young one, Valentina. Lovely legs. A natural athlete, I would say. Runs like a gazelle."

"Yes," agreed Ernie. "And our Caspar Hansen is courting one of them. She's a *very* pretty girl."

"Ah, yes! I met her after one of our games," said Sir Fabian. His eyes lit up. He was more interested now. "Robinson, you sort it. Get together with the Commercial Manager and whoever else...... Report back with a decision. And I'll get my Sports Producer to talk to you as well. See what we can sort out. Perhaps

I ought to cast my eye over these women if what you say is true. Any more items? No? That's it, then. Thank you gentlemen."

Arnie finished off his notes for the minutes of the meeting. The Directors were joking about women's football, ribald laughter accompanying comments full of sexual innuendo whilst he was contemplating life with just one testicle - that's if he had much life to look forward to at all. Still, he had his job to do - at least, he did so far, as Sir Fabian seemed to have forgotten about having fired him before the start of the season. Mind, he couldn't afford to become complacent. As long as he was still on the payroll, he ought to carry out his job as efficiently as possible. He made his excuses and left to see to the final details for the first match in the next stage of the Champions League. Wanderers were grouped with Feyenoord, Lazio and Real Madrid and were the favourites with most bookmakers to win the Group.

Feyenoord were something of a disappointment. As the first opponents in the next stage of the Champions League, they had been expected to provide really stiff opposition and New Stamford Stadium seethed with pre-match excitement on the Wednesday evening of the game. In the event, Wanderers swept into a three-nil lead within half an hour, Seamus O'Hooligan leading the charge, Georgi Strupinski adding the second and Johann van Dyke popping up to meet a Macca free kick whilst all eyes were on Seamus and Georgi. The Wanderers players eased off the gas in the second half and although Feyenoord pulled one back late on, they were never in it.

A one-nil win over Bradford the following weekend, a Sunday game to allow an extra twenty-four hours for Wanderers to recover after their midweek exertions, gained Wanderers their first Premiership win since the five-nil thrashing of Manchester United, but it was not seen as a turning point by the pundits. Bradford were just very poor, and were beaten by an own-goal in a dismal game unfortunately shown live on Digital Sport One. The Wanderers, commentators kindly suggested, had their thoughts on the tiresome trip to Japan for the Toyota Cup match against Iniquitos, the South American Champions.

Sir Fabian didn't get around to seeing the women play that month. His Saturday night and Sunday morning close inspection of Talulah's naughty bits was a ritual he was loth to miss, leaving him too exhausted to go to their game on the Sunday afternoon. He therefore missed their demolition of a strong Tranmere side, goals from Laura Kitson, Gina Perry and an over-the-moon Kizzie Wong giving them a 3 - 0 win. Kizzie Wong was brought on in the second half to replace Josie Smith who was due to start her suspension for being sent off at Charlton, just to see how she would slot in, and with Wanderers comfortably ahead two-nil with ten minutes left, she scored her first Premier League goal for the club. Janine's kick had been headed on to Kizzie by Penny Rickard. Kizzie had drawn a player and laid the ball wide to Valentina on the right. Valentina's long legs sped her up the wing until she was level with the penalty spot. Kizzy had moved forward, eager to have more of the ball, and was well-placed to gather Valentina's pass. A big defender was leaning all over her, but Kizzie ducked her shoulder to the left, back-heeled the ball gently between the defender's legs and darted round to her right, finding herself free and facing the 'keeper.

The 'keeper charged towards her.

Kizzie, a diminutive girl in the local Comprehensive's Sixth Form, put her right boot under the ball and scooped it high over the astonished 'keeper and watched ecstatically as it dropped *just* under the bar for an outstanding goal of sheer brilliance and audacity.

She was buried under a sea of yellow and blue.

"Saw it on the telly," she explained afterwards, sitting happily in the plunge bath, all soap bubbles and suntan. "Some Croatian or someone..."

The women also went to Merseyside a second time for the season and came back with three more points from a one-nil win over Everton on a rain-soaked pitch during ninety minutes of heavy rain. It was a Sharon Onslow special header from the edge of the box again, from another Penny Rickard corner.

They were still second, still two points behind Arsenal, still with a game in hand.

Chapter 20 - Problems with the Toyota

Not many soccer fans remember when or why, but for many seasons the European and South American Club Champions have played against one another for the unofficial title of World Club Champions. With the organisation of the FIFA tournament in Brazil it was not clear how long this fixture would continue. Played as the Toyota Cup ever since the Japanese adopted it as a way of increasing interest in soccer in Japan, it presented Wanderers with an unwanted extra fixture in November, at a time when Wanderers' Premiership results had left them out of touch of the leading pack. Sir Fabian wasn't pleased about the league position but the world-wide advertising opportunities of the Toyota Cup had been pointed out to him by the Digital International Board.

"You know who the Wanderers have got to play, FB?"

"No - who?"

"Iniquitos of Brazil."

Sir Fabian was none the wiser. "So?"

"They're the new giants of Brazilian football, and they're owned by the Asteroid Corporation."

"Ootgers!" Sir Fabian spat out the name with the venom of many years bitter dislike. Wilhelm Ootgers had locked horns with him back in his Rumpy Pumpy Club days. Ootgers had opened up a similar club very close by and the Rumpy Pumpy's profits had been quite seriously reduced until Fabian – as even *he* called himself in those days - had arranged for his rival's club to be wrecked by some hired thugs - an easy thing to organise in Johannesburg's clubland. Ootgers had known who was behind it, of course, and had attempted to retaliate. Sir Fabian had anticipated it, though, and laid a trap for Ootgers' men, routing them before they could do any damage.

The bitter rivalry between the two men had escalated from that moment. Any time either man suspected the other of being about to take over a new business, he would try to interfere in some way, buying shares in the same company being a favourite tactic. As each man had become more wealthy with a bigger and bigger business empire the rivalry continued. Blankopf bought a tobacco giant and opened up sales to the Third World: Ootgers did the same. Ootgers bought a tabloid newspaper somewhere, like 'The Globe' in the UK, Blankopf bought another one in the same country, like 'The Universe', plus another one somewhere else. Blankopf bought an oil company, Ootgers bought an international chain of service stations that wouldn't retail the products of Blankopf's company. Blankopf set up his satellite TV enterprise, Ootgers did the same. So far Ootgers hadn't bought a football team, but having seen *the* most desirable club in the world bought by Blankopf before he, Ootgers, had the idea himself, buying any other club, like for example Manchester United, Juventus, Palmeiras or Real Madrid, would be second best.

Until one of his Directors had pointed something out to him at the end of Wanderers' treble-winning season.

"Blankopf owns Wanderers. They'll play in the unofficial World Club Championships in Japan during next season, against whoever wins the South

American club championships. Should be easy to buy them - nothing like the problems Murdoch had trying to buy Manchester United - and then you can have some fun pitching your team against his. You could refuse to play against his team if they are sporting the Digital One logo. You could have our logo on your team's shirts so that we're advertised the same as he is. You could have a bit of fun threatening not to play if Digital One have bought the televising rights. No match, no TV revenue."

Ootgers thought it over and liked what he thought. He instructed the Director to look into it. By the time the Toyota Cup was in its planning stages, Ootgers' company, Asteroid Corporation, had successfully bought control of Iniquitos of Brazil who had won the South American Championship.

Digital International had already negotiated with Toyota and FIFA for the TV rights. The match did not have world-wide interest but Digital's Board hoped that by giving the game coverage out of all proportion to its importance a lot of people around the world would tune in. The fact that Wanderers were playing should guarantee a few tens of millions of viewers for a start. Iniquitos were not particularly well-known outside of Brazil, but that would only serve to encourage Wanderers fans to tune in. They'd sense an easy victory and as the majority of their fans had only started to support them because they won things, they'd pay to tune in.

Now Sir Fabian himself met with the game's organisers.

"We'll not televise any adverts for the Asteroid Corporation," he told them. "I'll not let my logo appear on the same screen as theirs."

That was obviously going to prove difficult as players from both sides were likely to appear together on the screen about every five seconds. This was politely pointed out to Sir Fabian by the Japanese businessmen across the table.

"Well, I'll not have that. They'll have to wear shirts without the Asteroid logo."

This, of course, was completely unacceptable to Asteroid.

"It'll be as bad for us," fumed Ootgers. "I'm buggered if Iniquitos will play if Wanderers have Digital's bloody logo on their shirts!"

There was consternation at FIFA and Toyota at the prospect of the game being cancelled because the sponsors, or in this case owners, of the two competing teams refused to take part in any game that served to promote their rivals. The newspapers in England picked up on it.

"Sponsors Row Over Advertising - Wanderers and Brazilian Unknowns may not play after all" - Daily Mail.

"Corporate Clash Eclipses Match - Such a clash of interests was inevitable" - Daily Express.

"Wanderers left Wondering! Non-event game may be a *real* non-event" - Daily Mirror.

"Digital have trouble with their Asteroids! Two media giants battle over big match advertising" - Daily Star.

"Satellite Wars! Satellite TV giants at odds over advertising at the Match No-one Wants To Watch Anyway" - The Sun.

"We'll Have To Go Topless! Wanderers topless supporter Wanda shows the boys how they'll need to turn out in ad-wars game: 'Get yer kit off, boys!' " - Daily Sport.

"Asteroid Corporation Threaten World Club Match! Media mogul Wilhelm Ootgers won't let Iniquitos face Wanderers" - The Universe.

"Digital International Won't Play Ball! Blankopf Blanks South American Champions" - The Globe.

* * * * * * * * *

Sitting in his bedroom in Woking, school nerd Cecil Thorneycroft sat scanning those same sports headlines on the internet. He spent many hours exploring the far corners of cyberspace on one of his two computers. Each afternoon, as soon as he returned from his Sixth Form College where he was studying A-levels in Pure and Applied Mathematics, Computing and Physics, with Further Maths as an extra purely out of interest, he would go straight to his room and wander off into cyberspace. He would browse late into the night, emerging in the morning with just enough time to swallow some cornflakes before heading off to College.

His day was spent poring over Maths problems and Physics calculations. There weren't many girls on the courses he was on, but even if there were, none of them would have been particularly attracted to his goofy, chinless, spotty, bespectacled appearance, his spherical head balanced atop on overlong neck interrupted by an over-prominent Adam's apple which seemed redundant since his voice had stuck on half-broken, squeaking and booming uncontrollably whenever he spoke; which was rarely, as he had no friends. He usually spoke only when explaining to his Maths or Physics teachers how to solve a particularly tricky problem.

He came into his own when Theatre Studies or the College's own Thrash Metal band wanted help with lighting designs and effects. He would quickly knock up a design on his computer, write a programme to produce a simulated display on screen so that he could test it before it was made, then, after suitable adjustments he would wire it all together, supervise its installation and happily operate it during performances.

At times like that, fellow-students would genuinely praise him and thank him; even the sensationally beautiful girls who tended to do Theatre Studies would show their admiration for him, sending him home happy but wistful. Happy that these untouchables had been so nice to him, wistful that to a nerd like him they were, truly, untouchable.

His mother, forty-one when he was at last born after twenty years of trying to conceive, hoped one day he would find a nice girl to settle down with. His father wished he had turned out to be a good sportsman, so was really very disappointed with his really quite exceptionally-gifted son.

"I worry about Cecil," he had once said to his wife. "His room is weird. He hasn't got a single poster of a girl up there at all. Micky's boys..." (next door) "...have Pamela Anderson all over their bedroom walls, and their mum has to stand their sheets in the corner and crack them to fold them before they'll fit in the washing machine."

"Oh, Clive, don't be disgusting!"

But it was true. His mother, much more reserved than his father, had thought it odd that ever since Cecil had gone through puberty, she had never had to face the kind of laundry that Rachel (next door) regularly complained about, albeit good-naturedly. When she went to clean Cecil's room, it was satisfyingly untidy - at least he was normal in that way - but his walls were covered with Maths formulae, plan drawings of aircraft, ships and tanks, and the pride of place was his print-out from the internet of the plans of how to build an atomic bomb. His calendar was not from The Sun or Daily Sport, but of photos taken by the Hubble Telescope of features in space. Add to that the fact that he didn't seem to have any friends and never went out, she was a bit worried about how he would get to meet any girls. Perhaps he would do that at University.

Cecil was intrigued by the conflict between Digital International and The Asteroid Corporation. Digital didn't want their cameras to show any images that promoted Asteroid, and vice versa.

"Simple!" he muttered to himself. He turned to his other computer and soon his fingers were flying over the keys and the mouse was driven for miles around its mat. After about an hour he sat back with a sigh of contentment. Looking at his watch he pressed a function button and saw that it was nearly nine o'clock in the morning in Tokyo. A few minutes careful searching on the internet threw up the e-mail addresses of Toyota and FIFA. He next spent quite a while rattling away on his keyboard, writing emails first to Toyota, then to FIFA. Once he had sent them, he showered, then went back to his room to await a reply at least from Tokyo, which was already at work. FIFA would be asleep for hours yet.

* * * * * * * * *

In an office at Toyota's promotions section in Tokyo an unscrupulous employee looked at the e-mail that had come from Cecil-Thorneycroft@currantbun.com.uk. Here was his chance of promotion! Carefully he composed a reply. "Thank you for your interest but the same idea has already been put into being by our technical department." He sent it, then deleted Cecil's message from the inbox.

He then went upstairs to seek an interview with his manager.

It was a simple enough idea which was easy to sell to FIFA.

"Funny," said the FIFA Official. "We had that very idea sent to us from someone in England."

The Japanese representative of Toyota's promotions section was deferential in the extreme. "It is very preasant that so many peopre think so highly of our humble undertaking. Fortunately one of my own emproyees has had idea in time for us to make start on ploject."

The "emproyee" in question was given the task of getting a prototype of the idea made, to show to representatives of Digital International and The

Asteroid Corporation. He had a cousin who was a manager in a low-quality plastic toy factory and within a week a half-sized prototype was mounted on the back of a small Toyota flat truck and driven to a small athletics stadium. All had been carefully planned by the unscrupulous employee who, already in possession of a one-off company bonus for the idea, was plotting with his cousin for false invoices to be submitted to FIFA so that the two of them could share a healthy profit between them.

Representatives of the two warring companies, Digital International and the Asteroid Corporation, could not be persuaded to come to the same demonstration, so it was arranged for them to miss one another by half an hour.

"If you will come this way," invited the unscrupulous employee, stepping respectfully aside to let the white man go ahead of him. Together they mounted the steps to the top of the modest stand parallel to the finishing straight of the running track. As they emerged from the stairway, the track was there below them. On the far side, parked about halfway along the orange-coloured back straight, was a flat truck with a large panel on it reading "Digital International - Winners in World Sport"

"What are you showing me that for?" asked the man from Asteroid, Giles Roberts.

"Prease don't take offence, Mr. Loberts. Prease to walk arong back of stand."

Mr "Loberts" walked grumpily in the direction indicated by the obsequious little son of Nippon. Mr "Loberts" didn't trust him at all. Had his grandfather overseen railway building in Burma during the war?

"Prease to observe advertising hoarding as we walk, Mr Loberts."

So Giles Roberts did, and as they walked along the stand the message on the advertising hoarding changed. "Asteroid Corporation - TV and Banking 24hrs Every Day!"

A little further on, and the hoarding's message changed back to Digital's, but after another few yards it showed Asteroid's name, and so the alternation continued as the two men walked the length of the stand.

"So, what's your point?" asked Giles.

"Prace Asteloid camelas where onry Asteloid advert is seen. You no see Digital advert on Asteloid TV. They put camelas where onry Digital advert is seen. Ha!"

Giles had to admit it was brilliant and would obviously work.

"What do Digital say?"

"No can say, Mr Loberts. Have not seen them. Spoke to Asteloid first, natularry." The unscrupulous employee was smarmingly ingratiating and Giles's flesh crawled.

"If they agree, how much will it cost to have them all round the pitch? You'd have to work out all the camera angles for us. I can't see them agreeing to co-operate with us over anything, even that."

"Of course." Another deferential bow. "Ret us discuss financial considelations....."

Half an hour after Giles Roberts had gone, Sebastian Green of Digital arrived at the little stadium and was conducted through the same demonstration, except that the unscrupulous employee slightly rearranged the flat truck so that when Sebastian first saw the advertising hoarding he saw Asteroid's advert. He was then invited to walk the length of the little stand and was as intrigued as Giles Roberts had been at the way the message changed every few yards.

"What do Asteroid say?" he asked.

"Aras, Mr Gleen, cannot say. Spoke to Digital first, natularry." Unscrupulous employee gave an ingratiating bow, once again hiding his expression which was hardly necessary as it was naturally inscrutable.

"We'd have to know where every single hoarding was so that our cameras can be put in the right place."

"Ha!"

"Can you do that without us having to work with Asteroid TV?"

"Ha!"

Sebastian had seen "Bridge Over the River Kwai" and knew what "Ha!" meant.

"How much?"

"Ah, so, Mr Gleen. Ret us discuss that over tladitional Japanese runch."

Chapter 21 - Advertising Impact

Digital's Sports channels showed lots of little snippets from Tokyo on all their football programmes, trying to build up interest in the game. They found hundreds of Wanderers fans in Japan and used them in their previews, decked out in Wanderers blue and yellow and singing the praises of Macca or Enrique Mouette. Asteroid TV's Sports channels had to pay Japanese youths to pose as fans of Iniquitos for use in their previews, but they got away with it because as few people outside South America knew anything about the Brazilian team, it was easy to assume that Iniquitos were at least popular in Japan.

The cameras of the two rival satellite companies were carefully set up around the National Stadium in Tokyo to make sure that whichever direction they faced as they followed the game, only their own advert was seen. It was discovered that ground level cameras couldn't read anything from the special hoardings, so both companies planned to have a couple of mobile cameras patrolling the touchlines.

Sir Fabian was kept informed of developments and was intrigued by the dual-message advertising hoardings.

"Who's idea was that?" he asked when Sebastian Green showed him the results of his visit to Tokyo.

"Some oily bastard in the Toyota Promotions Department," replied Sebastian. "I'm sorry, I just couldn't take to him."

"Oily or not, he had the idea and saw it through. See if we can get him."

Headhunting was common practice in Sir Fabian's circles.

"How does it work?" Sir Fabian was always interested in technical matters.

"Simple," explained Sebastian. "Just a huge version of those silly things you sometimes get in cheap Christmas crackers."

Sir Fabian hadn't seen the inside of a cheap Christmas cracker since he was about ten. His last Christmas cracker had been decidedly expensive, a cute little Polish girl who burst out of the huge cracker supplied for him by an exclusive escort and massage establishment in Pimlico that he had been a good customer of for several years (when he fancied a change from his Gentleman's club in Knightsbridge). Sebastian could see that Sir Fabian didn't understand.

"Those little pictures that changed when you moved them, like an eye that was open when you looked at it from one direction and shut from another direction, so you could make it wink just by moving it to and fro. They are made up from two images sort of cut up into thousands of strips and then set in plastic at different angles."

"Dunno what you mean," said Sir Fabian. "You're sure it bloody works?"

"Yes, I've seen it. Like I said, I walked the length of the little stadium they used for the demonstration and the advert kept switching from ours to theirs and back again. It was very effective. From one angle, a perfectly clear advert for one thing, from another angle, perfectly clear for the other one."

"Hmmph!" Sir Fabian didn't like to think what "the other one" advertised.

On the day of the game, the stadium was packed to its 58,856 capacity and the atmosphere was - well, jolly rather than partisan. Neither team had more than a couple of hundred fans who had been prepared or able to afford the time and money to fly to Tokyo for such an unimportant match. True, the world-wide appeal of Wanderers United meant that a large part of the crowd were there to support them, but being far-flung fair-weather fans they weren't capable of creating the kind of atmosphere that seeps into the very pores of the players to lift them like nothing else can.

The two teams came out, anthems were played, introductions were made, neither team really having a clue who they were being forced to shake hands with (the President of FIFA). Only as the two teams lined up did the twenty-two players on the field feel a little burst of competitiveness. This was our part of the world against theirs. It's not an important match but we don't really want to lose.

Wanderers lost the toss and kicked off, and a desultory affair of a first half unfolded as both sides, fearful of losing but not adventurous enough to launch themselves into a full-blooded assault on their opponent's goal, failed to produce a single shot on goal.

At half-time with the score thrillingly locked at nil-nil, word had reached Ronnie from On High. Sir Fabian, still not a football expert, nevertheless recognised a rubbish match when he saw one. He sent word to Ronnie, via his mobile 'phone from a hotel room in New York (where he was on account of one of his many business commitments), that things had to improve. Business commitments had made it impossible for him to spare the time to travel to Tokyo with the team.

What he actually said was, "If that lot don't buck their fucking ideas up they'll all be sacked!"

"You can't do that," advised Sefton. "They have contracts!"

"Well we've got to do something," fumed Sir Fabian.

"Why don't we stop over in Bangkok and visit your massage parlour if we win?" suggested Cecil, who quite fancied a free massage and shag himself as Sir Fabian's guest, never mind the players.

"Bloody good idea!" said Sir Fabian. "Double win bonus and a stopover in Bangkok if we win, straight home and double training if we lose!"

Ronnie didn't like interference from the Board, and indeed had never had to suffer it until now. However, as neither he nor Joker regarded this game as remotely important he was prepared to overlook it this once.

"Way-ay, lads, I'm up fer that!" said Macca after Ronnie's brief and unorthodox half-time talk. Some of the interpreters looked a little uncertain about the incentives on offer, especially Ellie, the delicious little babe who translated into Italian for Antonio and Jesus. What was *she* going to do in Bangkok while the players were strumping their way through the delights of Sir Fabian's massage parlour? She was, after all, the only female to have travelled with the Wanderers party on this particular occasion.

Unbeknown to Wanderers, there was a similar reaction from Wilhelm Ootgers to the terminally boring first half. He had made it known to the Iniquitos players that if they didn't pull their socks up they would all be given free transfers. Most of them were quite sure they would find another club quite easily but not so sure they would get anything like the wages that Ootgers was paying them, so it was game on!

From the restart the two teams threw themselves at one another like gladiators. The ball was whipped around the park at breakneck speed, crafted from end to end in flowing football interrupted only by bone-crunching tackles. The poor referee was taken by surprise and at first had difficulty adjusting to the new and unexpected pace of the game. He missed several early challenges that were straight out of a horror movie. Tempers naturally frayed until the referee started to get on top of things and booked Jesus Bastardi for nearly cutting one of the Iniquitos strikers in two, followed quickly by the booking of the Iniquitos right back for something a rugby union referee would have considered a high tackle on Manuel Sardhinas; as a result of which, he had to be substituted by Milo Opec.

The second half was only ten minutes old when the almost bisected Iniquitos striker saw his chance for revenge on Jesus close to the Wanderers goal. It was almost a wrestling drop kick from behind as Jesus was shepherding the ball safely out of play close to his goal for a goal kick. Down he went like a sack of coal and pretty soon he was engaging his assailant in a two-man brawl. The struggling, snarling men thrashed around just off the pitch and before they could be separated they had fallen onto one of the huge advertising boards positioned on the ground so as to be visible to the many cameras around the stadium.

There was a crunching of cheap plastic as the combined weight of the two footballers laid waste to the advert. Almost all the players rushed to the spot to pull them apart and as the cameras zoomed to capture the scene order was gradually restored and the crowd of players broke up, just leaving the referee and the two combatants in the picture. The two players were sent off, a process that took two or three minutes bearing in mind the language barrier and the protestations of the two combatants. All this time the mangled remains of the advertising board were in clear view behind them. This happened to be one of the clever dual-message adverts produced by the unscrupulous employee of Toyota, based on the idea stolen from Cecil Thorneycroft in Woking. Its structure had been laid to waste by the two fighting footballers, the many separate plastic strips scrambled and reoriented so that across the world on TV screens tuned into Digital Sport One, the advert read, albeit rather crookedly:

"git Corpor ation   B o nking   our ver a!"

With both teams reduced to ten men the game opened up even more and yet remained balanced on a knife edge. Iniquitos hit the bar. O'Hooligan hit the post for Wanderers. Sum Wun had a shot cleared off the line, Papa Médecin cleared off the Wanderers line. Antonio la Pazbaq pulled off a stupendous save from point blank range, Macca saw his free kick somehow clawed out from under the angle of the Iniquitos goal. Each time play swung towards the Wanderers goal, the mutated advert swung into view.

Digital Sport One employees weren't very happy with the reworded message. They anticipated a reaction from Sir Fabian, who was bound to be watching, and began to think about what could be done.

"What the hell can we do about it?" asked the Senior Editor. "Sir Fabian will expect to see our ad every time we have a shot of that goal."

"All we can do," suggested the Assistant Editor, "is get the cameramen to drop their shots so that the bloody ad isn't visible."

It proved very hard to do in practice. The ground-level touchline camera at the Wanderers end was instructed not to follow play any more but to keep his camera directed across the pitch towards the far post where any action was likely to bring the offending slogan into view through the cameras up in the stands. That didn't work too well: players often got in the way of the action and the idea had to be quickly abandoned.

Blankopf, watching the game on his hotel TV, was certainly not happy with what he saw. Not at what he saw on his bed: Sharon looked as fetching as ever. It was what he saw on the screen. He was on his 'phone straight away to Tokyo for the second time in twenty minutes.

"What the fuck is going on? How did that happen?" he bellowed across the ether.

"What's the matter, Blanky?" asked Sharon, trying to see what the problem was without dislodging the big blobs of spray cream now beginning to melt on her breasts. Sir Fabian had just finished constructing walnut-whip sized swirls of the stuff over each of Sharon's nipples when the battered advert had first come into view on his screen. He had been loth to take time away from his business commitments whilst in New York but a bit of forward planning made him decide to have Sharon fly over so that he could kill two birds with one stone - see his team murder Ootgers' rabble and have a shag with someone who understood his - well, outstanding problem, as it were. Sharon was always happy to fly over to the States on her own; once or twice she found Stewart the gorgeous Virgin air steward on the same flight and always took the opportunity to pick up where they'd left off the first time they met. All Blanky would want was a bit of horizontal gymnastics (with him horizontal most of the time) and then she would be able to do a bit of shopping before jetting back to Heathrow.

Sir Fabian had popped a Viagra and was doing quite well for him when he had shown a bit of annoyance at the silly game on the TV. A quick 'phone call later (something about Bangkok and bonuses), he had fetched the spray cream and got to work. Now something else on the TV had upset him and the cream was in danger of sliding off onto the bedclothes.

"I don't care what you do about it but just *think of something bloody quick!*"

"Blanky! The cream! It's slippin' orf!"

Sir Fabian was still taking no notice. There was nothing for it: Sharon scooped the cream off herself and ate it. Quite nice, really, but a girl had to watch her figure.

"Can you see what's happened to that bloody advert behind Wanderers' goal?" yelled Sir Fabian at Sharon.

"No I can't," answered Sharon. "Wha's 'appened?"

"Just bloody watch until the other team attacks again!"

So Sharon did, and pretty soon saw a glimpse of the offending advert.

"There! There! Did you see that?" Sir Fabian was obviously beside himself. Which Sharon though was a bit mean because he was supposed to be beside - or on top or underneath - her.

"Well, no....."

The screen showed a slow motion action replay of a shot put in by an Iniquitos player. "Oooh, Blanky! Woss it say that for? 'Oo's Vera?"

"*I* don't bloody know, you silly tart! Two players crashed into it and it ended up looking like that!"

"I don' understand. How c'd they change the wordin' on an advert. I mean, them Italian ones are like on a roller-blind, but yer couldn't make 'em say somefin' diff'rent."

It was too complicated to explain to Sharon. If only the dozy Editor would stop showing slow-motion action replays from that end of the ground!

The game continued to ebb and flow with chances either end so that the Wanderers' goal with its news about Vera got plenty of exposure. Wanderers thought they had scored with twenty minutes left. O'Hooligan's ball forward to Sum Wun gave the Chinaman the chance to slide the ball under the body of the advancing 'keeper only for the linesman to rule him offside. The cameras revealed that he was wrong. Minutes later and the ball rested in the Wanderers' net - the far side from the main cameras so that the offending advert had plenty of airtime - but any Iniquitos celebrations were cut short by the other linesman's flag. This time the cameras showed it to have been the right decision.

With the added incentive derived from a feeling that they had been robbed of a goal the Wanderers' players raised their game, if that were possible, and any Iniquitos player unwise enough to dwell upon the ball was challenged with extreme malice aforethought. It wasn't long before Pickaxe was in the ref's book for catapulting an opponent into another of the unscrupulous employee's cheap plastic versions of Cecil Thorneycroft's stolen idea. The unfortunate player required treatment while the game carried on (him being off the field of play) and when, after a few minutes, he wanted to return, the cameras picked him out on the touchline where he had been bundled out. Behind him was another minced message from the damaged advertising board:

"ital i o n   nation -   24 sin s   every day"

There was obviously some reaction to that in Italy amongst the many viewers who could understand a little English.

As this latest advertising disaster appeared on his screen, Sir Fabian's agitation increased and he stopped paying any attention to Sharon.

"Blanky, I'm cold. Cum on, luv, turn the telly orf an' 'ave some cream."

"Sorry, Shaz. These dick'eds have fucked me right off." He looked disconsolately downwards. "Anyway, me Viagra's worn off! Put something on, love, and watch the rest of the game. Or have a bath."

Sharon quite liked a bit of football especially when there were some nice thighs and bums to watch, so she pulled the quilt around her own exquisite body and snuggled down beside Sir Fabian.

" 'Oo's winnin'?"

"No-one. No score, quarter of an hour left. We'd better win, or the buggers'll be sorry."

"Well then, I spec they'll apologise."

Sir Fabian shut his eyes and shook his head. Bloody hell! There she goes again!

"Blanky?"

"Ssh! What?"

"Why've yer still got yer socks on?"

The game continued to ebb and flow with passion. Although most professionals in a match that had to end in penalties if necessary would become cautious as the ninety minutes approached lest they leaked a late goal, just occasionally even they become caught up in the heat of the action and continue to slog it out. Thus it was with Wanderers United and Iniquitos. Ronnie and Joker on the Wanderers' bench and their counterparts on the Iniquitos bench screamed at their teams to hold things steady at the back, but in vain.

Despite all the endeavour, the full time whistle arrived with the match goalless. Extra time began and both managers, having preached caution, despaired as the two teams once more locked horns.

A shot from Georgi Strupinski was saved and Sum Wun, following up, put the parried ball over the bar. Antonio la Pazbaq then acrobatically tipped a screamer over his bar, then watched helplessly as a defender crashed the resulting corner against a post. Just before the end of the second period of extra time, Macca challenged the Iniquitos 'keeper for a ball he had no chance of winning and the 'keeper squared up to him. Although no blows were struck, a milling mass of players gathered next to the Iniquitos goal, pushing and jostling over the line until another of the obviously fragile special advertising boards was trampled. As they broke up, the referee blew time and it was all to be decided on penalties.

After a suitable interval the two captains were called to the centre to toss for the choice of which end the penalties should be taken. Iniquitos won and chose the end where the ball had been when the game ended with all that jostling. That meant that Wanderers had to take the first spot-kick, so the Iniquitos 'keeper took his place on the line and the cameras of the world framed the scene.

Wanderers won 5 - 4 on penalties, Antonio la Pazbaq saving the tenth kick to make him the hero. He had dived to his left to make the save right at the base of the post. He stood, triumphant, waiting for his team mates to reach him from the half way line. All the TV cameras took in the scene. Behind him was the third mangled advert, its drunken wording clear to the millions watching:

"digital international - Wanking 24 hours Every Day."

Chapter 22 - Third Round Drama

Although the Toyota Cup hardly figured as a high priority fixture in the minds of the Wanderers United players and management, the flight back via Bangkok proved exhausting. Well, not so much the flight itself rather than the stop-over. True to his word, Sir Fabian had arranged for the team to be entertained at his "Little Vixens" massage parlour in downtown Bangkok. There was almost a riot as the girls recognised Johann van Dyke. Porn films were constantly on view around the club so his face - not to mention the rest of his body - was well-known. They all wanted "a go" of him so he was certainly kept busy. The other players were not slow to avail themselves of the delights on offer, though Ronnie and Joker didn't join in. They took Ellie for a bit of a tour of the teeming city and engaged in a different sort of debauchery at one of the top Thai restaurants in town.

"I decided that Jesus and Antonio did not need me to translate for them," remarked Ellie over her starter of Gung Choop Pang Tord (deep fried prawns in batter with a sweet chili sauce). Ronnie couldn't help thinking how sexy her English sounded, with its Italian lilt and her tinkling giggle. His Tord Man Plaa (minced white fish with green beans formed into little omelette shapes with a very spicy curry paste) was threatening to burn away the roof of his mouth, so he couldn't do much other than smile tightly.

"Yes, well, most of those girls speak English," observed Joker, relishing his Pik Gai (chicken wings marinated in oyster sauce and fried with garlic), "but they'll not be doing much talking!"

Ellie blushed and looked down at her plate.

Ronnie drank some water. "Ah jus' hope the silly bastards tek notice o' Bones's wee chat an' use the condoms," he croaked.

Ellie's blush deepened. Bones, the club doctor, had given the team some dire warnings about HIV and other sexually transmitted diseases and had somehow produced handfuls of condoms for each player. Ellie had had to translate everything for the two lusty Italians who both made it clear that they wouldn't mind a session or two with her.

"D'yer not 'ave ter give little ones, laik, ter the Chinamen, Bones?" asked the ever-tactful Macca. As interpreters muttered their various translations there were one or two titters within the group. The two separate interpreters for Lim Po of the People's Republic and the Taiwanese Sum Wun became somewhat animated, as did the two players themselves. It even seemed as if, for the first time, Sum Wun and Lim Po actually spoke to one another. Eventually one of their interpreters spoke up.

"We say Doctor Bones need condoms as big as bin riners," he said.

"Bin rine.... oh, bin *liners*." Bones looked puzzled. "I'm sorry - I don't follow you."

"Bin riners for biggest prick in room - Macca!"

The laughter was much louder for this and Macca kept quiet.

"Well, if there's one thing footballers do usually look after, it's their health," said Joker, "talking of which, this Thai food is supposed to be healthy, isn't it?" He was looking forward to the rest of the meal almost as much as the players - and some of the accompanying Directors such as Cecil Norris - had been looking forward to the Thai dishes they were getting stuck into.

At least they all slept well on the homeward flight, but it was no surprise to Ronnie and Joker when Wanderers were stuffed 4 - 1 in Sunderland's Stadium of Light on the Saturday.

"Cross between jet lag an' shaggin'," sighed Ronnie afterwards. "Wha' ye mait call shag lag!"

"That and the fact that they just can't adjust to the different competitions," suggested Joker. "Look at our fixtures for the next two months. We've just come back from bloody Tokyo and we go to sunny Sunderland. Tomorrow we fly to bloody Rome for Lazio, then back to sodding Hull for the cup. Leeds at home, Southampton away, Sheffield Wednesday at home, then we're off to bloody Rio. It's like a bloody yo-yo to these boys."

"Aye, that twat Blankopf didn'ae knaw wha' he wuz doin', an noo mistake!" growled Ronnie. "Th' old team never had nae trouble, eh? D'ye remember we scraped hame one-nil at Juventus and then were at hame tae Southampton the Sat'day and beat 'em six-nil? This lot wuid beat Juventus an' lose tae the laiks o' Southampton."

In the event, in Rome, Wanderers had to settle for a goalless draw but it gave them four points from the first two Phase Two games, so there was general contentment in the Wanderers camp.

Ronnie and Joker were secretly worried about the FA Cup Third Round tie at Hull, a team that had pulled off the odd cup shock in the past. They weren't the only ones.

"I've never known such an inconsistent team," grumbled Sefton on the 'plane back from Rome. He was glad Malcolm liked sitting near the tail like he did. If anyone survived an air crash, it was usually people sitting at the back.

"You can say that again," agreed Malcolm, comfortable in his aisle seat, chosen deliberately because it was just in front of the toilets. "We don't seem to be able to win the games that look easy on paper, but then we're still in with a good chance of winning the Champions' League."

"If we can win it again, Sir Fabian might be happy whatever happens in the league," said Sefton.

"That won't do," sighed Malcolm. "It has to be the FIFA tournament or nothing." He glanced nervously round to check that the nearest toilet was still vacant. The up and down performances of Wanderers were playing havoc with his bowels again. "He told Ronnie to build a *world* beating team. The Champions League is small beer to him. Mind, he won't be very happy if we don't win everything we're in. But the way results are going lately, we'll struggle to beat bloody Hull! 'Scuse me...." He struggled out of his seat and disappeared into the toilet.

Sefton couldn't help wondering if Malcolm had eaten anything that had disagreed with him, moving so quickly like that.

As things turned out, Malcolm wasted the movement, so to speak. The foray to the bleak Humber Estuary on December 11th was an anticlimax,

Wanderers winning the tie against the Nationwide Division Three side by a resounding six goals to one. Three goals in each half (O'Hooligan 12, 59; McGrath 26; Sum Wun 39; Milosovitch 47; Genitile 78) arose from a comfortable romp, and not even Hull's goal spoiled the afternoon, arising as it did from a hit and hope 35-yard volley in injury time that Antonio la Pazbaq tried unsuccessfully to save with his "mooning" technique.

"Only taim Ah've seen someone blushin' on all four cheeks at once, man!" laughed Macca in a buoyant changing room afterwards.

* * * * * * * * *

Some 350 miles away to the South West as the seagull flies the mood in one changing room was nigh on hysterical. Having ridden their luck in all previous rounds, Cornish side Porthleven had done it again. This time, Conference side Hereford, they of the historic victory over Newcastle in 1972, were the victims; though at least the game hadn't quite followed the same pattern as Porthleven's previous FA Cup games.

Much-fancied Hereford won the toss so chose ends, giving Porthleven the formality of kicking off. This they did, to the accompaniment of a huge roar from their many times bigger than normal crowd. Charlie Legge rolled the ball to Gary Bannister and set off towards the Hereford goal. Bannister laid it back to captain John Burrows who squared it quickly to fellow-midfielder Adrian Bleasedale. Legge had meanwhile made a beeline for the Hereford goal. A Hereford striker had quickly moved in to close down Bleasedale but he deftly side-stepped the challenge and hit a long ball towards the Hereford box. On TV replays later, it looked all too simple. The ball flew over the advancing defence and fell neatly to Legge's feet as the two central defenders looked as if each thought the other should have been tracking the man in gold and black. Charlie Legge was well-used to one on ones with goalkeepers and slid the ball past Hereford's custodian. The referee's watch showed thirteen seconds. So did the watch of the Radio Cornwall commentator.

"Unlucky thirteen for Hereford, then, and what a sensational start for Porthleven!" he yelled excitedly into his microphone. "It's Porthleven one, Hereford United nil, and not one Hereford player has touched the ball yet, until their 'keeper picked the ball out of his net."

Pensioners the length and breadth of Cornwall were on the edges of their upright armchairs, elevating armchairs and commode armchairs, their radios permanently tuned in to the local BBC station. On touchlines at every game in the County the word went round, and out to the players who themselves had only just started their games: "Porthleven are one-nil up!" Even at rugby matches, a much better supported game than soccer in Cornwall, the news spread round the crowds.

From the restart Hereford mounted an attack on the Porthleven goal which appeared to last for about forty-four minutes. They pounded away at the home defence, won corner after corner, found 'keeper Gary Penhaligon in outstanding form, hit the bar three times, the left post twice, the right post once, but to no avail, so that the teams went in at half-time with Porthleven still one-nil up.

That Hereford would eventually overcome Porthleven's defence and luck was in no doubt. Young Treve Hocking was feeling as glum as anyone else around the ground. He looked up at Denzil Chegwidden. "We aren't going to win, are we, Mr Chegwidden?"

Denzil shared the doubts of just about everyone else in the ground. Porthleven had ridden their luck in all previous rounds but Hereford, seven leagues above them in the Pyramid System, had produced by far the most ferocious assault on Porthleven's goal of all those games. However, he didn't want to upset Treve.

"Well, 'ee never knaw, boy. Us c'ld 'old out again. 'Ee jus' 'as ter 'ave a bit o' faith."

Treve wasn't so sure.

Neither was the Radio Cornwall commentator. "I can't see the Porthleven defence surviving such a comprehensive going-over for another forty-five minutes," he told his decidedly mixed audience. Ancient buttocks had moved precipitously close to the edges of assorted geriatric seating; players and spectators at soccer and rugby matches around the county were united in their amazement that Porthleven still led the Conference side by that early goal to nil.

At the Bude v Sticker match in the East Cornwall Premier League, one spectator, wearing one of those baseball hats with a built-in radio, turned to the other one. "Still one-nil," he said. "The Radio Cornwall bloke reckons they'll cave in, second 'alf."

"Is it Tommy Matthews?" asked the other spectator.

"Naw. Iss the other one; 'ee frum Lunnon!" said radio-hat man.

"Oh, don' worry about 'ee, boy," said his companion. " 'Ee's allus wrong."

"Arr!"

And so it proved. Hereford's assault on Porthleven's goal continued with the same ferocity as in the first half. Denzil Chegwidden consoled himself with the thought that at least after ninety minutes the wear on his lovingly-tended playing surface would be even. The end Hereford was now defending was a quagmire from their having camped in it during the first half. By contrast, the other end hadn't been played on until now. He was shaken out of his reverie by a loud outburst of anger from the crowd.

Penalty!

"Woss that for?" he asked Treve.

"Dunno!" wailed a distraught Treve. "Stevie Jewell tackled matey and I thought he'd knocked the ball away for a corner. Ref's given a penalty!"

The ref was surrounded by a crowd of gold and black shirts. He eventually emerged from the throng and made for his linesman. Or, rather, Assistant Referee. It didn't make any difference: it was still a penalty.

"The referee's pointed to the spot," yelled the Radio Cornwall commentator. "A harsh decision."

Many of the listening geriatrics made unscheduled use of their commode chairs; groans went round the watching crowds at the county's rugby matches.

Amidst a storm of booing, the Hereford captain stepped up to take the penalty, and buried it in the corner of Porthleven's net.

"That's it!" yelled the Radio Cornwall commentator "Now Hereford have made the breakthrough, I'm rather afraid the floodgates will open."

"Thank Gawd fer that," said the spectator at Bude with the radio hat.

"Thank Gawd fer what?" asked the other spectator.

"Hereford scored, but this bloke sez they'll gedda hatful."

" 'Ee's allus wrong, boy."

"Arr!"

And so it proved. After that fiftieth-minute penalty the Porthleven goal continued to lead a charmed life. Denzil Chegwidden couldn't help thinking how long it was going to take him to wash all that mud off the goal posts and cross bars, so often were they struck by the ball.

It was in injury time when, with a replay looming, yet another desperate clearance launched the ball into the Hereford half. It was a longer clearance than most: the ball had already been beaten out as far as the Hereford back four one of whom played a sloppy ball forwards that was intercepted by Mark Hope. It was his boot that sent the ball towards the no-man's-land between the last defender and the penalty area. The Hereford 'keeper, unemployed since the distant memory of picking the ball out of his net, was perhaps a fraction of a second late reacting. Once it became obvious that the ball was going to carry to him, he started towards it; as had Charlie Legge. Spectators on both touchlines, with the benefit of the side-on view, could see from the flight of the ball that Legge had no chance of reaching it. The 'keeper had only to take a few steps, really, as the bounce of the ball would take it to him.

Except the ball didn't bounce. It stuck in the quagmire of mud churned up by Hereford's first half seige of Porthleven's goal. The 'keeper hesitated, uncertain what to do, then started to sprint towards the ball. His feet slipped in the mud and he stumbled. Charlie Legge, by contrast, had just kept on running, chasing what had been a lost cause until the ball stuck. He reached it yards before the 'keeper and scooped it out of the mud, lofting it high over him. Time stood still. Many swore that the ball stopped in mid air for a second or two. Others said it was like watching a video on slow forward. Nevertheless, eventually the ball dropped and, after an agonising amount of time, found the net. The crowd went wild. The Radio Cornwall commentator lost his voice. At least half-a-dozen 999 calls went out from aged listeners who collapsed with excitement: fortunately, there were no fatalities, but there was a small peak in cases of temporary incontinence. Bude were playing out a nil-nil draw with Sticker. The spectator with the radio hat leapt in the air.

"Ye-ess!" he yelled. Twenty-two brassed-off players looked over to him.

"I'll 'ave whatever 'ee's 'ad," said one centre half to the opposing striker.

"How long left?" asked the other spectator.

Radio hat man clamped a finger over his earpiece, his faced creased with concentration for a few seconds.

"Dunnaw," he replied. "Bleddy bloke's lost 'is bleddy voice. They've gone back ter the stoodio!"

145

Hereford had time to equalise again - at least five minutes during which they won six corners and hit the framework twice more. But time ran out. The whistle went and virtually the whole crowd was on the pitch. Denzil Chegwidden winced. The pitch would take weeks to repair! Oh, sod it! He jumped over the rail and joined the rest, all trying to find someone in a yellow shirt to congratulate.

Hence - eventually - the near-hysterical atmosphere in the Porthleven dressing room.

In the clubhouse, and amongst the spectators making their way home, there was naturally talk of who Porthleven might get in the next round. Many tuned into Radio Cornwall in their cars. The commentator had got some of his voice back and was pointing out that, once again, his attempt at a prediction had failed. However, it was he who mentioned that as Wanderers United, as expected, had beaten Hull City, it would be some lucky team's fate to be flown out to Brazil to play them in the next round, together with a Jumbo-jet full of supporters. It had been a rumour for weeks, and confirmed in the "Daily Universe" only that week, as well as on the much less widely received Digital Sport One satellite channel.

"What a prospect *that* would be!" he croaked. "I'm not sure Radio Cornwall's budget would run to sending a reporter out for *that* game!"

Chapter 23 - The Fourth Round Draw

"Look, it's not as if we haven't done this before!" The Floor Manager was getting annoyed at the antics of the gang of men putting the finishing touches to the makeshift studio being constructed inside the Banqueting Hall at Wembley Stadium. "That bloody background panel is flapping around like something out of Cell Block H!"

Tarquin, balanced on the platform on top of a tall stepladder so that he could hold the offending panel in place, swore under his breath. "Bitch!" he said. He'd spent many happy months down under on the set of Cell Block H and couldn't understand why a few wobbling prison cell walls caused so much comment. Mind, it hadn't all been plain sailing. Some of those actresses had been hard cases, but at least he'd been able to advise one or two about how lesbians behave. Oh, what was that butch bloody Floor Manager saying now?

"Can't you fix the bloody thing up there somewhere, Tarquin, you wanker?"

"What do you suggest I attach it *to*, luv? I don't happen to have any fucking skyhooks in my pocket!"

"Yes, well, we know what you *do* keep in your pockets. We'll have to try to hold the damn thing steady from behind. Can you do that, Tarquin?"

Well, it wouldn't be the first thing I've held steady from behind, thought Tarquin. "I'll try, luv. A length of four-by-four would help." Abandoning the wavering panel, Tarquin climbed down. Honestly, all this fuss for a bloody football match. Load of butch men kicking a bag of air around. He set off to see if there was a suitable length of wood on the lorry outside.

It was Sunday 12th December. The specially-constructed temporary studio was more or less ready for the draw for the fourth round of the FA Cup. The lighting, cameras, seating for the invited representatives of the clubs involved and the special transparent "mixing bowl" for the numbered balls were all in place. It was just the false walls that provided the background behind the celebrities making the draw that were causing the problem. The Floor Manager couldn't understand why they'd had to erect the studio in a different part of the Banqueting Hall from where it was for the third round draw. The flats had rested against the walls of the Hall then but this time they had to be free-standing. He sighed. That's what the road crew were for, though God knows how that faggot Tarquin had wormed his way in. But then again......

Tarquin returned with the end of a length of four-by-four over his shoulder. The crew's foreman was carrying the other end. He was a big, muscular bloke who obviously worked out and he always wore that odd leather peaked cap. The two disappeared round the back of the troublesome panel and there was a thud as they put the length of four-by-four down. Tarquin reappeared briefly to fetch the step ladder.

The panel wobbled.

"Can't you get it up any further?" came the invisible Tarquin's indignant plea.

"I'm only using one hand!"

"Well use *both* hands, luv. I can't get my end where I want it."

"I can't use both hands. You told me to hold you steady."

"Well I'll take the risk if it means you can get my end up far enough."

"It's a bit hard. How's that?"

"Yes - yes: *nearly* there. Oh, balls! It's slipped out!"

"Sorry! I'm in an awkward position with that in the way."

"Let me change my grip. There! Is that any better?"

"Yes, that feels a lot better. Are you ready for me to try again?"

"Phew! I hope you manage it this time. I'm getting knackered up here!"

"Right: brace yourself! Uuuuuuurgghhh!"

"Higher. Higher! *Higher! Yeeeeessss!*"

The panel vibrated in time to the banging sound that came from behind it.

Tarquin's voice again: "Ooooh, at *last!* I thought I'd never get it in. Still, thanks, luv. I'm glad you came."

" 'Sa'wright. I've done something to my back, though. I was beginning to think we'd never get it up. Fag?"

Tarquin and the foreman emerged red-faced from behind the panel, both inhaling deeply on newly-lit cigarettes. They were greeted by a huge cheer and round of applause from the rest of the crew, all sitting and laughing in the seats facing the set. They never knew why.

* * * * * * * * *

That evening, the specially-invited audience gathered excitedly, most barely looking at the lights, cameras and special equipment for making the draw as they had been present for the Third Round draw. New to the audience was the Porthleven groundsman Denzil Chegwidden. He was there because the team's manager had gone skiing. He'd planned the trip in the summer because Porthleven had no league fixture for the Saturday after the Third Round of the FA Cup. He'd had to leave the scenes of hysterical delight after the win over Hereford for the drive up to Luton to catch his flight to the snow. So in his place, accompanying Chairman Len Williams and Secretary Vidal James was Denzil, in recognition of all the hard work he had done in getting the pitch ready, especially for all the epic FA Cup games and, more to the point, repairing it afterwards.

So Denzil was full of curiosity and didn't know where to look first. Not only were there the cameras, lights and other TV Studio paraphernalia, but so many famous faces from the world of football. There was David O'Leary of Leeds United, John Gregory of Aston Villa, Peter Reid of Sunderland, Matt le Tissier of Southampton, Joe Royle of Manchester City and, the icing on the cake, no lesser footballing celebrities than Ronnie Bone and "Joker" Wallace of Wanderers United - it was amazing to find himself in the same room as these men whose faces he so often saw on Match of the Day.

It was ITV and Digital One Sport whose cameras were covering the Fourth Round draw. Denzil blinked at the posse of TV people who rushed to and fro in apparent chaos. Clipboards seemed to be compulsory. His amazement was compounded when one of the posse approached the Porthleven contingent and asked them who they were.

"Porthleven," replied Len Williams, proudly.

"Aaaaahhh! *Won*derful! We've been waiting for you. Follow me, please!"

They were led to the front row of the banked seating. "Would you like to sit here, boys?"

"Why's 'ee sat us 'ere?" whispered Denzil to Vidal James.

"We're the stars, Denzil," replied Vidal. "Whoever we get, they'll want to interview us."

"Interview.....? What, on *telly?*" Denzil looked horrified.

"Nothin' to it, Denzil. Just like talking to Tommy Matthews on Radio Cornwall."

" 'Ee tried ter talk ter me about the pitch las' season. Oi didn't loik it much."

"Just be yourself, boy."

"Now!" said the man with the clipboard. "Shane Parkhurst wants to have a word with you."

"Who?" asked Denzil.

"Digital One Sport," answered Vidal. "Their top man."

"What does he want?" asked Len.

"Well, you're celebrities, luv, I expect he wants to ask you who you fancy."

Shane Parkhurst, Digital One Sport's chief football correspondent, breezed over to them.

"You must be the Cornish lot," he gushed.

"Ye-es..." Len Williams sounded uncertain.

"Curiosity value," Shane gushed on. "Everyone loves the underdog, that's what the FA Cup is all about, and you can't get much more of an underdog than you lot, eh?"

There was no answer to that. Each of the men from Porthleven felt not a little miffed at Shane Parkhurst's bluntness.

"I want to record an interview to be shown ahead of the draw. Who's it going to be?"

"You're good at talking, Vidal. How about you?" Len turned to Shane. "Vidal's our Football Secretary. Our Manager is on holiday. Gone skiing."

"Holiday?" Shane looked puzzled. "An odd time for a football manager to go on holiday, in the middle of the season."

"Well, like you say," replied Len. "He didn't expect to be needed at the FA Cup Fourth Round draw. We hadn't got a league fixture next Saturday, so he booked his holiday."

Shane shrugged. Used to dealing with Premiership clubs, he wasn't on the same wavelength as these part-timers from the back of beyond.

"So it's you, then?" He spoke to Vidal.

Vidal shrugged his shoulders. He didn't mind; in fact, he quite liked the idea of being on satellite TV even if not that many people watched it. Perhaps he might get interviewed by ITV as well. That would be a lot better!

"Yes. What do you want to know?"

"*What's* your name?"

"Vidal James."

"Bloody strange name!" Shane Parkhurst, once again, was blunt.

"Not as common as Shane, though." Vidal decided he didn't like this jumped up TV man.

The interview was brief, as indeed it had to be to fit in with the tight schedule for the broadcast.

"So, Vidal James, Secretary of no-hopers Porthleven from Cornwall," beamed Shane into the camera. "Who do you fancy for the Fourth Round?"

When Vidal didn't reply, Shane was forced to turn away from the camera and look at him.

Vidal looked suddenly surprised. "Oh, sorry. Were you talking to me?"

Shane looked thunderous. "Cut!" he hissed at the cameraman. "Of *course* I was talking to you! I'm *interviewing* you! Who did you *think* I was talking to?"

"Well, tell the truth, I wasn't sure. Usually when someone's talking to me they look at me as well." Vidal hadn't been too impressed by Shane Parkhurst's camera hogging style.

"We'll try again, shall we?" Shane nodded to his cameraman who wearily began to record again. He'd certainly drawn the short straw, having to work with bloody Shane Parkhurst. He looked into the camera even more than Jonathan Ross.

"This is Vidal James, Secretary of tiny Porthleven from way down there in sunny Cornwall." Shane became his bubbly, beaming public self, as opposed to his real self, once again. "Tell me, Vidal, all this must be a bit of an eye-opener for you, sat amongst all these big names in football." A change of question should throw this awkward customer from pasty-land.

Staring into the camera, Shane couldn't see Vidal's withering look in his direction. "Well, no, actually. We were here for the Third Round draw."

Shane actually turned to face Vidal, a forced smile fixed to his face. "Of course," he gritted. He gave up. He had more important people to interview. "Now, who do you boys fancy in the Fourth Round?"

"Well, Plymouth away would be nice," replied Vidal.

"Plymouth?" Shane, back facing the camera, gave it a puzzled look. He had expected Vidal to opt for Arsenal, Liverpool or, of course, Wanderers United. "Why Plymouth?"

"Local derby," explained Vidal. "Lot o' support for Argyle in Cornwall, so it'd cause a lot of interest."

"One of the teams here will have to fly to Brazil to play Wanderers United. I don't suppose you'd fancy that much?"

"Well, none of us has been to Brazil so I suppose it would be an experience. We'd have problems getting the whole team there because I don't expect they could all get enough time off work to make the trip."

"Would Porthleven withdraw if they draw Wanderers, then?"

Len Williams cut in at that point. "We'd ask 'The Universe' to sub the boys' lost wages so's they could all go. We wouldn't want to take a weakened side!"

There was no way that Shane Parkhurst could faze the men from the only non-league side in the draw, so he cut his losses.

"Well, there you go, these no-hopers from Cornwall refuse to be overawed by the occasion. We'll soon find out who they have to play as the draw is about to start."

"No, boy, you'm wrong," Denzil struck up. " 'nother 'arf an hour yet. Got a dodgy watch, 'ave 'ee?"

Editing would cut out his comments, of course, and Shane had simply provided a link to slot into the start of the live broadcast. An ITV cameraman, just making some test shots, captured it all, however. His sound man was also recording. It was later stored away by an editor who thought it would make a great out-take for future use. It would need some bleeping, though, as Shane turned on Denzil.

"Shuttup, you fucking moron! This was recorded to play just before the live fucking broadcast! *Cut!* God help you all, you carrot-crunching wankers!" And off he stormed.

Len, Vidal and Denzil sat down. "Oi don' even *loike* carrots!" said Denzil.

The draw took place in the recently established manner, with two famous ex-footballers drawing out the numbered balls whilst an FA executive placed them on a board in front of him in "home" and "away" positions.

The balls were tipped into the see-through container and stirred around.

"Iss loike bingo," whispered Denzil.

"Shh!" went Vidal and Len in duet.

"And the first ball out......" announced the man from the FA.

"Number fourteen" announced Famous Ex-footballer number one.

"Grimsby Town....." revealed the FA man for the benefit of the viewers. All the team representatives in the audience had a list.

"Number four," beamed Famous Ex-footballer number two.

"Will play Bolton Wanderers."

"Number eighteen...."

"Manchester City...."

"Number fifteen."

"Will play Leeds United." Some "oooh's" and "aaah's" from the audience. A giant-killing opportunity for sleeping giant Manchester City?

"Number thirteen...."

"Gillingham....."

"Number five."

"Will play Bradford City." Even more reaction from the audience. Apart from Porthleven, Gillingham had been a surprise package so far in the cup.

"Number one....."

"Arsenal...."

"Number sixteen."

"Will play Leicester City." An all-Premiership draw! That caused a ripple of comment around the room.

"Number thirty...."

"Wrexham...."

"Number eight."

"Will play Cambridge United." Not much excitement there, except for the managers of both teams who could each entertain the possibility of progression to the last sixteen.

The tension grew as more and more teams came out of the pot: *who* was going to end up with a free trip to Brazil for themselves and a Jumbo Jet full of supporters?

Liverpool v Blackburn Rovers, Charlton Athletic v Queen's Park Rangers, Aston Villa v Southampton, Plymouth Argyle v Portsmouth: no exciting local derby for Porthleven, then, but a tasty south coast derby between two naval towns with a long rivalry. Fulham v Wimbledon, Tranmere Rovers v Sunderland, Newcastle United v Sheffield United, Coventry City v Burnley: there were six teams left. Len Williams, Vidal James and Denzil Chegwidden shifted uncomfortably in their front-row seats.

"Number twenty-five...."

"Sheffield Wednesday....."

"Number thirty-one."

"Will play Wolverhampton Wanderers."

"Bloody hell!" It was getting to Vidal.

"Number eleven...."

"Everton...."

"Number six."

It was hard to hear the voice of the FA official identifying team number six - Birmingham City - because everyone in the room knew then who the last two teams in the draw were. The two Famous Ex-footballers had to raise their voices, as did FA man.

"Number twenty-nine....."

"Wanderers United...."

"Number twenty-three!"

"Will play Porthleven!"

Pandemonium broke out. Len, Vidal and Denzil were immediately surrounded by reporters; Digital One Sport and ITV cameras zoomed in on them. Hands appeared from all around them to shake their hands or clap them on the back.

Porthleven had been drawn against the biggest, most wealthy and successful club in the world, which was heart-stopping enough, but they had to be flown to Brazil to do it!

Chapter 24 - Rio Bound

The calendar was quite different for Wanderers United and Porthleven between the Fourth Round draw and the Fourth Round itself. As things turned out, Porthleven didn't play a single game. A scheduled League match at Newquay was postponed due to a waterlogged pitch; they had no fixture the following Saturday and the next Saturday after that was Christmas Day. Their New Year's Day match was also postponed and they had to fly out to Rio the Friday after that.

The Porthleven camp were philosophical.

"At least no-one has played badly because they're thinking about going to Brazil," observed manager Alan Carey to his assistant, George Torrance.

"And we've got no injuries to weaken the side," George added. "Len persuaded 'The Universe' to sub the wages for everyone that needs it. They threatened to name any employer who wouldn't let a player go with us on the front page under a suitably critical headline! It seems to have worked!"

Wanderers, on the other hand, had five matches. The thoughts of most players were on the FIFA tournament and Wanderers' results reflected this: a draw at Bradford, home defeat by Leeds United, away defeat at Southampton and home draw against Sheffield Wednesday left them floundering in twelfth place.

"What the hell's going on?" Sir Fabian Blankopf, forever in any one of a number of the world's centres of commerce, was once again bellowing down his 'phone to Sefton Perkins.

"Well, like you say, F.B.," replied Sefton, without believing it himself but hoping he sounded convincing, "the World Club Championship is the thing. We set our stall out in Tokyo. Our domestic competition is a bit of a distraction what with Rio to concentrate on, not to mention the Champions' League. We're right on course for that as you know."

"So what are you saying - the Premiership isn't important?"

This was clearly a ridiculous notion to any red-blooded English football fan. Sefton, like any other Premiership director, understood the importance of doing well in the Premiership: the sheer necessity of qualifying for the Champions' League which brought such huge financial rewards. Of course, Wanderers had won that last season so automatically qualified for this season's competition, but if they didn't win it this season then they needed to qualify via the Premiership.

"Well, F.B., let's just say it doesn't figure that highly in our minds as the other competitions we're in." A downright lie couldn't do much harm.

"Hmm." Sir Fabian didn't seem convinced. "What's this stuff I've been hearing about some village side we've got to play?"

A chance to deflect Sir Fabian's interest away from the Wanderers poor league form. "Ah, that! Well, I'll tell you what, F.B., but your idea of getting your paper to pay to fly our FA Cup fourth round opponents out to Brazil to play us has really turned out well. It could have been the Arsenal or Liverpool which would have been good enough for publicity. A team from a lower division would have been even better - the romance of the cup, you know - but we've drawn some tiny little village side from down in Cornwall, the furthest they've ever got in the cup, the last non-league side left, the lowest-ranked side ever to have reached the fourth round - it's the stuff dreams are made of. It couldn't have created more interest than if Prince Charles dated one of the Spice girls."

"What's that? Prince Charles? *Which* Spice Girl? Why haven't any of my fucking papers picked that up?" Perhaps Sir Fabian hadn't been concentrating too closely on what Sefton had been saying. Sharon had just come out of the shower and was uninhibitedly doing some exercises before she put any clothes on.

"No, no, *no!*" Sefton looked to the Heavens and shook his head. "I said that us getting drawn against the last non-league side in the FA cup has created more publicity than we could have possibly hoped. I made that up about Prince Charles and the Spice Girls."

"Made it up? Never mind, most of our headline stories are made up. I'll get on to my newspaper blokes immediately." Sharon was just finishing touching her toes ten times, her back to Sir Fabian. He put his 'phone down and immediately picked it up again, punching out a number. "Bloody hell, Shaz, why d'you stand like that to do yer exercises?"

"Eh? Oh, sorry, Blanky, luv. I didn't face yer as yer was on the 'phone. I di'nt want ter distract yer by flashing me tits an' me 'a'penny, so I turned me back!"

Sir Fabian chuckled as he listened to the ringing tone at the other end of his 'phone. "Thanks, Shaz, that was very considerate of you."

Sharon beamed with happiness. She didn't say anything as Sir Fabian was speaking again.

"Get me the Editor..... Piers? Now listen, you moron. I've just heard something about Prince Charles....."

* * * * * * * * *

The Wanderers party left for Brazil on New Year's Day. They flew in first-class luxury on a British Airways Jumbo Jet and upon arrival at Rio were transferred to their luxury hotel by luxury coach. Manager Ronnie Bone had always insisted on the best for what turned out to be his treble-winning side of the previous season even though many of them were happy to eat fish and chips out of newspaper on journeys back from away games.

This new bunch of international has-beens and misfits expected luxury. Never mind. It amounted to the same thing. They were off to Brazil to play against the world's best club sides (allegedly) with a team that he and Joker had put together with the express purpose of making Sir Fabian bloody Blankopf and the Wanderers United Board of Directors regret the day they decided to sack the two of them. Neither Ronnie nor Joker would have been that surprised at the mid-table position of the team at the turn of the year. It was the performances in the Champions' League that had gobsmacked them to the extent that they couldn't rule out the chance of doing well in Rio. "Doing well" is football parlance for winning.

"D'ye think oor bubble'll burst this trip?" asked Ronnie, sat next to Joker at the back of the First Class section.

"I guess it has to eventually. We've been dead lucky with injuries. I can't believe it. There's Antonio's knee, Caspar's punch-drunkenness, Sum Wun's knee, Lim Po's shoulder, then there's Pickaxe's tendency to get sent off, Jesus's habit of causing trouble by sampling his team-mates' wives, Manuel's drinking problem, Enrique's record of attacking the opposition's bench, Macca's.... well, let's face it, he's just a fat, boozy, womanising twat, and Georgi has upset players in the past, borrowing money after gambling losses and not paying it back. We certainly put together a right crowd, didn't we!"

"Aye, an' no mistake! We tho't Seamus was past it, he's bin knocking in th' goals, Papa's another one - Ah'm gettin' a mite worried aboot yon bastard. He's real spooky, ye ken?"

"I know what you mean. There's definitely something suspicious about him but he's certainly had his moments. Pity about Heinrich, though."

Heinrich Schickelgrüber was afraid of flying, of course. Although for Champions' League games in Europe he travelled by road, he'd had to be left behind for the trip to Rio. He was one of the kingpins in the Wanderers' defence, sweeping behind them one moment, bursting forwards to supplement the midfield or even the strikers the next. He offered Ronnie and Joker another option in the tactical battles of modern football.

"Aye, but it cannae be helped. Och, shite! Look oot!" Ronnie had spotted Sir Fabian making his way down the 'plane towards them.

"Well, you two," sprayed their Chairman. "Are we going to win this world championship thing or what?"

"O' course we're gonnae win it. Wha' sort o' a question is that?"

"I just wanted to hear you say it," sprayed Sir Fabian. "It's what I told you to build a team for."

"Ah know. We're no' doin' so bad so far, eh?"

"You've hardly set your own League alight!"

"Oh, *that!*" said Joker. "Well, we knew you wanted us to win the FIFA tournament, and the Champions' League, so the league games give us an opportunity to try things out - you know, like very extreme training games."

Ronnie was a bit taken aback at Joker's outrageous explanation of what was really the inability of the team to treat the Premiership games - which to the cosmopolitan squad did indeed have little meaning - as seriously as the Champions' League. "Aye, tha's the strategy, Sir Fabian," he agreed. "D'ye no' like it? Wuid ye like us tae do it diff'rently?"

Rugby was Sir Fabian's game. Sefton and the rest of the Wanderers board had convinced him that Ronnie and Joker were the best managing team in the world. The crucial point had been that no other manager in the world had appeared willing to take on the magnificent side that they'd assembled, so he couldn't sack them.

"No, no. I'm sure you know what you're doing." But his need to be The Man In Charge surfaced. "It's your balls if you screw up, though!" With that he moved back to his seat nearer the front.

Ronnie and Joker exchanged bemused looks.

"Where d'ye find *tha'* load o' bollocks from, laddie?"

Joker chuckled. "Fuck knows! Worked, though, didn't it! Do you fancy 'a wee dram'?"

Ronnie chuckled back. "Aye, why not!"

The 'plane flew on to Rio and the party were installed in their hotel with no unsavoury incidents. Since the ill-fated flight to Venice for the pre-season friendly there was a strict "no women" rule. Mind, for a trip away as long as this one it was a bit mean. Especially as it wasn't observed by Sir Fabian who had not only brought Sharon with him but Jenny as well.

"His 'Personal Assistant' and 'Chauffeur'," explained Johann van Dyke to Caspar Hansen who was already feeling decidedly uncomfortable in the Y-front district at the thought of being parted from Sharon for fifteen whole days and (groan) nights.

"At least we won't have to watch them perving around the hotel pool," he said. "Blankopf has had his yacht sent over to Rio and they'll all be on that."

"Just as well he won't be at the hotel with us," nodded Johann. "He's a bloody wanker."

"Except he'll be the only one of us not having to," moaned Caspar.

The Wanderers had a pleasant few days acclimatising themselves to the Brazilian summer and doing a bit of light training ahead of their first game against Necaxa, which they won comfortably. Porthleven's adventure began in Cornwall the following day.

Chapter 25 - Concorde!

The tiny airport terminal at Newquay belies the potential of the airport itself. It is part of RAF St. Mawgan, a fully operational airfield capable of dealing with any conventional aircraft in the world. Hercules transport 'planes frequently land there, not known for their short take-off. Even the giant Russian military transport 'plane, the Antonov An225 had landed there for an air show, although to be fair it needed less than half of the 2.2 miles needed by Concorde to take off. The St. Mawgan airstrip is easily long enough for the Concorde, though: it can land and take off with no problems. It is the terminal that is not really designed to cope with the numbers involved.

It was Friday 7th January when the specially chartered Concorde landed at Newquay, a rather short hop from Heathrow for such a magnificent aircraft. The terminal was packed with the Porthleven team and officials with their wives, girl friends and children, as well as well-wishers and press.

Prominent amongst the press present was the contingent from 'The Universe'. Banners and posters advertising the paper were everywhere inside and outside the terminal so that it was impossible for any photos to be taken that didn't include this free plug. Technology meant that most rival papers removed the posters from their own photos with just a little bit of computer-enhancement, but this wasn't so easy for the TV cameras.

Because of the intense local interest, all local TV and radio stations were covering the event. BBC Radio Cornwall had even wangled a reporter into Porthleven's official party. They managed to keep this from 'The Universe' who would not have been too happy with a breach of what they imagined was their "exclusive" coverage of the trip. Tommy Matthews was well known in local football, so it was easy enough to get him included in their party as one of the club officials. As the Concorde was due to arrive in Rio late on Friday UK time, it was going to be easy for Tommy to 'phone the studio for a live link-up during Radio Cornwall's Saturday afternoon sports programme.

Digital International's cameras and reporters claimed the prime positions, of course, and there would even be one on board the Concorde. In a glare of TV lights, Shane Parkhurst, Digital Sport One's chief football correspondent, was interviewing the Porthleven Manager, Alan Carey.

"Well, Alan," he beamed, looking into the camera as usual rather than at the man he was talking to. "What are your thoughts as you prepare to lead your team onto the 'plane for the footballing experience of a lifetime?"

"Just that we're all going to enjoy the trip in Concorde, do some sightseeing, play some football and just try to do ourselves justice." Here was a man not given to overstatement.

"If I can just bring in your top goal-scorer," effused Shane, still camera-watching and reading from (in his case at least) the appropriately named idiot board which bore the top goal-scorer's name, "Charlie Legge. Chas, do you expect to score a goal against the Wanderers?"

"Its Charlie, not Chas," replied the young long-haired man standing next to his manager.

"What?" said Shane, his camera-hogging face showing a slight draining of confidence.

"I was telling you I'm not called Chas. Everyone calls me Charlie," explained the poker-faced young player.

"Yes - er - *Charlie* - you are the top scorer...."

"Eighteen so far," revealed Charlie.

"....so how many goals - pardon?" Shane was looking decidedly uncomfortable now and actually looked away from the camera for a second to glance in Charlie's direction.

"I've scored eighteen goals in league and cup games so far this season. I can read the questions too, you know." Still poker faced, Charlie made the merest movement of his eyes towards the idiot board.

"Read the.... Ha ha ha." (Shane didn't sound amused.) "Who do you...."

"Ryan Giggs."

"....admire most.....what?"

"Ryan Giggs. I read the question again."

"Er - right - er - we'll just go to our camera on the tarmac for another look at the 'plane..." Shane, visibly unnerved, beamed desperately into the camera.

In the editing truck outside, the Digital Sports One outside broadcasting editor chuckled with great satisfaction at the transmission monitor in front of him. Allowing as long a delay as he dared, he ordered a switch to camera four and the transmission monitor showed a wobbly view of the Concorde outside the terminal. The camera one monitor showed Shane Parkhurst's face contort from his camera smile to a snarl of rage aimed at the young Porthleven footballer.

"You stupid fucking yokel," he raged at Charlie. "You're supposed to wait for me to ask the bloody questions, not read them yourself!"

"Oh, sorry," said Charlie. "I'll know next time."

"There won't *be* a next time, you dozy carrot-crunching fucking peasant!"

"Excuse me?" Charlie's expression showed mild concern.

"You heard me, or have you got pasties in your ears, you ignorant Cornish twat! I hope you lose seventy three nil. Fancy sending *me - me* of *all* people - to the arse end of the country to cover *this*."

"Are you calling Cornwall the arse end of the country?" asked Charlie.

"Fucking right!" Shane's camera face was long forgotten.

"Well, that's not very friendly," said Charlie. "You might upset a few Cornishmen saying things like that."

"Like I *care*. You're all a bunch of straw-chewing, sheep-shagging wallies down here."

"Sheep shaggin's Wales, mate," said a large man standing just behind Charlie. It was Mickey Faithful, Porthleven's sweeper. He stepped forward and grabbed the disgruntled Shane by his lapels.

"An' we di'nt chew much straw down Crofty." Micky had worked down Cornwall's last open tin mine after he'd left school, until made redundant when world tin prices forced its closure. " 'Ere, boy, 'ave a Camborne kiss!"

Mickey felled Shane with a head butt to the nose and all hell broke loose.

In the editing truck, the editor was gleefully recording everything that camera one was seeing. A quiet word through camera one's headphones made sure that not a detail was missed, although the shots of Shane on the floor clutching his flattened, bleeding nose were sometimes obscured by the legs of people milling around.

"You sthupid bathtard!" squealed Shane from amidst the tangle of legs around him as several of the team struggled to move the incensed Micky away. "I'll have youth for that!"

Other, more successful, interviews were taking place amidst the crowd. BBC TV's Spotlight South West had goalkeeper Gary Penhaligon being interviewed by their local reporter Justin Leigh, doing an infinitely more professional job than Digital's Shane Parkhurst. For one thing, he was actually looking at Gary as he asked him about his excitement at the prospect of flying in Concorde, seeing Rio, playing against the most prestigious club side in the world and his rôle in Porthleven having reached the fourth round of the FA Cup in the first place.

Carlton TV were replaying highlights of Porthleven's progress to the fourth round (there had only been cameras watching them from the first round proper) in between shots of the inside of the terminal building and the crowds outside, with a voice-over commentary. Their producer had quickly summed up the problems caused by all the 'Universe' posters and banners around the place. A couple of 'phone calls led to the arrival of a Carlton van loaded with a home-decorator's scaffold tower. Once it was erected and their cameras were mounted high upon it, their downward angle meant that none of the 'Universe' posters came into shot. The Carlton producer and his editor (in Carlton's editing truck outside in the car park alongside Digital's) were delighted. As the editor of 'The Universe' watched the tapes of all the coverage later that day his sentiments were slightly different.

There was a gradually increasing air of excitement in the terminal building. Excitement wasn't what Shane Parkhurst was feeling, though, as he was being patched up by a young St John Ambulance Brigade cadet, chuffed to bits to be treating a well-known TV sports presenter but becoming increasingly dischuffed as the man's real personality became all too obvious.

"Carethul, you sthupid clumthy thod!" raged Shane as the spotty lad in his slightly oversized uniform tried to wipe the traces of dried blood from the famous face.

"Oi'm bein' as careful as Oi can, Mr Park'urst," he explained. " 'Ee don' want thiz 'ere droid blood all over yer face, do 'ee?"

"Jutht get a thuckin' move on. Good gweith, ith everybothy a bloothy peathant down here?" The lad, a volunteer after all and not deserving of the TV star's vitriolic insults, felt enormously let down. He'd thought this bloke to be such a hero, with his fast "in your face" presentation and apparently unlimited knowledge of football. Seeing him have all his questions on an improvised autocue had been his first let down. Hearing him go on like this was the last straw.

"Yer nawse is busted," he informed the seething Shane, slightly surprised at how pleased he felt at having to deliver this diagnosis to the odious man. "Orl Oi can do is patch 'ee up an' suggest you geddun X-rayed." In the Cornish way, he put the emphasis on the "rayed" rather than on the "X".

"Exth *rayed?*" mimicked Shane. "Chrith, you peopleth can't even *sthpeak* pthroperly! *Oooochth!* What thid you do that for, you bloothy *oaf?*"

The St John's lad had taken out a nice big bright pink fabric sticking plaster and quickly slapped it across Shane's assaulted hooter.

"Proper job!" he beamed. "That'll do 'ee. No need ter say thanks. It's what we're 'ere for!" With which he rose and made off through the crowd back to the first aid post.

Shane, already beside himself with rage, tenderly touched his face and recoiled at the apparent size of the plaster applied by the first-aider. He found his way back to his camera team.

"We've got tho get thome more interviewth done," he said to the producer, camera man, sound man and lighting man. They were trying not to laugh at the appearance of Shane, who they all knew was just about as vain as any TV presenter could be. Which is very. Without the other three knowing, each man decided to say nothing to Shane about his appearance: the huge fabric plaster, pink against his sunbed-assisted sun tan, the ripped Yves St Laurent shirt where the Porthleven sweeper had grabbed him and the blood all over the same shirt and the Pringle jumper.

"Right!", "Right!", "Right!", "Right!", they each said.

"Who can I interview nextht?"

The producer consulted his clipboard. "There's their goalkeeper. We've got a set of cue-boards for him. He's likely to be the busiest man on the pitch. He's already been interviewed by the local BBC"

"He'th the one. Get him, fatht ath you can. Get the right cue boardth up."

The producer went off in search of his man whilst the camera man sorted through the bundle of idiot boards and found one marked "Porthleven Goalkeeper Gary Penhaligon"

The tall, heavily-built, dark-haired 'keeper came back with the producer. "This is Gary, the goalkeeper. Gary, meet Shane Parkhurst, who I'm sure you have seen on TV."

"No," said Gary, trying not to laugh at the appearance of the battered Shane.

"Oh, well, never mind. Shane will ask you a few questions on camera if you don't mind. Okay?"

"Yea, right."

The producer pushed and manipulated the goalkeeper into position alongside the Shane who had obviously forgotten how horrendous he looked.

"Ready for camera one, OB?" said the producer into his throat mike. In the editing truck, the editor looked at the image on the camera one monitor. There was Shane in glorious close-up, tanned face, large pink plaster spread across a flattened nose, a little blood seeping through it, the ripped and bloodied shirt, the blood-stained jumper: "Ready camera one: camera one - *go!*"

It made classic TV, shown on programmes such as Chris Tarrant's and Clive James's all over the world for many years afterwards. The normally unflappable Gary Penhaligon found it hard to keep a straight face, especially as the four TV men behind the camera were almost crying with suppressed laughter at the sight and sound - or "thight and thound", as they recalled in bars and at parties for ages afterwards - of a struggling Shane Parkhurst interviewing in his usual way, ignoring his interviewee as he camera-hogged with his now dreadful face. It was when he asked Gary if he thought his back was strong enough to cope with picking the ball out of the net as often as he'd have to that it finally went wrong.

"Well, my back may end up feeling like your face looks," replied Gary

"Thorry?" queried Shane.

"Completely knackered!" explained Gary, finally giving in to the laughter that was breaking out around him. As everyone on camera except for the bemused looking Shane doubled up with mirth, the camera wobbled and then the scene suddenly went blank for a second before there was another shot of the Concorde still waiting patiently on the tarmac. A voice off camera (actually that of the editor in the editing truck) apologised for the loss of transmission and assured the viewers that normal service would be resumed........an advert for tampons cut in.

Shane Parkhurst was never heard of again. He grew a beard whilst recovering from nervous exhaustion, reverted to his given name of Duane Smitherham and got a job as a trainee manager with Tesco's.

Chapter 26 - To Rio?

The excitement of the events in the terminal were soon forgotten by the Porthleven players, officials and their relatives as they settled into their seats on Concorde. None of them had ever flown in it before. Many of them had never flown in anything before. There were lots of nervous and excited eyes peering out of the tiny windows as the beautiful aircraft taxied away from the terminal building and made its way to the western end of the runway. The watching crowds were several deep at the perimeter fence, some waving, many wearing the black and gold of Porthleven.

Concorde stood a moment at the end of the runway and then with a deafening roar began her take off. Soon, she was a graceful shape in the eastern sky, showing her unique lines to the people at the airport as she turned right and climbed away. The sky was unusually clear for a Cornish January meaning that as the 'plane crossed the southern coast over Dodman Point, the passengers were treated to spectacular views of the Cornish countryside and coast. By prior arrangement, the flight path took Concorde round The Lizard and back up the coast for a flypast over Porthleven itself. Hundreds of villagers who had not made the trip up to Newquay to wave their team off lined the harbour front and cheered as Concorde gently waggled her wings as she flew on a more northerly course now, passing Hayle and St Ives before turning west around Zennor and taking the bearing for Rio.

Out over the Atlantic the pilot opened up and soon the speed indicator at the front of the passenger cabin showed Mach 2.

"Ladies and gentlemen," intoned the pilot over the intercom, "Welcome aboard Special flight BA701 to Rio de Janeiro. This is your pilot Captain Ed Latimer speaking. Your co-pilot for the trip is Captain Trevor Watson. Now that our little air display over Cornwall is over I can inform you that we are flying at sixty thousand feet and as you can see from the display in the passenger cabin we are flying at twice the speed of sound. We have surprisingly good weather with little or no prospect of any delay and should be arriving in Rio in approximately three and a half hours time, where the weather is fine and the temperature an hour ago was thirty degrees Centigrade, that's eighty six degrees in old money."

A ripple of gasps and happy laughter ran through the passengers. It had been a bracing thirty nine at Newquay, pleasantly mild for that time of year. Through many heads ran the thought that perhaps there should have been some sun blocker in their luggage after all.

"Please enjoy the flight. You will find the flight attendants amongst you fairly soon, serving your meal and they will help you if you need anything."

Once Concorde has lifted her nose and the pilot has got his foot down (or rather, pulled the throttles right back) there is very little to do. The windows are tiny and at more than eleven miles up there is not a lot to see, except for the amazing spectacle of the curved horizon, a bit of a let down for any member of the Flat Earth Society who happens to fly in Concorde, but a breathtaking sight for anyone else. The cabin is narrow, the seats in pairs either side of the aisle, and boredom can soon set in. However, for this particular load of passengers the excitement level was so high that they hadn't had time to get bored yet.

The flight attendants began to serve the meal. There wasn't the usual salmon. Someone at 'The Universe' had actually had a good idea and arranged to have smoked mackerel served as the starter.

"They like mackerel in Cornwall," he had said as he prepared to contact BA and arrange for it to be on the menu.

"Woss this?" asked a weather-beaten Arthur Faithful, father of Micky Faithful, near the back of the 'plane as the pretty young flight attendant put a plate of smoked mackerel on his fold-down table.

"Smoked mackerel, sir. I hope you like it."

"Where's it from?" The man looked a little stern.

"Er - fresh from Grimsby, sir, or so I'm told."

"Grimsby."

"Yes, sir."

"You know where we're from, don't you, flower?"

"Er - well, yes, sir. Cornwall."

" 'Es. Someone needs their arse kickin, my 'ansome. Fancy serving Grimsby fish to Cornishmen!"

"I'm sorry, sir. Would you like something else?"

"Only yer 'phone number, sweet'eart! Then Oi c'n invite 'ee down and treat 'ee to some *real* Cornish food. It'll do. You've got some Cornish beers on board, though, haven't 'ee? I'll 'ave one later, but right now I'll 'ave a glass of champagne. Well, you do on Concorde, don' 'ee?"

The flight attendant smiled at the man, who had looked a tough prospect when he asked about the mackerel but had turned out to be so good natured. "I'll bring it to you as soon as possible, sir." A few minutes later in Concorde's cramped little galley she remarked how pleasant the passengers were. "Aren't they lovely?" she said to her colleague. "I might have a holiday in Cornwall if they're all like this."

Children, dads, some mums and most of the players were taken in twos to the flight deck to stare at the tightly packed mass of dials and switches in front of the two pilots.

The front few seats were occupied by the party from 'The Universe' and Digital Sport One. The cameramen from both tended to get in the way as they photographed the players and there had to be some shuffling about so that the manager, chairman, captain and various others could be interviewed on tape for broadcasting as soon as the pictures could be beamed back to the UK where, naturally, the sporting public was captivated by the whole event. It all helped to prevent too many of the passengers from getting bored.

Except for Siggy Klein and Norris Leverhulme, slumped in seats 1A and 1D respectively, right at the front of the passenger cabin. Siggy was a technician with Digital Sport One and was distraught at having to be parted from the seventeen-year-old sixth-former from the exclusive Lady Ellen girls' public school (fifth in the national league tables for A-levels) with whom he frolicked most evenings. The fair Rachel, for that was her name, had a surprisingly sophisticated understanding of what made forty-two year old men like Siggy tick. Always reluctant to wear her uniform at school, she was more than happy to wear it when Siggy called.

With both parents heavily involved in the City and never home before eight in the evening, Rachel had plenty of time to entertain Siggy. She had a way of stripping whilst shagging him that never failed to get the best out of her lover. That he was a year older than her father mattered not a jot to Rachel. Being the father of her school's Head Girl, an easy to despise toady named Margaret who behaved just like everybody's worst idea of a power-hungry prefect, Siggy was a deliciously tempting proposition for Rachel to shag. They had met when Siggy was working with a Digital Sports One outside broadcast crew recording a lacrosse international at Lady Ellen School. There had been immediate chemistry between them and when Margaret swooped up and greeted "Daddy" before threatening to put Rachel in detention for talking with the TV crew (expressly forbidden by the Headmistress), Rachel set her mind on seduction.

It had been easy. She knew Siggy was divorced (Rachel sometimes felt deprived compared to her friends because her parents had been married for nineteen years). She crept back after Margaret had gone off to terrorise pupils elsewhere, slipped her address and 'phone number into his hand and said: "I fancy older men like you, I'm seventeen, not a virgin and my parents never get home before eight. Call me!"

Siggy called that afternoon at half past four and was shagging her by five. That he shagged her non-stop for over an hour was a complete turn on for Rachel who had never been continually serviced for more than a few minutes at a time (by much younger partners, it has to be said) and thus the affair began. Siggy missed her like hell and wouldn't be able to see her for a week. He decided to 'phone her.

Norris Leverhulme, across the aisle in seat 1D, was a reporter with 'The Universe'. He was also dismayed at the prospect of a whole week without a shag. His partner was one of the girls regularly featured in 'The Universe'. Chelsea Winner was her professional name, much more appropriate that her real name, Celia Postlethwaite. Sex with her was absolutely brilliant as far as Norris was concerned. She had a flawless skin, angelic face and a monumentally statuesque figure atop long, long legs. She didn't enjoy sex. She didn't dislike it, she just did it because that's what you do if blokes are going to take you out. Norris was nice looking and a newspaper photographer, so he got good money, could afford to take her to nice places and had many contacts in the glamour photography line so that she got lots of work. Norris was feeling horny and decided to 'phone her.

Deep in the electronic heart of the speeding Concorde, just a few feet from seats 1A and 1D, a small disturbance occurred as a salvo of rogue microwaves bombarded it. There were confused and conflicting transmissions from within Concorde to and from a satellite thousands of miles out in space which interfered with those from the navigation satellite communicating with Concorde's guidance system. Silicon chips hesitated and paused, stuttered and reprogrammed. The VOR location system stuttered briefly and lost the Rio beacon. It searched for it. It found a signal and locked on again. The autopilot received slightly different instructions now and responded accordingly.

In the cockpit, the pilot and co-pilot missed the slight flicker of the Automatic Pilot warning light and the Aircraft Deviation light. They were being captivated by the rare wonder in the expressions and voices of the succession of passengers who visited them. They were used to the braying arrogance of the people wealthy enough to fly Concorde regularly and the assumed knowledge about supersonic flight of those who scraped together enough for one of those £499 joy-rides. Here, though, was a 'planeload of genuinely pleasant and unassuming people from the Cornish fishing village they had flown over, all amazed at finding themselves on board at all and disarmingly polite, almost shy, towards the two supersonic pilots. They could be forgiven, therefore, for not noticing the almost totally indiscernible change of course made by the Concorde. The on-board computers were happy that they had everything under control. She now flew in a very, *very* gentle arc, anticlockwise, that took her further and further away from the bearing for Rio.

The two 'phone calls went on for over an hour, until one of Siggy's colleagues, Eddie Stevens, a camera man who had been videoing lots of interviews, returned to his seat at last.

"What the hell are you doing, Siggy? Don't you know you're not supposed to use mobile 'phones on a 'plane? And you!" He had seen Norris across the aisle. "For Christ's sake, hang up, both of you!"

Whether the explicit sexual content of both calls had any effect on the reactions of Concorde's electronic navigation system will never be known. All the pilots knew was that, at about the time they were due to contact air traffic control at Rio they were called up by Capetown asking them to identify themselves. The chaos on the flight deck can only be imagined. They were lucky to get clearance to land because there was the mother and father of anticyclones bearing down on the airport. It was a rocky landing in the increasing turbulence; routine flight simulator stuff for the pilot, just a bit bumpy. A tyre blew on the port undercarriage as they braked to a halt, still routine procedure for the flight deck, and there they were: the Porthleven football team were in Capetown with a fierce storm about to close down the airport. Wanderers were in Rio. It was a headache, and no mistake.

Chapter 27 - Stranded!

The Concorde passengers were escorted through the lashing rain into the terminal building. Although they had their warm clothing from when they had boarded at Newquay, they didn't have any waterproofs, though being Cornish they didn't worry about that. What this group *was* worrying about was the Captain's announcement as they made the approach to what they had expected to be Rio de Janeiro. Capetown? What was going on?

"Oi wuz once on a 'plane diverted to Birmingham instead o' Bristol," said Denzil Chegwidden to Vidal James sitting across the aisle from him. " 'Ow the 'ell are we goin' to get to Rio? They'll 'ave ter fly us over termorrer."

"Whaddidee mean, 'technical problem'?" asked Micky Faithful, his large frame uncomfortable in Concorde's confined spaces. " 'Ow can a technical problem make us 'ave ter land on another bloody continent?"

There were similar loudly articulated questions being asked up and down the cabin but of course, no-one had the answers.

Except right in the front row immediately facing the bulkhead between the passengers and the flight deck, where Siggy Klein's Digital One Sport colleague Eddie Stevens had a very good idea what had caused the problem.

"You complete fucking *moron*, Siggy! I thought *everyone* knew you don't use mobiles on aeroplanes!" he hissed under his breath, his fear of being overheard battling with his desire to wring Siggy's neck. He was thankful that the cabin noise in Concorde prevented those behind him from overhearing.

"It wasn't only me," whined Siggy. "*He* was using his 'phone as well!" He nodded in the direction of Norris Leverhulme, whose name he did not yet know, sitting in the window seat across the aisle. "And anyway, you don't *know* it was our 'phones."

"Of course it bloody was! We've ended up in bloody South Africa, for Christ's sake. Bloody Columbus navigated more accurately than that."

"I don't see why you have to bring a TV detective into it," moaned the disgruntled Siggy.

"TV detec.... that's bloody *Colombo*, you complete tosser. I'm talking about Christopher Columbus, the explorer who discovered America. Didn't you learn anything at school?"

Siggy felt insulted. "I'll have you know I won the Physics prize in...."

"I'll give you fucking Physics! Your Physics has landed us in South Africa, like three thousand bloody miles off course!" Eddie leant across the aisle to address Norris. "Oi! You!" he called in a stage whisper. Norris looked up. "D'you realise that your bloody 'phone call is probably the cause of this cock-up? Yours and this wanker's here?"

Since being told to hang up by Eddie, Norris had been kicking himself because when reminded, he did remember something about not using a mobile on an airliner - mobiles and laptop computers, he'd recalled. Still, nothing drastic had happened - the 'plane hadn't gone into a steep spiral or anything horrible like that so he hadn't given it another thought. Until the Captain's shattering announcement, that is, when he went cold with realisation.

"Do you think they'll find out?" he asked.

"I shouldn't wonder," said Eddie. "I mean, it's a pretty big cock-up, isn't it! Perhaps the black box will tell them something. Whatever it is, only us three know, so we'd better keep shtum about it. This lot," he indicated the rest of the passengers, "will crucify us if they find out. It's the biggest thing in their lives, this trip to Rio to play Wanderers. We'll just have to hope we can get there tomorrow."

But, of course, then came the rough landing through the approaching storm and the announcement by the Captain when they had taxied to the terminal that a tyre had burst and he would do what he could about getting a spare as soon as possible. It was when the party realised that theirs was the last 'plane to land before the airport was declared shut because of the storm that doubts began to creep into peoples' minds about getting to Rio for the game.

The doubts became certainties when a BA employee, hastily summoned to the scene to deal with the unexpected turn of events, addressed the Concorde passengers in the VIP lounge to which they had been ushered.

"Ladies and Gentlemen, I'm sorry to have to inform you that we cannot be certain when we will be able to arrange for you to fly on to Rio."

"Fly on! I like that," whispered the Porthleven Assistant Manager George Torrance to Alan Carey, the manager. "He makes it sound as if this is a planned stop-over!"

"Ssh!" hissed Alan. "Listen!"

"The pilots and our ground staff have tried to sort out what caused the technical problem that interfered with the 'plane's navigation system. Whatever it was, they need to be reset and tested. They can't be tested without a test flight, and this storm..." the BA man uncomfortably indicated the rapidly worsening conditions outside. "....makes any sort of flight out of this airport impossible for what looks like at least forty eight hours. We have arranged accommodation for you in the Capetown Hilton and in a short while there will be coaches to take you to your hotel. In the meantime, if you would collect your luggage in the normal way....if I can help anyone with any specific requests, I will."

"Excuse me! Norris Leverhulme, 'The Universe' newspaper in the UK."

"Oh." The BA man looked a little cautious. "I can't make any comment to the press at this stage."

"I just wondered what had caused the problem. Was it an electric storm, or solar flares? What sort of thing has caused this to happen before."

"I'm sorry, sir. Until our technical boys have analysed the read-outs from their test apparatus, no-one can be sure."

Alan Carey spoke up. "If you can't get us to Rio in the Concorde, can't you bring in another 'plane to get us there? If it had escaped your notice, we're due there on Monday to play an FA Cup match."

"Remember I said that this airport is likely to be closed for anything up to forty eight hours."

"We're fucked, boss," Said Micky Faithful standing at his manager's elbow.

Still addressing the chap from BA, Porthleven's manager went on. "We'll need free 'phoning facilities. There's a lot of 'phoning to be done."

"Of course, sir, I'll see to it immediately."

There wasn't anything else to be said. Norris had hoped to be told that the fault was definitely something other than his (and the other chap's) mobile 'phone. He'd have to wait, but at least he could file an exclusive to 'The Universe'. The match itself, a combination of the Wanderers' FA Cup opponents being flown out to Brazil and the dream situation of having a completely unknown non-league side having got as far as the fourth round at all, was the hottest sporting story since England's world cup win in 1966.

The 'phone lines were buzzing between Capetown and the UK. The Porthleven Secretary, Vidal James, called the FA to inform them that they were unlikely to get to Rio in time for the match. It was the worst 'phone call he'd ever had to make.

Chapter 28 - Decisions at Lancaster Gate

The magnificent Maracanã Stadium in Rio de Janeiro can hold 160,000 spectators, but for the majority of the FIFA World Club Championship games it had echoed with emptiness. In the clubhouse at Porthleven after the Fourth Round draw there had been a few good-natured drunken discussions about how their lads would react to playing in front of a crowd that size. Alcohol can convince people of a lot of things and some locals did briefly imagine that the stadium would be full for the Wanderers-Porthleven game.

In the event there wasn't going to be the chance to find out. The FA had contacted their Brazilian counterparts over the question of a venue and the latter seemed reluctant to sanction the use of a top class stadium for an English FA Cup game. They eventually suggested the ground of São Cristóvão, a minor league club in Rio, whose small stadium held no more than five thousand fans at the most, probably less since part of its terracing collapsed during one game some years ago.

An FA Official was quickly flown out to inspect it to make sure it met the requirements of the FA Cup and check that the playing surface was suitable. It was declared suitable by a decidedly myopic Official once it was understood that all signs in the ground should have English translations printed beneath them. The various omissions such as suitable toilets for female spectators and the unfortunate gap-toothed appearance of that collapsed terracing were overlooked and the match was scheduled for Monday 10th January, kick off 8.30 pm local time, 6.30 pm in the UK. That would allow Digital Sport One to cash in on what they imagined would be a terrific amount of interest in the fixture, and they advertised it as a pay-per-view event.

On the Saturday, São Cristóvão had a league game against the modestly named Portuguesa da Ilha do Governador, whose few fans were not noted for ever setting up much of a chant in support of their team, probably through lack of breath. The crowd of a few hundred were treated to a mind-numbing 0 - 0 draw and actually looked forward to this odd fixture that was going to take place on the Monday. Then came the news that the team flying out had somehow ended up in South Africa and that there was some doubt about whether they could make the fixture at all.

The consternation at Lancaster Gate was extreme when the news reached them that Porthleven were stranded in Capetown. A meeting of the FA's top brass was hurriedly called.

"We'll have to reschedule the game," said the Competitions Secretary.

"We can't," said the Treasurer. "We've already bent the rules just to please that Blankopf bloke."

"We didn't bend the rules at all," the Secretary disagreed. "A neutral venue was agreed by the Council. That's allowed in the rules."

"Well, yes, but we had to be a bit flexible about some of the ground facilities," persisted the Treasurer. "What was it about concrete, paving slabs or other suitable material being available around the pitch for spectators? We decided that sun-baked earth was 'suitable' just because it is as hard as concrete. And one chemical toilet in a tent is to be the women's toilet facility, isn't it?"

"All that is irrelevant," interrupted the Chairman. "It isn't Porthleven's fault. If a team was held up due to unforeseen weather conditions or something, we'd allow an extension to the deadline."

"Yes, but this is quite different," the Competitions Secretary exclaimed. "We've got Wanderers out in Rio, looking set to win the World Club tournament, this Cornish team in bloody South Africa, grounded by a burst tyre and a hurricane; and the Fifth Round due to be played on the twenty-ninth. If we allow both teams time to get back home, it'll be pushing things too far if there has to be a replay."

"A replay? Are you serious?" The Press Liaison Officer laughed. "Like, Porthleven are going to hold Wanderers to a draw. Come on!"

"I know, I know, but we have to allow for a replay. We can't schedule our games on the basis of predicting the results in advance. Think of the precedent it would set."

"You're right," sighed the Chairman. "Well, you're both right, actually. Porthleven aren't going to earn a replay, but we have to make a decision on the basis of not predicting the result. As I see it, we can't do anything about the situation without extending the deadline."

"Yer could simply stage a walk-over," suggested Mavis Grubb, the tea lady who just happened to have wheeled her trolley into the meeting.

"What? Oh, thank you, Mavis," said the Chairman, taking the proffered cup. "And I'll have one of those jam doughnuts, please. What did you say?"

"Wanderers could 'ave a walk-over, like that Scotland game in Estonia the uvver year."

"Oh. Right. Well, yes, they could, couldn't they. Thank you, Mavis. That is an option we haven't - er - discussed yet."

"Well, Wanderers will murder that li'l Cornish side, won't they. This way, they still go aht the Cup but wiv their pride intact." Mavis busied herself around the meeting table, shifting agenda papers aside to make way for the cups of tea she was putting down, like a mother organising her sons. The Competitions Secretary had taken two doughnuts and a flapjack.

"Now that's naughty," scolded Mavis, taking a doughnut back. "Fink of yer blood pressure. All Wanderers 'ave ter do is kick orf, score a goal, there's no-one ter kick orf fer the uvver side so the ref abandons the game. Nah, accordin' to yer rules, an abandoned game 'as ter be replayed on the same grahnd two Wednesday's later. Wan' a top-up, luv?"

The Chairman's cup was empty and Mavis, in full flow, still didn't miss such things. A Queen amongst tea-ladies, was Mavis. She refilled the Chairman's cup.

"Well, yer can't do that, can yer," she went on as she poured. "An' there ain't time ter get it played out in Rio even when that Cornish side *can* get over 'ere. So, look at Rule 12(g). That says yer can do what yer like, reely. So, Wanderers kick orf, score a goal and yer declare it a one-nil win fer Wanderers. All above board an' accordin' ter the rules, see. Yer could prob'bly get

Wanderers ter go dahn and play a friendly against that Cornish side at the end o' the season ter make up fer their disappointment at not playin' against all them stars. They'd make some money on the gate, too. Lovely place, Cornwall. Me and my Reg went to Newquay once. Smashin' place. Jus' fink. If Wanderers play a friendly dahn there, under instructions from the FA, like, yer could go wiv 'em. Yer'd like it, you mark my words. Ooh, me veins! I mus' get me weight orf me feet. I'll come back fer the cups later. Tar-ar!"

She waddled out behind her rattling trolley. The assembled might of the Football Association looked at one another in silence for a few seconds.

"That's it, really, Gentlemen, isn't it?" said the Chairman eventually. He had been surreptitiously peeping into his copy of the FA's Competitions Rule Book to check Rule 12(g). Mavis had been right. She usually was. "I think that's an excellent idea! A walk-over and a friendly at the end of the season to make up for it. I think on balance the Porthleven people will be happy with that."

"We'll have to get the Council to back the decision," warned the Treasurer. "How do we do that in time?"

"Get 'phoning," smiled the Chairman. "We'll get them to agree by 'phone and ratify it at the next Council meeting!"

Which is what they did, with most Council members seeing the sense of the idea. The Cornwall FA Member wasn't too happy until he got a reassurance from the Chairman that Wanderers would be instructed to play an end-of-season friendly at Porthleven. "Okay, boy," he agreed. "Proper job!"

The decision was conveyed to both teams, separated as they were by the Atlantic Ocean. Contacting Wanderers at their hotel in Rio was straightforward. Getting hold of Porthleven was a bit harder. No-one knew quite where they were. In the end, as a long shot, the Competitions Secretary rang the Porthleven Clubhouse number. A bored-sounding barman (who *was* bored - just about everyone with the slightest interest in the football club had gone on either Concorde or the special Jumbo Jet) gave him a mobile number belonging to Vidal James, the Secretary. This proved to be successful and Vidal listened with interest to what the Competitions Secretary had to say.

Ronnie and Joker in Rio couldn't have been happier, really. They'd already got two good wins under their belt against Necaxa and Vasco da Gama and the match against Porthleven would have been an unwelcome intrusion, carrying the risk of an unwelcome injury or two.

The Brazilian FA was almost beside itself with anticipation that it could be a really top notch English team that would get drawn to play against Wanderers. Manchester United would have been the favourite, at least in Rio, but they were already out of the FA Cup, knocked out by Wimbledon in the Third Round. What about if it was West Ham, the club of that most honoured of English players in Brazil, Bobby Moore? Except they'd been knocked out already as well, as had that team with the funny sounding name that Juninho played for.

Ronnie and Joker would have shrugged their shoulders and got on with it if the opposition had been of that kind. But a totally unknown minor non-league side? It was almost an insult. If it had happened at any other time - say, in the third round - then the little team from Cornwall would have played at the New

Stamford Stadium in front of an all-ticket 65,000 capacity crowd, lost ten-nil and gone home with more money than they knew what to do with.

But Ronnie and Joker wanted to win this FIFA World Club Championship now they were there, and playing even a weakened side against Porthleven laid themselves open to the possibility of injury to some of their key players, so it wasn't worth it. Hence their delight at the FA's decision.

When Sir Fabian got the news, though, he was not happy at all.

"Whaddya mean, the game may not be on? We've got millions riding on this, in TV rights and pay per view income." Waddilove had not relished calling Sir Fabian on his mobile number (you never knew where he was or what time zone he was in) to break the news. He tended to shoot the messenger.

"I'm just passing on the message, F.B. It seems some technical problem ballsed-up the Concorde's satellite navigation system or something, and now a hurricane has closed Capetown down."

"Hurricanes don't happen in Capetown," snorted Sir Fabian with the tone of a man not to be contradicted. Which, of course, as far as he was concerned, was what he was. And as far as just about everyone who worked for him was concerned, too.

And he should know, thought Waddilove.

"Where are you now, Sir Fabian?" he asked. "Have you got a TV handy?"

Sir Fabian had. He was actually at his Wimbledon home.

"If you turn your TV on now to Digital Sport One you'll see for yourself, F.B." said Waddilove. He was watching it at that moment on the TV in his office.

Sir Fabian grabbed for the remote control and switched channels. " 'Ere, wot did yer do that for?" squealed the naked Sharon, lying tummy-down on her bed watching a repeat of "Goodnight Sweetheart".

"Shuttup, Shaz. Something's happened to the 'plane we flew out to Rio."

"Oh, God, it 'asn't crashed, 'as it?" Sharon looked genuinely upset as she lifted herself up on one arm, half-turning to face Sir Fabian so that he was treated to a glimpse of one of her exceptionally beautiful silicone-implanted breasts.

"No, no, nothing like that. The bloody thing has landed in Capetown."

"Oh. So?" Sharon's knowledge of Geography was limited to the topography of men's bodies and the Circle and District line stations around Knightsbridge and South Kensington.

"It's in bloody South Africa, not Brazil!"

"Oh?" Sharon was none the wiser.

"Listen!"

On the TV screen, Digital Sport One's reporter Harry Edwards was talking to camera. He was inside the Capetown airport terminal and behind him there was a window showing a black sky outside and rain running in a torrent down the glass.

".......are being transferred to local hotels at the airline's expense. But the real tragedy beneath all this can be summed up by what you can see behind me." Harry turned dramatically and the camera panned to one side of him and zoomed in on the weather outside. "This airport is shut, possibly for as long as two days, because of the effects of Hurricane Sharon, by which time it would be too late to get this brave little team to Rio in time for their once-in-a-lifetime match against the mighty Wanderers United."

"Ooooh, Blanky! They've named an 'urricane after me. Did *you* do that?" Hearing the hurricane named on one of Sir Fabian's TV channels made her suspect that it was all down to him, the soft old darling! He might have difficulty keeping it up, but he did know how to romance a girl. Fancy having a hurricane named after you! If she could only see the look on the face of Mr Clutterbuck, her old Geography teacher.

"Shuttup, Shaz!"

Isn't that sweet? Now he's all embarrassed, he's trying to cover up by pretending to be all severe. She turned completely on one side now, favouring him with a full frontal. Might as well let him see what he was paying for.

".......but one rumour doing the rounds is that someone used a mobile 'phone whilst on the flight, which upset the satellite navigation system on board. It has to be said that only people who regularly fly could be expected to know that mobile 'phones should not be used in an aircraft in flight, but of course many of the passengers on *this* flight were not what you could call seasoned travellers."

The muffled retort of "Bollocks!" could just be heard off-screen at this point. Denzil Chegwidden, the Porthleven groundsman and seasoned trans-Atlantic traveller, was outraged when he heard that.

Harry went on. "That *is* only a rumour, I have to emphasise," he said, with just the merest of glances in the direction of Denzil's comment from behind the camera, which he was sure must have been heard on air. "There could be other explanations, such as a magnetic storm that the Concorde may have flown over, or an electromagnetic disturbance in the atmosphere caused by the solar wind or unusual sun-spot activity. Whatever the cause, the team are stranded here in Capetown and we can only hope that the FA Cup fourth round tie between Wanderers and Porthleven can take place perhaps after both teams return to England."

"Harry - Harry - er - what are the chances of that happening, seeing as how the only way the FA would allow Wanderers to play in the FA Cup *and* the FIFA World Club Championship was if this tie was played this week, meaning that only the timely and generous intervention of 'The Universe'..." - owned by the same man as his TV channel, so earning the Digital Sports One Chief Sports Presenter Dennis Robbins, back in the studio in Milton Keynes, Brownie points for the free plug - "...made the tie, and Wanderers defence of the cup they won last year as part of their treble, possible?"

There was the slightest of delays as the question sped via satellite to the ears of Harry Edwards in Capetown, lengthened as he interpreted Dennis's long and convoluted question.

"Well, you do have to ask yourself that question," replied Harry. How the hell do *I* know, he thought. Those tossers at the FA will probably say that Wanderers must go through on a walk-over. "It is hard to say. It would only seem just for the game to be rescheduled until the two teams can at least find themselves on the same continent - by which, of course, I mean when they are back in England next week. It's the only fair and logical solution really."

Sir Fabian grumbled and cursed for a while. The FA Cup game in Rio was to have been one of his special moments. He had intended to milk the fixture as much as possible. Only his intervention, using his tacky tabloid 'The Universe' to foot the bill for the Concorde and two Jumbo Jets full of supporters, had made it possible. He personally had conveyed the offer to the FA so that not only could Wanderers play in FIFA's World Club Championship and help England's case for staging the 2006 World Cup, but they could also defend the FA Cup. It would have given him some brilliant publicity in support of his attempts to gain British citizenship. Now it had all blown up in his face. How the fuck could a bloody Concorde en route to Rio end up in Cape Town? No point wasting time wondering: it had happened. He supposed that Wanderers' opponents would just forfeit the game, so the opportunity had been snatched from his grasp.

"Damn!"

"Never mind, Blanky. Just fink of that team, flyin' aht ter play a game an' endin' up in the wrong place. They'll miss their game of football nah, won't they! They won't know what ter do wiv themselves."

"I was going to get a lot out of this game, Shaz. All that organisation, getting the match on, arranging the flights and everything, all that's wasted." Not that he had actually done any of the donkey work. True, he had been to speak to the Minister for Sport and had made one or two personal 'phone calls to FIFA and the FA - calls set up for him by his staff, of course; but the real work had naturally been delegated.

"Well, p'raps someone'll give 'em a game wherever they are now," suggested Sharon, stretching for the remote to put "goodnight Sweetheart" back on.

"Who cares what they bloody do with themselves?" fumed Sir Fabian. "I don't care if they kick a ball around in the arrivals lounge....."

Suddenly his face brightened. "Shaz? Your a bloody genius again!" He went over to the bed where Sharon was still innocently displaying her surgically-enhanced charms for him to admire, which he now began to. Sitting by her and laying a fond hand on her tantalisingly curved hip, he said those three words a girl loves to hear.

"Where's me Viagra?"

Whilst it had time to work, he got busy on the 'phone. He spoke at length with the editor of the 'South African Universe', owned coincidentally by Digital International.

At Lancaster Gate, of course, and unbeknown to Digital Sport One's Harry Edwards, the decision had already been made. The FA Competitions Secretary had spoken to Arnie Robinson of Wanderers and Vidal James of Porthleven. Arnie passed the news on to Ronnie in Rio. Vidal passed the news on to the rest of the Porthleven party in the bar of the Hilton where BA had put them up until the storm over Capetown blew itself out and a replacement tyre could be flown out and fitted.

"Bummer," said Gary Penhaligon, the 'keeper, summing up everyone's feelings.

"You'd think they'd postpone it 'till next week," moaned Micky Faithful.

"Can't do anything about it," said manager Alan Carey. "They *might* do what the bloke from the FA said, and come and play us at Gala Park at the end of the season. That'd be something."

"Yea," said midfielder and captain John Burrows. "Look on the bright side. We're going to lose one-nil. That'll look great in the record books in years to come. 'Wanderers United 1, Porthleven nil,' " he said in his best James Alexander Gordon voice. "Ooh, close one! Better than - well - whatever the bloody score might have been!"

A bell boy approached the table where Alan was sitting. "Excuse me, sir. Are you the manager of the football team?"

"Yes, son, what can I do for you?" Alan smiled at the young coloured boy in his smart uniform.

"Two things, sir, May I have all your autographs, please? And there's some reporters here to see you. Shall I show them in?"

"Yes, okay." He turned to those around him. "I suppose we ought to face the fact that we're going to get quite a bit of attention due to this cock-up! We'll keep them waiting a bit, though, while we give you your autographs."

The overwhelmed bell-boy coyly produced a new-looking autograph book and pen from his pocket. Alan took it round and made sure the entire squad signed it. He signed it last and handed it back to the bell-boy.

"There you go, son! You're very welcome. Now, where's those press boys?"

The bell boy, beaming, went out and returned with two rather seedy looking men. Obviously reporters.

"The reporters, sir," announced the bell boy. "Thank you very much, sir." He looked at the ten pound note in his hand, his tip from Alan, and wondered how much it was worth. He was well pleased when he went into the hotel's bank to change it.

"We're from the 'Universe'," said the less seedy reporter. "We've got a proposition for you."

"Oh? What sort of proposition?" The Porthleven manager was suspicious. Obviously these two characters were just after a story of some kind.

"We know about you," went on the more seedy-looking reporter. "You're the no-hope side supposed to be in Rio to play Wanderers United in some cup competition, yea, and you're stranded here because of some balls-up and the storm, right?"

"That's about it, though we'd prefer 'non-league' to 'no hope'," replied Alan.

"Well, you ain't going to leave here in a hurry, are you, but here you are, expecting a game of football. Well, we can arrange one for you tomorrow, against a local side from a black township. Play a friendly against them, make a lot of friends, nice bit of publicity, how about it?"

Some of the players within earshot were perking up and showing some interest.

"Sounds like a good idea," said left wing-back Nigel Thwaites.

"Better than kicking our heels round here feeling sorry for ourselves," agreed Micky Faithful, the sweeper.

"I say let's do it," said Justin Harrington, right wing-back.

"Me too," centre-back Stevie Jewell chipped in.

"We'd have to clear it with our FA," cautioned Secretary Vidal James, "but as long as they say it's okay, then we can."

"What d'you think, boys?" said Alan, loud enough for all the team to hear. There wasn't one dissenting voice.

"Well, lads, there's your answer. We'll have to leave it to you to organise it all. Just let us know when you're going to pick us up and provide enough transport for all of us - eighty or so plus the media boys. Three coaches? I presume your paper's paying for all this?"

"That's all taken care of. You get clearance from your FA and we'll do the rest."

Surprisingly, it only took a 'phone call to get clearance from the FA. Somebody there must have felt that a goodwill friendly played by the hapless non-league side would salvage something from the débâcle they found themselves overseeing.

Probably because of the enormous amount of world-wide publicity surrounding Porthleven, Sir Fabian's Editor of the 'South African Universe' was able to fix a game up in no time at all in Capetown's Newlands Stadium, used for rugby and soccer, and such was the interest that a crowd of over 25,000 turned up to watch the game with Nelson Mandela and Archbishop Desmond Tutu as the guests of honour. Their opponents were a youth team from Capetown Province and the game ended a good-natured three-all and raised hatfuls of cash for the township kids. Back in the UK, Sir Fabian's tabloid "The Universe" blasted the story of Porthleven's predicament and their hastily arranged charity match across most of its pages.

"Porth in a Storm!" screamed its front page, with library photos of Table Mountain, Concorde, Nelson Mandela and Arch Bishop Desmond Tutu scattered around. "Porthleven, the footballing minnows from Cornwall who have bravely battled against all the odds to reach the FA Cup Fourth Round for a dream tie against football's mightiest club side were powerless against the forces of nature that stranded them in Capetown. Yet the gallant English boys...." (there was some reaction to that line in Cornwall) ".....bounced back with a hastily-arranged charity match against local Township boys - thanks to our sister paper in Capetown, "The South African Universe" - in front of a huge crowd which included former President Mandela and Arch Bishop Tutu. Story in full on page 2. See also pages 4, 5, 6, 8, 10, 12, 13, 14, 18, 19 and 20."

Such is the British sporting public's interest in both the unusual and the underdog, not to mention an unusual underdog, that "The Universe's" circulation soared that day.

And at least Radio Cornwall's Tommy Matthews had a game to report on.

Chapter 29 - The Walk Over

The groundsman at the flyblown little ground of São Cristóvão was not exactly a recognisable counterpart to Porthleven's Denzil Chegwidden. Stumbling slowly across the threadbare pitch, he burped up gas from his lunchtime intake of cheap beer and surveyed the playing surface. Bald but smooth. Much like his head. He peered at the ground beneath his feet. Or as close to his feet as his huge beer gut, with its stained, holey vest stretched over it, allowed. Like a billiard table! Well, better than the billiard table at the tatty little bar where he did most of the development work on his beer gut. There wasn't much for a groundsman to do on a minor league ground in Rio. Without the wherewithal to pay for regular watering such as the major clubs could, the sparse growth of grass that grew in the closed season was soon worn away by the players' feet in the earlier games. Once the surface was rolled flat when the ground was slightly softened by closed season rains, it remained flat and hardened like concrete. The main problem for Alfonso Alvarez, for that was the fat man's name, was keeping the white lines visible.

A small hot breeze eddied across the ground and raised a little cloud of dust from the dry surface. With each such breeze a little of the dry lime on the white lines blew away. Alfonso sighed and changed the direction of his slow stumbling, making for his hut next to the tumbledown grandstand.

Sitting on the bottom step of the little terrace next to the end of the stand was a small boy. Mario Marino was twelve years old but looked younger. Undernourished from birth and brought up in the shanty towns outside Rio, he longed to play for São Cristóvão when he was old enough, just as Ronaldo, hero of all boys his age and much older, had done. It wasn't São Cristóvão's only claim to fame. In 1926 they had won the Rio State Championship and in the 1960's had been mentioned in the same breath as the England team by no less a man than Garrincha (what he actually said was "England - that team who play in white shirts just like São Cristóvão."). Now they languished in Rio's second division.

Mario had only heard about the days when the emerging genius of the boy Ronaldo had been preserved by only allowing him to wear the number 11 shirt in the second team. This was to protect him from the rough and tumble of the first team games. Mario wanted to be like Ronaldo. São Cristóvão have no "replica shirts" on sale and even if they had, little Mario wouldn't have been able to afford one. He made do with a non-descript white T-shirt on the back of which he had used a battered ball-point pen to clumsily inscribe "Ronaldo" above the number "11". He wore it as he played football with the men on the open spaces in his shanty town and on nearby beaches - all barefoot football with threadbare footballs on impossible surfaces. Mario was allowed to play with the men because, quite simply, he was good enough. With no school to go to, he spent a lot of his time helping Alfonso around the São Cristóvão ground. Sometimes Alfonso paid him a few centavos. He was carefully saving all the money he could scrounge. He wanted to buy some football boots. Perhaps even some football socks.

"Hi, Alfonso," he greeted the big man. "What are you doing today?"

"Hey, Mario! I'm doing the lines again, as usual." Not much help needed there, of course. What could he find for Mario to do today that would justify a few centavos? Of course!

"And because of this special game we're having here tomorrow, the goal posts and cross bars will need to be painted. I'll fetch you the paint and brush."

He went into his battered clapboard groundsman's hut, which young Mario always admired because it was much bigger and more sturdy than anything he had ever lived in, and soon the stuttering rattle of the engine of his little groundsman's tractor could be heard. Out he came, riding side saddle on the metal seat, keeping an eye on the trailer groaning along behind, one of its two wheels very much in need of a puff of air in its tyre.

"Jump on, Mario," invited Alfonso, and the two of them rode in tatty splendour across to one of the goals. Alfonso unloaded a paint-splattered wooden step ladder, a paint tin and brush. "There you are, you know what to do," he said and Mario jumped off the truck and began to manoeuvre the ladder into place. Alfonso also dismounted and shambled back to the hut to fetch the lining machine.

Special match! Ha! Why pick this ground? Why not the Maracanã stadium where the famous Wanderers were playing all their World Club Championship matches? It didn't make any sense to him, but he was getting a bit of a bonus for having to get the ground ready so why should he worry? He had been instructed to tidy up the back row of seats in the grand stand and rope it off from the rest so that the "world's press", he had been told, could sit there. He had already removed the seats from the next row down, again as per instructions. This was to give the "world's press" an uninterrupted view of the game, which as far as Alfonso had heard was not even likely to take place. He also had to make sure that the gap left by the collapse of some terracing years ago was really securely fenced off.

He pottered along behind the marking machine, his slow gait suited to the job of making sure there was plenty of white on the lines. Alfonso may not have looked the part but it had to be said that his touchlines were just as ruler straight as Denzil Chegwidden's. When Mario had tried his hand he realised just how hard it was to create a straight line. Alfonso had finished by the time Mario was through painting one goal. He put the lining machine back into the hut and then went to inspect Mario's work.

"That's looking good, Mario. You've done a good job." He could touch in the bits the lad had missed later. "You going to do the other one for me?"

"Yes, please!"

They loaded the ladder and paint onto the trailer and headed off to the other end. Alfonso let Mario drive. Unfortunately, neither paid much attention to the trailer and just as they were slowing down in front of the other goal there was suddenly a jarring accompanied by the sound of rending wood.

"Stop, stop!" shouted Alfonso, turning round towards the sound. A spade had slid off the trailer and got jammed between the truck and trailer, digging into the baked soil, the wooden handle breaking under the strain.

Cursing as he got off the truck, Alfonso was quick to reassure Mario. "Not your fault, Mario. I should have been watching it. I can fix it." He wrenched the shattered spade free of the truck and trailer and surveyed the damage. "Well, perhaps not! You can move the truck now, Mario."

When Mario parked the truck next to the unpainted goal he came back and looked at the gouged pitch. "Oh no! What will we do?"

"No problem. We'll just scrape it level and fill it in. Don't worry. No-one will know it happened."

With the help of another spade, Alfonso did the job, but had quite a bit of dry, dusty soil left over.

"Why is that?" asked Mario?

"Well, you can never get the soil back into the hole you dig it out of," explained Alfonso. He scooped up the surplus soil and threw it behind the goal. "You get on with the painting. I've a few things to get on with." He wandered off and left Mario to it.

Eventually, Mario finished his painting and put everything back onto the trailer. He looked around to see if he could see any sign of the damaged pitch.

He couldn't help thinking what a clever bloke Alfonso was. He had to search quite hard to find the place where the repair had been made. He bent down and felt the ground. Where the gouge had been was just a patch of ground that was soft to the touch, where the replaced soil was not as hard as the sun-baked stuff around it. Mario pushed his fingers into the soft dirt to probe the extent of the damage, then used his palm to smooth it over again. Good as new, he thought. What a clever man!

* * * * * * * * *

The fixture had attracted huge interest right from the start. First of all, Wanderers' defence of the FA Cup had been assured right at the start of the season when 'The Universe' stepped in with its offer to fly their opponents out to Rio to fulfil their fourth round commitment. Then there was the fascinating progress of tiny Porthleven to the first round proper, then the second, then the third fuelling speculation about what would happen if they reached the fourth round: could *they* be the Wanderers' opponents? Then came the drama of the fourth round draw:

"Number twenty-nine....."

"Wanderers United...."

"Number twenty-one!"

"Will play Porthleven!"

The tabloids had gone crazy at that point, of course. First of all finding Porthleven, then sending teams of reporters down to find the manager, coach and players, photographing them at home, at work, at training, during matches: they could not move for the press. The village pubs didn't object, of course. Trade was well up on normal December and January figures. Even the broadsheets gave up large amounts of space in their Sports sections to publicise the tiny Cornish village side, although their photographs were much more aesthetically pleasing and their grammar was much better than in the tabloids.

After the media scramble at Newquay's tiny airport, the arrival of the Concorde in Capetown, thus stranding the team thousands of miles from the venue, whipped the topic up to the screaming front page headline stage, and the FA's decision to stage the fixture even though Porthleven weren't going to be there had sports editors the world over apoplectic with delight. In England, even the World Cup victory in 1966 hadn't been as big a story.

"F.A. Spoil Giantkillers' Biggest Day!" - Daily Mail.

"FA Cup Match in Brazil Off!" - Daily Express.

"Nuts In Brazil! - FA Decide on Walkover Farce!" - Daily Mirror.

"Walkover Farce Decision by FA Nuts!" - Daily Star.

"Minnows to be Walked Over in FA Cup Farce!" - The Sun.

"Nuts to the Pasty Boys as FA do FA about Cup"! - Daily Sport.

"Silver Lining for Porthleven - They'll Only Lose 1 - 0!" - The Universe.

"Cup Decision Outrage Denies Minnows Their Big Day!" - The Globe.

Consequently, the world's press turned up in their hundreds for the walk-over, occupying far more than just the back row of the modest São Cristóvão grandstand. Then there were the several hundred fans flown in on the two Jumbo jets, one flying out of Birmingham with the three hundred and fifty lucky Wanderers fans on board, the other out of Newquay with the Cornish contingent.

All the passengers were winners in The Universe's special draw.

"Win a Free Trip to Rio to Support Your Team!" ran the special page a few weeks earlier. "Just collect twenty tokens, stick them on the special card (look in tomorrow's edition), fill in your name and address and state which team you support - Wanderers United or Porthleven. Then post it off......." - the usual format for a tabloid's special competition. Not surprisingly, far more entries came in from Wanderers fans. An alert sub-editor noted how many of the applications from "Porthleven" supporters came from anywhere but Cornwall.

"There are a lot of Cornishmen around the country - around the world, even," said one knowledgeable colleague.

"Yes, but I reckon some Wanderers fans are trying it on, don't you?"

"Probably," agreed the knowledgeable colleague. "We'll have to examine the Porthleven entries carefully."

They put all those with Porthleven addresses in one pile. There were just over three hundred, some from the same address as obviously husbands and wives, fathers and sons - and daughters - had all bought extra copies of The Universe in the hope of getting a place on the 'plane.

"I reckon we should give all them a place," said the sub-editor.

"So do I," smiled his knowledgeable colleague. "Dig out all the others with Cornish addresses and pull 'em out of the hat for the remaining places."

Which is what they did. It resulted in a 'plane full of a happy band of supporters taking off from Newquay just a few hours behind the team's Concorde. There was a friendly family atmosphere, what with almost everyone on board knowing everyone else. A few Cornish songs were sung and there was even a light-hearted chorus of "We're on our way to Wembley!" which petered out into good-natured laughter.

The Wanderers' 'plane was filled by drawing out the winners from the thousands of entries. There was an entirely different atmosphere, with many passengers over-imbibing at the airport and on board.

"It's worse than an Alicante charter-flight," gasped a harassed flight attendant between dashes up the aisle loaded with the next order for drinks. "Bloody football fans!"

Naturally, there was consternation amongst both sets of fans when news of Porthleven's plight reached them, especially amongst their supporters. However, as they'd been flown out specially, virtually all of the two sets of supporters went to the ground, knowing that they were going to witness a piece of football history and years later would be able to say "I was there!". The tatty little ground was packed, because there were quite a few Wanderers fans out in Rio for the FIFA competition, as well as a lot of locals, who turned up for the same reason.

In the cramped home dressing room, some broken clothes hooks hurriedly replaced by Alfonso, plus some extra ones so that there were enough for all the team and substitutes to have one each, Ronnie addressed the team.

"Ah dinnae know what tae say, lads," he began. "Ah think that all o' ye should ge' a touch o' the ball before ye score. Then we all get changed again an' gae back tae the hotel!"

The tiny dressing room could barely accommodate fourteen players, and then only if they didn't all try to get changed at the same time. A Premiership side has sixteen players, the manager, assistant manager, coach, goalkeeper's coach, physiotherapist, doctor, kit man and boot man, plus members of the squad injured or just not picked who are there anyway as part of the build-up. Wanderers also still needed several interpreters, so the conditions in the dressing room were rather like a Northern Line carriage in the rush hour. There was certainly no room for Papa Médecin's black candles, silver crucible and chicken's blood.

The interpreters babbled their version of Ronnie's few words as arms and legs struggled to divest themselves of clothing and pull on kit. There were various cries of pain or indignity as elbows accidentally dug into ribs, stomachs, noses, eyes and bollocks.

"Fuckin' 'ell, boss!" complained Macca. "There's not enough room to swing a mouse in 'ere! We've 'ad injuries in training and even kicking in, but never in the bloody changing room! Can't yer no' get rid of someone?"

"Yeah, ye're right, Macca. Look, lads, jus' the eleven Ah've named plus me an' Joker stay in here. Everyone else, vamoose! Scram!"

The interpreters interpreted but made no effort to leave with the rest of the squad and non-playing staff.

"Come on, folks, piss off! The sooner we get this farce over and done with, the sooner we can get on with our preparations for the South Melbourne game." Joker added his contribution to the proceedings. The interpreters again interpreted and stayed put. Joker tried again.

"Ellie, love. Why aren't you people leaving?"

Jesus Bastardi and Antonio Genitile had both been enjoying the close physical proximity they were forced into with the petite, elegant young interpreter from Cunning Linguists

"How else will our boys know what is going on?" she fluttered in reply. The interpreters tended to regard the player or players they translated for as their own.

"Okay! Listen up," said Ronnie through gritted teeth. "Translate this next bit and then get the fuck oot! We kick off, we pass th' ball tae ev'ry player so ye all ge' a touch, then we pass it aroond goin' upfield, makin' sure we pass *backwards* all the time - no fuckin' offsides, ye ken - and....Sum Wun will score. Then the game is abandoned and we all come back in here, get changed and go back to the hotel. Right? Then explain that all ye interpreters have got tae leave 'cos there isn'ae room fer ye all, an' ye'll see 'em afterwards. Then fuck off out. Please!"

The babble of voices grew, and there was clearly some dissent.

"Pliss! Lim Po, he wan' know, why capitalist running dog score goal?"

"Oui, Kwasi, 'ee ask why you not choose him to score?"

"Tak! Georgi vant to know same sing!"

"Oh, for Christ's sake!" sighed Ronnie. He screwed his eyes shut and shook his head as if to shut out the problem.

"I' be sure, boss," said Seamus O'Hooligan. "Write our names down on slips of paper and pull a name out o' the hat!"

Opening his eyes again, Ronnie let out another sigh. "Thanks, Seamus. Translate!"

The suggestion met with grudging approval. Paper was sought, names were scribbled and the São Cristóvào trainer's bucket, found underneath one of the benches along the walls, was brought out to act as the "hat". The slips of paper were dropped in, Ronnie shook it in exaggerated fashion and then held it up for Joker to pick a name out.

"Macca!" he announced, and a ripple of mock cheers passed through the room.

"Fust raffle Ah've won in years, man!" said Macca and, dignity satisfied all round, the players carried on changing as best they could.

"*Now*, interpreters, will ye *please* leave?" asked Ronnie. The room became less crowded and there was less chance of an injury as the players finished changing.

The referee blew his whistle to summons the teams - well, *team* - out onto the pitch - no dressing room buzzers at São Cristóvào - and the team stood ready to file out.

"Let's get this farce over, then," said Ronnie, and he led them out.

A loud roar greeted the Wanderers team as it filed out into the sunshine. Mainly it was cheers from their fans and from the interested neutral locals, but there was some booing, albeit good natured, from the black and gold bedecked Porthleven contingent.

The team lined up for a photograph and then went and kicked in as if they were to play a normal game. Jesus Bastardi went to the centre circle when the referee blew.

"Hey, Jesus," called Macca. "What happens if you lose the toss?"

It had been decided in advance at FA Headquarters that no toss of the coin would be necessary. Wanderers could kick whichever way they wanted. The famous figure of the schoolmaster referee solemnly greeted Jesus.

"Which end do you want to score in?" he asked.

Jesus had not liked the booing of the Porthleven fans. It wasn't in the Latin temperament to understand the good natured demeanour of the Cornish, despite the influx of Mediterranean genes into the Cornish gene pool when Spanish crews invaded Mousehole and its immediate surroundings in the sixteenth century. He'd show them for booing the Wanderers!

Nodding towards the end of the ground with the black and gold in greatest profusion, he said, "We kicka *that* way!"

As his team had headed towards the other end for the kick in, no change of ends was necessary and so the team just shaped up for their kick-off.

The referee counted the players, signalled both linesmen, or rather "assistant referees" - checked his watch and blew for the kick off.

In the dug out, Ronnie turned to Joker. "Ah've got a bad feelin' Joker. Ah didn'ae impress on them how important it is not tae foul up. We cannae let the ball go oot fer a throw in, eh?" He laughed mirthlessly.

"No worries, boss," replied Joker. "I think the whole thing is a bit of a laugh, really! A nice bit of relaxation in the middle of a hectic week. This could have been a full game, with the chance of injuries, and it *could* have been against Arsenal or Chelsea. Just relax and enjoy it!"

Sum Wun had kicked off, rolling the ball to Georgi Strupinski (he certainly wouldn't pass it to Lim Po!) who laid it back to Enrique Mouette. Enrique pushed it back to Kwasi Ankoma who then set a cross-field move in motion, passing square to Antonio Genitile. By now, the crowd, in festival mood, was cheering every pass, the cheering getting louder with every ball. Genitile flicked it on to Jesus Bastardi, thence to Papa Médecin who rolled it back to goalkeeper Edmun Edmunsen. He side-footed the ball forward to Macca ten yards outside his penalty area, who turned and took the ball a couple of paces forward before placing the ball to his right, into the path of Jerome McZane. McZane played the ball up the right channel to Lim Po who could only see Sum Wun immediately inside him, so he wasn't about to pass to him. Instead, he lofted the ball across to Georgi Strupinski who brought a gasp out of the crowd as he appeared to have difficulty controlling the ball as it bounced unusually high on the bone hard pitch close to the touch line.

In the dug out, Ronnie winced. Joker reassured him again. "It's all right, boss. Relax!"

Strupinski knew that Macca was the selected scorer and looked for him. Macca had taken an exaggerated route wide to the right in a simulation of a blind side run. He was looking to Strupinski and as their eyes met Macca pointed to where he wanted the ball. Remembering that the ball had to be passed back to avoid the offside rule, Strupinski took the ball to the by line and sent over a cross. Macca spurted in to meet the ball about ten yards out in front of goal. The ball's trajectory brought it down towards the point where Macca would meet it. Macca placed his right foot firmly down and swung his left foot back to meet the ball as it hit the ground.

The ball hit the ground *exactly* where Alfonso had filled in the gouge made by the falling spade. It hit *exactly* the point where the rock hard ground met the softer filled in bit. It hit the edge nearest to Macca, so it stood up rather than bounce predictably. Macca's foot was already swinging. There was nothing he could do. Boot met ball in less than ideal directions. The ball skidded off the outside of Macca's boot and flew wide of the goal into the crowd - the yellow and black bedecked crowd - behind.

A huge cheer emerged from about five hundred Cornish throats. A loud "Oooooh!" echoed around the rest of the ground, turning into a howl of disbelief.

The referee signalled a goal kick. The players stood in disbelief. Macca stood open-mouthed in amazement. Then, creating images that Digital Sport One's cameras captured in close-up which were circulated round the world to be reproduced in sports pages everywhere for years to come, Macca's face creased up and crumpled as he burst into tears. The schoolmaster blew his whistle again, pointing over to the players' tunnel. "Match abandoned: there's no-one to take the kick!"

Jesus Bastardi, as captain, ran up to him. "Whaddya mean, abandon?" he raged. "We gotta win!"

"It's a goal kick, and as the other team can't take it, the game can't be restarted, just like it can't if the floodlights fail. So, match abandoned. It's up to the FA now."

He started to walk off, joined quickly by his assistants. It was only as he was disappearing into the tunnel that the full impact of what had happened dawned on Ronnie.

"I told ye ah had a bad feelin' aboot this," he said to Joker. "What the fochin' hell happens noo?"

In the stand, the officials from the FA (for three had been sent: why not cash in on a junket like this?) sat in stunned silence. The booing and laughter from around the ground, including the singing and chanting from the Porthleven supporters, faded from their senses.

"The *stupid* prat!" said one eventually.

"How did he miss?" asked the second.

"The ball seemed to bobble as he shot," explained the third. "He couldn't help it."

"What a *wanker*!" said the first.

The team gradually came to and began to sulk off the pitch. The watching crowd saw captain Jesus Bastardi put a reassuring arm round the blubbing Macca's shoulders and whisper a few encouraging words in his ear, like you see happening when a player misses the vital kick in a penalty shoot-out. His comforting words only seemed to make Macca feel worse.

"What *can* you say to someone in a situation like that?" said the third FA official, viewing the touching scene of sportsmanship with some sympathy.

"You useless-a, fuckina drunk, fat-a stupid-a *cunt!*" murmured Jesus into the distraught Macca's ear, ruffling the tearful player's hair good-naturedly and looking sympathetic for the sake of the cameras he knew would be focussed on him. "We get inside, I punch you fuckin-a fat face-a to *pieces!*"

The second FA official took a sealed envelope out of his inside jacket pocket. He had been given it on the Q.T. by the Competitions Secretary just before he left.

"Open it if there's a problem," had been his laconic instruction.

He slit open the envelope and read the few words on the single sheet of paper.

"The score nil-nil stands, as one-nil would have stood if that's what had happened," he told the others. "The replay is on Tuesday January eighteenth, kick-off seven-thirty. It can be played at Porthleven, or if they choose, at Wanderers."

"Well, someone had his crystal ball well polished for the occasion," said the first FA official. "We'd better tell the teams. I'll do it."

"I'll tell the press," said the second.

"And *I'll* tell the Porthleven fans," said the third. And I'm going to enjoy that, he thought. He was a Manchester United fan!

Chapter 30 – Replay

"We drew!"

"What?"

It was the evening of Porthleven's successful game against the Township boys and the players and officials were enjoying the dinner held in their honour. Vidal James's 'phone had gone and he had a brief but animated conversation with the caller. Then he hung up and relayed the news.

"We bloody held them, nil-nil!"

"What are you going on about?" Alan Carey was as mystified as the rest of the gathering. So Vidal explained what had happened at the walk-over. As he did so just about everyone's mobile went. They all knew people who had flown to see them in Rio. They were all being 'phoned with the same news. It turned into a mad evening.

Vidal received another call, though, from the FA.

"We've got to decide about the replay," he announced. "Where do we play?"

It wasn't a hard decision. The Porthleven Football Club Committee were all there, so held a Committee meeting straight away. The issue was, play the replay at the magnificent New Stamford Stadium in front of 65,000 and go home with over £300,000 to spend, or play on their own ground in front of no more than one and a half thousand spectators with perhaps £60,000 to put in the bank.

"It's no contest, lads," said the treasurer, looking at the figures he had scribbled on the back of a menu.

"I say ask the lads," said the Chairman. "Money isn't everything."

"Think of the clubhouse we could build!" replied the treasurer.

"No need to," said the Chairman. "We've the FA grant, the Lottery grant, and we need £81,000 in matched funding. So far we've already raised - what - £22,000? Bingo! Three hundred grand won't let us do any better in the league than we generally do already. We'll have the new clubhouse and brilliant changing facilities. We'll be able to run entertainments that'll bring in all the money we need. It's not practical to think about moving up the pyramid. Look what happened to Saltash, Liskeard and Falmouth. Did OK, but it nearly broke them. We're even further off the map and when the cash ran out we'd be nowhere. I say ask the lads. Let them decide. If they go for playing away, so be it."

So they polled the players, and they were virtually unanimous.

"Bring 'em to Cornwall, boss!" said Micky Faithful. "Bugger travellin' all the way up there fer a stuffin'. Think 'ow many o' our fans won't be able ter take the toime to go all that way for a midweek game. Lerrum see Wanderers at Gala Park!"

And that was it.

Next day, they flew home in the Concorde. No-one used their 'phone during the flight.

When they landed at Newquay, the Chairman fought his way through the throng of radio, TV and newspaper reporters to a quiet corner of the gent's toilets and made a 'phone call. It didn't take long. He simply informed the Competitions Secretary that Porthleven Football Club would play the replay on their own ground. He even suggested that to overcome the ticket problem, they should only be available to passengers on the two Jumbo Jets. Presumably the airline had a list of passengers they could use. The Competitions Secretary thanked the Porthleven Chairman for his call and said that the suggestion about the tickets was worth looking into.

The Wanderers Directors were not so pleased.

"Where on earth *is* it?" asked Malcolm Black. He was thinking, they've only got outside toilets down there, haven't they?

"No problem," replied Jack Grimethorpe. "I've been down that way a few times in my trucks. It's on the south coast, past Helston and a few miles before you get to Penzance."

"Penzance I know," said Sefton Perkins. "We went to the Scilly Isles once. We got a boat from Penzance. Bloody terrible crossing: rough as hell. We were all sick as dogs!" The stay on St Mary's had been a wonderful holiday once Sefton's family recovered from the effects of the meeting of the tides between Land's End and Scilly, spoiled only by the prospect of the trip back. "How far from Penzance?"

"About ten miles this side," replied Jack.

"Well, I think it will be a nice break," said Ernie Arscott.

"I agree," offered his younger brother Reginald. "There was a lovely article in the Saga magazine about Cornwall's hidden treasures, only revealed in the glory of Cornwall's winter sunshine. We'll go a day or two early. It will be a nice break."

The Directors were sitting by the pool of their hotel in the swankiest part of Rio, basking in the sunshine (well, not the Arscotts. They were sheltered from the worst effects of the Brazilian summer sun by the shade of a large patio umbrella)

"Nice break? Nice break? What the blood and sand d'you call *this*?" Dick Fossett spread his arms wide to indicate their plush surroundings. "Ten days out 'ere like this?"

"What did the FA say, Arnie?" Sefton attempted to bring some sense into the discussion.

"Well, after he gave me an earful for having made such a monumental cock-up of something a junior school girl's team could have done - honestly, he made *me* feel responsible for that silly fat sod's miss - he told me that Porthleven have elected to play at home, the date is Tuesday the eighteenth of January, kick-off seven thirty." Club Secretary Arnie Robinson looked a little disconcerted. "He went on to add that he hoped we'd find the place but doubted it seeing as how we have a multi-million pound team that couldn't find an open goal."

"Well you must admit," Cecil Norris chipped in. Drawing nil-nil against an absent team was a first. Thank goodness they didn't put eleven traffic cones on the pitch for us to play against. They'd have beaten us!"

"How did Sir Fabian take it?" asked Malcolm, who felt a colonic spasm coming on.

"Ah, well, not the reaction you may have anticipated," reported Arnie.

"Didn't he spit blood? That McGrath clown made us a bloody laughing stock. Never mind that we only have to draw with that Australian side and we're in the Final, this is going to stay with us for the rest of the season!" Malcolm's spasm got worse.

"We-ell, he wanted to know whose idea it was," explained Arnie.

"Idea?" Sefton's interest was aroused. The rest looked mildly curious, too.

"Yes. Whose idea to have Macca miss so there would have to be a replay?"

"You've still lost me." Jack spoke for the rest. Malcolm winced with the pain in his gut.

"Whose idea it was," repeated Arnie, slowly, " to create even *more* interest in the FA cup game by making the walk-over into a draw so that there would have to be a replay, doubling the potential TV revenues of the game. He thought it was a master stroke!"

"Good grief!" gasped Sefton.

"Holy shit!" chuckled Dick.

"He doesn't miss a trick, does he!" laughed Ernie.

"I suppose if it *had* been staged like that it *would* have been a great idea," mused Malcolm, whose spasm suddenly ceased.

Arnie looked a little embarrassed. "Well actually I allowed him to form the impression that it had been *my* idea," he admitted. "Remember, he told me I was sacked the day he arrived, and I've been sort of working my notice ever since. I thought that at least *some*one ought to get something out of this farce - other than bloody Digital International, that is."

"Now wash your mouth out, Arnie!" laughed Sefton. "Remember he pays your wages!"

"Yes, but for how long in my case?" Arnie sounded worried.

"Well, lads, I don't think we need to disabuse Sir Fabian of his impression that Macca's balls-up was Arnie's idea, eh?"

No-one seemed to disagree. Especially Malcolm, whose colonic spasms had stopped entirely.

The pregnant silence that followed was broken by the arrival of a white-jacketed waiter. "Excuse," he addressed Sefton. "Pliz come witha me, Señor Perakin."

"What for, lad?"

"Pliz, polizia wisha to spik witha you."

"Police? What on earth for?"

"They noa say, Señor."

Sefton lifted his heavy frame off the sun lounger and followed the waiter into the hotel. He was led to the foyer where he was introduced to a swarthy-looking man in a long coat that seemed unnecessary in the Brazilian summer weather.

"Señor Perakin?" he enquired.

"Per-kinz," corrected Sefton. "Who are you?"

"I-a am Ina-spector Dominguez," replied the man in the Colombo mackintosh. "You are-a ze *Vice* Presidente of-a ze Wanderers futobul club, si?"

"Vice *Chairman*, actually. Same sort of thing. What can I do for you? Do you want autographs of the team for your children? No problem."

"Zat would-a be nice, but eet iz not-a so nice ze reason I am-a here. Your Presidente, 'ee is-a Señor Blankopf?"

"That's right, but he's not here at the moment. He isn't staying at the hotel. He's on his yacht. It's moored in some marina somewhere. I'm not sure where it is but I can find out quickly enough, unless I can deal with the problem."

"Pliss, Señor, 'ee *is-a* ze problem!"

"Why, what's happened?" Alarm bells began to ring in Sefton's head. Surely he wasn't dead? That would cut off his finance straight away and Wanderers would be up a creek without a paddle and no mistake.

"Señor Blankopf ees in-a custody. 'Ee 'as been - ah - indiscreet. Pliss, will you-a come with-a me to ze Police-a Station?"

"Indiscreet? What do you mean?" At least the bastard wasn't dead. Indiscreet? What did that mean. I'll bet it's a woman.

"Is a woman involved?"

The inspector gave a shrug and turned both hands palm upwards as he grinned grimly.

"Of-a course, Señor."

"Thank God for that! I'll just go and put some different clothes on," said Sefton. "I won't be more than five minutes." He was relieved. Only a woman, that's OK. He's so rich, he'll be able to buy his way out of trouble.

* * * * * * * * * *

"Fancy barging in on me when I was with a hooker!" Sir Fabian raged. "I couldn't understand what was going on at first. A bloody police raid, I ask you! Mine was a bit of all right, too, but we'd hardly finished our bloody drink when the bastards burst in. We'd hardly finished getting our kit off, more to the point. I mean, it wouldn't have been so bad if it had been afterwards. When the bloody police broke up the party she started to gabble at me, then she started screaming about 'Reals'. I thought she was having a go at me about Wanderers because she was a Real Madrid fan or something. Silly bloody cow. She actually still wanted me to pay her even though I didn't lay a hand on her and we were being bundled into a bloody black maria!"

Sefton listened, bemused. With Sir Fabian's alleged background - if even half the newspaper articles written about him were true - it was odd that he had been so careless as to visit a brothel. And what was he doing anyway, knocking off a pro when he had that beautiful blonde bimbo of a 'Personal Assistant' constantly on call? I mean, it was different in *his* case. *His* wife was a different thing altogether. She wasn't exactly pretty any more, nor was she actually ugly. She was sort of in between – pretty ugly. That's what Sefton generally told business associates who hadn't actually met Doris. It was an old joke but it often broke the ice. It also helped to justify the odd occasion when he 'phoned an interesting-looking number from a particularly eye-catching card stuck up in any of the telephone boxes around King's Cross whenever he had to go to London on business. That *was* different, but Sir Fabian had no excuse.

"And the *next* bloody thing I know is, I'm being bloody charged at the police station and all the time this bint is screaming and yelling at me for not paying her and threatening to have the law on me! Bloody deranged! And here I am!"

'Here' was a dingy, grey cell, straight out of 'Cell Block H', except here the walls were not hardboard. Grey walls, wooden table and chair, hard wooden bed with a thin, inhospitable mattress and one stained and patched blanket to match the rock hard pillow. There was a stench of urine coming from a suspiciously stained corner of the cell, hard to explain as there was a perfectly adequate chipped enamel pot under the bed.

"What did they charge you with?"

"Fucked if I know. Like I understand what they're jabbering about anyway! Shaz will be wondering where I am. She'll be worried as fuck!"

"I'll let her know where you are," offered Sefton.

"Christ! Don't tell her why! Make something up!" She'd throw a wobbler and no mistake. Might even walk out on him! He couldn't bear that. Not just because those tits had cost him a fortune, but because they were so perfect. Like the rest of her. Apart from her voice, but then when she was doing a Monica Lewinski that wasn't a problem, especially as she did it so well. Christ, she was better than that bloody hooker, come to that! Which he hadn't done, of course, the police having arrived some minutes too soon.

"She's bound to find out eventually," said Sefton. "The press are already gathering outside. They know something is up."

"Bastards! Well, still don't tell her. It'll be better coming from me, if I can get out of here before the news breaks. *Bastards!* I thought that nil-nil draw was enough for them to get their teeth into. Clever bloke, that Arnie. Shrewd man. You're wrong about him working his notice. I'm overruling you. We're keeping him on and giving him a pay rise. D'you know, he's responsible for our new line in merchandising? Club coloured knickers for the lady fans! Or for blokes to buy their birds. Selling like mad! That tight-arsed little Commercial bloody Manager of ours wanted to veto the idea! Silly tart! How can a bird with such fantastic thighs be such a fucking prude, eh?"

Sir Fabian was rambling on. He wasn't in control of the situation and he wasn't used to that. "I thought we'd come out of this smelling of roses, deliberately arranging it so that this nobody bloody team from wherever it is can have their dream of playing against Wanderers. I thought we'd get a lot of brownie points for that. Instead of which, just because I pop into a whore house for a bit of rough, something most of them have probably done every night since they got here, the bastards are onto it like rats up a drain pipe."

"Well, I'll let Shaz know you'll be delayed. I'd better prepare her for you not getting back tonight. Shall I invite her to join us at the team hotel?"

"Yes, do that."

"I've had an idea that might help you, too. I won't be long." Sefton went to the cell door and banged on it. Bloody hell, how often had he seen that done on

TV and films? "Oi! Let me out!" He couldn't resist it! A policeman came and let him out.

* * * * * * * * * *

The press went wild, of course, especially in England, *especially* the titles not owned by Sir Fabian.

"Club Chairman in Hooker Row" - Daily Mail.

"Wanderers Boss Wanders" - Daily Express.

"Lady of the Knight" - Daily Mirror.

"Blankopf's Brothel Bother" - Daily Star.

"Escort Girl Shame of Wanderers Chairman" - The Sun. (The headline writer got a bollocking for such a feeble effort.)

"What was FB doing with his Digitals, then?" - The Sport.

"Urgent Need for Tighter Privacy Laws" - The Universe.

"Blankopf Bonks Brazilian Bird!" - The Globe.

With so much of the press always looking for reasons to knock Wanderers, Sir Fabian's visit to a Brazilian knocking shop - and not even a particularly high class one at that - was like manna from Heaven. All his business connections were mentioned, his companies listed, his ownership of the Rumpy Pumpy Club in Johannesburg dragged up. There were many photos of him with Sharon accompanied by much (fairly accurate) speculation about why she was seen so often at his side.

As for Sharon, it had been possible to keep the actual details from her, of course, but she had greeted the news of Sir Fabian's "little bit of bother", as Sefton described it, very calmly.

"Will 'e get aht termorrer?" she asked in her nails on a blackboard voice.

"Probably," replied Sefton, grateful that the 'phone he was using reduced the penetrative effect of her vocal cords. "I may have speeded things up a bit by sending one of our players' interpreters to the police station to help him. Should help to avoid any more misunderstandings. Anyway, he'd like you to join us at the team's hotel tonight. I've arranged for his chauffeur to pick you up at seven so that you can be with us for dinner. Better than you being all alone on that boat."

"Ooh, fanks," trilled Sharon. Brilliant! She'd go and find the Navigator and see how long it took her to talk him into a shag. Her record where he was concerned was three and a half minutes.

She didn't manage it: it took more than five, because the Navigator, ever mindful of how much he enjoyed his job, insisted on making a 'phone call to the police to see if Sir Fabian was likely to be on his way. Mind, having found out he wasn't due to be even interviewed until the morning, the Navigator was able (unknowingly) to easily break Sharon's previous endurance record, set in the crew's cabin of the Virgin Jumbo Jet, more than trebling the time and leaving her wide legged and eyeless. Well, her eyes remained shut with a combination of ecstasy and exhaustion.

Wow! What was she doing, planning to go to the team's hotel that evening? She'd rather have more of the Navigator. He persuaded her to go, though, as Sir Fabian expected it. He also wanted to go and visit a particularly attractive lady he had met at the marina who had invited him aboard *her* yacht for - er - drinks.

Chapter 31 – Comparing Notes

Shaz went ashore to meet up with Sir Fabian's car. Not his stretch limmo from England, of course; just a normal sized limmo, but still driven by Jenny.

"All right, Shaz?" Jenny and Sharon actually got on quite well, but they rarely found themselves together without Sir Fabian.

"Yeah, brilliant, ta," beamed Sharon, still in a bit of a whirl after her forty-five minute romp with the Navigator.

"You've been bonking that sailor again, haven't you!"

"Yeah! 'Ee don' arf know 'is way arahnd a gel's norty bits!"

"Well, he *is* a navigator," punned Jenny.

"Yeahri know 'ee is," replied Sharon, several feet below the pun. Jenny didn't think any the less of Sharon for being so thick. She recognised that Sharon simply had talents in a different direction. Like they used to say at school, "everyone is good at *some*thing, it's just a matter of finding what it is". Total bollocks, of course, thought Jenny. It was bloody obviously not true of some people. She could remember lots of girls she had been at school with who were completely useless at everything and were likely to spend their lives achieving bugger all. They were the ones who often got pregnant first, usually before they were sixteen,

"Which proves the point," one of her more woolly-minded friends had once said in a heated sixth form common room debate. "They *were* good at something!" So much for different points of view.

But Jenny thought that Sharon, whilst not academically bright, was certainly no fool. She was, after all, the constant companion of one of the richest men in the world. Even before she'd met Sir Fabian in the Pimlico Sporting Club, she was earning well above the average for her age, male or female, by virtue of her lap dancing. She had a talent for moving her body, whether for dancing or anything else, a gift that Jenny could understand after taking her own mother's advice.

Sharon sat in the front with Jenny, who skilfully threaded the large car through the reckless Rio traffic.

"You're not bothered about Sir Fabian, then?" she enquired.

"Nah, Ah'll see 'im termorrer. That Sefton man said 'ee'd sent someone dahn the cop shop to sort it all aht!"

"Yes, but she's a bit of an old slapper by all accounts. Over forty if she's a day. A prossie! Why did he bother when he's got us?" Jenny didn't know that Sharon was unaware of the exact nature of Sir Fabian's "bit of bother". Sharon *did* know that Sir Fabian got frisky with Jenny and she wasn't particularly bothered by that. After all, sex with him was always a flop, often literally despite the Viagra. If he was being entertained by Jenny then Sharon wasn't having to fake her orgasms. She could get decent sex more or less whenever she wanted, so that was all right. Mind, she was beginning to realise how much she had been missing out.

She'd thought she knew what good sex was after her first time in the bald-tyred Capri. Later, good sex had been what she'd had from the lad with the fluffy dice. Much later, it was what she did with the assistant bar manager at the Pimlico Sporting Club. Later again, with Stewart the Virgin Air Steward on the Jumbo Jet. But after this afternoon's session with the Navigator, she suspected that her entire sex life since the Capri had been worse than most girls got. Not being a keen reader, she'd never read the problem pages and sexual advice columns in teenaged girls' magazines.

"What d'yer mean? What old slapper?"

"The one Sir Fabian got into grief over."

"Nah, gel. Dunno wot yer talkin' abaht!"

That was when Jenny realised that Sharon hadn't been told the full story. She was in too deep now, so she enlightened Sharon.

Who screeched with laughter when Jenny finished. "Daft ol' git!" she spluttered, between laughs. "Cort wiv 'is trahsers dahn! Serve the old bugger right! Poor Blanky, though. I bet 'ee don' arf feel showed up!"

The two girls, worlds apart intellectually but totally on one another's wave length, chuckled together. Sharon quietened down first.

"Jenny?" she asked.

"What?"

"That Roger you're shacked up wiv over in the staff flats."

"We each have our own flat," intoned Jenny, mimicking one who was repeating rehearsed answers.

"Yeah, right, an' I'm a virgin!"

"Well, that's the official arrangement. So one night it's my place, the next night his, or something like that. What about him?"

"Is 'ee good?"

"Good?"

"Shaggin', yer daft cow!"

Jenny became dreamy eyed. "Mmm, yes!"

"Kin I as' yer a question? It's a bit personal, like."

"Seven inches. Not gynormous, I know, but it's what he *does* with it..."

"Nah, not that. Mind, seven ain't bad. Not *that* bad. Nah. What I wanner ask yer is, what's the longest yer've dunnit for?"

"What, non-stop, fully joined up shagging?" Jenny's brow furrowed. Then it brightened. "Neither of us went to watch the Man United game, you know, in October when we beat them five-nil. We had it on telly, and Roger started more or less as they kicked off. He said he'd give me an orgasm for every goal scored. He made me go on top for the second half - he made some pathetic joke about changing ends and I said, no, I wanted him to keep shagging. So - ninety minutes, plus half time, say fifteen minutes, plus injury time, probably five minutes, so that's a hundred and ten minutes!"

"Bloody 'ell! 'Ow many hours is that?"

"Er, well, one hour and fifty minutes. Ten minutes less than two hours. And five orgasms, too, don't forget. I wanted him to be out here for the FA Cup game to do the same thing."

"Why?"

"What do you think the score would have been against that non-league team?"

"Dunno. Loads, I s'pose." Suddenly, Sharon shrieked with laughter as the penny dropped. "Oooh, Jenny! Loads of orgasms!" Then she became serious again. "But 'ee shagged you for nearly *two hours*? I bin missin' out, gel!" And she told Jenny of her own modest experiences.

"I know just the bloke for you, then." said Jenny.

"Oh? 'Oo?"

"Johann van Dyke, the Dutch boy in the team."

"Boy? 'Ee's over firty, ain' 'ee?"

"Figure of speech. I'll introduce you two properly and explain your problem."

"Wot will 'ee do abaht it?"

"Hung like a donkey, stamina of a point to point horse!"

"Woss one o' them?"

"Keeps going for hours. He used to be in porn films until he was actually making more money playing football. Which isn't easy."

"Ooooh, Jenny. I dunno which one 'ee is. Is 'ee good lookin'?"

"Passable."

Sharon looked forward to dinner that night and hoped poor old Blanky wouldn't be too uncomfortable in his cell. She thought about him, picturing his surroundings in her mind. As her mind was inspired by many episodes of 'Prisoner Cell Block H', she would have been surprised at just how accurate her imagination really was. This was another continent, though, and didn't some of these South American countries torture their prisoners? Didn't they freeze them sometimes? She had faint recollections of something to do with prisons and something else about "chilly in South America". And didn't they chain them up?

"I'd 'ate ter be chained up," she said as her thoughts surfaced.

"Oh, Johann doesn't do that. Well, not unless you ask him," Jenny assured her.

Sharon, not quite back on the same planet, looked vaguely puzzled at Jenny's reply but didn't pursue it. Her mind was still racing.

"Will they use ice to make 'im cold?"

Jenny mistook the " 'im" for " 'em". "What, your nipples or your naughty bits? He might well do that if you're into that. Roger screwed me with an ice pop once. Sensational! A raspberry one. He said I had a raspberry fanny that night. I said, well it couldn't be cherry, could it. I lost that years ago!"

"You're *mad*, you," said Sharon, brought back to earth by Jenny's revelations. Though why she'd started on about ice pops Sharon couldn't fathom.

"They *don't* torture 'em in prison 'ere, do they?"

"No. Sir Fabian will be OK. He'll probably get bail, and then have to pay a fine and what's that to him, eh?"

Sharon, reassured, smiled happily and looked forward to seeing how this Dutch footballer measured up.

Chapter 32 - A Hatful of Arseholes

After the anticlimax of the nil-nil draw against the absent Porthleven, there was the simple matter of the third group game in the World Club Championship. Having competently disposed of Necaxa in front of about 7,000 spectators lost in the vast emptiness of the Maracanã stadium and then beaten Vasco da Gama in front of a crowd of some 140,000, Wanderers just needed to draw with rank outsiders South Melbourne from Australia.

For this game, around three thousand curious football fans scattered themselves around the Maracanã. The press almost outnumbered them.

"Just as well we're not playing the whole of Melbourne," commented Malcolm as he took his seat in the Director's box, the seat at the end of the row nearest the way out so that he could get to the toilet quickly if necessary. "We might still struggle after Monday's fiasco!"

Next to him, Sefton just smiled. "Cheer up, Mal. Things are going well. We're going to win this tournament, we're going to have a nice little trip to Cornwall and we've created loads of publicity which keeps Sir Fabian sweet - just enjoy the game!"

The Australians were more used to the heat than most of the Wanderers team and started brightly, making up for their lack of skill and tactical sophistication with effort and muscle. They put Antonio la Pazbaq's goal under early pressure and he had been forced into making a couple of saves early on. With Heinrich Schickelgrüber left back in England due to his fear of flying, Antonio Genitile and Jesus Bastardi were the twin centre backs. It was only in the tenth minute that a lunging challenge by South Melbourne's no-nonsense striker Gary Morgan left Antonio on the ground clutching his weak knee in pain. Off he went and Caspar Hansen took his place. Lim Po was next to go, his shoulder dislocated in the eighteenth minute by a challenge with the 'keeper. Sum Wun replaced him and lasted five minutes, his bad knee twisted tackling a central defender some two feet taller than he was.

In the Wanderers dug out, Ronnie was getting a bit agitated. "Fochin' 'ell, Joker!" he moaned. "We'll no' have a team fo' the final a' this rate!"

"Stick Pickaxe up front," suggested Joker. "Give 'em a bit of their own back."

"Aye, mebbe ye're right. Get stripped, Pickaxe. Play up front. Put yerself aboot, son, ye ken?"

"Right. Do you want me in between Seamus and Georgi?"

"Tell you what," suggested Joker. "Play in front of them. Cause a bit of mayhem. Tell them to play more down the centre behind you, picking up the pieces."

Pickaxe went on and relayed the new instructions to the team.

Next to go was Caspar, a head to head collision with Gary Morgan leaving the latter walking away with a grin on his face.

"That's another Pom down!" gloated Morgan, oblivious to the fact that hardly any of the Wanderer's players were actually Poms. Caspar's punch drunk brain was concussed, and off he went.

"On you go, Enriqué. Tell Jesus to play with three at the back and you play off them, okay? Me and Ronnie'll join you in a minute!"

"Pas de problème, patron," said Enriqué as he waited for the referee to wave him on.

Turning to Edmun Edmunsen, who was the replacement goalkeeper that day and the only sub left on the bench, Ronnie asked: "Where d'ye fancy playin', Ed? Right wing? Centre fochin' forward? Ah tell ye, Joker, Ah've no' met a shambles like this before!"

Joker simply looked on and chewed rapidly like all managers and coaches do during games.

On the pitch, things were about to get worse for Wanderers. They'd won a corner on the right and Enriqué went to take it. Pickaxe took up a position right by the Australian 'keeper with the obvious intention of making things difficult for him.

"Awright, Pom?" enquired the 'keeper of the rough-hewn Pickaxe. Pickaxe just glared back.

"Come on, mate, I'm only tryin' to be friendly."

Pickaxe carried on glaring. Enriqué was about to take the corner.

"Well, fair do's, yer Pommie bastard. I don't wonder you ain't smilin'. I've seen yer wife, mate - ugly as a hatful of arseholes!"

Pickaxe gave a roar of rage and nutted him. All hell broke loose as players from both sides struggled to pull Pickaxe and the 'keeper apart and inevitably they all began to struggle with one another. The referee was blowing and blowing on his whistle to no immediate effect and it was several minutes before order was restored.

The Australian captain confronted the referee.

"Did yer see that, mate? He nutted our boy! Yer gotta send 'im off fer 'is own protection!"

The referee had seen the head butt and needed no help from the players. Out came his red card and Pickaxe walked.

"Well, tha's fochin' marvellous," raged Ronnie. "We get this far through the season wi' hardly a blip, an' it all happens in half a match! I dinnae believe it!"

Joker went to meet the fuming Pickaxe as he came off the pitch. "Why d'you do it?" he asked? He and Ronnie had seen the head butt too. "We said put yourself about, but we kind of assumed you realised we didn't mean get yourself sent off!"

Pickaxe was heading for the tunnel. "He insulted my missus!" he snarled without breaking stride. "I'll have him later, the cunt!"

The half time talk was brief.

"Papa," said Ronnie through the Haitian's interpreter. "Ye'll have tae weave some magic on the right side, son. Milo?" Another interpreter looked up. "Let Papa go past ye an' when he does, drop in behind him, okay? Georgi?" The Polish interpreter sprang into life. "Drop intae midfield an' start switching wi' Enriqué doon that right channel, yeah?"

"Oui, patron, je compris."

"'Ee say 'ee unnerstan', monsieur Bone," translated the man from Cunning Linguists.

"Noo, lissen, everybody," shouted Ronnie. All the interpreters perked up at the same time. "All we need is a draw. Ah cannea stop the Aussies kickin' ye off the park, but Ah want the rest o' ye t'at least avoid gettin' sent off, okay? Look on the bright side. Wi' Pickaxe off, ye've all got more room tae play. Try ten minutes o' one touch. Treat it like a trainin' session. Get possession, *keep* possession. Okay, they're as big and strong as fochin' kangaroos, but they're aboot as bright, too, so jus' go oot an' do yer stuff."

Which is what they did in the second half. Mind, things did seem to get gradually easier as the half progressed. One by one the South Melbourne players on the left faded out of the game, pulling out of tackles, not contesting 50:50 balls and even putting passes astray. Three were replaced and the team rallied a little, but soon the substitutes' games went to pieces, too. It led to Wanderers having a field day on their right side, Papa Médecin in particular apparently allowed as much room as he needed. His efforts were rewarded in the eighty-first minute when Macca, completely knackered but unable to come off for lack of an outfield substitute, found the energy to plant one of his archetypical free kicks *just* inside the top corner for one-nil. Just a minute later, when he had just failed to reach a pass from Papa Médecin which went for a goal kick the Australian 'keeper decided to have a chat.

"Bit lucky with that free kick, Pom!"

"Noo, mate, noo luck! Skill, man! Ah just aimed fer ya mouth, son, an' its way too big ta miss. The only thing Ah've seen bigger is yer old lady's cunt!"

The 'keeper's genial mask slipped and his face contorted with rage. He aimed a punch at Macca and missed, but Macca went over like a felled tree anyway and the 'keeper was sent off.

The rest of the game passed off without further incident apart from Papa Médecin's utterly brilliant run from the edge of his own penalty area all the way down the right wing and into the box to score easily past the substitute 'keeper. The expression "ghosted past the defence" seemed totally appropriate as the South Melbourne defence let him through as if he and the ball were invisible.

It did seem strange that when the final whistle went and the teams left the pitch, some of the South Melbourne boys behaved as if they didn't know the game was over, being in a complete daze. They tested negative for drugs afterwards and soon seemed to recover, though they all seemed surprised that the score had been two-nil and not a goalless draw. Their medics put it down to dehydration, though their boys ought to have been used to that. In the boisterous Wanderers dressing room, Papa Médecin carefully packed away his assortment of bones, feathers, sticks and little phials of red liquid that the rest of the team still thought of as his "lucky charms".

"Brilliant goal, Papa," beamed Ronnie. Papa exchanged a few words with his interpreter.

" 'Ee say, 'ee 'ope 'is magic you ask for at 'alf time was okay!"

"Yeah! Magic goal, son, magic!" replied Ronnie.

Mais d'accord, thought Papa.

Then there was the inquest into Pickaxe's sending off and Macca's part in the Australian 'keeper's dismissal.

"Come on, Pickaxe, he's never even *seen* your missus!" said Joker to a rather subdued Pickaxe, miffed that he was going to miss the final.

No, but I 'ave, thought Jesus. An' she is-a *ugly!*

The atmosphere was very jovial, though, despite the injury list and the knowledge that Pickaxe would be suspended for the final, but Wanderers had reached the final in style, three wins out of three, and could look forward to it with glee.

The directors had joined the throng in the dressing room, too, and had brought down some champagne.

"You know," said Sefton in a quiet corner to Ernie, the older Arscott brother, "Some people say the Australians have no culture, but they're wrong. Such a rich use of the English language! Ugly as a hatful of arseholes indeed!"

Chapter 33 - Flying, Man!

There wasn't much time to sort out the injuries in time for the final, which was only two days later.

"If only we had Heinrich here," said Ronnie, thinking aloud, really, but echoing Ronnie's thoughts too.

"Pretty long drive," remarked Ronnie. "Let's see, noo. Across tae France, across Europe, Russia, then tae Siberia an' a ferry across the Bering Straits, doon through Alaska an' Canada, then it's a straight road until ye turn left at Chile and pop through the fochin' Amazon. Ye'll get a route fra' the A.A., ye ken!"

They were on the coach heading back to their hotel. "If only we could get him on a 'plane, though," said Joker.

"Ye'd have tae drug the bastard!" grunted Ronnie. "Any ideas, Bones?"

'Bones' was the unoriginal nick name of the Club Doctor, Miles Bletchley-Crewe. He had read Medicine at King's College Hospital in 1969, playing as much soccer as he could during his student years; though he was more enthusiastic than good. He went the usual route through Houseman, then Senior Houseman, and decided he'd like to specialise in Sports medicine after his weekend stints in Casualty uncovered a genuine enthusiasm for treating the many sprains, contusions, lacerations and fractures suffered by amateur sportsmen and women of all ages. So much more satisfying than patching up idiots who had crashed motorbikes or had accidents joyriding, and quite frankly not as depressing as dealing with other branches of medicine that had more frequent contact with death.

He became a Registrar, then Senior Registrar at which point he set up a very successful sports clinic in South London in the early 1980s, building it up into a thriving organisation with such a good reputation that occasionally some professional clubs sent players there for treatment.

When he heard that Wanderers were looking for a new Club Doctor to replace their retiring one, he applied like a shot and was gobsmacked when he got it. The salary was huge, he went to all their matches which satisfied his undiminished passion for football and lived in a superb house that went with the job. His wife Linda, a teacher until their first child was born, happily went along with Miles's career moves and even got to as many of the home games as she could. She wasn't particularly sporty. She just loved the atmosphere and excitement. And the foreign trips, of course. With both children now in University she had plenty of time on her hands to allow her to join her husband if Wanderers played abroad. She'd not bothered to go back into teaching again. Who would?

"What was that, Ronnie?" asked Bones, leaning forwards from the seat behind.

"Ah jus' said it'd be nice if we cuid somehow drug Heinrich an' get 'im on a 'plane to play in the final."

"Well, Doctors prescribe tranquillisers to people who are afraid of flying," replied Bones. "Ten two-milligram Diazepam tablets usually cover the average flight to Tenerife and back."

"Couldn't Heinrich do that?" asked Joker.

"Well, I did try to talk to him about that very thing when he joined us," said Bones, "but he didn't even want to discuss it. It'd be different if he wanted to do that. It might take a stronger dose, and of course a long haul flight is more difficult."

"I hate dentists." Malcolm had been listening from the seat behind Bones.

"Well, a lot of people do," observed Bones.

"Wha's that tae do wi' Heinrich?" asked Joker.

"Well," explained Malcolm, moving forward to sit alongside Bones. "He doesn't like flying, I don't like dentists. I have to take a tranquiliser just to go for an inspection, never mind when I go to have a bloody filling or something. One bloke tried to pull out one of my molars with just a local anaesthetic. I passed out and when I came round the bloody dentist was panicking because he couldn't find my pulse." He held up one of his wrists. "I've got the type of wrists that you can't find a pulse in. Well, he was shitting himself. He thought I was dead! After that he dropped me from his list and I found this other guy....."

Wha' the bluidy hell has this got tae do wi' Heinrich's fear o' flying, thought Ronnie.

".....who sent me to hospital to have the thing out using intravenous valium."

"So?" enquired Ronnie.

"Really?" said Joker.

"Oh, yes?" said Bones.

"Brilliant stuff! Just a little prick on the back of your hand...."

"No' the fust time ye've had a wee prick in yer hand, eh laddie?" joked Ronnie.

"Yes, very good, Ronnie. They pump this stuff into your vein and you don't feel a thing. What's even better, you don't even remember anything about what they do to you - no pain, nothing."

"That's right," added Bones. "Valium and other similar drugs have amnesiac properties, but as far as the dentist is concerned, the patient is fully conscious. He'll move when you ask him, you know, 'Open wide' and all that. Are you thinking what I think you're thinking, Malcolm?"

"Depends what you are thinking," smiled Malcolm. "Could we dope Heinrich to get on the 'plane?"

Bones looked thoughtful. "You'll have to let me think about that one: it'd hardly be ethical. I'll make a few 'phone calls, call in a few favours. I'll get onto it as soon as we reach the hotel."

* * * * * * * * *

Heinrich Schickelgrüber was sitting quietly in the comfortable lounge of his club house listening to a recording of Hitler's most famous and stirring speeches, when the 'phone rang.

"....Ehr kommt! *EHR KOMMT!*" screamed der Fuehrer from Heinrich's Bang and Olufsen speakers.

Heinrich turned the tape off, got up and went to the 'phone. "Ich komme, *ICH KOMME!*" he mimicked.

"Vot are you doink? Hef you started wizout me?" called his wife Eva from the kitchen where, clad in black leather bra, briefs and suspenders with black fishnet stockings and black stiletto heels, she was finishing the ironing.

It was the Arnie on the line. He had hurriedly flown back to the UK.

"Sorry it's so late," said Arnie, "but the - er - clinic got onto us. You - er - need to come in so that they can - repeat a test or something......" His voice trailed off. He wasn't very good at lying but Ronnie and Bones had been most explicit on the 'phone. His mouth was dry and he couldn't swallow even though he wanted to. Oh, God, that's a symptom of throat cancer, isn't it? Would they be able to see a growth in his throat if he went to Casualty? Why did they call it Accident and Emergency now? If you had throat cancer you'd find it hard to say "Accident and Emergency", so how could you be expected to....

"Repeat tests? Vot tests?"

"I don't know. They'll tell you at the clinic."

"Vitch clinic?"

"Er - come to the club and I'll take you there. Er - you'll need a change of clothing in case they want to keep you overnight. For the tests."

"Can't it vait until tomorrow mor4nink?" He didn't like to think of Eva having gone to all that trouble for him tonight without being - well, you know - thanked properly. After all, she had done his Wiener Schnitzels just like his mother used to.

"No, no!" blurted Arnie. "You'd miss your 'pla......plointment!"

"*Was?*"

"You'd miss your appointment."

"It iss after ten o'clock at night," complained Heinrich. "Vot clinic sees people at zis time?"

"Please, Heinrich, just come to the club." Arnie was getting desperate. All the Brownie points he had earned for 'his' idea to stage a nil-nil draw in the FA cup walk-over could be wiped off if he didn't get Heinrich to Bones's medical mates in time to get him sedated, down to Heathrow and onto the 'plane. He didn't yet know of Sir Fabian's decision to keep on with a pay rise. "Do you want me to come and get you? It would give you time to put a few things in a bag."

"How long vill you be?"

"Twenty minutes?"

"Okay. You come here. Gootbye."

"Who vos zat on ze 'phone?" asked Eva, emerging from the kitchen.

"Ve haf tventy minutes only, Pumpernickel," Heinrich replied. "Zen I hef to go to ze clinic for ze club."

"Clinic?" Eva looked alarmed. She also looked alarming. Seventeen stones dressed like she was is pretty alarming.

"Nuzzink to vorry about, Pumpernickel," he reassured her. "Look. I verk okay, huh?" He took her hand and placed it on his groin.

"Ooooh, Heini!" Eva quivered with excitement, which was a lot of quivering. "Tventy minutes? Ve haf a kvick vun, ja?"

Ten minutes later, Heinrich repeated his parody of those words of Hitler, which made him think irreverently about what - or who - Adolf might have had hidden behind his lectern for that speech.

Heinrich was ready with his overnight bag when Arnie arrived in his Mondeo. Well, the club's Mondeo, actually, but who was to know. Arnie's unease was evident to Heinrich who interpreted it to mean that there was actually something seriously wrong. After all, why else would he have to go to this clinic so late at night? It was therefore a quiet journey.

Arnie soon swung the car into a dark car park and parked alongside three other cars that were there. He led Heinrich towards the only light visible in the building, showing through a door. They went in. Arnie went straight to another door at the far end of the corridor they had entered. He knocked and they went in. Heinrich nervously followed behind.

Inside, the room was brightly lit and obviously a treatment room of some kind, with lots of bits of medical hardware around the walls, including a couple of desk top computers flickering benignly. There was a desk with three men in white coats seated behind it and there was also the obligatory examination couch.

Arnie introduced the three men to Heinrich, Doctors Grey, Schwarz and Blanc. Somehow, perhaps because he was a bit worried about what might be wrong with him, Heinrich didn't smell a rat. It wouldn't have been much help if he had. They were their real names.

"Vot iss ze problem, chentlemen?"

The three men looked at one another as if each would rather not be the one to answer. Eventually, Doctor Blanc spoke. "Nothing to worry about, Mr Schickelgrüber. We have been engaged by Wanderers just to solve a little problem that has come up."

"Problem? Vot iss wrong wiz me?"

"Actually, nothing we can't deal with," replied Doctor Grey. "We just want to do a little test following up something Doctor Bletchley-Crewe talked over with us."

The Doctors were choosing their words very carefully. So far, so good. Bones had certainly had a long talk with his three colleagues - on the 'phone from Rio earlier that evening; and what they were about to do certainly *could* be regarded as "a test". Also as somewhat unethical, but the agreed fees had been huge and were to be paid in cash.

"Vot did Bones talk about?"

It was Doctor Schwarz's turn to speak.

"Stress."

Clearly a man of few words.

"I do not hav zis - stress. I am not heppy viz not playink in Brazil, but..." Heinrich did not want to voice his fears.

It was just what the three Doctors wanted to hear. "Oh, really?" said Doctor Blanc. "Are you saying that you wish you could be playing in the FIFA tournament in Brazil?"

"Vell, yes, of course."

"Well, never mind, eh," purred Doctor Grey. "We'd better get on in that case. Would you roll up your sleeve, please? We want to do a simple blood test."

That wasn't exactly a lie, either. They would take some blood and test it with a bog-standard testing stick, just to cover themselves. Just in case Heinrich kicked up afterwards.

Doctor Grey skilfully took a small sample of blood from Heinrich's arm and transferred it to a labelled specimen tube, which he sealed.

"Now we want to give you a little something to help you relax so that we can commence our - er - test," explained Doctor Schwarz, a man of not so few words now. "Would you just lie on the couch, please?"

Normally, Valium type drugs are administered through a vein in the back of the patient's hand. They couldn't easily do this to an unsuspecting Heinrich so Doctor Schwarz gave him a quick jab in the arm. "You may feel a little out of it for a while," said the good Doctor, whose voice became more distorted and distant to Heinrich's ears.

Heinrich's faced relaxed into a bland, beaming expression.

"I think he's ready, Mr Robinson," said Doctor Schwarz. "You get his stuff into your car, we'll do what we have to do here."

Arnie left, and a few minutes later, the three Doctors emerged into the dark car park walking with Heinrich between them.

Arnie's heart went into his mouth. "He's supposed to be....."

"Don't worry, Mr Robinson," said Doctor Blanc. "He's out." In a slightly louder voice, he spoke to Heinrich. "You haven't a clue what's happening, have you, Heinrich?"

"Was? No, ant I don't care, eezer!" He giggled uncharacteristically. He saw Arnie in the car and came to a halt, clicked his heels and raised his arm in a Nazi salute. "Herr Robinson! Heinrich Schickelgrüber reportink for duty!" He turned to Doctor Blanc. "Be careful! Herr Robinson iss *fery important man* in ze orkanisation!" he whispered loudly.

"What organisation is that, Heinrich?" asked Doctor Blanc.

Heinrich looked suddenly doubtful. "Sheiss!" he eventually whispered loudly again. "I don't know. But still - vatch out!"

"You'd better get in the car, Heinrich," urged Doctor Grey.

Heinrich dropped his salute, relaxed, shrugged his shoulders and said "Okay!" as he climbed into the back seat.

He sat between Doctors Schwarz and Blanc whilst Doctor Grey sat in front next to Arnie.

Arnie drove like mad to get to Heathrow. He had to stop a couple of times to allow the good Doctors to top up Heinrich's dose, easily done as they had inserted a cannula into a vein on the back of his hand whilst Arnie was loading the car.

Arnie dropped them off right outside Terminal 4 but they barely made the flight to Rio, though they did have time to top up Heinrich's dose before actually getting onto the 'plane. They settled into their first class seats, Heinrich not aware that he was on a 'plane at all, of course.

"Better do up your seat belt, Heinrich," advised Doctor Grey from the seat alongside him.

"Vy zey hef seat belts in zis coach?" he asked.

"Oh, that's been the law for ages now," explained the Doctor truthfully. "And - er - these modern coaches are very fast, for motorways, you know."

The 'plane set off down the runway.

"Vow!" exclaimed Heinrich. "I see vot you mean!"

It took off.

"Mein Gott, vot a steep hill!"

It was a fairly uneventful flight, that's if you don't count Heinrich's bursts of singing. No-one understood what he was singing because he sang in German. No-one, that is, except for a very, *very* elderly businessman seated nearby, flying, as always, under an assumed name, adopted when he evaded the advancing Russian army in Berlin in 1945. A tear came into his eye as he listened to Heinrich's pharmacologically enhanced singing: "Wir fahren gegen England, wir fah-ren ge-gen Eng-ger-*land!*" Ach so! Zey vere such dreams ve had in 1939, he thought. Brazil had been kind to him, though, and he couldn't wait to get back to the bar of his Alter Kameraden club.

The Doctors had worried about getting a drugged Heinrich through the immigration checks at the other end, but they needn't have. The man they had to get past was a fervent football fan - not at all unusual in Brazil, where organised football coaching starts at the age of five - and he recognised Heinrich Schickelgrüber straight away.

In broken English, he welcomed the footballing hero. "Señor Schickelgrüber, welcome to Brasil! But, I theenk you no like flying, no?"

Heinrich, eyeing the man's uniform, clicked to attention and gave the salute again. "Heinrich Schickelgrüber reportink, Herr Reichsmarshal! You are correct, sir. I do not like flyink. Zat is vhy I hef come by coach. Zey are very kvick on ze autobahns zese days." He indicated the three Doctors with him. "Zese are my friends. Ve hef been singing on ze coach und now ve play football. Sieg Heil!"

Spinning on his heels, he goose-stepped away - straight into a wall.

Doctor Schwarz burst out laughing. In perfect Spanish, he said to the immigration officer: "What a brilliantly funny man! Do you know, he's kept us in stitches all the way from London. You don't often think about what international footballers might be like off the pitch, do you? I think when his playing days are over he will be able to make his living on TV! Do you want to see our passports?"

"Just to stamp them, señor. He's joining the team for the final, yes? I'm a Rio Plate fan myself, so I'm not sure if I want Corinthians to win or not. Thank you, señor." He stamped their passports. Heinrich's had been with Arnie in the Secretary's office along with all the other players' passports - that way the club could make sure that they were always up to date.

Bones was waiting at the exit gate when Heinrich emerged, still goose stepping, with the Doctors in pursuit clutching their flight bags.

"Hello, Heinrich. Nice journey?" greeted Bones.

"Bones!" Heinrich pulled up sharply. "Vot are you doink here? Vhy aren't viz ze boys in Brazil?"

"I just thought I'd come and meet you. How are you feeling?"

"Fine, sank you. Ve haf eaten a nice meal on ze coach. Vere do ve go now?"

"I've got a car waiting." Bones addressed his medical colleagues. "Okay, boys? Any - er - problems?"

"No, Miles, he seems fine. He'll need a boost fairly soon, mind. Now we've got him here, what's the plan?"

"To be frank, I'm not sure. Just getting him here was the most important thing. Let's get to the car. You can give him his boost there."

They guided the still goose-stepping Heinrich into the car where he happily co-operated once again whilst the Doctors administered his boost. He sang a little more on the car journey to the hotel before settling down for a nap.

When Heinrich opened his eyes it was light. He was lying fully dressed on a bed in a room he didn't recognise. He felt absolutely brilliant, like he'd never felt before. This was because not only had he never had medical treatment under Valium sedation before, but as a very health conscious young footballer he had certainly never experimented with mind altering substances.

He got up and went to the window. There was a beautiful panorama of city and sea before him which he didn't recognise. He was startled by the sound of a toilet flushing. Turning round he saw Bones emerging from a door.

"Oh, hi, Heinrich. How are you?"

"Neffer felt better, sank you, Bones," replied Heinrich. He rubbed his right hand. "My hant iss sore, zat iss all." He giggled, but didn't know why.

"Good...."

"Bones, vhere are ve? You vere wiz ze team in Rio. Vhy haff you come back? Zey need you, surely, wiz all zee inchuries?" He wanted to giggle again, but in view of the seriousness of his team's situation over there in Brazil, he controlled himself.

"Well, Heinrich, that's the point. I *haven't* come back."

"Heffent come beck? But here you are!" He couldn't control the urge to giggle at this.

"Well, no, Heinrich, here *you* are!"

"Vhere am I?" Another giggle.

"Rio."

"Rio? Brazil?" The giggling was getting hard to control. "Don't be silly. How did I get here?"

"On a 'plane, Heinrich."

Heinrich heard the words but they didn't register. He couldn't have flown, he didn't like flying. No, he was *petrified* by flying. But Bones was telling him he had just flown to Rio. He remembered the coach trip and the sing song, and he had some recollection of eating a very pleasant meal on the coach, but...

"Ze meal!" Heinrich wasn't giggling now.

"Meal?"

206

"Ze meal on ze coach. Zey don't serve fife course meals on coaches! Zat vos a *'plane*? How did I get on?" What was even more of a puzzle to Heinrich was that he didn't really care. In fact, the fact that he didn't care seemed so funny that he giggled again.

Bones saw that Heinrich was still partly under the influence of the Valium, so he decided to come clean.

"We needed you here, Heinrich, and you - er - you *did* say to the Doctors who brought you that you wished you could play in Brazil. You agreed to us carrying out a test. The test, or experiment, really, was to see if we could get you here, on a 'plane, without you having to worry about it. It worked. You're here, and you're laughing."

Heinrich tried to digest all this but his mind was still too far off the ground to cope, so he ignored it.

"I play in ze final tomorrow, zen?"

"That's the idea." Though how the hell we're going to get you back to England afterwards I really don't know, thought Bones.

Chapter 34 - World Champions!

And so the day of the first FIFA World Club Championship Final dawned. As forecast months earlier by many soccer pundits, Wanderers were there, and to make sure of a packed Maracanã stadium there was also a Brazilian team involved, Corinthians. It was just what FIFA had hoped for. It wouldn't have mattered if Vasco da Gama had been there instead of Corinthians. What really sold the game world wide was the much hoped-for appearance of the most widely followed team in the world, Wanderers United.

FIFA's personnel proved to be more agreeable to Digital International's style of doing business than the FA or Premiership League officials had been and it had been easy for Sir Fabian to secure the world-wide television rights. Digital had out-bribed the Asteroid Corporation which was faced with trying to think of something else to screen on its sports channels during the Rio final. Actually, they didn't do too badly. One of Ootgers' minions had pointed out that in England, perhaps half the football fans followed Wanderers, but the other half hated them for their continued success, so they ran highlights of the 1966 World Cup Final and Manchester United's first European Cup win and weren't far behind Digital International in viewing figures on the day.

Sir Fabian was beside himself with pleasurable anticipation, of course. Whilst his multi-billion dollar international business deals were meat and drink to him, the excitement he felt at being the owner of one of the two teams in the World Club Championship Final was something else. It certainly had an effect on his blood pressure so that with the added effect of his customary Viagra, he was quite perky when he woke up on the day.

"Oooh, Blanky, 'ave you been overdoin' them tablitts," squealed Sharon when she woke up alongside Sir Fabian with something unexpected pressing into her delicious rump.

"I just feel good this morning, Shaz," explained Sir Fabian. "Why don't you climb on for a minute or two?"

Well, at least Blanky knows his limitations in that department, thought Sharon. "Yer know jus' what ter do ter please a gel, don'tcher, Blanky!" She'd put up with his usual gasping efforts the night before, happy that the police had got to him before he had got to the hooker. I mean, she could have had all sorts of diseases. Sharon hadn't made a fuss. She had been altogether too worn out to bother after her session with Johann van Dyke. It had been fascinating hearing about his exploits as a porn movie star. Not that he had bragged about it. Sharon had had to draw it out of him, so to speak, and he had modestly related a few choice memories to her. It turned the whole session into an educational experience when she was forced to ask him what he meant by some of the things he told her about. He'd found that a demonstration was better than a mere description and Sharon took part enthusiastically.

"You could earn a fortune in the porn industry," he had told her, meaning it. "I could get you in just like that."

"Ooh, no, I don' fink so, Johann. I mean, I like *doin'* it. I jus' don' fink I'd like uvver people *watchin'* me do it."

Johann hadn't pushed the point. Girls who tried out but weren't comfortable being watched by the film crew and backstage staff never made it and always looked wrong to the discerning viewer. He just carried on with his unexpectedly pleasant romp with the Chairman's bimbo, and decided that his earlier opinion of her as, well, just that, a bimbo, was a bit harsh. Sharon was obviously a tart with a heart, like so many promiscuous girls are; just looking for affection, but in her case clever enough to have landed herself (literally) in the lap of one of the richest men in the world. It was at the end of the session that things went wrong. Sharon had gone to the bathroom of Johann's luxurious room. She was just tidying herself up after an exhausting session - during which the Navigator's three-quarters of an hour was beaten out of sight - when Johann came in behind her and turned her round for a stand-up quickie. Seconds into the bout, his foot slipped on some water on the floor and his left leg flew sideways. Down they went in a heap, and Johann was left on the floor clutching his groin.

"Shit!"

"Wossup, Johann?"

"Help me up, please!"

Sharon was, of course, a very fit girl and had little difficulty helping Johann to his feet. She supported him as he limped to the bed and sat down.

"My groin!"

Sharon's hands flew to her ha'penny. His groin? Surely his willy hadn't snapped off inside!

"Oh, Gord! Let me see!" She expected blood. She looked down and saw his willy, lying limply against his thigh. It was the first time she had been relieved to see one in that state.

"You'd better go. I'll have to get the club doctor. Don't worry, I'll just say I slipped in the bathroom."

"Well," giggled Sharon. "Yer did!"

Despite himself, Johann smiled at her. "I won't be able to play against South Melbourne, you know!"

"Oh, Johann, I *am* sorry!"

"Don't be silly. It was my fault entirely. I just fancied a quick one!"

"Well, when yer better, we c'n finish it orf properly! If yer'd like to, that is?"

"Yes, I would. You'd better go now so I can get the doc."

That session had left her extremely sore but had opened her eyes even more to what was available, sexually speaking. Sir Fabian's unexpected priapic intentions on the morning of the World Club Championship Final were not exactly welcome until she thought about how *little* she had to do to stay by his side. He spent days away from her on business, giving her ample opportunity to make plenty of liaisons with the various dishy men that she encountered. So she jollied him along that morning, faking two orgasms instead of the usual one just because he was obviously in such a good mood. She wondered if Johann's groin would be mended in time for the Final. How long did it take for a groin to mend? She asked Sir Fabian.

"I don't bloody know, Shaz. I seem to remember blokes from my Rugby playing days were out for a few weeks with it. Why?"

"Er - oh, well, that Dutch bloke 'as one, don'ee? It'll weaken the team, won' it?"

The news the previous day of Johann's injury had not exactly pleased Ronnie and Joker.

"I don't know, Shaz. I do know they got Schickelgrüber over, so that'll help."

It did more than help. The inclusion of Heinrich meant that Ronnie and Joker could field quite a strong side allowing for the absences of the injured Genitile, Hansen and van Dyke. Lim Po's dislocated shoulder had been popped back into place and a pain-killing injection had sorted out Sum Wun's knee for the time being.

Wanderers were used to playing in front of huge crowds that were largely against them and it did not worry them overmuch. All were current or former internationals, so the hostility and atmosphere were part and parcel of their footballing lives. True, Papa Médecin spent longer than usual mumbling over his larger than usual collection of oddments on the bench next to where he changed, but as they marched onto the pitch behind Ronnie and Joker they just felt the right degree of adrenalin rush. No adrenalin, and the mind and muscles wouldn't work to their full potential. Too much and you could just freeze on the day. Just enough: look out, opposition.

The Maracanà was packed to its 160,000 capacity.

"All yer family came, then, Seamus," yelled Macca in Seamus's ear. Seamus yelled back.

"Half of 'em couldn't get tickets because all your illegitimate kids got 'em first!"

At the rear of the file of players, Papa Médecin hadn't stopped mumbling since he left the dressing room.

After the presentations Jesus Bastardi led the team to the end that had the biggest showing of blue and yellow for the kicking in. Summoned to the centre for the toss-up there were more photos, then he lost the toss. It didn't really matter, there was little advantage to be gained either end.

Wanderers had Antonio la Pazbaq in goal, a back four of Papa Médecin, Jesus Bastardi, Heinrich Schickelgrüber (still perhaps a little bemused at being there) and Kwasi Ankoma. In midfield they had Macca playing on the right, Milo Opec and Enrique Mouette in the centre and Manuel Sardinhas on the left. The two strikers were the fairly common pairing of Seamus O'Hooligan and Georgi Strupinski. On the bench, Edmun Edmunsen was the reserve 'keeper, resplendent in his specially-commissioned blue and yellow bobble hat. Stefan Milosovitch and Jerome McZane completed the list of fit players that could reasonably be called on as substitutes. Lim Po sat there as well, his re-located shoulder still sore and well strapped up. He could be called on to make up the numbers in case of injuries, as could Sum Wun. Ronnie and Joker were reasonably happy.

"We'll still have 'em," Ronnie shouted to Joker as the two sides faced up for the kick-off.

"I reckon so," yelled Joker back into the ear of his boss. "Back in July, we'd never have believed anyone if they'd told us we'd be here now, eh?"

"Aye. Greavsie's right. Funny ol' game!"

The first half was a bit of a disappointment as each team was afraid to take the initiative for fear of a mistake giving a chance to the opposition. Antonio la Pazbaq had two easy saves to make whilst at the other end Georgi Strupinski and Seamus O'Hooligan had just one half-chance each, though the Corinthians 'keeper did have to work a bit to keep out a Macca free-kick.

At half time Ronnie switched Macca inside and put Milo Opec wide, talked about how the Corinthians' two chances had come about, telling his midfield to watch for the advance of the Corinthians' sweeper, and asked for more crosses from the by-line as the other 'keeper seemed uncertain about balls drifting away from him. As the players were called out for the second half, he and Ronnie gave the customary individual gee-up to each player.

"Bit more of your ol' magic this half, eh, Papa? Magic? Un'erstand?"

"Ce n'est pas si facile aujourd'hui, patron," muttered the Haitian full back in reply. His boss obviously didn't understand. It was probably best that he didn't, but working his voodoo against such a huge adverse presence as the massive Maracanã crowd took a lot out of him. Still, all his team mates were doing their best in their own individual ways and it was up to him to do likewise.

The deadlock continued until a quarter of an hour from the end. True, Papa Médecin had begun to make a few runs down the right, making a little more headway each time, it seemed, as the left-side players in the Corinthians team appeared to become more and more bemused by his skills, but the real breakthrough came when one of his runs ended with a corner to Wanderers on their right. Heinrich Schickelgrüber went up for the corner and Macca put over a pin-point kick that was tailor-made for Heinrich. He charged in to meet it and collided heavily with the Corinthians' goalie. His elbow, whether by accident or design, made a crunching contact with Heinrich's face as he went to head goalwards. The ball skidded off his forehead as he collapsed in a heap in the goalmouth. The full back on the post knocked it away for another corner.

When Bones picked Heinrich up he was spluttering blood and spitting enamel. He was obviously out for the rest of the game and was helped off. Some reshuffling was necessary as Jerome McZane was brought on. While all this was going on, Seamus O'Hooligan went back to talk to Jesus Bastardi. Communication wasn't that easy as Jesus' English was so poor and anyway Seamus's English was so heavily accented. Seamus certainly didn't speak Italian. But Seamus indicated the use of an elbow by the opposing 'keeper and the bits of broken tooth being spat out by Heinrich. Jesus frowned and slowly advanced for the next corner as, with Heinrich off and the substitution made, play could resume.

Jesus advanced into the box and planted himself not in front but behind the Corinthians' 'keeper. Close-up cameras showed him to be apparently shouting instructions to his team. The 'keeper was shouting too. Then, just after Macca took the kick, the 'keeper, bellowing with rage, turned on Jesus and punched him.

Pandemonium! A struggling mêlée quickly developed in the goal mouth and it was many minutes before order was restored. The Corinthians' 'keeper got his red card and they were forced to bring off a striker and replace him with their substitute goalie whose first job was to pick the ball out of his net after Enrique Mouette's spot kick.

Often the ten men will rally, especially with a big crowd behind them, but Corinthians seemed unable to rouse themselves. Papa Médecin continued to ghost his way freely up and down the right wing and in injury time he threaded his way all the way into the Corinthians' goal area to make it two-nil past a mysteriously immobile goalkeeper.

So Wanderers were the first official FIFA World Club Champions! For the players, the medals ceremony was just a dream. Jesus received the trophy and the Wanderers' supporters went wild as their team did a lap of honour, passing the cup from one to the other in the customary fashion - footballing history was made!

In the dressing room ages later, Papa smiled happily to himself when Ronnie congratulated him on his performance and goal.

"Ah asked ye fer a bit o' magic an' ye delivered! Brilliant!"

But the main talking points were the 'keeper's assaults on Heinrich and Jesus.

"How's Heinrich?" asked Seamus of Bones.

"Two broken incisors, a canine and a premolar, plus a lot of lacerations inside his mouth," replied Bones. "He's in a lot of pain. The nerves are exposed in the broken teeth, and that's on top of the bone and tissue damage."

"Jus' the job, then, man," Macca butted in, just out of the shower and flamboyantly towelling his wedding tackle dry.

"How's that?" asked Bones. "Hardly just the job, a mouthful of broken teeth and a load of stitches needed in his mouth."

"Nae, mon. Think on. 'Ow did yer gerrim t' Rio? Doped, reet? Well, gerris teeth fixed here, laike, an' gerrim 'ome the same way!"

Bones looked thoughtful. "I see what you mean. He'll be expecting his teeth to be fixed and he'll need at least a local for that..... thanks, Macca! You're not just an ugly face!"

"Haway, mon! Anythin' t' oblaige, laike!"

"What happened to make their 'keeper go for Jesus?" asked Joker. Translations flew around the dressing room as Jesus explained.

"The 'keeper, he-a Spanish. I learn-a good Spanish at Calvados. I tell-a him thing about his-a wife. Is not-a my idea!"

"What did yer say, canny lad?" asked Macca.

"Le dije que su mujer era tan fea como un sombrero lleno de aguje ros de culo," said Jesus.

The Spanish interpreter from Cunning Linguists translated.

"Jesus told the goalkeeper, his wife, she is as ugly as a hatful of arseholes!"

Chapter 35 - Playing under lights

Preparations at Porthleven's little Gala Park ground were hasty, to say the least, when word came through that the FA Cup fourth round replay was to be held there. With all of the Committee and virtually everybody else associated with the club in South Africa when the news broke, things were very quiet around the village.

Morwenna Tregunna was taking advantage of the deserted state of Gala Park, though. A Helston girl, she was happily entertaining Able Seaman Prosser to a vertical knee-trembler in the little covered terrace which runs along part of the touchline. It was he who had brought them there, knowing of the location because his service football team from the Royal Naval Air Station at Culdrose played Porthleven's reserves.

"Iss a bit public, ennit?" complained Morwenna. "Those people in they bungalows up there can see!"

"Only if it were daylight and they 'ad binoculars," the Able Seaman reassured her.

"Well, awright, if yer sure," said Morwenna, giving in too easily to her desire to strump the matelot.

Some fumbling and "ooh"ing and "ah"ing later and the Able Seaman and Morwenna were connected. It wasn't the most noteworthy of couplings, being somewhat hurried because of the imperfection of the surroundings.

"Ow! Mind! You'm on me foot!"

"Ouch! Bloody 'ell, lift yer skirt up properly, 'Wen. The hem's sawing me 'ampton off!"

" 'Ere, 're you wearin' a condom?"

"Yea, I 'ad it on ready." How many maidens fall for that one?

"Oh. awright, then!"

"Yer too low down, 'Wen!"

"I'm on tip toe already. Yer'll 'ave ter bend yer knees!"

Not for the first time Morwenna regretted finding a bloke who didn't have anywhere decent to take her. Occasionally she'd find a lad with a flat or cottage, though they tended to be students. They had a bed for shagging but no money to give a girl a good time. The ones with the money, in Helston at least, tended to be ratings from RNAS Culdrose, but they lived on the base and couldn't take girls back there; or else they lived in married quarters.

As for Morwenna, she still lived with her mum and her mum's latest boyfriend and, like most of her classmates, would do so until she was first of all eighteen and could just leave home, and secondly had a bloke in tow that she could move in with. Only the clever girls who went to University could look forward to moving away from home. Morwenna's GCSE results had not been encouraging.

Employment prospects beyond some kind of minimum waged job were poor. Life was depressing if you looked at it like that, so she had filled her days since her sixteenth birthday the previous July by seeing how many blokes she could shag. She was in competition with her three best friends, all modelling themselves on the characters in "Sex in the City", except in their case it was "Sex in the Town, Village or Country". Able Seaman Prosser was proving to be reasonably satisfactory even if his choice of trysting place was a bit draughty.

Over in the almost deserted clubhouse, a couple of locals were lazily supping pints. Roger Wearne was a Staff Nurse and hadn't been able to take the time off to go to Rio on the Jumbo Jet. Billy Rosewarne was a market gardener whose domineering wife Rita simply wouldn't let him go.

"Brazil indeed! I don't care if it *is* free, I never heard of anything so daft in all my life, going half way round the world just to watch the village football team. An' I don't *care* if all your mates are going, I'm not going to let it be said that you're as daft as *they* are. An' if their wives are going too, then they're no better than they ought to be. The very idea! How long are they going to be away? A week? A week! The 'plane and hotel might *well* be free but you can't be away in a place like that for a whole *week* and not spend a fortune, it'll be boozing with the same old bunch every night for a week, not just Thursdays and Saturdays like it is now, though Lord knows why I let you do *that* on what *you* earn, an' that's *another* thing, how can you take a week off work *now*? You can't have a week off without pay so it'd have to come out of your annual holiday. What am *I* going to do while you're away, have you thought of that? Just like all men, selfish to the core, think only of yourselves, you go and watch that silly football team *every week* and it still isn't enough for you, you want to go on some blooming silly jaunt to *Brazil*, if you please, and when, might I ask, have you ever taken *me* anywhere for the last fifteen years, eh? I suppose you think our honeymoon in Benidorm was enough, don't you, though Lord knows, it was too much for you if my memory serves me right, too tight most nights to be much use to me and then so badly sunburned you ended up in *hospital*, for Heaven's sake, the humiliation of it, having to come home off my honeymoon on my own because you were still in hospital, my mother was *absolutely right* about you when she said....."

Billy's nickname for Rita was Pearl. Nickname, not pet name. Pearl, because Billy reckoned Rita had missed her vocation.

"She ought to 'ave bin a pearl diver in the South Seas," he moaned in the clubhouse one night. "She can nag without drawin' breath fer *ages*. I reckon she can 'old 'er breath longer than any other bugger! Perfick fer pearl divin'!"

The 'phone went behind the bar, and the bored-looking barman answered it. After a few seconds and a glance towards Roger and Billy, the barman said, "Well, Vidal, there's only Roger and Billy here. They can do it, can't they, if I give them the keys?"

Vidal, just about to board the homeward-bound Concorde, agreed.

"Okay. Easy enough. I'll ask them." The barman leant across to his only two customers. "It's Vidal. He says, the replay is going to be played here, of all things, and he wants the floodlights checked. Can you do it? You know how they work, don't you?"

Billy nodded. Over the years he'd often helped Denzil Chegwidden, the groundsman.

"Yea, Vidal, Billy says he'll do it. Nice trip?" The barman started back from the ear piece. "Well, there's no need to be bloody rude," he said, and hung up. "He wants you to go over and put the floodlights on and make a note of which ones have gone. They've all got to be working next Tuesday for the replay. Just put them on, let 'em warm up and jot down which ones don't work. Here." He handed Billy a pen, pad and some keys. "Bring it all back and I'll get onto the people who replace the lamps."

Billy and Roger made their way through the darkness across the lane from the clubhouse and through the gates of the football ground itself. They unlocked the door to the pavilion-style changing room block and crossed in the darkness to the toilet. There, Billy put the light on to reveal the switch boxes for the ground's floodlights.

" 'Ere, boy," said Billy, "I'll purrem on, you go an' see which ones don't light up."

He stretched up, inserted the keys and threw the switches on the 440 volt boxes.

In the little bit of covered terrace, Morwenna and Able Seaman Prosser were getting there or thereabouts. Both had their eyes tightly shut, their earlier problem of unequal height overcome by Morwenna having hoisted both legs either side of the Able Seaman's waist whilst he held her up by the combined effects of his leg strength and the way he forced Morwenna's back against the concrete wall at the rear of the windswept little structure.

"Yes! Yes! *Yes!*" exclaimed the Able Seaman.

"Oh! Oh! *Ooooh! Oh bloody hell!*" shouted Morwenna who, with her head just over the Able Seaman's shoulder facing out across the pitch, became aware of a gradually increasing intensity of feeling, no more than a girl could reasonably expect, really, as well as a gradually brightening light even though her eyes were still shut. She just thought the effect was something to do with her ever elusive genuine orgasm until the light became so bright that even in her state of heightened sexual excitement she sensed something was wrong. Opening her eyes, she was almost blinded by the glare of the floodlights on the other side of the pitch.

"Oi! *Oi!*" she yelled at Able Seaman Prosser.

Almost there, A.S. Prosser simply yelled back. "Yea, go on gel, go for it!"

Morwenna hammered his back with ineffectual fists and desperately writhed her body to and fro, trying to disengage herself from the thrusting sailor. He mistook both of these as exhibitions of unbridled passion.

"Yea, baby, yea, let it come!"

Morwenna battered his ears. "Stop, stop you bleddy bugger, everyone can see us!" With a superhuman effort she managed to force herself free, timing an extra special shove to coincide with one of Able Seaman Prosser's outward movements. She collapsed down to one side of him as he consummated their act into thin air.

"Uuuuuunnff!" climaxed the disengaged Able Seaman, inseminating the concrete wall.

"You bugger, you ent wearing a condom! You beastly bastard!" To say that Morwenna was indignant would be an understatement. Not only was the rotten bugger riding her bareback but they were under bloody floodlights. "Why 've they turned they lights on? Don't it mean they'll be comin' out ter play football? 'Ow c'n we geddout of 'ere wivout bein' seen?" Morwenna was desperately readjusting her clothing, halfway through which she suddenly remembered the rows of bungalows on the hill beyond the far floodlights. She felt like she was dressing on stage and modestly turned her back.

Able Seaman Prosser had the advantage of already having his back to the imagined hordes of spectators peeping through their curtains. Hurriedly packing a still rampant hampton can be a hazardous business with a zip fly and so it proved for A.S. Prosser.

"Yeeoooooww!" he screamed, instantly regretting the force with which he had pulled on the zip. And "Ooooohmigod!" as he yanked it in the opposite direction. The joke round the mess had always been that this didn't happen to blokes who were circumcised. How he wished, through the waves of pain that assailed him, that he was bare headed; though it felt like he was now, if the pain was anything to go by. He winced as he tucked his mangled member into his spanking-schoolgirl patterned jockey shorts and zipped up carefully.

To be fair to Able Seaman Prosser, he was extremely confused. His coitus had been rudely interrupted, their bonk had apparently been about as public as a live show on the Reeperbahn and he had just circumcised himself without an anaesthetic. And now this silly bird he had picked up was giving him GBH of the ear'ole into the bargain.

Over in the pavilion, Roger Wearne was jotting down a note or two on the barman's note pad. "Okay, Billy, you can switch off now. Only two not working, I've noted them down."

Click! And the lights on the covered terrace side went out.

Click! The whole ground was plunged into darkness, all the more intense for being in immediate contrast to the brilliance of the lights.

Stumbling a bit in the dark, Roger and Billy locked up and went back to the bar.

In the trysting place, Morwenna and Able Seaman Prosser were now completely blind and blundered into one another as they staggered about.

"Now what?" asked Morwenna of no-one in particular.

"I think it's time I got you home," answered A.S. Prosser from the gloom, regaining some semblance of normality despite his disorientation caused by the sudden blackness and the searing pain.

"Where *are* you?" hissed Morwenna, flailing her arms about as she tried to locate her erstwhile partner, aiming in the direction from which his voice had come. She made contact.

"Aaaaargh! You stupid cow!"

Her windmilling arm had caught him right in the privates. Or ordinary seamen's, as they might say in the Navy. Whatever, it was bloody painful. A punch in the goolies usually is, of course, but A.S. Prosser's were particularly delicate.

"Oh, for goodness' sake, woss the madder with 'ee, boy?" Morwenna asked. All she wanted now was to get home. "Come on, less go while the lights is out."

Their eyes becoming gradually accustomed to the dim glow from the street lights of the village, Morwenna and her sailor made their way to his G-reg Escort and drove off towards Helston. The draught blowing in through a small rust hole on her side hadn't bothered Morwenna on the trip out, but for the trip home she was particularly aware of it. She'd not been able to find her knickers in the panic. Not that she was that worried. None of her frilly ones had been clean when she was dressing to go out. The only clean ones she could find had been a pair of her long neglected school knickers.

Chapter 36 - The Media Descend on Gala Parc

The Committee members of Porthleven Football Club had an idea; the people who travelled up to Newquay to see the team off on the ill-fated Concorde trip had some idea; the three hundred or so villagers who had flown to Rio on the Jumbo Jet had a bit of an idea; but the rest of the villagers, especially those running small businesses, had absolutely no idea of just how much of a media circus would descend on their little haven of peace on the south Cornish coast. With only a few days' notice of the fixture, Sports Editors on newspapers, radio and TV stations up and down the country were thrown into a panic, all anxious to get their reporters, radio cars, cameras, outside broadcast vans, mobile satellite transmission facilities and so on to Porthleven. Except for the BBC, of course, who had sent just one camera to record the First, Second and Third Rounds for "Match of the Day".

Most pressurised of these over-worked media persons was the Chief Sports Editor for Digital One Sports, only too aware that this event was not only unique in sporting history but involved Digital International's bullish, bullying owner Sir Fabian Blankopf who had let it be known that he expected absolutely *no* cock-ups; more than that, he expected any event involving Wanderers United to receive a complete one hundred per cent effort. The Chief Sports Editor, Wayne Smitheram, had almost had a heart attack watching the performance of that complete tosser Shane Parkhurst live from Newquay as the Porthleven team and officials departed on Concorde. Somewhat placated by Parkhurst's immediate resignation (he would tell Sir Fabian he had summarily sacked him), he was now faced by having to put maximum effort into broadcasting a game from a completely unknown corner of Cornwall. He'd have to find a suitable replacement for Shane, of course. But hell! Why not do it himself? It was ages since he'd fronted an outside broadcast. Why not do the whole thing from the ground? He quite fancied a trip to Cornwall.

A quick briefing with his immediate team resulted in one of the producers, Greg van Dam, being sent off to sort out accommodation and reconnoitre the ground so that he could work out the placement of the cameras, commentary position and so on. The trouble was, the BBC were doing the same for their Match of the Day team, likewise Asteroid Corporation Sport, Sky Sport and Eurosport. Transworld Sport also wanted to get in on the act, and all sent their people down to first of all find Porthleven and then book hotels for their crews. Carlton TV's South Western division and BBC's Spotlight were a bit better placed for getting themselves organised, especially Spotlight who had provided the pictures of the earlier rounds for "Match of the Day". Best organised of all were the BBC's Radio Cornwall. They had often reported from Porthleven's ground, always by 'phone because its position at the bottom of a narrow valley meant that no outgoing radio signals reached it. For an FA Vase match once, they had pulled out all the stops and parked their main radio car at the top of the hill overlooking the ground and used a radio mike from a position on the grassy bank overlooking the half way line. It had worked very well and their reporter on the day, Tommy Matthews, had been able to give a full match commentary of exceptional quality. The various media teams planning their descent on the sleepy fishing village knew nothing of this.

When Greg van Dam swung his car into the car park by the Porthleven clubhouse he liked what he saw. The ground itself, on the opposite side of the road, looked spacious with a wide, flat pitch. He could see a natural grassy embankment along one touchline and some kind of covered area opposite. Eight tall floodlight pylons towered into the clean Cornish air. It had all the atmosphere of a "proper" football club - no Mickey Mouse set-up, this, which is what some wags back at the studio had told him to expect.

"They clear the sheep off before kick-off," one had suggested.

"And put the cows in another field so they can use the cowshed as a grand stand," added another.

"No need to drain the pitch. It's got a one in four slope!"

And so on.

Greg crossed to the gate of the ground itself and found it unlocked, so he went in. No-one challenged him - a bit different from every other ground he had been to! Sure enough, the pitch was wide and level with plenty of space beyond the touchlines, neatly enclosed by a post and rail fence. Immediately behind that was a concrete hard-standing about a yard wide. Behind the goal his end there was some flat car parking space - he immediately pictured the Outside Broadcast vans parked there - and a single storey building that he assumed held the changing rooms. The far end seemed to have a small grassy embankment and on the other side of the pitch there was a low concrete structure extending some way either side of the half way line.

He headed over to this covered area, ducking under the railing to cut across the pitch. Stakes and ropes cordoned off the goalmouths, a sign that perhaps boys occasionally came into the unguarded ground for a kick-about. He tried to imagine that happening at Anfield, Old Trafford or the New Stamford Stadium! The pitch was well-maintained, flat, without divots and almost completely grassed, no mean feat for mid-January. Obviously some groundsman was doing a first class job. He saw signs in the covered area of recent activity. Someone was in the middle of putting in seats, including a fenced off area on the half way line.

"They're putting in seating for the officials plus a few extra spectators," he thought. The little club was gearing itself up for the match of its life. Ducking under the rail into what was becoming a little stand, Greg turned and surveyed the pitch, already sorting out in his mind's eye where his cameras would go and taking pleasure in the fact that there was plenty of room between the touchlines and the fence for some mobile cameras to give really atmospheric close-ups of play on the wings.

It was time to make contact with the natives, so he headed along the stand towards the changing room block. As he glanced around, he saw a little scrap of blue cloth in the corner of the stand. He didn't know what made him do it, but he stopped to pick it up. It was a pair of knickers. Smiling as he turned them over in his hands he saw a sewn-in piece of white cloth with red lettering embroidered on it. He looked closer. "Morwenna Tregunna", he read.

* * * * * * * * * *

On the Saturday before the replay, with Porthleven having flown back on the Thursday, it was business as usual in Cornish football. Except, for Porthleven, it wasn't, because the media circus had already started to invade their lives. They were big news. They had made the headlines just for reaching the Fourth Round of the FA Cup. Even if they had been drawn at home to Aldershot and lost they would have been the centre of attention in the soccer world for at least a week or two because of their fantastic achievement.

But they had not only reached the Fourth Round, they'd been drawn away to the richest, most feared and powerful team in the world which had won the FIFA World Club Championship only that week; before that, been the team to be flown out to Rio under special arrangements, courtesy of 'The Universe', just so the game could be played, got stranded in Capetown where they played a much-publicised friendly against the under-privileged boys from the Capetown slums (in front of a huge crowd that included Nelson Mandela and Arch Bishop Tutu and raised a lot of money to help improve the sporting facilities for the boys' community); and all the time conducted themselves with such friendly dignity that, being in the world's spotlight, they had won themselves friends on every continent.

The village of Porthleven lived off that for years afterwards as tourists from all over the world with the merest interest in soccer stopped off there, drank in its pubs, ate in its restaurants, sampled its ice creams, enjoyed the delights of its harbour and just had to pop along to Gala Parc - just to see it.

No wonder, too, that Gary Lineker went down to Porthleven to front "Football Focus" that weekend.

It all caused a bit of disruption at great rivals Falmouth, too, as cameras followed Porthleven there for their Cornwall Senior Cup game, for that was their fixture that Saturday. The match certainly provided lively entertainment for the world's sports fans as first of all there was a forty minute delay in the first half whilst an ambulance was called to remove a Falmouth player with a suspected broken leg. Porthleven's skipper John Burrows was sent off for the challenge, having given his side an early lead. Charlie Legge headed a second goal but in injury time Falmouth were awarded a controversial penalty. The kick was taken by Falmouth's Mark Rapsey who, keen to get the game restarted, got into a fight for the ball with Porthleven's Stevie Jewell for which both were sent off. It was Falmouth's first defeat of the season in a match that had Gary Lineker commenting: "....and you don't often see games as action-packed as that in *any* division!"

Action replays, never before available in football at that level, revealed that the referee had been right: it *was* a penalty!

There had been interviews before the game, interviews after the game and much analysis of what the outcome of the replay would be. The consensus was that Porthleven were in for a right stuffing.

When Porthleven's Committee met in their clubhouse on the Monday evening they barely recognised the ground. Vans of all shapes and sizes were parked in the area next to the changing rooms, many with large satellite aerials facing down the pitch towards the harbour - due South. Cables criss-crossed everywhere and there were boom cameras all over the place. Technicians were fitting miniature cameras inside the goals and setting up microphones all round the touchlines; men and women were running to and fro, more often than not with mobile 'phones clasped to their ears, usually arguing over which company should have its cameras where; the BBC, Sky, Digital International and the Asteroid Corporation were all more or less duplicating, or rather quadruplicating, all camera positions - the chaos was total.

"Blimey, Vidal," exclaimed Len Williams, the Chairman. "What are you going to do about all *that*?"

Vidal scratched his head. As Secretary, he felt he ought to be involved somehow. "Dunno, boy," he eventually said. "Let's go and have a pint."

So they did, leaving the TV boys too it. Mind, they *did* find the clubhouse rather crowded, with braying TV producers, technicians, camera men, presenters, commentators, link men, make-up girls - it read like that huge long list that no-one reads at the end of a modern film. Len and Vidal fought their way to the bar. Despite the crowd, they were quickly served.

"Well," said Len, looking round. "At least we'll make some money!"

"Yes," agreed Vidal.

"You from round here?" enquired a brash, chinless individual sporting a cravat and indescribably patterned shirt.

Len and Vidal nodded, supping.

"You'll make some money out of all this, what?" guffawed Cravat.

" 'Ess," nodded Len, taking an instant dislike to Cravat and slipping deliberately into broad dialect. "We shall 'ave ter get a bigger money box, shan' us, Vidal."

" 'Ess, boy," replied Vidal, taking his cue from Len. "I see'd a *ten poun' note* jus' then. Wen' right across the bar, there. True 's I'm standin' 'ere!"

"*Ten Poun'?* Did barman 'ave enuff chenge, moi 'ansome?"

" 'Ess, 'ee tekked a lod o' cash ternight, pard. Ent naw-one paid 'un wi' chickens or brocc'li ternight. Orl cash, boy."

"Jolly good," said Cravat, moving away to bray at some colleagues.

"What a prat!" laughed Len.

"Yes, boy. Shame we didn't have no straw to chew, just to finish him off!"

The Cornish are the kindest people in the world, but they don't suffer fools gladly.

"Seriously," said Len. "Is everything all fixed up for the game?"

"Just keep your fingers crossed," suggested Vidal. "Denzil's done a fine job on the pitch. We've been lucky with the weather, he's nearly finished the seating and all the extra gate people, programme sellers and tea people are lined up. I've got scaffold people coming in tomorrow to put up a bit of staging opposite the stand for Tommy Matthews. The other commentators will have to make their arrangements with him. We've got lots of raffle prizes. Here." Vidal fished in his pocket and pulled out Morwenna Tregunna's knickers. "Know her, do you?"

"Morwenna Tregunna." Len shook his head, chuckling. "Where d'you get them?"

"One of those TV boys handed them in. Says he found them in the stand! We'll have to ask the players if they know who she is. We could make them a raffle prize for them in the dressing room. Cause a laugh, buck 'em up a bit!"

"We need a pennant to exchange before the game," said Len.

"Don't you dare, boy, don't you dare!" And the two men laughed into their beer.

Chapter 37 – So Who Ate the Fish?

The Wanderers United team had flown back from Rio the day after the World Club Championship Final, making a triumphant touch down at Birmingham Airport where they paused on the steps down from the 'plane for numerous photos, the new trophy held aloft in traditional fashion. The sports media made much of the fact that their next game after playing against what could now be described as the second best team in the world was an FA Cup Fourth Round replay against a team who, according to the pyramid system, came from a league nine levels below the Premiership.

Naturally there was intense interest in the game. In a competition famed for throwing up many surprises which upheld the notion of the "romance" of the FA cup, this was the romance of the century. Brave little no-hope Porthleven were ignoring the lure of big money by choosing to play the game at home, as was their right.

"Now for the Minnows!" - Daily Mail.

"Porthleven in for a Storm!" - Daily Express.

"£40 a man country boys take on United's millionaires!" - Daily Mirror.

"The Cup Stops Here! (For Cornwall's Pride)" - Daily Star.

"Our Haul of Cups Runneth Over - Wanderers to Gobble Up Minnows" - The Sun.

"Our Topless Cornish Crackers Give Their Support!" - Daily Sport.

"Should No-hope Clubs be Banned from FA Cup?" - The Universe.

"Wanderers due a Shock Setback?" - The Globe.

There was little time for the Wanderers team to do much more than transfer the spaced-out Heinrich Schickelgrüber and his accompanying doctors into a car so that he could come down off his second Valium trip on the drive to Cornwall. A chartered 'plane awaited the rest of the team at Birmingham and they were soon on their way to Newquay, though a modest Dash Seven was now their transport, not quite in keeping with their status and not nearly as glamorous as the Concorde that brought Porthleven home. Mind, at least Wanderers were being brought from where they were supposed to have been and were unlikely to go too far off course.

The pilot of the Dash Seven emphasised the point just after take off.

"Good afternoon, ladies and gentlemen and welcome aboard Brymon Airways Special Flight BA701 to Newquay. This is your pilot speaking, Captain John Foster, your co-pilot is Captain Gerry Reynard. We shall be flying at a height of fourteen thousand feet and will follow the M5 to Bristol and then the north coasts of Avon, Devon and Cornwall to ensure that we don't get lost. Please inform one of our flight attendants if you lose sight of land as that will mean we have flown too far, in which case we'll turn round and come back. We should arrive at Newquay some time today. The weather there is clear at the moment, the temperature on the ground a balmy eleven degrees. Oh, and well done in Rio, by the way, it's a pleasure to be your pilot. Any chance of some tickets for your game at home to Chelsea? We hope you enjoy the flight and will charter us again."

A ripple of gentle laughter passed through the passengers as the interpreters translated. Spirits were high and the jokes flew round. The two flight attendants brought round a snack; scones, jam and Cornish cream. One of the attendants, a tanned girl with dark hair and eyes, stood at the front of the passenger cabin and reached for her microphone.

"Ladies and Gentlemen, Lizzie and I would like to draw your attention to the light snack we have brought round, a traditional Cornish treat including genuine Cornish clotted cream from a creamery near to Redruth." There was the merest hint of Cornish in her accent. "The correct way to eat it is to cut the scones in half, then spread the jam, with the cream on top of that. Don't put the cream on first. That's what they do in Devon, and that would never do! I hope you enjoy it. If anyone fancies seconds, just ask and we'll see what we can do!"

"Ah wouldn't mind seconds o' you, love!" yelled Macca, temporarily forgetting that he was still under the threat of Jesus Bastardi's "contract" out on him.

"Ah, now, me darlin', you n' me have somet'ing in common, do we not?" said Seamus as the dark Cornish beauty walked past his seat,

"Oh?" she diplomatically enquired. "And what would that be?"

"Whoi, and aren't we both Celts, moi love?" He put out an arm to stop her.

"Well, yes," replied the dark Cornish beauty in the uniform. "We must be careful to avoid in-breeding, then, mustn't we!"

A few seats back, Johann van Dyke was appraising the flight attendant, looking magnificent in her uniform, and sketching out an idea for a porn movie script that he would discuss with his colleagues in the industry as soon as he could. In this little 'plane, and with the American market in mind, he would call it "The Half Mile High Club".

* * * * * * * * *

The Wanderers stayed in a hotel in Falmouth where they had been able to arrange for their food to be prepared by their own small team of chefs. This had become the norm for International sides playing in World Cups, but with such a lot at stake these days and with so many temperamental and over-paid players, the Wanderers Board had sanctioned the idea for the entire season. All meals just before every game were planned by prepared by their team of chefs who always went with the team to the hotels used for away games even in the UK.

There were four of them: Dick Stone, Anthony Dansfield, François Saussice and Roger Odgers. Between them they prepared a number of carefully balanced meals under the watchful eye of Nita Worrell, the club's nutritionist. They bought only the highest quality ingredients, and for games abroad took gallons of mineral water not just for use in preparing and cooking the food but also for doing the washing up in, too. There had to be no danger of food poisoning upsetting the team. To be doubly sure, samples of all dishes were set aside and frozen, to be kept long enough to establish that no illness had been caused before the samples were thrown away. The idea was that if any player came down with anything they could have the food he had eaten analysed to see if it was the source of the problem.

On the day of the replay a light lunch rich in protein and carbohydrate was planned as usual and a pleasant concoction of local sea bass and rice was prepared by Roger. It was declared a total success even though it was a change from the usual routine of fillet steak.

The team travelled through the winter landscape to Porthleven, their coach grandly ushered into the car park next to the clubhouse. There wasn't room for it by the pitch because most of the room was taken up by all the TV and radio vans. The team and its entourage of management, medical staff, Directors and interpreters were then led across to the changing rooms, cramped by Premiership standards but palatial compared to the ones at São Cristóvão. The players themselves had already been to the ground on the Sunday for a bit of light training and to familiarise themselves with it.

Excitement grew as the tiny ground was packed at least an hour before kick-off with the fifteen hundred or so souls lucky enough to have got tickets. They had been ushered between the unruly mass of TV company vans with all their criss-crossing cables, most of which broke the standard broadcasters' health and safety rules regarding the positioning of cables where the public may walk. Their tangled presence only served to maximise the atmosphere of anticipation. The various TV and newspaper cameramen were in brightly-coloured tops, milling to and fro, providing extra entertainment for most of the spectators.

Attracting most of this attention was the camera suspended above the little hastily-organised stand. Digital International had parked a gantry lorry – a "cherry-picker" - in the road alongside the ground. Their camera installed in the bucket, it and the cameraman had been hoisted into the night sky and then poked between two of the pine trees that shielded that side of the ground from the road. The arm of the gantry and the bucket on the end, with the camera and cameraman precariously installed, appeared like a giant dinosaur's neck and head through the foliage, providing by far the best vantage point of all. The Sports Producers of the other TV companies were all kicking themselves for not having had the idea themselves. Digital's Greg van Dam thanked providence that he had driven past a Highways gantry lorry with its team of street-light maintenance men to give him the idea. It had certainly put one over on bloody Asteroid Sport! Never mind that he'd had to offer the cameraman a big bonus to spend two hours suspended in a bucket on a January night with a cold wind blowing in from the nearby sea.

"And take an empty bottle with you," he had suggested to the put-upon employee.

"What for?"

"I don't want you sullying Digital International's name by pissing on the crowd!"

Music from the nineteen sixties played over the PA, the normal pre-match sound at Porthleven. A Mexican Wave was started and the atmosphere of expectation was enhanced when, almost an hour before kick-off, the floodlights came on. This was at the request of the various TV crews to give their pictures that bit extra.

It had worked out quite well for the groundsman Denzil Chegwidden, too. He had been intercepted, on his way to making yet another inspection of his near-perfect pitch, by Gregg van Dam.

"I say, excuse me, you're the Groundsman, aren't you?"

" 'Ess, boy."

"I must say you do a brilliant job. Have you seen Man. United's ground these days? Yours puts it to shame.!"

" 'Ess, I knaw."

"Look, would it be possible for you to put the floodlights on now? Just so we can get our cameras adjusted, you know. Best quality pictures and all that!"

"We don' usually put 'em on 'till jest before the teams comes out," replied Denzil. "Costs a lot in 'lectric, see?"

"Oh - er - yes. Well," Greg reached into his pocket. "Would this cover it?"

He proffered a £20 note. Denzil looked at it calculatingly; calculating that the soft-handed media man from upcountry would have no idea how much electricity the floodlights used or how much it cost, which was not more than £10 for a whole game.

"We-ell....." he began, his weather-beaten face creased by doubt. Another £10 appeared. " 'Ess, that'll cover un, boy. Thanks. I'll see to it."

"Thanks awfully." Greg had run off to tell his outside broadcast editor to be ready for the lights.

Denzil strolled past the Sky TV van. Technicians were busy inside and out.

"Awright, my lover," hailed Denzil.

A harassed looking girl with a clipboard clutched tightly against her non-existent bosom looked at him.

"What?" she enquired.

" 'Ow can 'ee see what 'ee's doin' in the dark loik that?" asked Denzil.

"Oh! Well, we've lights in the van, but we can't see much outside!"

" 'Ess. Id'll be bedder when us puts the floodloits on," prompted Denzil.

"Floodlights? Oh, of course, the floodlights." She turned to yell to someone in the van. "Mike, the floodlights. They could put them on now, couldn't they?"

"Of course, Roz. Brilliant. See if you can arrange it," came the muffled reply.

'Roz' turned to Denzil. "Can you do that? It would give us time to make our pictures, well, just that much better, you see."

"Well," replied Denzil "The 'lectric is some dear fer they lights...."

He made another £30 out of Sky, and when he had extracted similar sums from the Asteroid Corporation, Carlton, the BBC and the Transworld Sport crew he went into the toilet in the changing room block and turned the lights on.

"Whad're 'ee doin', Den?" asked a lady stacking cups behind the tea bar.

"TV boys wan' them early ter 'elp adjust their picture quality."

"Fair enough, boy. Should've got 'em ter pay!"

"Oi did," grinned Denzil. "Thirty quid *each*!"

"Thirty.......you bugger, Den, proper job! You keep un, boy. Extra match bonus!"

"I'll buy all the boys a drink after the game, 'owever many we lose by!"

The tea lady chuckled away to herself. That Denzil! He had his eyes open when *he* was born, and no mistake!

A buzzer sounded in both dressing rooms. This was it!

* * * * * * * * * *

In the Porthleven dressing room there were a few white faces with tense jaws. In the Wanderers dressing room there were one or two green faces with tense buttocks.

Enrique Mouette's was one of the green faces.

"Je suis malade," he moaned to his interpreter. "Je m'excuse...." He dashed off in the direction of the toilet and soon the sounds of vomiting could be heard. This clearly sent the other green-faced players over the edge: Antonio la Pazbaq and Edmun Edmunsen both stood suddenly, clasping their hands to their faces and looking wildly towards the closed toilet door. Antonio ducked into the shower and Edmun quickly followed him. Both could be heard being violently sick. Georgi Strupinski, Lim Po and Seamus O'Hooligan followed their example and soon the dressing room air was pervaded with the pungent odour of fresh vomit.

Macca chuckled. "Wey-ay, lads! Smells like the bogs at the end of a good night at Stringfellows!"

"Open the fochin' windows fer Christ's sake!" demanded Ronnie. "Wha' the foch is gaein' on? Wha's the matter wi' ye all?" He was getting, to say the least, a little uneasy.

"Who else is feeling ill?" asked Joker.

Muttered translations revealed that Heinrich Schickelgrüber was still feeling woozy, but as he was being "rested" for this game it didn't matter too much. For a man who had been pumped full of Valium for hours on end twice in the last week, and recently had four teeth removed, he was doing well to string a sentence together while standing up, never mind actually feel okay. Jesus Bastardi needed no interpreter. Just as the referee's buzzer sounded, he puked without warning all over the bench next to him, where unfortunately Papa Médecin's pre-match ritual paraphernalia were arranged. The black candle went out, of course, and the feathers on his chicken's feet looked unlikely to be of any further use at all.

"Mon Dieu!" he wailed, cut off in mid-incantation. His interpreter paraphrased the tirade that followed. "He's not very happy with that."

"Aye, the carrot fairy strikes again," chortled Macca.

227

"Shuttup, Macca, you're not helping!" snapped Joker. Papa Médecin demanded a translation. "What do you mean by 'carrot fairy'?" asked his interpreter.

"Why, man, ev'ry time yer sick, laike, there's always carrots in it, even if'n you's 'aven't eaten any, laike!" explained the rhinoceros-skinned Macca.

"I thought I told you to belt up!" snarled Joker. "This is serious. That's - what - seven so far. Can we get the ref to delay the kick-off?"

"Tha' depends," growled Ronnie. "Who else feels ill?"

No-one else appeared to be feeling sick. The echoing sound of retching from the showers had stopped and some of the afflicted were showing their faces again - though these still tended to be green.

"Enrique," asked Bones, digging out some schooldays French. "Tu es bien maintenant." Enrique's interpreter went into automatic mode. "The doctor is asking you if you feel okay, Enrique. Oh - sorry!"

"Oui. Je sera bien a jouer," replied Enrique.

"He's okay to play."

"Y' still look fuckin' terrible, man!"

"Yes, thank you, Macca, you really are helping, you know," admonished Bones.

"Doan't fuss, man. It's only a bit o' puke, laike. It's laike that filum, the one in the aeroplane. Who 'ad the fish an' who didn't. The two pilots did. Din ye remember?"

"Aye, well, we *all* had the fochin' fish, ye pillock. Noo - *belt up!*" Ronnie was definitely not pleased. "Bones, you'll have tae check the food later. The lads seem okay after they've thrown up. Joker, go an' get the ref. Even a ten minute delay will help, just tae get the lads feelin' better."

Joker departed, finding the Porthleven team crowded into the central area between the two dressing rooms, waiting with the well-known schoolmaster referee, the two assistant referees and the fourth official. Joker approached the referee. "We've got a problem," he said. "Seven of our team have just been ill. Thrown up. Can we delay the kick-off?"

"There would have to be a very good reason," replied the referee.

"We've had lads throwing up just as the buzzer went. Come in and see for yourself. The smell should convince you!"

The referee shrugged his shoulders. "Okay, I'd better take a look."

In the Wanderers dressing room no-one else had been sick, but two others, Milo Opec and Papa Médecin were beginning to feel off colour.

"Puke in Bastardi's bag, man, get yer oan back," whispered Macca. Papa didn't understand him, of course. Nor did he care much. He couldn't be sure that his woozy feeling wasn't to do with his defiled pre-match altar. Never mind that the others thought that they were just his quaint lucky charms. What did they know about placating the souls of the undead so that they didn't throw themselves in front of him or any shots or passes he made in order to foil his efforts? They'd looked after him so far but only because he had been so conscientious with his rituals. Indeed, at his home he had been responsible for the demise of more chickens than his nearest branch of KFC. He clutched his little plastic bag of chicken blood and, as usual, when no-one was looking, he pushed it out of sight up his sleeve ready to sprinkle it surreptitiously before him as he ran onto the pitch. That merely strengthened the voodoo, though. His vomit-caked altar offerings had to be somehow cleansed of what after all was a rejected meal. If a human rejected a meal, it certainly wasn't good enough for the souls of the undead, so he could be in trouble.

On balance, he hoped it was the fish.

The referee came into the dressing room and immediately recoiled at the smell. "Bloody hell, I see what you mean!" he said. "How many of your players are fit?"

"Bones?" prompted Ronnie.

"Well, seven have thrown up, once each, and that seems to be all it is. Two more are beginning to feel ill, so they'll probably need to throw up and then after a few minutes they'll probably be reasonably okay again."

"Well, you know the rules. As long as you have seven fit players...."

"Ah know," interrupted Ronnie. "We'll be oot in five minutes if tha's okay wi' you."

"Okay," agreed the ref. "Can I suggest you keep someone here at the dressing room door in case anyone is struck down during the game? Not nice, throwing up on the pitch." He turned to address the players. "Run off, shouting to me as you go and that'll be okay. You'll have to return to the field of play in the approved manner, of course, at the half-way line. As if this fixture hasn't been plagued enough! Okay, Ronnie, let's be fair and say ten more minutes to get yourselves sorted. I'll have to put a report in, of course, but that's routine and I can see - well, smell - the sick..... there won't be any problem as far as the FA's concerned. You'll need some medical certification, I imagine. I'd better go and talk to Porthleven."

He went out into the lobby and when the situation was explained to the Cornish team they agreed to wait ten minutes. Vidal James went to the little room in Moaners' Corner, where the PA was housed, and announced the short delay. The various TV crews began to sweat. Digital One Sport and Sky were broadcasting live and a delay to proceedings would cause complications. Neither had allowed for extra time, so their timings were tight.

Back in the visitors' dressing room Papa Médecin suddenly dashed for the single toilet and repeated Enrique's earlier vocal efforts.

Five minutes later the buzzer went again and Wanderers gathered themselves together to leave. Milo Opec had been sick just after Papa Médecin and that seemed to be it.

This time, both teams gathered in the area between the two dressing rooms and filed out side by side behind the referee and his assistants. Up until their hastily arranged game in Cape Town, the sound that greeted them would have been the loudest the Porthleven team had heard. They hadn't the ghost of a chance of winning, but here they were, entertaining the wealthiest, most successful team in recent footballing history, not in a promised end-of-season friendly, but in a serious match. It was a proud moment.

Chapter 38 - One – nil

The teams filed onto the pitch and went through the ritual kicking-in and centre circle toss of the referee's coin for choice of ends or kick off. John Burrows won the toss and chose to kick against the wind for the first half, which meant defending the clubhouse end.

It wasn't obvious to any of the spectators, but several of the Wanderers team were definitely off-colour. They had to kick off and as the two sides lined up to face one another, Georgi Strupinski and Seamus O'Hooligan took their places at the centre spot with the ball. The referee counted the players on both sides. Behind Georgi and Seamus was a midfield of five, mainly due to Wanderers having few fit defenders to select from. From left to right, they were Manuel Sardinhas, Enrique Mouette, Milo Opec, Macca and Jerome McZane. Their one central defender was Jesus Bastardi, captain that day, with Kwasi Ankoma and Papa Médecin on either side. Edmun Edmunsen was in goal, wearing his woollen bobble hat to protect his grade one hair cut from the cold wind blowing from the harbour, from where there was what even the locals in the crowd regarded as an unusually strong smell of rotting fish and seaweed.

Facing them were the part-timers of Porthleven from the Jewson South Western League. Gary Penhaligon was in goal and forecast as likely to be the busiest player on the field. There were three central defenders: Darren Holsey, Dave Larsen and Stevie Jewell. Justin Harrington was the right wing-back with Nigel Thwaites on the left. John Burrows captained the side from midfield in the company of Mark Hope, Adrian Bleasedale and Gary Bannister. The lone striker was Charlie Legge. Micky Faithful was on the bench with Ian Rowe, Peter Gamble and Paul Ainscough.

The whistle went and Seamus pushed the ball sideways to Georgi. He turned and played the ball back to where Manuel Sardhinas should have been, only he wasn't. Instead he was streaking goalwards like a man possessed. With a hand clasped over his mouth. The smell of rotting fish had just tipped his stomach over the edge and he was heading for the changing room. He gesticulated wildly at the referee as he ran past him and disappeared into the changing room.

Charlie Legge, meanwhile, had run into the gap using his exceptional pace, reached the loose ball and hit a first-time shot from some forty yards out. At his level of football, most times such a shot would have missed the target by quite a margin or fallen tamely into the goalkeeper's arms. This shot was going high until the strong wind resisted it enough to slow it down. Edmun Edmunsen was, as is often the case with goal keepers, several yards off his line for his own side's kick-off. He was also experiencing a new wave of nausea, so wasn't really concentrating as much as a player paid as much as he was should do. The wind from the harbour behind him smelled strongly of rotten fish and something worse besides, and his stomach churned. The ball actually clipped the crossbar as it went in. Porthleven were one - nil up in mere seconds!

Charlie Legge was buried under a mountain of gold and black shirts whilst the Wanderers players looked around in disbelief. Kwasi Ankoma was the first of them to move. He ran over to the referee, pointing towards the Porthleven end.

"And Ankoma has spotted something, I'm not sure what," shrilled Digital Sport One's commentator Terry Prosser. "He's trying to draw the referee's attention to something...now he's running off! I didn't see a red card - this is sensational - Wanderers are in disarray, Manuel Sardhinas off the field of play right from the start, apparently ill, and now Ankoma is following him to the dressing room... all I do know is that only three players have touched the ball and Porthleven, unbelievably, are leading World Club Champions Wanderers by one goal to nil!"

In the Wanderers dugout, both Ronnie and Joker had their heads in their hands. Beside them Antonio la Pazbaq was feeling even worse. Lim Po had just thrown up on his football boots.

Georgi and Seamus kicked off again, this time Georgi making sure that Milo Opec was where he wanted him to be before he played the ball to him. The nine men of Wanderers played the ball around, their superior skills allowing them to bide their time until Kwasi and Manuel eventually returned to the field of play via the halfway line in the approved fashion, much to the confusion of Digital's Terry Prosser, who to tell the truth wasn't the most observant commentator on the circuit, getting by on the strength of his dramatic voice alone.

Wanderers began to look the side they were despite their intestinal difficulties. They tested Gary Penhaligon a couple of times, and the way he responded made one or two managers sit up and take notice when they watched the highlights later. Hadn't Nigel Martyn of Leeds and England started in the same league as this Porthleven side?

The next victim of the carrot fairy was Jerome McZane. As the vomit rose in his throat he had to make the run for the changing room, yelling "I's goin' to t'row up, man!" at the referee as he went. His path took him across the Porthleven penalty area in what looked to everyone like a penetrating run as Enrique Mouette, spotting him, played a great ball into his path. Jerome ignored the gift and kept going, off the pitch and into the dressing room. Gary Penhaligon, fielding the easy ball, was as puzzled as anyone in the ground. Shrugging his shoulders, he gave it some air and watched the ball disappear satisfyingly over the half way line despite the wind. It wouldn't be too long before it was back, he thought.

He was forced to rush out and go down at the feet of Seamus O'Hooligan just a few minutes later and once more felt relieved to have safely fielded the ball. He had noted that banging the ball high and hard towards the centre of the Wanderers' defence was quite effective. In the videos they had watched, the Wanderers' defence had proved to be very good in the air, but today he was sure he detected almost a reluctance by Bastardi and Médecin to head the ball, and the same went for most of their midfield and the two strikers as well.

Indeed, Bastardi was the next to be excused, leaving just as Jerome McZane returned looking decidedly grey. Bastardi had to meet a route one ball and headed it firmly away. Bloody hell, he felt ill after that and felt another bout of vomiting coming on. By now, the tolerant schoolmaster in the middle was used to the coming and going of the Wanderers players. He and the huge centre back exchanged glances and he surreptitiously waved his permission to the player to leave the pitch. Off ran Bastardi, the crowd also becoming used to the antics of the Premiership giants.

A wag soon had the home fans adapting the old Manfred Mann hit: "If you've gotta go, go now, because you've got to have a shite!" It wasn't entirely clear to the crowd what the nature of the Wanderers' players problem was, so no-one could blame them for drawing the wrong conclusions. It was clear to Ronnie and Joker, though, that the vomiting was going to be affecting the team for a while yet, and it was allowing the little Cornish side to match them in all parts of the park. And they were one-nil down, and the match was being beamed live all over the world.

Ten minutes before half time Wanderers made the breakthrough the form books demanded. Again it was Enrique Mouette who set the move up. Manuel Sardinhas to his left saw a way of getting round behind the Porthleven defence. He took Enrique's precise pass on the outside of his left foot, a beautifully weighted first touch that set the ball up perfectly for his strike with the outside of his left foot that bent the ball around Gary Penhaligon and into the far corner of the goal. Manuel's celebrations were strangled in his throat, however, as he realised that his shot had also curved around the fleet figure of Jerome McZane darting diagonally across the goal, once again en route to the Wanderers' vomitarium.

The Wanderers fans in the crowd saw nothing of this, they were too busy cheering the goal. Their joy turned to anger as they realised that the goal had been disallowed. The linesman's flag was up - or it would have been if the man holding it hadn't recently been renamed the assistant referee. If the renaming was done in an attempt to reduce the level of abuse directed at the men with flags, it failed pretty dismally. Presumably some genius at the FA thought that as yelling "Oi, assistant referee, are you blind?" was a bit of a mouthful, such unwarranted verbal assaults would peter out, without giving due regard to the conservative nature of the average abusive fan who would, for the sake of convenience, continue to call him a linesman. The one with the flag up in this case was having a few old fashioned adjectives added in front of the old-fashioned name. The referee ran over to consult him.

"The number eleven wasn't offside, was he?" he asked.

"No, it was the number twenty-seven. I know he was running for the bog, but he was right in front of the 'keeper as the shot came in. He must have distracted the 'keeper, so he was interfering with play."

"Yes, right. Offside, then. No goal."

He signalled the free kick and of course there were the predictable reactions from the opposing factions in the crowd. The Wanderers players were not happy, of course, and a number of them pursued the referee. He waved them away. Referees don't change their minds anyway, and the players weren't to know that even as they protested, the action replays being beamed world wide showed that Jerome McZane had clearly run across Gary Penhaligon's line of vision in an offside position as Manuel Sardinhas shot.

"Good decision by the linesman!" bawled Terry Prosser. Commentators certainly didn't bother to try to get their tongues round such a user-unfriendly name as 'assistant referee'.

In another five minutes the half-time whistle went and, unbelievably, Wanderers went in a goal down.

In their dressing room Ronnie put Bones in charge. "Who's still feeling like a puke?" he asked. Seamus O'Hooligan, Georgi Strupinski, Milo Opec, Edmun Edmunsen, Antonio la Pazbaq, Jesus Bastardi and Lim Po all did.

"It's that bhluddy wind, Doc," complained Seamus. "What the fochin' bejasus it smells of, Oi don't roightly know but it 'ud make a statue puke! Fresh sea air my arse!"

"Right, lads, line up." Bones made all the ill players swallow something. Almost immediately they began to retch and the showers took the brunt of it.

"Don't worry," said Bones, seeing Ronnie and Joker looking worried. "I'm clearing their stomachs. Then I'll give them something to settle things down." He had got busy on his mobile early in the first half when he saw how things were progressing and was soon in touch with a local doctor who brought what he needed to the ground.

As the coughing and gasping players emerged from the shower, Bones gave each one an injection. "That'll hold it for an hour. You should all start to feel better soon."

"Worra boot the game, boss," asked Macca. "Any changes, like?"

"Nae changes, lads," replied Ronnie. "Let's hope the Doc's jollop will pull us through. Nae wurries, boys. Jus' gae oot an' do 'em!"

In the home dressing room there was an air of unreality, but the manager was bringing them down to earth. "Vidal tells me a doctor's car arrived just before half time bringing something to their club doctor. He's probably going to get them back on their feet for the second half. Just do your best, lads. We've had a good run."

"Club doctor?" quipped Charlie Legge. "Have we got one?"

"My missus always gives me a seeing to after a game," answered Micky Faithful. "Does that count?"

"Flo who cleans the clubhouse looks like an old witch," observed Ian Rowe. "Perhaps she could be our witch doctor?"

"We can get Denzil to run his mower over your bollocks," called Mark Hope from the toilet, having a pee.

"What's that got to do with a club doctor?" someone yelled back.

"Nothing," came the muffled reply. "I just thought it would be a good idea!"

Alan Carey thought it prudent to hold down the high spirits. "Come on, lads, focus again. If they are fitter for the second half we're going to be busy. Darren, Stevie, Dave, watch the ball holding up in the wind. We won't pull back and try to defend our lead, that'll just be asking for trouble. Let's just play our game and close them down tight. And learn, of course, boys. These are the cream, the best. Let's learn from them. Do your best. And Micky?"

"Boss?"

"Let Mark out of the bog now!"

The buzzer went and it suddenly went quiet and tense in the dressing room.

"Go and enjoy it, lads!" exhorted Alan.

"Come on, boys!" shouted John Burrows, as captain taking on the responsibility for leading the team. "Concentrate! Let's do it!"

And out they went.

Chapter 39 - TV Trouble

During the half-time break, the crowd buzzed with excitement. In the small, roped-off section in what had recently become the stand, the Wanderers Directors and officials were being treated to tea and pasties brought out to them by a posse of specially recruited tea ladies. They were a disgruntled group. They had been told by Joker about the players' problem as he passed their position on his way to the dugout.

"I can't believe this," said Sefton, munching on his pasty. "What a cock-up. If we lose this one, Blankopf will blow a gasket. He might even pull out, even though we're the World Club Champions!"

Malcolm's intestines gave a protesting gurgle and he desperately contemplated the distance to the nearest toilet. "Oh, you don't think so, do you?"

"We-ell, no, I suppose not, but what a complete bloody farce after the nil-nil draw."

"If the players are fit to carry on, we'll do it. We only need two goals, after all," said Cecil with confidence. "Look, here they come."

The crowd cheered loudly as the two teams came onto the pitch for the second half.

In his position on the scaffolding opposite the stand, Digital Sport One's commentator Terry Prosser was watching the scene live as well as on the small monitor he had in front of him. It was no easy task, for with the main camera perched over the stand on the end of the gantry, the TV picture showed the opposite view to his.

"And an atmosphere you could cut with a knife prevails at this quaint little Gala Parc ground down here in Cornwall," he blathered. "There appear to be no changes on either side, so whatever it is that has afflicted the Wanderers players, it can't be too serious, though it has obviously affected their performance. And Porthleven kick off to get the second half under way. That's Legge, the goal scorer, back to Burrows, put under immediate pressure by Mouette, who has in fact fouled Burrows. Mouette isn't happy with that decision, he's arguing the point with the referee - it looks like he's being booked for dissent...."

Terry consulted his monitor to see exactly what was happening, along with millions of Digital Sport One viewers world-wide. They saw the image wobble and pan dramatically away before being blocked by a close-up of a swathe of foliage, followed by a brief close-up of the car park full of TV vans, dishes on their roofs, and a clear image of an Asteroid Corporation van before the editor in the Digital Sport Outside Broadcast truck reacted and switched to a ground-level camera.

In common with the millions of viewers, Sir Fabian, watching events on his TV in Johannesburg, where he was on business, wondered what on earth was going on. The first-half performance had been bad enough but Sir Fabian was particularly angry at the sight of the Asteroid Corporation van on his TV channel. He reached for his 'phone.

* * * * * * * * *

Karenza Chynoweth was not a happy person. Lumpy and overweight, with big bones and flesh to match, she inwardly railed at a world that worshipped either matchstick thin models or curvy feminine women. She could aspire to be neither. She seethed at adverts in magazines or on TV that sold fitness videos, make-up or in any way used glamorous women to promote any product whatsoever. She knew that even if she won the lottery, no amount of plastic surgery could make her in the least bit attractive. She had been shunned for being fat and ugly at school, where fate played a cruel trick on her by giving her a particularly uncomfortable adolescence. Plagued by acne and crippling period pains, she became bitter and depressed.

She had not even been blessed with a particularly good brain. Certainly not A-level material, she gained a very moderate crop of GCSEs and went to College to do a GNVQ course in Social Care. Her work experiences had taught her that her appearance was not conducive to a career in Care. Old people and toddlers alike just could not take to her. Some even seemed frightened of her unfortunate appearance. At the age of nineteen she found a perfect job. She became a traffic warden.

Based in Helston, she was particularly vigilant whenever she saw an even remotely attractive woman driver just a minute over time in a restricted parking area. Women with young children were not immune. If they had children, then they already had more than she felt she could ever hope to have, so she showed them no mercy or consideration. She had found two cars in a car park one day, both with well out-of-date tax discs. She waited for the drivers. The first was a young woman, pretty, and Karenza booked her. The next car's driver arrived moments later. She was a frumpy, fat, ugly, middle aged woman with a hairy wart on her nose and no sign of any rings on her fingers.

"Just thought I'd wait and point out that your tax seems to have run out." It was three months out of date.

The frumpy, fat, ugly, middle aged woman with the hairy wart and no rings looked flustered and blushed. "Oh my God," she said. "I'm so sorry. Now you mention it, I remember the reminder coming. I just put it on the sideboard and forgot all about it." A look of panic spread across her face. "Oh, no, I wonder if I paid the electricity bill?" She looked at Karenza with pleading in her eyes. "I suppose I'll get a big fine for this now!" Tears sprang into her eyes.

"Now, don't get upset, madam." Karenza felt genuine sympathy for the frumpy, fat, ugly middle aged woman with the hairy wart and no rings. It could be like looking in a mirror in a decade or two from now. "Look, if you apply for your road tax now you can fib on the form and say the car was off the road for the last couple of months. That way you've saved a bit of money!"

The frumpy, fat, ugly, middle aged woman with the hairy wart and no rings looked so relieved, Karenza's spirits were lifted even more than they had been by the earlier booking of the young pretty woman.

"Just make sure you do it soon: today, if possible. We're just here to help!"

At this unlikely statement from a traffic warden, the frumpy, fat, etcetera muttered her thanks, got into her car and drove away.

Karenza had been specially drafted in to the nearby village of Porthleven to help keep the roads clear on the night of the match against Wanderers. A huge amount of extra traffic was expected and the roads immediately around the ground were to be kept clear of all parked vehicles. A couple of local farmers had unwittingly made this easier than it might have been by cashing in on the event and using fields next to the main road as "overflow car parks".

Karenza had strolled, traffic warden style, around the harbour, placing parking tickets on a couple of cars that were ignoring the "Police - No Parking" signs. She wandered round the bend into one of the two classified roads out of Porthleven - the one by which Porthleven's ground was situated. It was already dark but up on her right she saw the lights of a parked vehicle. Her eyes glittered in the dark. Another victim? She approached the vehicle and saw the legend "Digital One Sport" emblazoned on it. Greg van Dam had acquired the gantry truck in time to have the company logo made up on panels that fitted the rear windows.

Sport! That was another red rag to Karenza. She had been too fat and lumpy to be any good at it. At school, PE lessons had been a nightmare, having to undress with all those normal sized girls, knowing she looked frightful in the silly PE skirt and top. She couldn't run, couldn't do gymnastics, wasn't even co-ordinated enough to do things like shot putt or discus: sport reminded her of the empty life she led because of her physical appearance. Sport was for beautiful, or at least graceful or co-ordinated people. Anyone who watched these satellite sports channels was looking at beautiful and gifted sportsmen and women all the time. Bastards!

She approached the cab of the van. There was no-one in it. With a grim sense of satisfaction she wrote out a ticket. As she fixed it to the screen a man approached.

"Oi!" he yelled. "What the hell are you doing?"

"Can't you read?" countered Karenza. "This is a no parking area. There's going to be a lot of people around for the football match tonight."

"I know, you silly cow. What d'you think this is here for?" The man was clearly going to be unreasonable.

"I have absolutely no idea," replied Karenza, politely as per her traffic warden training. "All I know is that you will have to move it."

"Don't be daft! It will have a camera on it to show the match!"

"Well, it can't stay there, sir. You'll have to move it!"

"Are you deaf as well as stupid and ugly? I've just told you, it will have a camera on it showing the match to millions of viewers all over the world. It can't be moved until the game is over."

Deaf, stupid and ugly. Right, thought Karenza. If that's how you want it. "You'll have to move it *now*, sir. You've already got a ticket, but since you have returned to the vehicle and are refusing to move it, I must warn you that it could be towed away."

"You can't tow it away, you dozy cow! Didn't you hear what I said? It will be used for a live TV broadcast to millions of people all over the world who have paid good money to watch just what we're showing. And you want to tow it away? Go away and frighten some children!" The man was extremely belligerent.

"You have been warned," Karenza informed the belligerent man as an idea formed in her mind.

To get the van towed away might take some time, but she'd do her best. She turned her back and talked into her lapel radio.

Karenza's Uncle Dereck was a bachelor. It probably had something to do with his being lumpy and overweight, with big bones and flesh to match, making him fat and ugly. He and his niece had a lot in common, but oddly enough they got on despite the fact that when they looked at one another they saw themselves. Rather than driving them apart, it seemed to draw them together, comrades in adversity, as it were. Uncle Dereck ran a garage in the nearby village of Ashton. Something like an hour after his niece's altercation with the belligerent man he listened to the voice at the other end of his 'phone with interest and readily agreed to the request.

It was around half-time between Porthleven and Wanderers that he drew up in front of the offending gantry truck in his breakdown lorry. There was a police car there as well. Karenza had wandered off after calling in hoping that the belligerent man would sense triumph and go away. She had returned and found the patrol car waiting and the gantry truck empty, it's crane-like roof appendage raised with its end poked out of sight through the cypress trees lining the football ground. The noise of the crowd swelled through the night air. On the other side of the trees was a blaze of light from the floodlights. Where Karenza and her uncle were, in the road, it was dark, all the more black due to the exceptional brilliance of the quartz floodlight bulbs.

Karenza approached the patrol car, in which a bored-looking constable was seated. "Hullo," she said. "Are you here to see the tow-away?"

"Yes," said the bored constable. "Can we get on with it?"

"You stay there," said Karenza. "I'll see to it. I know the tow-truck driver. He's my uncle."

"Oh, right, thanks," said the bored constable, starting his engine and closing his window. It was winter after all. Might as well put his heater on and keep warm. He'd have given a lot to have been one of the officers on duty at the match.

Karenza went over to the breakdown lorry. "Hi, Uncle Dereck! You should have heard what the driver called me! Deaf, stupid, ugly, a dozy cow - he was horrible! Let's get it towed away."

"What's on the roof?"

"Only a camera. If we move it, it may make someone from the TV company realise we mean business. Think they can come down here and do what they like!"

Uncle Dereck backed his lorry up close to the front of the gantry van and began to sort out the towing rig. Getting into the gantry truck was no difficulty:

Uncle Dereck had a mass of assorted keys and seemed to know which ones to try. He let the handbrake off so that he and Karenza could roll the front wheels into the towing cradle.

Up in the bucket the cameraman felt a lurch. His camera hadn't been on air at the time - it was coming to the end of half-time and the editor in the van behind the goal - where he was no doubt nice and warm, thought the precariously perched camera man - was beaming out close-ups of the crowd from the mobile cameras around the pitch. At least it had given the cameraman time to relieve himself into the bottle thoughtfully provided by his producer.

As the teams came out for the second half, the editor was still using the pictures from the mobile cameras for some dramatic close-ups. The camera man in the gantry cradle didn't have time to wonder what caused the lurch: the second half had started, some twonk had committed a foul and then argued the toss with the referee. As he was being booked for his trouble, his camera came on air as the editor asked him for a close-up of the booking. He zoomed in on the scene and then his world went pear-shaped.

Suddenly his bucket was dragged sideways and he was buried in a mass of pine tree branches. They pulled and pushed him to and fro and then, to his horror, as the cradle continued to scythe sideways through the tree tops, he felt himself being lifted out of the cradle. One of the branches, on a pine tree bent almost at right angles by the errant gantry bucket, had hooked him up by the hood on his Arctic jacket. After the bucket had moved on to cut its swathe through the adjoining trees, the one by which the camera man was suspended straightened up, whip-like, catapulting the him, screaming, at a steep angle up into the air.

By some miracle he reached the apex of his trajectory, thereby becoming virtually motionless for a fraction of a second, just by the top of one of the floodlights. He instinctively grabbed hold of it and hung there, petrified and confused. As he came to his senses, he realised where he was and how incredibly lucky he had been. Most people unexpectedly stranded eighty feet above the ground on a slender aluminium pole would feel anything but lucky, but the cameraman had a perfectly good head for heights and realised that he was at least safe, even if he was rather embarrassingly stranded. Until he realised that he could actually reach the ground safely. Locking his arms and legs around the pole, he released his grip just enough to begin sliding down.

No-one noticed him. The game was too absorbing. Everything was going fine even though the pole got wider as he descended. The cameraman was still able to control his speed until he reached the ground. The pylon stood between the touchline and the spectators' enclosure so his sudden appearance did surprise a few people. The cameraman, relieved to find himself down and in one piece, just smiled at the crowd and made his way to the Digital One Sports outside broadcast editing truck. He didn't know what the bloody hell had happened but he was unhurt and might as well get warm.

Outside with the breakdown lorry, Uncle Dereck was forced to stop. Cables that had hung unseen straight down from the gantry bucket had now swung the bucket backwards and he could see them now that the bucket was pulled through to his side of the trees. He climbed into the cab of the gantry truck and after starting its engine (using one of his selection of keys) soon had the gantry and its bucket properly stowed away on the roof. He'd also found that the cables had connecting pieces in the bucket, so he pulled them apart and threw the cables into the trees.

"Told you there was a camera on it," said Karenza. "They'll be keen enough to get that back!"

Uncle Dereck climbed up to secure the bucket. "Here!" he shouted down to Karenza in the gloom. "There's a bottle of Lucozade up here. You want it?"

"Oh, thanks!" called Karenza. Uncle Dereck threw it down to her. Karenza, feeling thirsty and seeing the Lucozade label in the dim light, unscrewed the cap to take a swig.

Chapter 40 - The Aftermath

Wanderers United ran out four-one winners in the end. Bones' administrations gradually took effect and although Porthleven exploited the high ball to good effect, they fell behind to an Enrique Mouette volley from outside the box and a Macca free kick after a clumsy challenge on Johann van Dyke by Darren Holsey. After that it was all over, really. As the Wanderers players felt better they began to play a bit and in the last ten minutes they really showed the Cornish side a thing or two. Georgi Strupinski rounded things off with two well-worked goals and that was it. Porthleven's great day hadn't been too much of a disaster, losing four-one to the world club champions. True, it was their heaviest defeat of the season, but what would anyone have expected? The statistical records wouldn't include reference to the Wanderers' medical problems. It would just go down as 'Porthleven 1, Wanderers United 4'. That, in the same season that Wanderers had beaten Manchester United five-nil!

In the Wanderers camp, people were not happy. "I want that bloody fish analysed," ordered Ronnie. Bones contemplated putting the wheels in motion. Back at the hotel he sought out the chefs and told them of the events of the evening. They, of course, hadn't been at the match but had been preparing a light supper for the team.

Roger Odgers spoke up. "I'll get the samples, Mr Bletchley-Crewe. They're in this freezer." He opened a large chest freezer, rummaged around and drew out a sandwich box. "They're in here." Bones took it from him and prized it open. Inside were several small plastic bags wrapped around unrecognisable bits of food. Roger picked out a couple of the bags. "These are the bits of fish cut off each piece of sea bass. Is that what you want?"

"That's it. I'll get them sent off. We should know in four or five days. I must say it looks to me like a sure case of food poisoning. I hope for your sakes it isn't anything you guys prepared."

"So do we."

Bones put the samples into sterile specimen tubes, sealed them and put them back in the sandwich box.

"These can't be dealt with until tomorrow. I'll collect them in the morning."

A few minutes later, in the hotel lounge, Bones talked things over with Ronnie, Joker, Nita Worrell the nutritionist and Arnie Robinson the club secretary.

"The only people to be ill were players," he pointed out. "Only Kwasi Ankoma, Macca and Pickaxe weren't affected."

"Your forgetting our casualties," said Joker. "Heinrich, Antonio and Lim Po weren't ill either."

"An' those six were all on th' same table," added Ronnie. "an' so were we. An' none o' the Directors were sick, eh? They were on another table taegether."

"Twelve players were ill altogether, and they sat at two tables," said Bones. "Bloody hell, it's pretty clear. Food served to those two tables had something wrong with it. We got food that was okay."

"A matter of luck, then," suggested Arnie. "It could have been any of us." He felt mightily relieved that it hadn't been his table. Goodness knows, he wasn't a fit man anyway. Just what havoc the germ would have wreaked on him didn't bear thinking about. Just as well it had been the fit young footballers who fell victim.

"Strange coincidence it was the two tables where the fit players were," said Nita.

"If ye believe in coincidences," growled Ronnie. "Ah smell a rat somewhere."

"We'll know more at the end of the week when the food samples are analysed," said Bones.

"Are you suggesting it was deliberate?" asked Arnie of Ronnie in a hushed voice. My God! He would have to watch everything he ate from now on! It was as if he expected the culprit to suddenly appear, bottle of poison in hand.

"All ah said was, its one hell o' a coincidence!" repeated Ronnie.

"Who do you suspect?" Arnie pressed. He felt like he was in one of those whodunit films. Ten Little Deaths on the Nile, or something.

"Steady on," advised Bones. "Best not to say anything rash. Even if the fish *does* turn out to be dodgy, it doesn't mean sabotage or anything like that."

"We-ell," muttered Ronnie.

"Look, we won," said Joker. "If anyone tried to nobble us, and I'm not convinced they did, well then, they failed. I told the TV boys that the problem had arisen only minutes before kick-off, which is true, and that at first we didn't foresee how many players would be affected or how badly, which is also true, and that we'd just dug in and not let anybody down, and *that's* true as well. We didn't disappoint our fans because we won, and we didn't let down Porthleven or the FA because we didn't mess them around. I think on balance we come out of this smelling of roses."

"Which is more than you can say for our dressing room!" added Bones with a grim smile. Joker had spoken to the press after the game because Ronnie wasn't in the mood.

At a table in the corner of the hotel's bar the Directors who had made the trip sat discussing the same topic.

"I tell you what," puffed Sefton Perkins. "We were made to look right idiots out there, players dashing off to be ill, playing like zombies. I don't understand why it wasn't postponed on grounds of ill-health."

"There is the point that despite being afflicted by illness we fulfilled the fixture and still won," suggested Dick Fossett. "Think of some Premiership sides that think their arses are dipped in diamonds. They'd have cried off all right."

"I agree," said Cecil Norris, who had been disappointed at the size of Porthleven's tiny stand. No point trying to sell them any new seats. They'd only want about a hundred. "Let's face it, we're going to be in the bloody Guinness Book of Records as the only team in the world to draw nil-nil against no opposition. We had to redeem ourselves somehow. You know how the tabloids like to pick on successful sides like us."

"Funny how it was only players who were sick," pointed out Jack Grimethorpe.

"What do you mean?" Malcolm Black was in a state of inner turmoil. He had been most uncomfortable at the tiny ground. The two flush toilets he had found weren't like the ones in the VIP lounges of Premiership clubs; nor were they at all close to the half-way line position prepared for the FA and visiting club officials. He had realised that if his bowels let him down he would have to wend his way through the tightly packed crowd either to a toilet block beyond the changing rooms or through even more of the crowd to the toilet off the changing room foyer. No luxury Director's box loo here, never mind his own personal one at New Stamford Stadium. A double dose of Imodium had been his only course of action, washed down with a glass of kaolin and morphine.

Panic had gripped his immobilised intestines as he watched the players dashing off one by one. He, like the home crowd, assumed they were being stricken with attacks of diarrhoea. On such a scale it *had* to be something they'd eaten, and the Directors had been eating the same food as the players. Now he worried that with the anti-diarrhoea medicines he had sealed some kind of germ into his gut where it would remain, happily multiplying, until the drugs wore off. Sweat broke out on his brow.

"I mean," said Jack, "If the whole team comes down with something that I'd bet Mars to a marble was food poisoning, but *we* don't, the injured players don't and Ronnie and *his* table don't, well, that's..." he shrugged. "......funny."

"I see what you mean," said Sefton. "You reckon someone deliberately served nobbled food to the team only? Bit far fetched, isn't it?"

"Yes, but not impossible. Odd coincidence, just the players getting it, that's all I say."

"Don't we check all the food prepared by the chefs?" asked Cecil.

"Yes," confirmed Sefton. "I daresay Bones is going to see to that."

Dick Stone, one of the chefs, entered the bar.

"Would you gentlemen like a spot of supper? We're ready to serve it in the Dining Room."

"Right, thanks, lad. I'm a bit peckish, I must say," said Sefton, lifting his frame out of his armchair. "What's on?"

"Fish and chips, Mr Perkins. Locally caught cod and my own special beer batter."

"Oh, great. A fish supper, eh, lads?"

Cecil and Dick rose to join him, but Malcolm and Jack stayed put. "N-not for me," stammered Malcolm. Not more bloody fish!

"I don't know....." said Jack.

"Come on, lads! You don't think the phantom poisoner is going to have another go, do you?" laughed Sefton.

Jack slowly rose. "I guess it'll be all right. I'm just being silly!"

"Well, I'm not hungry," lied Malcolm. "You go ahead. I'll have an early night."

The four Directors left him to it. After they had left the room, Malcolm went up to the bar. "Four packets of crisps, please: two plain, two salt and vinegar. A Kit Kat, a Twix, a Toffee Crisp and one of those spicy sausage things in the foil packet there."

His pockets packed, Malcolm went up to his room. He 'phoned room service for a pot of tea.

"Would you like some biscuits or a sandwich, sir?" asked the pleasant voice at the other end.

Bugger! In his panic, he hadn't thought of that! Surveying his range of chocolate bars, crisps and the sausage, he thought he'd prefer a sandwich. Cheese would be safe. "Have you got cheese?"

"Cheddar, sir?"

"Yes please."

"Branston pickle?"

"Oh, yes!" Even better!

"Would you like it toasted?"

"Oh, marvellous! Yes please, and some biscuits."

"Certainly sir."

Thus Malcolm had his supper in his room whilst others enjoyed succulent cod and chips downstairs. Not everyone, though. Neither Arnie Robinson nor Ronnie Bone could face fish that night. They went out and hailed a taxi which took them to the nearest MacDonald's. Which wasn't that near!

The players had all been advised by Bones to have just warmed milk with a little honey and sleep it off. Naturally, Macca, Quasi and the three injury-list players felt no qualms about the fish and chips. Macca entertained his table by throwing chips ever higher in the air and catching them - well, most of them - in his mouth. And, canny lad that he was, he asked for and got a second plate of fish and chips.

"Noa point wastin' good food, mon," he explained through half-chewed chips. "Some o' the lads 'ave skipped theirs. Ah mayt as well 'ave it, eh? Ah doan' knoa wha' they're worried aboot." He held his plate up for all to see. "Look, mon. Noa carrots!" He laughed so much at his own joke that Antonio next to him had to clap him on his back to help quell his coughing fit. Others seem to have been slightly put off their food at this reminder of the carrot fairy's activities that day.

A bit later, in the hotel's kitchen, the four club chefs finished off their tidying up. They cleaned their own equipment to maintain their close control over everything to do with the players' food. They had naturally talked about the players falling sick, even to the point of noting the coincidence of who had and had not been ill. They were agreed that it was nothing to do with them, of course. They were done for the day, and knocked off. Roger Odgers went out for a breath of fresh air before he turned in. When he was well away from the hotel he took out his mobile and keyed in a number.

"Hi, it's Rog. All right?..........................Whose idea was the pong? The players told us about it. Rotting fish?"

The voice on the other end explained. "That were our cousin Anthony."

He pronounced the 'th' as in 'thesis' in the Cornish way. " 'Ee 'ad the idea when 'ee see'd which way the wind blawed. 'Ee sluiced out 'is 'olds an' 'is mate fetched up some rottin' seaweed wi' 'is tractor an' parked alongside the quay. They say 'ee smelled 'ansome! Yer fish were orl roit?"

"Yes, the fillets we served to the team were what you might call well hung! I disguised the flavour with a rather clever little sauce of mine. All the specimen bits were cut off the fresh ones. Four-one wasn't bad, eh?"

"Naw, not bad. An' stop talkin' posh, Rog. Mether wouldn't knaw 'ee, boy!"

Roger laughed. True, his accent had all but gone as he had worked in various top class London restaurants and hotels after qualifying from the catering course at Camborne Tech. He didn't get back home very often.

"I'll see 'ee termorrer before oi go," he lapsed, for his brother's sake. "G'night."

Chapter 41 - A Saturday Night and Sunday Morning

The fact that many of the Wanderers United squad were still feeling delicate after their intestinally-affected performance in Cornwall made their 0 - 0 draw at Aston Villa four days later something of a success - a point gained rather than two lost. A draw at Coventry the following Wednesday was, on the other hand, a game thrown away, Sum Wun having scored twice in the first half only for two defensive errors to let in Coventry for what was for them a vital point. Wanderers United, FIFA World Champions, languished in mid-table. When it came to their FA Cup Fifth Round tie at home to Leicester City, though, the team clicked into top gear and eased through to the Quarter Finals with a 2 -1 win that had the home fans singing the Wembley song long after the final whistle.

It kept Sir Fabian happy, too. He had been agitating after the two draws. Having become World Champions, he couldn't see why Wanderers weren't sweeping all before them. He had managed to get to the Leicester game and the win took the edge off his impatience a bit.

"You have to remember, Sir Fabian," explained a not particularly convincing Sefton, "these Premiership games are small beer compared to Rio and the Champions' League." They were enjoying a drink in the Boardroom after the game, Sir Fabian with his customary Fosters, Sefton with his pint of best. Sharon was sipping at a Campari and soda, not really listening to all that boring old chat about football. She was more interested in the football*ers*. She perked up when Johann van Dyke came in, hoping to attract his attention. She fancied a return match after her Thrill in Brazil - or as Jenny James described it, a "second leg-over".

"Well, even if those managers of yours are using the English league games as practice sessions for the more important games, they ought to be winning some of them," sprayed Sir Fabian.

"Well, I think the main thing is to make sure we're in the more important tournaments each season. We'll be in the next FIFA one as winners, and when we win the Champions' League we'll be in that again." He used "when" to inject a note of confidence into what he was waffling to Sir Fabian. He decided against pointing out how important it was to be at the top of the Premiership just in case they *didn't* win the Champions' League again this season. He wasn't to know about the problems Liverpool faced five years later.

"Hmmph!" was all Sir Fabian could say in response. He didn't understand this soccer thing at all. In rugby, the best club side in the world would mangle any other team in its domestic league.

Malcolm Black came in, looking worried. He had spent most of the game on his secret toilet, perched high above the pitch in his special guest box behind its camouflaged door. As Wanderers had won he was feeling a little better, confident enough to make his way round to the Boardroom. On his way his mobile had rung. It was Bert Barnard, his right hand man at Consolidated Solids.

"I had a check round during the game," said Bert. "I'd like you to let me have a proper look at the stand sometime this week when it's empty."

"Oh? Why?" Malcolm's confidence in the continence of his bowels faded a little. Well, a lot, actually.

"Well, it's been a while, and I really think it would be wise to see if there are any signs of deterioration. There was a lot of vibration from stamping feet today. It's all right when Wanderers lose. The fans don't create much vibration then. But too many wins and we could have a problem."

"Oh God! O.K., I'll see you here first thing Monday if you like. Nine o'clock?"

"O.K., Mal. See yer."

Hence Malcolm's worried expression when he entered the Boardroom. He was safe enough. There were the Directors' executive toilets just outside the door. Sefton beckoned him over.

"Malcolm, on our way ter Wembley, eh?"

"Looking good, Sefton, looking good."

"Then why have you got a face like a smacked bum?" demanded Sir Fabian.

"Have I? Perhaps it's my natural expression," blustered Malcolm. "I mean, we won! What could be better?"

"Well I've just been telling Sefton here. We should be winning *more*!"

God help me if we do, thought Malcolm. A run of straight victories might have the bloody stand down.

"Tell you what, Sir Fabian, how long are you here for? The girls have got a game tomorrow. Why don't you give 'em a look?"

Sir Fabian thought it over. People kept on telling him he ought to watch the women's team play. He didn't like being told what to do, but the thought of a couple of dozen sporty women running around was tempting.

"What time?"

"Two-thirty kick-off, Sir Fabian."

"Where do they play? We don't let them play here, do we?"

"We agreed to let them play one or two games here when the pitch can take it and perhaps for an important game, like against one of the top sides. They're playing on our training pitch, just beyond the car park behind the New Millennium Stand."

Sir Fabian made a decision.

"I'll meet you here at two o'clock! Sharon?" He looked around for her. She'd been with him when he first came in; now where was she? He spotted her over near the bar talking with his red-headed chauffeuse and one of the Wanderers players. He went over to them.

"Shaz, what are you planning for tomorrow, only I'm coming here in the afternoon to look over one or two things with that greasy little bloke from the Board."

"Ooo, that's awright, Blanky, luv. C'n I 'ave Jenny 'ere ter drive me ternight?"

"Yea, I suppose so. I'll be going down to London on business. May even stay over. You can entertain yourself O.K., can't you?"

Sharon sure could. She had been sizing up the chances of getting Johann van Dyke to herself as Sir Fabian interrupted. Now that Sharon knew that he wouldn't be home that night and that he wanted her to entertain herself, she could make Johann an offer she hoped he wouldn't refuse.

In London that night, Sir Fabian headed for his gentleman's club and the undeniably erotic charms of Talulah, who was torn between dejection that she was destined to spend time with the fat, salivating tycoon and anticipation of the £100 tip he usually gave her. By the time they were together in the "private conference room" the Viagra was taking effect and the session began.

"I like this place," he said, breaking off for a minute. Coming up for air like the great fat whale you are, thought Talulah. "What place, Sir Fabian?" Did he mean London, the club, the room, her groin?

"In Rio when I tried for a bit of personal attention it all got out of hand. All over the bloody papers. You *must* have read about it!"

Talulah had - and had only then made the connexion between him and Wanderers United.

"Well, you always were a ladies man!" she flattered. It was a house rule. The men who patronised the club paid a great deal of money for the quality and discretion of the girls as well as for the plush facilities. However distastefully gross they were, they had to be made to feel like the studs most of them believed they were. "If you are going to be a bit of a lad, you'll get into trouble somewhere along the line!"

"I thought Shaz would go mad, but she didn't seem to mind."

"Well, she must think like I do, that there's more than enough of you to go round!"

This Talulah girl knows a thing or two, thought Sir Fabian. Top shag, top brain. It wouldn't be any good his trying to replace Sharon with her: she was too bright. His constant companion had to be flea-brained to put up with going with him wherever he had to go as well as with his taste for other women.

He ate, licked, slurped and sucked his fill and made as best use as he could of his Viagra-induced condition, then snored and snorted his way through the night. He breakfasted in his normal way whilst Talulah, once more straddling his face, counted the minutes to when he would take his leave. Not forgetting the occasional fake orgasm, she writhed and wriggled convincingly until he decided to stop.

"Gotta go, Talulah!"

"What, already? Goodness, is that the time?" Thank goodness!

"Sorry to let you down but I've got to go. Business calls!"

"What, on a Sunday?"

Sir Fabian laughed. "Well, you work on Sundays, don't you?"

Talulah had to laugh. Touché! Sir Fabian got dressed, put two fifty pound notes into her hand and left. Ugh! thought Talulah. He hadn't even showered! She dived into the shower herself, then dressed in her Falmer's and a sweat shirt, grabbed her Nike bag and checked out.

"Cheerio!" she flung at the receptionist. "I'll see you Tuesday!" She always took Mondays off. Mondays were slow anyway.

She ran round to the basement car park and leapt into her dark green MGF. Minutes later she was speeding towards her destination, about an hour and a half away.

Sir Fabian had used his mobile to summons Roger, his other chauffeur, and was a bit further away from the club than Talulah, heading for New Stamford Stadium, also, coincidentally, about an hour and a half away.

Chapter 42 – a Small World!

"Right, Mal. Lead me to the ladies!" Sir Fabian had decided, after his customarily superb night with Talulah, to wallow in the spectacle of sporty women in flimsy football kit. Being such a ladies man (Ooh, that Talulah certainly was a good judge of blokes!) he couldn't wait to get amongst the womens' team. Who knows, there might be one or two likely conquests there for him to charm.

"I should have said yesterday; you'll need some decent shoes, Sir Fabian. And have you got a coat? No heated executive box this afternoon! We'll be on the touchline."

Watching a game from the touchline! Sir Fabian had fond memories of doing just that in his youth - though that was in South Africa and the ground was invariably dry, the weather warm; and besides, it was rugby. He viewed the low, scudding clouds outside as they blew threateningly across the sky.

"No, I haven't got a coat with me. I never need one."

"Doesn't matter. We usually use our Stewards' coats. They're in the Stewards' Room near the tunnel." Malcolm looked at Sir Fabian's immaculate expensive-looking shoes. Nodding down in their direction, he said: "They'll get a bit mucky. I think there are some Wellington boots down stairs as well."

"I'll be O.K. What's a bit of mud, eh? I've got girls in Bangkok and Jo'burg who wrestle in the stuff! This women's game should be a bit like that, eh?"

"I'm not sure they'd like to hear you saying that, Sir Fabian," ventured Malcolm. "They'll be playing to win, you mark my words!"

"The bloody men could learn a thing or two from them, then," growled Sir Fabian.

The door to the Boardroom swung open and the Arscott brothers came in, with Cecil Norris just behind.

"Hello, Mal. Thought we'd find you here," said Ernie, the elder Arscott. "Sir Fabian! Coming to watch the ladies, eh?"

"Bloody right! How many more of you old pervs come and watch them, eh? Do they swap shirts after the game? Eh? This cold weather must make 'em stand out, eh? *And* it looks like rain! I hadn't thought of that. Twenty-two wet T-shirts! I can't wait. Let's go!"

"They do wear bras under their shirts, Sir Fabian," said Cecil who, at thirty-four, didn't really think he was as much of an old perv as Sir Fabian was. "And they're sports bras, too. No black lacy Wonderbras!"

"Well, never mind! Come on; let's go before you talk me out of it!" Sir Fabian's only motive in taking time out to watch the women play was lechery. As the figurehead of a huge multinational collection of assorted enterprises his time was at a premium. Money and sex were his two main incentives. Where he could combine the two, he did.

The group of men made their way down to the corridor beneath the stand that ran from the changing rooms to the players' tunnel to kit themselves out with the distinctive blue and yellow Wanderers United Stewards waterproofs. Then they went out to the car park and headed for the playing fields beyond.

* * * * * * * * *

The Wanderers United Ladies team were all keyed up for their Women's National Premier League game against Everton, who were fifth in the table to their third. To lose would close the gap between the two sides to just one point...

"....and that would never do, girls," said manager Marty Fozzard amidst the scene of thighs gleaming with liniment. Get yer shirt on, Sharon, for goodness' sake!"

The statuesque figure of the tall, nineteen-year-old centre-back dominated the centre of the small changing room alongside the Wanderers United training pitch. With her height and suntan, in shorts, socks and bra, she was a glorious sight for any red-blooded male to behold.

"That's not a sports bra, Shaz!" admonished Lou Purdey, the team's playmaker who rivalled Sharon in the legs department. "You'll have black eyes by half-time!"

"Forgot," replied Sharon. "It's in my bag." Her hands went behind her back.

"Shaz!" Marty stopped her short of unclipping the inadequate item of lingerie. Well, inadequate for a girl about to run her guts out for ninety minutes; adequate for pleasing the eye of her boyfriend, the Wanderers United centre back Caspar Hansen.

"If you must do that, me'n Rex'll go outside for a minute. You know the rules."

At each game, the team would assemble in the changing room. Marty would announce the line-up and then say "Right! Shorts and tops, quick as you can, then let us know." The team were supposed to change as quickly as possible into their shorts and shirts first, without bothering with socks, ankle straps, shin pads, boots, laces and so on. Those could be dealt with once they were all decent enough for Marty and Rex to go back in and talk tactics. The girls all knew the routine by now and ignored it at their peril.

"Fine! Fine!" chorused several of the girls.

"Oh, fuck off!" Sharon responded. The fine was fifty pence in the hat for the end of season booze-up. Any infringement of the unwritten conventions was a fifty pence fine. Sharon hadn't been ready for the team talk.

"FINE AGAIN! A QUID!" yelled just about everyone in the room.

"Oh - *sugar!*" Sharon knew as well as anyone else that swearing was another fifty pence.

Marty and Rex waited outside the door of the boisterous room.

"Well, you can't fault the spirit," observed Rex. "Barbara says they are really on the crest of a wave at the moment, despite losing last week." Barbara was his wife as well as the captain of the side.

"We need a win, though," replied Marty. The team had drawn two and lost one in their last three games and lost some ground on Arsenal and Doncaster Belles at the top of the league.

"Well, we beat Everton in November," Rex pointed out. "We'll be all right today. Hullo, here they come." He had seen the brightly-coloured coats of the Directors making their way across the field. "There's five. Who's the fifth one?"

Led by Malcolm, the party of Wanderers United's luminaries headed for Marty and Rex.

"Hullo, lads!" called Malcolm.

"Mr Black. Nice to see you all again," replied Marty. "Hope we can serve up more than a draw this time!"

Malcolm turned to Sir Fabian. "These are the two lucky chaps who manage the women's team, Sir Fabian. This is Marty Fozzard, the manager, and this is Rex Holden who helps him out. His wi..."

"Manage the women's team, eh?" sprayed Sir Fabian. "Lucky bastards! D'you manage them one at a time or just jump in the bath with all of 'em?"

"Well, actually....." began Marty.

"I can't wait to see 'em in action, especially in this cold rain. I expect you two bastards need the odd cold shower. Where d'you look when they're changing, eh?"

"Well, we always...."

"I guess it depends on whether you're a tits man or a thighs man, eh? Me, I'm a thighs man, so I'll be O.K. all through the game, eh? The tits men will have to wait until they're in the showers!"

The changing-room door opened a few inches and a tousle-haired head appeared.

"Shaz is decent now, Marty."

"Right, Valentina." Marty turned to Sir Fabian. "Time for the final talk, so you'll have to excuse us. Thanks for coming and I hope you are impressed enough to come again." He and Rex went inside and shut the door.

"Depends how many times I come *this* time, eh, boys?" foamed Sir Fabian, who was getting quite excited at the prospect of the game. Hidden beneath the hoods of their Stewards' jackets, the others winced. O.K., they were all bucked up at the sight of some of the women who played, but there were limits!

In the dressing room, Marty was addressing the girls.

"We're honoured today, girls," he began. "The usual United Directors are here, but they've brought along the bloke who bought the club last summer - Sir Fabian Blankopf."

"What, that bloke who owns Digital International TV and all those newspapers?" asked Janine, pulling on her goalkeeper's gloves. Being the eldest of the team she probably kept abreast of the news more than most.

"That's him," said Rex, "and he's a complete pillock! He's practically drooling out there at the prospect of seeing you play. He came out with the old 'swapping shirts' line. Where do we look when you're changing, that sort of thing."

"I can tell you where *he* looks when I'm changing at home," said Rex's wife Barbara. "Probably at the newspaper!" There was general laughter around the room. She and Rex had been married for fourteen years.

"Still, he's the man with the money," said Penny Rickard, the lesbian policewoman who played in midfield or at the back. "Put on a good show, girls, and there might be something in it for us."

"Good point, Pen," agreed Marty, "but he's a lecherous old git. Got some Essex piece in tow all the time. Called Sharon, actually."

"Whoooo-ow! Go, Shaz!" some of the team laughed.

"Oh, fuck off!"

"FINE! PAY UP!"

Sharon smiled and shook her head. Bugger! One pound fifty!

"Sir Fabian Blankopf?" asked Lou.

"Yeah, don't look so worried," said Marty. "He's only here to letch!"

A buzzer sounded.

"Right, girls!" shouted Marty. "Let's do it!"

The team filed out and headed for the pitch. Everton Ladies were close behind them. Sharon and the sixteen-year-old Valentina Materazzi stopped off at the touchline where Sharon kissed Caspar and Valentina kissed Stevie Grigg, now with Aston Villa but present at as many of the games as possible.

"Woah! Don't we all get a kiss, girlies?"

Sir Fabian had taken one look at Sharon's long, lean, tanned legs and become smitten.

"They're their boyfriends," hissed Malcolm. "That's Caspar Hansen, our centre half. He's been knocking off that girl for months. She's a centre back, too."

"Pity!" Sir Fabian scanned the other players. "Wow! Look at *that*! Who's the Chink?"

"That's Kizzie Wong. She's *seventeen*, Sir Fabian." Malcolm emphasised her tender age as if to suggest she was off-limits. Wrong move.

"Seventeen, eh? I *bet* she is! My favourite age! I love 'em. No need for me to go all the way to my club in Bangkok, eh? And look at the thighs on that number seven! Bloody hell, I'm going to enjoy this! Who is she?"

"That's Lou Purdey. She's the engine-room, really. Most of our attacks are set up by her."

"She can make an attack on me any time she likes," leered Sir Fabian. "Give me a look at her engine room as well, eh?"

Malcolm shuddered.

The game started and the fifty or so touchline spectators soon forgot the cold, blustery showers as the game ebbed and flowed. Everton had lost one-nil on their own turf and wanted to put that right. Just on half-time Penny Rickard misjudged a cross and the Everton number nine nipped in and scored. There were some pursed lips and furrowed brows on the faces of the Wanderers girls as they marched in for the break.

"We'll do 'em in the second half," said Cecil Norris, who had his eye on striker Gina Perry. She had spent the first half on the subs' bench. "We'll have the wind behind us."

Caspar Hansen and Stevie Grigg joined the Directors.

"What's the opinion of the professionals, then?" asked Ernie Arscott.

"Yes, we'll be O.K.," replied Caspar.

"Yes," agreed Stevie. "No worries."

"You going to come back to us, Stevie?" Reggie Arscott hadn't wanted the old treble team to be broken up. Stevie eyed Sir Fabian. He, of course, knew what had gone on and why Ronnie and Joker had split up the team.

"Well, you know how it is, Mr Arscott. I enjoyed it here. I'd come back tomorrow if the old team could be put back together. As it is, I'm happy enough at Villa. We're doing better than you in the league. And I can watch Valentina play most games, too. Life's not bad!"

The teams came out for the second half, the Wanderers girls all wearing determined looks, frowning with concentration. Sir Fabian, who had thoroughly enjoyed the first half, looked closely at each of the players, trying for eye contact. They marched past him, none paying any attention to him, something Sir Fabian wasn't used to. Young Valentina even ignored Stevie - not that he was worried. He understood that she was keeping focused on the next forty-five minutes. She was closely followed by left back Zoë Pryde, 'keeper Janine Morris, striker Laura Kitson, midfielders Barbara Holden and Lou Purdey deep in conversation, centre backs Penny Rickard and Sharon Onslow - she ignored her Caspar, too. Then came Kizzie Wong and....

Sir Fabian started. He looked round at the retreating figures of the numbers six and seven. Now it was his turn to frown.

He was much quieter during the second half in which the Wanderers pressed Everton more than they had before half-time. Eventually, Kizzie Wong broke through the centre as Laura Kitson and fellow striker Elaine Richards dragged their markers apart. Kizzie nutmegged the sweeper and slid the ball wide of Everton's startled 'keeper for the equaliser. One-all and twenty minutes left! Kizzie was mobbed by the team and the small group of spectators went wild.

The outcome was inevitable. It was just a question of how the winning goal would be scored. It was, in the end, a classic Wanderers United Ladies goal. Gina Perry, on for Laura Kitson who'd taken a knock, launched an eighty-fifth minute corner from the right high towards the top of the Everton box. The majestic Sharon had started her run as Gina started hers and met the ball high at full speed some fifteen yards out, powering the ball into the top right corner of the net with a header that made Caspar wince - but glow with pride. When she got the right ball, timed her run right and got her header on target, no-one stopped them!

Wanderers couldn't add to their lead, but the whistle went and it was three points in the bag! Faces now wreathed in smiles, the team trooped happily off. Caspar embraced the muddied Sharon, kissing the mark on her forehead made by the ball as she scored the winner. A shy-looking lad of about seventeen ran up alongside Kizzie and patted her on the back.

"W-well done, Kizzie!" he stammered.

Kizzie turned in surprise and smiled at the lad. "Oh! Hello! Thanks! I didn't know....."

Red faced, he was gone. Kizzie looked after him, gave a small smile and then turned to respond to other congratulations from spectators and team alike.

Valentina was walking towards the changing rooms arm-in-arm with her Stevie. It was a happy throng if you ignored the glum-faced Everton players. Sir Fabian sought out the number seven with the magnificent thighs. There she was.

"Hey! Number seven!" What had Malcolm said? Of course! Lou. Lou Purdey. "Lou Purdey!"

Lou stopped and turned round. She was hot, sweaty, muddy and elated. Her hair was a wet, matted mess and she had a small cut on her cheek. She smiled at Sir Fabian.

"Hullo, Sir Fabian."

"Hullo, Talulah! Fancy seeing you here!"

"I heard you were here," said Talulah. "You won't let on about our – business arrangement, will you?"

Sir Fabian was a lecherous old bastard, but even he saw no point exposing Talulah's sideline to the world. Besides, if he did, he'd probably never get to pay for her services again.

What a small world, though!

Chapter 43 - Going Down

Wanderers United didn't have much to celebrate after the cup win against Leicester City. They lost their next two Premier League games, both one-nil, to Spurs away and then Everton at home on successive Saturdays. Real cynics amongst their followers began to doubt their chances in the FA Cup Quarter Final at home to Gillingham from Nationwide Division Two. After all, Gillingham had beaten Bradford in the previous round and Wanderers were gradually heading towards Bradford's end of the Premiership. The Nationwide Division Two side, however, had reached their peak and slumped to a disappointing five-nil defeat in front of the Wanderers' customarily huge crowd in their state-of-the-art stadium.

Or some sort of state. Back after that win against Leicester, Bert Barnard had met up with Malcolm to have a look at the New Millennium Stand. Malcolm's guts were in turmoil at the prospect of what they might find. Funny how he'd been perfectly all right the previous afternoon. It just went to prove how much effect stress had on his irritable bowel syndrome. Somehow, he always found watching the girls very relaxing.

It was easy enough for the two men to examine the structure of the stand without arousing any suspicion. There aren't too many people around a football stadium on a Monday morning. The groundsmen potter about repairing the playing surface and the office staff are in, but the stands are usually empty unless Christine Goodley, the Commercial Manager, happened to be showing prospective Hospitality Suite clients around - unusual that early in the morning.

All the various types of private boxes on the different levels of the stand allowed Bert plenty of cover to unscrew panels or examine spaces over false ceilings so that he could look for new cracks or check on those he'd found earlier in the season. His diagnosis was grim and Malcolm, a builder himself, remember, saw little evidence to contradict him.

"Bloody hell, Mal," said Bert, sucking through his teeth like a plumber just asked to give an estimate. "I reckon it really is a matter of how well you do. When you win, the crowd makes more noise and jumps up and down more. When you lose, they don't. If you do badly, attendances will go down which means less stress on the structure. It could last to the end of the season, but at some stage we'll have to pretend to discover the problem and shut the bloody stand!"

Malcolm paled visibly. If Wanderers won most of their games, the stand could collapse before the end of the season. It didn't bear thinking about that it might collapse when filled with some twenty-two thousand fans. If, on the other hand, Wanderers' season went to pot and they won nothing, Sir Fabian would pull out with all his cash and they'd be ruined. They wouldn't be able to meet the astronomical wages bill or afford to demolish and rebuild the jerry-built stand, which would have to be done. His colon responded predictably and he winced with pain.

"So the bloody thing is going to fall down sooner or later! Bloody hell, what a fucking mess! What can we *do?*"

"Emigrate?" suggested Bert.

"That might be all we *can* bloody do!"

"Well, as they say up North, 'before yer do owt, do nowt'," advised Bert. "I can keep an eye on the worst cracks. I can even bodge up something to hide some of the symptoms. Bit of filler here, new, slightly bigger ceiling tiles there, that sort of thing. I'll just look regularly and more often. Look, I don't like football but you'd better put me on your guest list for your private box so that I can check after every match. I can mooch about checking everywhere and keep you posted."

"I'll fix you up in one of the Arscott's boxes," said Malcolm. "I'd rather keep my box to myself. My guts, Bert..."

"Yeh, right. I'd almost forgotten your secret throne! All right, is it? I suppose if it's a crappy game it's just the job!"

The two men departed, Bert back to the yard, Malcolm intending to join him later after seeing to one or two things that Arnie Robinson, the club Secretary, had called him about. A few silly letters to sign, replies to letters from fans: critical fans, irate fans, sanctimonious fans, fans offering all sorts of advice. They all got replies - unless there was no address. It didn't take long.

"Is that all? Well, see yer, Arnie. All right, are you?" Oh, bugger! Mistake! Arnie, chronic hypochondriac that he was, was never all right. He began to tell Malcolm about his latest series of symptoms. Malcolm was very late getting to his builders' yard.

On the day of the FA Cup Quarter Final the five goals against Gillingham hadn't brought the ecstatic reaction from the capacity crowd that a similar-sized win against a Premiership side would have done, so there wasn't anything for Bert to report after he did the first of what became his regular checks.

The defeat at home to relegation-fodder Watford on the following Saturday continued the Wanderers' slide down the table and although the players didn't seem that bothered, the Board were beginning to get jittery. All the talk of the need to win something on the flight to play Marseille in the Champions League fell flat as they flew back after a 1 - 0 defeat. Fortunately, or so the rest of the Board thought, Sir Fabian hadn't been around much after the Sunday of the women's match against Everton. He'd spent a lot of time chatting with midfielder Lou Purdey and then taken his leave.

"I wouldn't mind," Cecil Norris had observed, "but he took the Steward's waterproof and wellies with him!"

"He'll be giving us grief before very long," predicted Sefton as the 'plane bumped its way through turbulence over France. Malcolm had already headed for the toilets, most thought to be travel-sick, but with the combined stresses of the Wanderers' poor results and Sir Fabian's likely reaction on the one hand and the state of the New Millennium Stand on the other, it was the other end of his alimentary canal that was causing him trouble.

Wanderers only had time to lose one-nil at Newcastle before taking on Marseille in the return Champions League match. The usual capacity crowd had an entirely different atmosphere about it as the teams lined up and when Seamus O'Hooligan curled in a corker on the hour they went wild. Wilder still when the final whistle went, so that Malcolm, perched up on his secret loo, was torn between running for his life from the stand and his fear of temporary incontinence en route.

On the following Saturday at home to Spurs, the same capacity crowd didn't seem to mind losing 2 - 1 which meant Wanderers had only managed two points from their last seven league games. Their slide down the table continued. In midweek, though, they nipped over to Holland and saw off Feyenoord in their next Champions League game, Georgi Strupinski scoring a second-half hat trick after the Dutch side had taken a first-half lead. Pausing only to lose 2 - 1 at Upton Park so that West Ham stayed comfortably in the top half of the table, Wanderers' next opponents were Lazio in the Champions League. They'd drawn 0 - 0 in Rome in December, but since then Lazio had been having a brilliant season. It didn't matter to the Wanderers players. In front of their usual sell-out crowd they won 2 - 1 with goals from Seamus O'Hooligan and Macca (a free kick) either side of Lazio's goal. The win meant that Wanderers were through to the Quarter Finals! More thunder in the stands, more diarrhoea for Malcolm.

The next two Saturdays brought further league defeats, at home to Southampton and away to title-chasing Leeds. Contrary to Bert's predictions, the persistently poor results in the league did nothing to reduce the attendances. All Wanderers matches continued to be full houses. Every post brought requests for tickets from all over the world.

Even Arnie Robinson had thought the gates would fall in the circumstances but the requests for tickets still poured in.

"You could have built the stadium twice as big and we'd still be full every game," he remarked to Malcolm one day, sweating a little as the sharp pain over his left eye persisted. The doctor had diagnosed sinus trouble but Arnie wasn't sure it wasn't a brain tumour. Still, he must soldier on. It was how he would want to be remembered. "That Arnie, eh? Crippled with pain as his incurable tumour got bigger, but he carried on. Like an ostrich egg, it was, sticking out of his forehead like that!" That's how Arnie supposed brain tumours ended up looking like.

"What - bigger?" gasped Malcolm. He pictured his New Millennium Stand twice the size and packed with fans as it began to collapse. "Sorry, Arnie - must - go!" He dashed for the nearest toilet. Arnie stared after him. What a rude departure! Anyone would think he was ill!

Sefton was in a paddy because Sir Fabian had 'phoned him from out of the blue. He had raged on about where Wanderers were in the Premiership.

After the long and uncomfortable conversation, Sefton had gone to the club and sought out Arnie Robinson.

"It's serious, Arnie. He was threatening to exercise his get-out clause. We'd be up shit-creek without a bloody paddle and no mistake! The whole squad would have to be sold because we wouldn't be able to afford the wage bill! I think I managed to calm him down in the end. Thank God we're still in the FA Cup and European Champions Cup. I mean, I know it's daft, but the Jekyll and bloody Hyde way that our United Nations shower is playing we could win both those cups, on top of being bloody World Champions and get relegated from the Premiership at the same time!"

Arnie was only half listening. He'd had a dull pain in the small of his back for a couple of weeks and was sure that he'd read somewhere that it was often the first symptom of spinal cancer. He'd 'phoned for yet another appointment with his doctor.

"*Yes* Mr Robinson, what can we do for you *today*?" asked the Receptionist with more than a hint of weariness.

"An appointment, please."

"What seems to be the trouble?"

"That's what I want the doctor to tell *me*!"

"Yes, but what makes you so sure you need to *see* the doctor?"

"Because he can't bloody diagnose me by telepathy. Will you just let me know when the next available appointment is, please?"

"Now look here, Mr Robinson. I believe you have been rude to me before. I don't have to put up with this, you know!"

"You would if I came down there to book an appointment!"

"Well, if you're well enough to get down here like that, there can't be much wrong with you!"

"Oh, so everyone in your waiting room at the moment hasn't got anything wrong with them? *That* should get the bloody waiting lists down all right!"

"There's no-one in the waiting room at the moment, we haven't got a surgery now."

"Well, no surprise there with you to make sure that only people too sick to move can make appointments. Look, I've got a pain in my lower back. I've had it for two weeks. The magazines all say if symptoms persist, see a doctor. My symptoms have persisted. I'd like to see my doctor."

"Have you taken paracetamol?"

"Wouldn't be much use if it's cancer, will it!"

"Or aspirin? Or Nurofen? Back pain is often inflammatory. Aspirin or Nurofen will be better."

"Not if it is cancer of the spine they won't!"

"Oh, *really*, Mr Robinson! It's a bit early to think it's that!"

"Oh, a bit early, is it? What, I take aspirin until I have a stomach ulcer, have that burst because you think it's probably indigestion, get rushed into hospital for emergency abdominal surgery, meanwhile all those nasty little cancer cells are multiplying and going walkabout around my body so that I get a load of secondary tumours - *then* can I see a doctor?"

The line had gone dead as the Receptionist hung up, leaving Arnie working out when he could nip away and visit the surgery in person. He'd been about to make his escape when Sefton collared him.

"I asked you what time Ronnie and Joker are due in today?" Sefton looked annoyed. "Have you been listening?"

"Yes, of course!" Arnie wasn't sure what he'd missed. "I - I just had a bit of a dizzy spell, that's all. Like you say, our results are very stressful. Er - Ronnie and Joker should be here now. Have you looked in their office?"

Sefton had. "No-one there," he said.

"What about their match-day office?"

"Bugger! Never thought of that. Give 'em a buzz, see if they're there, will you?"

Arnie dialled the number. If Ronnie was there Sefton would go down to see him and he could still get to the surgery and take that bloody Receptionist on face to face. Mind, if it came to blows, he wouldn't be much good, not with his back.

Ronnie was there: Sefton went down. He poured out the whole story of Sir Fabian's telephonic tirade.

"You've got to try to get some results out of those fucking morons in the Premiership," he concluded.

Some of the fucking morons were drifting by, gathering for a tactical talk. One of them, Caspar Hansen, had been politely waiting outside Ronnie's match-day office, waiting for a word with him about his next fitness check. He'd heard every word of the brief exchange between Sefton and Arnie. Bloody hell! Sell the team? Couldn't pay the wages? That would be awful! If he had to go abroad, he'd be split up from his Sharon! She was a student and had her course to finish. He forgot all about seeing Ronnie about his fitness check, his head full of dark thoughts about being parted from the love of his life.

After the tactical discussion Ronnie made the point that Sir Fabian was not happy about the team's Premiership position. He didn't elaborate about the financial repercussions that would follow his withdrawal from the Board.

"Heads wid roll, ye ken, an' I dinnae mean Joker an' mysel'!" was all he said.

Caspar thought about telling the rest of the team what he'd overheard outside Ronnie's office but then decided not to, at least for the time being.

He did confide in Sharon that night, though, as they lay together in his bed. The thought of being parted from her had made Caspar particularly attentive and passionate and Sharon lay there in a daze of delight, floating gently down from the last of the peaks of ecstasy to which Caspar had expertly guided her. Now he was just absent-mindedly tracing his hand up and down her body in soft, gentle sweeps from her breasts to her thighs.

"Oooh, Caspar! That was the best yet! I don't think I could ever bear to be parted from you. I know I'm a bit young, and still have more than two years to do of my degree, but I just never want to leave you. I never thought about marriage, but suddenly, right now, right here in your bed, after..... well, you know; well, suddenly the idea doesn't seem so daft or old-fashioned."

"Oh, Sharon!"

"What?"

"Well, I feel the same, but I overheard something I don't think I was supposed to. It seems that Sir Fabian may pull out of the club because he's not satisfied with our performances in the Premiership."

"But you're World Champions! What more does he want?"

"Well, let's face it, we're doing really badly in the league. We get it together for the FA Cup and the Champions League but I have to admit, I don't think

I'm the only one who finds it hard to get worked up about playing Leicester or Southampton when we've got Lazio or Feyenoord in the Champions League. I mean, we're in the Quarter Finals. We've got Barcelona on Thursday, then our FA Cup Semi-Final at Wembley, then we're at home to Coventry! Which of those excite *you* the most? But Blankopf's got a point. If we're that good we should be on top of the Premiership by a mile."

Sharon snuggled into his neck and sniffed his Calvin Klein.

"Never mind!" she sighed. "We've got each other. What does it matter that old Blankopf isn't happy?"

"Because if he pulls out, the club won't be able to pay our wages so they'll sell us - and they'd almost certainly sell me abroad!"

"Come again?"

Caspar ignored the opportunity for a one-liner. He wasn't feeling in a comical mood.

"I'd be sold to a Spanish or Italian club, or somewhere even further away. We'd be split up!"

After what she had just said to Caspar, Sharon was appalled.

"Well, you lot had just better pull your socks up and start winning some Premiership games! In the meantime, let's forget about it. I know just the thing."

Her head disappeared below the duvet as she slid down the bed, tracing a line down his chest and six-pack with her tongue as she went.

Caspar forgot about Sir Fabian for a while.

Chapter 44 - A Change of Mind

The atmosphere in New Stamford stadium was amazing that Thursday night of the Champions League Quarter Final First Leg between Wanderers United and Barcelona. It was almost sparking with static at full-time when few people could remember having been in the midst of such a level of noise and excitement. Wanderers ran out three-one winners on the night (a Macca free-kick, an Enrique Mouette thunderbolt from outside the box and a towering header by Jesus Bastardi from a Macca corner). It took a long time for the stadium to clear, but when he could, Bert Barnard went round checking the New Millennium Stand. There was evidence that some of the cracks in the structural concrete were widening.

As he had been expecting that to happen Malcolm was already in the agonising throes of his syndrome when Bert reported back to him.

"How soon before we have to put our hands up," he called, his voice a little muffled behind the camouflaged door in his private guest box.

"Perhaps half-a-dozen games like today's; perhaps less. Lose a few and it'll go a bit longer." Bert heard a groan from behind the door.

"I'll leave you to it, Mal. Next Wednesday, isn't it, next home game? Cheerio!"

Before that game, though, there was the small matter of the FA Cup Semi Final. This was at Wembley against Newcastle United. It was a tight game with Newcastle equalising Sum Wun's opener before half-time, but Enrique Mouette unleashed a bit of his Gallic magic to win the game for Wanderers some eight minutes from time.

Between that high and the second leg of the Champions League Quarter Final there were two Premiership matches to fit in - Coventry at home and Sheffield Wednesday away. Both were desultory affairs, both lost by Wanderers, both by one-nil. They slid further down the table and Sir Fabian was not happy. He flew in from Hong Kong to London and made a bad-tempered stop-over at his Wimbledon Common house.

"You'd better arrange to visit your folks or something, Shaz," he said as his blubbery body caused his huge bath to overflow.

"Oooh, Blanky, ta, luv! I fort yer'd wan' me ter stay wiv yer orl the time. Yer in a bad mood, ain'tcha, luv, 'cos Wanderers aren't doin' very well. I fort they wuz World Champions or sumfink?"

"That's history, Shaz."

"Are you sure? I mean, I know I wasn't much cop at school, like, but I'm sure we never dun football in 'Ist'ry lessons!"

Oh, bloody hell, there she goes again, thought Sir Fabian.

"Just get dried and into bed, Shaz! Leave the business to me. You just take care of my pleasure!"

So she did.

At about the same time the other Sharon, centre back for Wanderers United Ladies, was at the end of a late girls' night out with the rest of the team -

something of a habit that had built up over the years that contributed to the tremendous team spirit.

Since their win over Everton, witnessed by Sir Fabian, the ladies team had played four league games, winning three and drawing one, and reached the quarter final of the Women's FA Cup. Janine Morris, the 'keeper, made some comment about the continued slide down the Premiership by the men's side despite their performances in the FA Cup and Champions League. They all had a big laugh about it; all except for Sharon, that is.

"Come on, Shazza, crack your face!" Penny Rickard noticed her serious expression.

"I'll tell you something," said Sharon. "If it gets much worse, Blankopf will pull his money out of the club. Caspar overheard Ronnie talking to one of the Directors about it. They'll have to sell the team because the rest of the Board wouldn't be able to pay their wages. They'd have to cut right back. Caspar would probably have to go abroad!"

"Well, that's what I *really* call coitus interruptus!" laughed Gina Perry.

"You might have a bit more energy for your football if you're not shagging so much!" added Josie Smith.

Linda Lawson, who worked for a bank, looked thoughtful and then cut into the babble of unsympathetic comments the rest were making about Sharon's love life.

"Hey, listen, girls! If Wanderers lose Blankopf and have to make economies, that would be curtains for us! We'd be back on the park as Midford Town Ladies!"

That shut them up.

* * * * * * * * *

Wanderers had to travel to Spain for the second leg of their Champions League Quarter Final, with that 3 - 1 first leg lead in the bank. Of course, Barcelona did have that away goal which could prove vital. Sir Fabian had decided to go with the team. If they lost, that would be it, he thought. The night before the flight out, he was in London and had dispatched Sharon to her mum's in Essex (Sharon had jumped on a train and headed for a leafy location an hour away where she was about to indulge in some multi-positional gymnastics with Johann van Dyke). He headed as usual for his gentlemen's club and a rendezvous with Talulah.

Talulah had been looking forward to it: which was something of a reversal of sentiments where she and Sir Fabian were concerned. True, she liked the £100 tip he usually gave her on top of the £250 fee passed on to her by the management of the gentlemen's club. She nearly had enough stashed away to give up working at the club, enough to provide her with a comfortable income for the rest of her life. She'd get an ordinary job, a respectable job, perhaps train to be a PE teacher, and concentrate on bringing up her ten-year-old daughter Miranda properly rather than farming her out between her mother and Miranda's father, from whom Talulah had been separated for nearly nine years.

No more having to fake pleasure at seeing, meeting, being with and having all types of sex with a procession of overweight, balding, sweating, panting businessmen who all either believed they were irresistible to women or were happy to rely on the theory, wrong in the case of most of her clients, that money is an aphrodisiac.

"Well, Sir Fabian, how *lovely* to see you! Why has it been so long? Ever since our game with Everton, in fact. I suppose I never talked about my football. What a coincidence, eh?"

Sir Fabian's dark mood over the Wanderers' poor league form was mellowed slightly by Talulah's greeting. If the men's team had a few players like her in it they'd be doing better! And fancy waiting in the private conference room dressed only in her Wanderers United Ladies shirt and a pair of the club-coloured knickers! Knockout!

They got down to their usual routine, Sir Fabian helped by his Viagra, Talulah by a different form of inspiration. It was as she was gently descending from her *fourth* fake orgasm (she normally only allowed three per client) that she deviated from her usual warm-down. She lifted herself from Sir Fabian's slavering mouth (as his tongue was clearly tiring) and snuggled down alongside him. A bit like snuggling down alongside an elephant seal, she thought, but this is important.

"Was that nice?" she cooed in his ear. Oh, yuck! She'd not noticed how hairy his ears were, and there was a great lump of wax in the one she was cooing in.

"Bloody great, Talulah! Or should I call you Lou?" This was fantastic! The girl really *did* fancy him!

"Why haven't you been to see us play again?"

"Just too bloody busy, Lou. I've had a bastard newspaper editor to sack in South Africa, an Aussie Rules soccer franchise to sign in Melbourne, a government minister to bribe in the Far East, a tobacco company to sell in New York, a mobile 'phone company to buy out in Denmark, a brewery to shake up in Germany and my Yacht was used for a Royal party by some minor nobs in Mexico."

"Oh, I see! That's a shame. We're doing ever so well, thanks to the coaching we get from Wanderers. Fancy you buying them, eh?"

"Hmph!"

"It looks like they're going to win the FA Cup *and* the Champions League thing, doesn't it?"

"Yes, well they're doing bugger all in your Premier League. If they lose any more games in that I'm going to pull out!"

"You? Pull out? That doesn't sound like the man *I* know! Eh?" Talulah giggled saucily in his waxy, hairy ear, giving him a playful nudge in the ribs – or where she judged they ought to be, under all that sweaty blubber. She hoped she sounded convincing. Perhaps she was good enough to be a Drama teacher! "Oh, I see what you mean! But what would happen if you did that?"

"I don't know and I don't care! Well, that's not true, actually. It would probably ruin the club. Bankrupt them. Kaput!"

Talulah sat bolt upright and looked dreadfully sad. Sir Fabian put out a hand and touched her arm. "What's up, Lou?"

"If that happened, it would be the end of our ladies' team! If Wanderers folded up, they'd disband their teams, wouldn't they? That includes us!" She burst into an uncontrollable bout of sobbing. Yes; perhaps a Drama teacher.

Sir Fabian sat up and put his great hairy arms around her. He wasn't very good in situations like this. "Now, come on, Lou. A girl like you would soon find another team to play for!"

Talulah's sobs became deeper. Gulping great lungfuls of air, she said, " No - I - wouldn't. - We'd have - to - pull - out - oftheleague - in - mid - season. - All - the - players - would - be - banned......" All lies, of course, but she was doing her best.

"It's business, Lou. The bloody team costs a fortune and I expect a good return for my investment!"

"B-but - they-re - *Wanderers*. - They - get - a - full - house - every - game! You wouldn't get any more money on the gate even if they *were* on top...." (Damn! She'd forgotten to sob for a minute, there!) ".....of - the - league. - And - I bet - there's - just - as - many - people - all - over - the - world - tuning - in - to your - satellite - TV - to - watch - them, - win - or - lose!"

Sir Fabian thought about that for a minute and then considered the sobbing girl in his arms. Those *magnificent* thighs! And after all, they *had* won the cup in Brazil, and before that, in Tokyo (thanks to his intervention, he felt) and seemed to win the important games.

Talulah played her final card. She seemed to be recovering from her tears now.

"As long as they stay in the Premiership, your money's safe, I'd have thought."

"Right, Lou. I've always marked you down as a smart girl. I reckon you're right. I'll stick it out to the end of the season. As long as Wanderers don't go down, I'll keep them. I won't sell out."

"Really, Sir Fabian?" sniffed Talulah. Bracing herself, she kissed him full on the lips - something the girls rarely did. Hugging his grotesque chest, she lied, "Ooh, you *are* wonderful! I'm *sure* Wanderers won't go down!"

"But *I'd* like to, Loo!"

In the circumstances, and because she didn't have to look as his face, she let him. She'd got what she wanted, even if she had worked very hard for it. If only the girls knew! They never would, of course, and she didn't want them to. She was glad her little plan had worked but couldn't wait for Sir Fabian to take his unshowered leave of her. Mind, to Talulah's amazement, the tip this time was £250!

Chapter 45 - A Pair of Cups

Sefton had been expecting Sir Fabian to be particularly objectionable on the trip to Barcelona but found him in a buoyant mood.

"Going to stuff these dagos, are we, Sefton?" he sprayed as the 'plane took off.

"Er, well, we've a 3 - 1 lead from the first leg, so even if we lose by the odd goal we go through."

"What's an odd goal?" Sir Fabian still had a lot to learn about soccer. "One that goes in off a post or something?"

Sefton explained.

Wanderers went a goal down inside five minutes when a long-range shot took a wicked deflection off Antonio Genitile's heel and left Edmun Edmunsen and his bobble hat diving the wrong way. He had nothing more to do for the half, though. Barcelona had to score a second time to win on the away goals rule, so began to get more adventurous in the second half. Ronnie had prevailed upon his wing backs to be ready to go forward and do their stuff if there was the chance of a break, and so it was, with five minutes left, that Papa Médecin ghosted down the right wing with Barcelona's defence apparently looking the other way until they all seemed to see him at once and made for him en masse, leaving Kwasi Ankoma in acres of space on the left to receive Papa's cross and tuck it home.

The small contingent of away fans went mad, as did the visitors' bench and the Wanderers' Directors who had travelled.

"That's it! That's bloody *it!*" Sefton was up on his feet, hugging Dick Fossett for all he was worth. Sir Fabian had stayed in his seat and surveyed the jubilation with surprise.

"That's only one each," he yelled over the noise around him (immediately around him. The rest of the stadium, except for the small section at one end with the Wanderers fans in, had fallen silent). "I want us to *win!*"

"They'd have to score *three times* to beat us now, Sir Fabian. You add the scores together. We are winning four - two now. We're through to the semis!"

Sir Fabian took some time grasping the idea of aggregate scores but by the time they were on the 'plane back home the next day he was happy enough.

He wasn't so happy a week later when Wanderers had lost their two Easter games, 3 - 2 at home to Middlesbrough and 2 - 1 away to Manchester United. A Manchester United player scored off the pitch as well, as Nicky Bickham renewed his acquaintance with Jesus Bastardi's daughter Juanita, who got him to add his 'phone number below his autograph. She had to promise not to have that tattooed over as well, though. It was ex-directory.

"But-a no-one eez going to see it there, Neeck," she had murmured.

"What about the tattoo artist?" Nick had asked.

"Ah. Sorry. I-a had not sought of zat!"

A further defeat at home to Liverpool left Wanderers really deep in trouble.

"Wanderers Slide Continues" - Daily Mail.

"Wanderers Falter Again - Relegation Looms!" - Daily Express.

266

"World Champs are Premiership Chumps!" - Daily Mirror.

"Going Down? Three Games To Go" - Daily Star.

"Wanderers Wobble On Brink!" - The Sun.

"Wanderers Have Already Gone Down, Claims Sixth Former Roxanne" - The Sport.

"Wanderers Concentrate on the Big Time" - The Universe.

"Wanderers Doomed!" - The Globe.

However, there was another trip to Spain for the first leg of the Champions League Semi-Final against Valencia. No-one could have envisaged just how many miles would have to be covered by Heinrich Schickelgrüber's car at the start of the season. He was getting so weary of the long, continental journeys he was almost moved to ask Bones to sedate him so that he could fly with the rest of the team. Almost, but not quite.

Wanderers and Valencia fought out a tense draw, Jerome van Dyke scoring from just inside the box to put Wanderers ahead, only for Valencia to equalise a few minutes later.

"An away goal, though, lads! Tha's no' so bad!" was Ronnie's verdict.

Sir Fabian wasn't so pleased, though. As far as he could see, Wanderers had gone seven games without a win. Another stop-over in London, en route between Canada and South Africa, had allowed him the opportunity to visit Talulah again, though, and his slightly weakening resolve not to sell up was strengthened again.

With the second leg only a week away it was no wonder that Wanderers couldn't concentrate on their Premiership game at Arsenal in between. A Macca free kick gave them a half-time lead and it looked as if they were going to hang on until *two* injury time goals turned victory into defeat, just like that.

There was little time for gloom as the team prepared for the visit of Valencia, though. The capacity crowd was stunned into silence as Valencia took a third minute lead, but they soon got behind their team and produced successive crescendos of noise that lifted the players to greater heights. Enrique Mouette equalised right on half-time and it was all one-way in the second half, Seamus O'Hooligan crashing in the winner with twenty minutes left. Wanderers played exhibition keep-ball from then on, each pass accompanied by loud cheering and stamping of feet. The whistle went and the noise, unbelievably, increased almost beyond the pain threshold. Wanderers were in the Champions League Final!

Bert Barnard had to wait a long time before the New Millennium Stand was empty enough for him to make his inspection.

"I don't know, Mal," he shouted through the camouflaged door. "You've got - what - *two* more games at home? As long as you lose them it'll be O.K., then we can pretend to find the problem as soon as the season ends."

Inside his secret toilet, looking down on the still brightly-lit rectangle of emerald green, Malcolm reached for his Andrex.

"Right-o, Bert!" he shouted. "Look, I'll see you in the bar in a quarter of an hour."

"Right!" - and Bert was gone.

Malcolm sat and pondered. What a predicament! If Wanderers lost the last two games it was very likely that they'd be relegated. He, along with the whole Board, was wondering how come Sir Fabian hadn't pulled the plug ages ago. Perhaps being in the FA Cup Final and the Champions League Final was keeping him sweet. No-one could see him sticking with the club if it was relegated, though. If only they hadn't sold out to him! They'd still have last season's team and would have probably won everything including the Premiership. Though in that case, his bloody stand would have collapsed weeks ago. More pains gripped his intestines and he checked that there was a spare roll of Andrex. There was! Funny how such a small thing can be a comfort amidst great adversity.

They lost at home to Derby. One-nil. It was to prove a life-saver to Derby, virtually ensuring their survival in the Premiership that season. The usual 65,000 crowd didn't seem unduly worried despite the fact that Wanderers dropped into the bottom three for the first time. They had two finals to look forward to before the last League game, which had been rearranged for the Saturday after the Champions League Final. It was only against Wimbledon, fellow relegation candidates. No pressure, then!

Wanderers beat Aston Villa 1 - 0 in the FA Cup Final, the last one under the twin towers.

"You know," remarked Sefton to the rest of the Wanderers Board as they watched their team parading round the historic old stadium with the cup. "No wonder they're having trouble raising the cash for the new place. Would *you* put any money into a Wembley without the twin towers? *I* wouldn't." The others all nodded in agreement.

"The Philistines have taken over everywhere," opined Ernie Arscott. "If it's traditional, get rid of it!"

"You're right," said Dick Fossett, a man who had played in a Wembley Cup Final just after the war. "Know what I reckon? If they just included some replicas of the twin towers in the new design – made of fibreglass or some such - so Wembley's Twin Towers were there for all to see, and there to be played under, investors would queue up for a bite! *I'd* buy into that!"

More nods of agreement.

It was only four days later that Wanderers added the Champions League Cup to their collection for the season. They beat Valencia 3 - 0 in the Stade de Paris with goals from Strupinski (39), Ankoma (67) and O'Hooligan (75). That made a bit of history, an English club successfully retaining the FA Cup and the descendant of the European Cup in the same season.

"Ah've got a guid feelin' aboot the Wimbledon game, Joker," said Ronnie after a bit of light training the day before that vital game.

"I know what you mean, boss," agreed Joker. "We haven't won a league game this year, which makes this last one a Very Important Match! And what has that team of God-knows-whats been doing all season?"

"Winnin' important matches!" they chorused.

Sixty five thousand fans took their places in the New Stamford Stadium for the visit of Wimbledon.

Chapter 46 - The End!

The bottom of the Premiership had Wimbledon on 33 points, Wanderers on 32, Sheffield Wednesday on 31 and Watford last with 24. Wanderers had obtained a special extension to their League programme on account of their excursion to Brazil and success in the Champions League. Few could have anticipated that it would be such a vital match. Quite simply, Wanderers had to win to stay up. Anything less, and they were down.

The tension in the Wanderers changing room was almost unbearable. In his corner, Papa Médecin's array of bits and pieces seemed bigger than ever. Macca wasn't making silly jokes. Sum Wun appeared to apologise to Lim Po when they both accidentally brushed against one another as they changed. When Stefan Milosovitch started to look around for his tie-ups, Milo Opec spotted them partly hidden under his bag and threw them over to him. Seamus O'Hooligan wasn't smiling. Barely a voice broke the silence. Ronnie motioned to Joker to come out into the corridor.

Pulling the door shut - a bit of a job as over the last month or so it had started to stick a bit - he whispered to Joker.

"Ah've got a guid feelin' again, laddie! Wha' aboot that atmosphere, eh?"

Joker nodded. "I know. They're really up for it. There's never been a feeling in the air like *that* before! Like we said. They can do it for the big ones, and this *is* a big one."

"Aye. Best go an' gee 'em up!" Ronnie had to push hard to open the sticking door. "We'll have tae get this fochin' door seen tae!"

Up in the New Millennium Stand the Directors' box was full to overflowing. Sir Fabian was there together with all of the Directors except for Malcolm. The old top scorer Dick Fossett looked across at the Wimbledon Directors, then turned to Jack Grimethorpe beside him.

"Seems a shame if Wimbledon go down," he said.

"Shame? It's them or us, boy. It won't be us!" retorted Jack.

"No, what I mean is, when this Premier League was set up, the wheelers and dealers behind it didn't intend for clubs like them to be in it. Bradford, Watford, Ipswich, little clubs, they weren't supposed to come to the party. Wimbledon have been, like, thumbing their noses at the big boys - us included, granted, for what - well, years. Ever since the Premier League started because they happened to be in the old First Division at the time. It'll be a shame to see them go."

"Well, I see what you mean, but there's no room for sentiment today, Dick!"

"The way we've been doing in the league since we got back from Brazil, Wimbledon must be feeling confident!" chipped in Cecil Norris, the other side of Jack.

The crowd, almost all there an hour before kick-off, broke from its singing and chanting to welcome its heroes onto the pitch. At the suggestion of Arnie Robinson, sitting at the back of the Directors' Box nursing a bad head cold that he was hoping wouldn't go onto his chest where it might develop into bronchitis and then pneumonia, the Wanderers women's team had preceded the men, carrying the FIFA World Club Championship trophy, the Champions League trophy and the FA Cup. There was a fourth trophy, too. They trotted them round the touchline as the men kicked-in. It just helped to raise the level of the crowd's frenzy a little more.

"Nice touch, Arnie!" yelled Sefton, turning to acknowledge the success of the idea. To Sir Fabian, he shouted, "That was Arnie Robinson's idea, the women with the cups! The fourth one is their Women's FA Cup. They won that, and were runners up in the league! Not bad, eh?"

"Women with cups! I like it!" He turned and nodded to Arnie. Arnie should have been pleased at such recognition from the Chairman but he had remembered that sometimes viruses could somehow infect the heart and be rapidly fatal. Arnie rarely enjoyed himself. Wherever he was, whatever he was doing, he usually felt symptoms that could be the first signs of something terminal.

The officials came out, the captains were summoned, the coin was tossed, the teams changed ends and the crowd lifted its vocal efforts into an ear-splitting ululation that might well have struck fear into the hearts of a team other than Wimbledon, outnumbered, outclassed and out-financed for all their top flight days. No problem, this, for them. Outclassed, maybe, but never beaten for spirit, Wimbledon kicked off and tore into the attack. They pinned Wanderers back and soon forced three successive saves out of Antonio la Pazbaq, back in the side after recovering from a severely bruised gluteus maximus sustained whilst repeatedly demonstrating his novelty method of saving shots for a Channel 4 documentary on Sporting Eccentrics. On ten minutes the Dons took the lead, Hughes crashing home a volley from ten yards. Antonio Genitile and Jesus Bastardi looked at one another as if to say "I thought you had him". After twenty-three minutes Hughes scored again. Antonio and Jesus had both gone for him and collided with one another to leave Hughes free.

Papa Médecin ran over to them and appeared to be shouting something to both men. They both just nodded back very slowly.

Wanderers began to push up and put pressure on Wimbledon's goal. Enrique Mouette skimmed the bar. The crowd bayed and stamped, sensing a break-through. Macca sent a free kick curling wickedly goalwards only for Sullivan to somehow tip it over for a corner. Louder noise, harder stamping. The corner came over, Heinrich Schickelgrüber banged a thumping header against the bar. Sixty three thousand fans (two thousand tickets had been made available to Wimbledon) stood and screamed and sang and stamped.

Wimbledon counter-attacked, the ball ending safely in Antonio la Pazbaq's hands. He threw it immediately out to Papa Médecin on the right touchline. Papa began to take the ball up the wing. On he went, the opposition backing off him like he had terminal halitosis. On and on he went as the crowd urged him forward with greater volume for each yard he covered. Deep into Wimbledon's half, and still no challenge. All possible targets were tightly marked as Papa reached the penalty area, his ears buzzing from the amount of noise the crowd was making. A defender at last approached and lunged for the ball. Papa went down. Penalty!

Macca ran over to Enrique.

"Let me have it!" he yelled.

"*What?*"

"*Let me have it!*"

"*WHAT?*"

"*LET ME......*" It was impossible to hear or be heard with the racket the crowd was making. Beneath the hysterical tones from the sixty three thousand sets of vocal cords was a low roar produced by sixty three thousand pairs of feet stamping rapidly just to make more noise.

Macca just picked up the ball, placed it on the spot, turned to Enrique and pointed to himself. Enrique nodded. Let the mad Englishman take it.

The sixty three thousand throats became suddenly silent as Macca shaped to take the kick. He made no mistake: the net bulged and many ears in the stadium hurt as the crowd, impossibly, got even louder.

Wanderers continued to attack for the rest of the first half but despite several near misses and because of some good goal-keeping by Sullivan it was still two-one at half time.

Up in the New Millennium Stand Bert went on a quick recce. Visiting as many suspect spots as he could without arousing suspicion, he made some worrying but not unexpected discoveries. He hurried along to Malcolm's Special Guest Box, but found the door locked. He was sure Malcolm was inside, but if he was shut into his secret loo he probably wouldn't be able to hear him knocking. He decided not to return to his seat in Ernie Arscott's box, but to keep monitoring the hot spots. If the worse came to the worse, he thought, he could always 'phone the police with a bomb scare to get the stand cleared quickly.

Malcolm could hear his knees knocking, though. He'd thought he was miserable when forced to play goal post with Clarence Draper by that sadistic bloody PE teacher of his, but that was bliss compared to how he felt now. The fans in the stand had made so much noise and stamped their feet so heavily that he could feel the vibrations where he sat. His intestines were imprisoning him on his loo. He wanted to leave, to flee, to hide, but he dare not leave his seat.

The teams came out and locked horns for the second half. Wanderers once again took the game to Wimbledon and brought the crowd quickly back to the boil with more near misses. The minutes ticked by, slowly for Wimbledon, holding on to their vulnerable-looking lead, too quickly for Wanderers, running out of time. Tempers flared and Enrique Mouette was booked for a foul.

With some twenty minutes left Ronnie and Joker agreed on a desperate plan. Off came Enrique - with a booking, they couldn't risk his getting sent off - and Antonio Genitile - his knee had somehow lasted the season, more or less, but it was still a possible weak link. The back five with wing backs became a back four. On went Pickaxe Smith in midfield - and Lim Po up front to make three strikers with Seamus O'Hooligan and Sum Wun.

Almost immediately Pickaxe ploughed his way through Wimbledon's packed defence, inflicting a few serious bruises and bringing a fine save out of Sullivan. Pickaxe continued to be a threat down the middle - a physical one, rather than a footballing one - but it gave the Wimbledon side something new to think about.

Then, with some six minutes left, an amazing thing happened. Wimbledon had broken out and threatened the Wanderers goal for two or three minutes - a long time when all of a sudden Wanderers could hardly get the ball out of their own penalty area. At last Macca put his foot on the ball and picked out Sum Wun who ran onto the pass out towards the right channel. He had to hold the ball up - not too difficult for some one only just over five foot tall with a low centre of gravity. Seamus O'Hooligan, dutifully deep to support his temporarily beleaguered defence, became available for a second or two but as Sum Wun spotted him he was quickly closed down. Lim Po had moved up away on the left, far beyond Seamus, and was unmarked and alone in a meadow of space. Sum Wun saw him, but looked for support elsewhere. On the bench, Ronnie, Joker, Enrique, Antonio, Edmun, Caspar, all the non-playing substitutes, Bones and the steward collecting spent water bottles all screamed their frustration. No-one could hear anyone else in the incredible din, but still Ronnie yelled: "He *still* won't fochin' pass the fochin' ball to fochin' Lim Po, the focher!"

Sum Wun, still screening the ball, then shrugged his shoulders. Well, it might have been seen as a feign to throw off his defender, but he did in fact shrug to himself and then launch a huge ball square into Lim Po's unmarked path. Lim Po simply took it round Sullivan and equalised.

He was, of course, buried under a yellow and blue heap until Jesus started to pull bodies off the pile and point angrily at his wrist and the centre spot - there was no time to waste!

Wimbledon immediately made defence-strengthening substitutions which also, they hoped, would cause enough of a delay to knock Wanderers out of their stride.

From the restart it was frantic stuff. Tender ears bled with the sound produced by the Wanderers fans. For hours afterwards, sixty five thousand pairs of ears buzzed as if they'd all been to see The Who play a come-back gig live at the Brixton Academy.

Ninety minutes were up. No-one could hear the two thousand Wimbledon fans whistling at the ref to blow time, but they were trying it anyway.

A corner to Wanderers, with Macca to take it on the right. Papa Médecin was one of the defenders who moved up to join the attack, but he stood between Macca and the packed goalmouth, facing the jostling, arm-waving mêlée. He leapt up and down and waved his arms in bizarre fashion and the players couldn't help noticing him. When he had the attention of most of them he pointed dramatically at them, staring. They stared back, the jostling forgotten. Papa turned to Macca and pointed and stared at him now, and Macca took the corner.

The ball flew off the inside of his left boot and curled wickedly towards the goal. No-one seemed to see it as it flew into the net. Krakatoa may have made a lot of noise, but not much more than the crowd inside New Stamford Stadium. No-one noticed Papa clap his hands with glee before he led the charge towards Macca. It took a while for the referee to prise the Wanderers players, subs and several fans off Macca so that he could first of all breathe, then get up and take his place for the restart.

Which lasted five seconds before the referee blew time. Wanderers had done it! Wimbledon, on the other hand, were out of the top flight after a brilliant fourteen-year spell, having become a league club only four years before that. There were tears down many faces at the Wimbledon end.

The Wanderers squad did a lap of honour and the crowd broke into a chant of "Champions!" Thump-thump-thump! "Champions!" Thump-thump-thump! It went on for ages.

Suddenly, in the New Millennium Stand, the PA system crackled into life.

"Attention, ladies and gentlemen! We must ask you to leave the New Millennium Stand as quickly and calmly as possible. We have received notification from the Police of a bomb threat and must take it seriously. Please leave the New Millennium Stand as quickly and calmly as you can!"

Stewards let some of the crowd onto the pitch and herded them to the other side. The stand quickly emptied, the Stewards being well-trained in such procedures. Bert Barnard, returning from the pay 'phones in the corridor behind the press gallery, headed for Malcolm's box only to be turned away by a steward.

"I must get back to Malcolm Black's box to make sure he's all right!" insisted Bert.

"Don't worry, sir, we have people responsible for that. His box has probably been checked already!"

"You don't understand, he may not hear you!"

"Someone will go into his box to see that it is empty."

"It's locked...."

"We have master keys, sir. Now, *please* move along!"

Bert, in fact, got swept away in the crowd.

On his secret loo, Malcolm's bowels reacted to the tense win by simply doing more of the same. Bomb scare! Piffle and poppycock! How many times did bomb scares turn out to be real? In London, perhaps, or Belfast. Not here. He'd just stay until his diarrhoea subsided, then find Bert and decide when it would be best to come clean about the state of the stand.

He looked out through his one-way glass at the other three sides of the ground, still filled with delirious, chanting, singing, stamping fans. He could feel the sound *and* the vibrations even where he sat.

And a creaking sound. And cracking. And he felt his loo sway beneath him. His next intestinal offering was out of fear.

The fans still filling the other three sides of the ground, as well as those on the pitch, were not immediately aware of anything happening to the New Millennium Stand. None had seriously expected the bomb scare to be real. They were too busy mobbing the team which had come back onto the pitch again as part of the evacuation.

Eventually, though, more and more people noticed the New Millennium Stand starting to sag. Chanting and singing were replaced by gasps and screams. The top deck of the stand suddenly settled downwards on top of the middle deck. That collapsed at one end, the two crumpled layers looking for all the world like the Titanic going down at the bows. The back wall fell forwards, adding to the cloud of dust that rose above the debris, partially obscuring the detail of what followed. There was plenty to hear, though, as tortured metal screeched and shrieked inside shattering concrete. Unseen panes of glass exploded musically to add dramatic effect, plastic seats broke with strange popping sounds and severed cabling crackled and sparked through the billowing dust. A thunderous vibration announced that the other end of the top two levels had given in under the added weight of the back wall and crashed down onto the lower level, which caved in under the pressure from above. The cloud of dust grew higher, its huge bulbous shape thrown into dramatic relief by the light of the setting sun. Two of the support columns fell sideways into the cauldron of dust - lucky, because had they fallen forwards they would have landed on the pitch where several thousand fans still watched in awe.

The rumbling and crashing stopped. The stewards, helped by many PA appeals, gradually cleared all the spectators from the ground. They certainly had plenty to talk about. As if the game hadn't been exciting enough on its own!

On the pitch, just the players and officials remained. Sefton was already talking to the Wimbledon Directors about compensation for all their players' clothing and possessions, now buried under a mountain of rubble and tangled metal.

"Jus' may luck, man," quipped Macca. "Ah's on a promise terneet, and the tart's 'phone number is in mah jacket!"

"Ye know why yon stand fochin' collapsed?" Ronnie asked Joker.

"Woodworm?" suggested Joker.

"Nae, laddie. It fochin' fainted because Sum Wun actually fochin' *passed* tae Lim Po!"

Papa Médecin was looking worried. He found his interpreter and brought him over to Ronnie and Joker. " 'Ee say, 'ee not responsible. 'Ee jus' tell Wimbledon defence to fall back. Fall back, fall back as 'ee run up wing. 'Ee no think 'is voodoo *that* good!" He nodded towards the cloud of dust billowing and beginning to settle over what had once been the New Millennium Stand.

"Wha' the foch's he talkin' aboot?" asked Ronnie.

"Don't ask," replied Joker. "Just don't ask!" Turning to Papa and his interpreter, he said, "Tell Papa not to worry. Well played!"

Sefton came over. He was looking worried.

"We're one light," he said. "Have you seem Malcolm Black?"

No-one had.

"Didn't he watch all the games from his special guest box?" asked Joker.

"Oh my God!" Faces turned towards the rubble.

"He could be under all that bloody lot!"

Some of the group began to move towards the stricken stand. Some policemen, quickly on the scene from outside the ground, tried to stop them going too close.

"You'll need special equipment to lift that lot. Sniffer dogs to find people, like in earthquakes!"

"Surely someone checked all the boxes," asked Sefton. Enquiries were made of the stewards and eventually the one responsible for checking the boxes was found.

"On my life, Mr Perkins, I unlocked his door and looked in. He wasn't there."

"Thank God for that!" said several people.

Then Macca's voice again.

"Ah c'n see 'im, mon!"

All eyes turned to Macca, then to the direction he was looking. Which was up.

"If'n he's as frightened as Ah would be, mon, he's in the reet place!"

The cloud of concrete dust was slowly clearing, some settling like snow, some drifting away on the air. Gradually the panorama of twisted metal, crushed seating and crumbled concrete became clearer. As did one of the three remaining support columns, standing up amidst the destruction like stripped trees on the Somme.

Near the top of the one Macca was looking at, some fifty feet above the rubble, was a little ledge, a fragment of what had once been a section of floor. On it was perched a seated figure, dusted white with powdered concrete, its trembling visible even from that height. A gust of wind blew some of the dust off. The figure's arms moved and began to knock more of the dust away.

There was a petrified Malcolm, trousers round his ankles, sitting high up on his secret throne, caught in the orange glow of the rays from the setting sun.

Afterthoughts from the author

The Premiership in the 1999-2000 season was, of course, won by Manchester United. Wimbledon were one of the relegated clubs, finishing third from bottom, so that at least was more or less as in the book. The Premiership has been less colourful since their demise.

Chelsea won the FA Cup that year, not Wanderers United, but Chelsea fans might have worked out why Chelsea never seem to get a mention during this account of the fictional Wanderers United's tortuous Premiership season......

Manchester United didn't fare too well in the World Club Championship that season, but I used their appearance as the basis for Wanderers United's fictional performances there. Mind you, even though Wanderers United won it, it didn't help England's efforts to stage the 2006 World Cup....

The next World Club Championship wasn't staged until 2005, replacing the Toyota Cup and - er - subtly renamed the FIFA Club World Championship Toyota Cup. Liverpool totally dominated the final in Yokohama against Brazil's Sao Paulo (something like seventeen corners to nil and three disallowed "goals") and yet lost 1 – 0. Such is football.

I ought to apologise to Charlton Athletic Ladies FC, real winners of both the Premier Womens' League and the AXA FA Womens' Cup in the 1999-2000 season (Charlton being known as Croydon that season). May the womens' game in this country continue to grow in popularity until attendances are regularly counted in tens of thousands rather than hundreds.

Apologies are also due to Real Madrid, the real winners of the Champions' League in 2000. It was they who beat Valencia 3-0 in Paris.

A word about Newquay Airport. At the time of writing, some doubt exists about its future. It doesn't bear thinking about that it could actually close down. It would be a massive blow to the Cornish economy if it did, and anyone who makes any decision that contributes to its closure, be it local politician, national politician, company director or any other category of interested party, should be utterly, utterly ashamed of themselves. Brymon Airways doesn't operate into Newquay now, but as of early 2006 AirSouthWest, Ryanair, Skybus, BMI and Monarch do. Check their websites.

In Chapter 26, all the references to Concorde being sent off-course by the mobile 'phones were made up just to help the story along. Modern aircraft navigation systems just couldn't let that happen: all sorts of warning lights and bleepers would alert the pilots! I still hate it when I see people using mobiles on 'planes, though. Mind, I hate people using them on trains as well.

Chapter 30 sees the Porthleven players deciding to play Wanderers United at Gala Park. In reality, no non-league player would turn up the chance to play in a 65,000 capacity state-of-the-art stadium; and the FA and police would never let a tiny non-league club stage an FA Cup match against Premiership opposition unless absolute security could be guaranteed. But it wouldn't have made such a good story!

Oh, yes: and the **real** story of how Manchester United came to miss out on the 1999-2000 FA Cup so that they could play in the 2000 FIFA World Club Championship is not that the Sports Minister, Tony Banks, came right out and said they'd have to pull out of the FA Cup like I have him suggesting to Sir Fabian Blankopf in chapter 16. In Manchester United's case, although it was clear that both the Government and the FA wanted them to play in the FIFA tournament, neither suggested United's withdrawal from the Cup; nor did Tony Banks. This arose when United's representative at a meeting between themselves, the FA, the Premier League and Tony Banks, held on 17th June 1999, stated that "something would have to give from the existing fixture list" for United to take part in the FIFA tournament. After various options were ruled out, such as extending the season (which somehow Wanderers United wangled according to the last chapter), tinkering with the date of the Charity Shield or giving United a bye to the 5th round of the FA Cup, the Manchester United representative said "that if something is to give from the fixture programme – then why not suggest that Manchester United do not play in the tournament altogether…!" At this, the FA representative agreed to put the idea to the FA Board, but doubted it would be accepted by the FA or by the sponsors. It was, of course, and the rest is history.

Printed in the United Kingdom
by Lightning Source UK Ltd.
109097UKS00003B/247-297